Daughters
OF THE SUN

Also by Ira Mukhoty

Heroines: Powerful Indian Women of Myth and History

Daughters
OF THE SUN

EMPRESSES, QUEENS AND
BEGUMS OF THE MUGHAL EMPIRE

IRA MUKHOTY

ALEPH

ALEPH

ALEPH BOOK COMPANY
An independent publishing firm
promoted by *Rupa Publications India*

First published in India in 2018
by Aleph Book Company
7/16 Ansari Road, Daryaganj
New Delhi 110 002

ISBN: 978-93-86021-12-0

12

Printed in India

To the memory of my parents,
Gobind and Nicolle Mukhoty

CONTENTS

Ambitious Siblings and a Shahzaadi's Dream
1631—1721

INTRODUCTION

India was ruled for over 200 years by the Gurkani, a clan that established an empire of such magnificence, size and wealth, that it became a byword for glory around the world. But the name by which the Gurkani became rightly famous was an aberration. The dynasty was a nomadic Timurid one, as the founder, Babur, proudly traced his lineage directly to the Turkic conqueror Amir Timur (also known as Tamerlane), who established an empire in the fourteenth century quite as glorious as Chinghiz Khan's. Babur referred to himself, and to his lineage, as Gurkani, from the Persianized Mongol word for guregen, or son-in-law, since some of the Timurids, including Amir Timur himself, had married Chingizid women, to add to their legitimacy. But Babur himself, and all of his descendants, male and female, were intensely proud of their Timurid lineage, very consciously evoking the Timurid charisma in various ways. Indeed, Babur thoroughly loathed his Mongol cousins, the Uzbeks, considering them brutish and uncivilized, and would have been horrified to know that his dynasty would become synonymous with an Anglicized form of Mongols—the Mughals of India.

It was while researching my first book, *Heroines*, that I realized the casual negligence with which we regard our history in India and the sometimes benign largesse with which we assimilate inaccuracy and fallacy as received wisdom. But the naming of things is important. It shapes the way in which we view ourselves and the place we occupy in the world. To name a thing is to magic it into being, to give it substance and weight. When the Europeans gave the name 'Mughals' to Babur's dynasty, they were negligently assuming a shared Mongol inheritance for all Central Asian conquerors. One of the women I studied for my collection of essays in *Heroines* was Jahanara Begum, among the most accomplished women of the Mughal empire. I discovered the exact depth of my ignorance at that point—an ignorance that was also inadvertently tainted with prejudice.

The misnomer of the dynasty is only the very beginning of an enormous amount of almost whimsical misinformation that surrounds the history of the Mughals. The empire of the great Mughals—from Babur's invasion at Panipat in 1526 to the death of Aurangzeb in 1707—coincides exactly with the arrival and settling of the Europeans in India for trade and more, the elucidation of that history and the way in which we view it even today is marked by the way in which those early Europeans experienced and interpreted Mughal rule. The Europeans kept meticulous records of all their transactions with the Mughal court. They wrote detailed accounts in their letters to their holding companies and they wrote memoirs and travelogues. Jesuit missionaries arrived at the same time and they too wrote extensively of their experiences and travels. On the other hand, from the Indian point of view, it was considered indelicate, indeed outright rude, to write about royal Muslim women who were expected to maintain a decorous purdah. The Europeans, not held back by any such need for decorum, were instead fascinated by the notion of the private space of the Mughal women and indulged in some truly fervid leaps of imagination when trying to conjure up that forbidden world—the Mughal harem.

An Englishman travelling to Mecca in the seventeenth century admitted that the first question a traveller returning from the East was faced with was 'what are the women like?' And yet, when European men interacted with the Mughal court, they found themselves distanced from the affairs of women at several levels: as men, European men, they were both physically and culturally separated from the world of women. The purdah of the zenana meant that the women and the household that they inhabited were prohibited to them. François Bernier, a seventeenth-century French physician and meticulous observer of Shahjahanabad, admitted that though he yearned to visit the zenana, 'who is the traveller that can describe from ocular observation the interior of the building?' Moreover, since they usually did not speak Persian or Turki, Europeans could only comprehend this beguiling world through an interpreter. The nuances of culture and comportment were therefore often inaccessible to them. They could not understand the reason for a Mughal woman's influence and power, attributing it to an emperor's weakness, or worse, to incest.

Daughters of the Sun

The resulting chimera creation, the 'Oriental harem', was therefore a lurid and sometimes fantastical mix of bazaar gossip, stray gleanings of fact and sexual fantasy. The most frequent portrayal of this 'harem', as it was consumed eagerly by a curious audience in Europe that was beginning to be fascinated by the 'exotic East', was that of a cruel, despotic and endlessly lascivious emperor surrounded by thousands of nubile young women competing for his attention and pining away in sexual frustration. Not only was this image eagerly adopted by Western audiences, it also trickled down into the Indian consciousness through the colonial experience and the European narrative of Indian history. Thus, to this day, there is a perception that Mughal women operated within a fixed zone of influence, the domestic harem, an immutable cloistered space in which they led restricted and unfulfilled lives, from which they could seldom escape, and to which only the emperor had access. As I discovered while doing my research on the women of the great Mughals, nothing could be farther from the truth. In fact, the zenana was an industrious, carefully calibrated and orchestrated world. The wanton world of the Europeans' imagination in which the women ruthlessly schemed against one another and wasted the hours of their days in frustrated languor was just that, a fantasy. The zenana was instead a busy, well-ordered place where each woman knew her place and her worth. It was a place where accomplished, educated women were prized; well-spoken, articulate and cultured women most likely to advance. There were intrigues, and jealousies, certainly, for how would there not be when hundreds and sometimes thousands of people lived together? But the overwhelming nature of the zenana was one of warm support and companionship, a complex, nuanced world of female complicity and understanding, one in which excellence was valued and women learned all the skills required to run a city, for there were no men within.

A much truer picture of a zenana was described by an Englishwoman, Mrs Meer Hassan Ali, who married an Indian man and lived for twelve years in a Muslim nobleman's household in the nineteenth century. 'A lady here,' wrote Mrs Meer Hassan, referring to an Indian zenana, 'would be the most unhappy creature existing, unless surrounded by a multitude of attendants suitable to her rank in life.' Moreover, 'they cannot imagine anything so stupid as my preference to a quiet study, rather than the constant bustle of a well-filled zenana… The ladies' society is by no means insipid or without interest', she further writes of the zenana. 'They are naturally gifted with good sense and politeness, fond of conversation, shrewd in their remarks and their language is both correct and refined.' She writes of the 'cheerful meeting of friends, the distribution of presents to dependents and remembrances to the poor; all is life and joy, cheerful bustle and amusement', and it is difficult to imagine a world more far removed from the claustrophobic, sexually charged harem of popular imagination. John Fryer, a physician with the East India Company (EIC), accidentally spied a zenana when the curtain separating him from his patients fell. He was surprised to find the women 'not altogether unemployed, there lying pared mangoes, and other fruits for confection and achars, or pickles; some samplers of good housewifery in needleworks; and no indecent decorum managing their cloistered way of living'. And so John Fryer found the women busy making achaars and doing embroidery, and he was amazed, for it was its very mundanity and industry that he found puzzling. The mystery, really, is how this pervasive notion of the 'harem' came to have such a tenacious hold on the modern Indian imagination.

The explanation usually given for the general dearth of information about Indian women is multi-layered: women were usually uneducated, so they did not transmit written histories; India, in general, tended not to emphasize written histories, preferring the oral tradition; moreover, physical evidence is fragile in India, subject to the tempestuous weather, eroded by time and the negligence of historians. But in the case of the Mughals, none of this holds true. The women were all, right from the beginning, some of the most educated of their age. Timurid girls were given the same rigorous education, in mathematics, history, physics, poetry, astronomy etc., as boys because the Timurids placed a very high value on calligraphy, writing and erudition. The Mughals were also memory-keepers par excellence of all Indian kings. They wrote memoirs and appointed court historians in enthusiastic numbers. As for the physical evidence of Mughal ambition and glory, India is fairly studded with examples of their vision, in sandstone and in marble.

The information is available, therefore, though it is often oblique, obfuscated or hidden in plain sight. This book is an attempt to recreate the dynamic, changing world of the women of the Mughal empire, from the time that Babur chanced upon the 'al-Hind' to the beginning of the eighteenth century which marked the end of Aurangzeb's reign—a period of almost 200 years. I have examined the lives and influence of some fifteen women who left their mark on India and whose lives impacted, to a greater or lesser degree, the luminous destinies of these Mughal padshahs. In the case of the earlier Mughals, it was the older matriarchs who were most influential, aunts and mothers like Aisan Daulat Begum, Khanzada Begum, Dildar Begum, Gulbadan Begum, Bega Begum and Maham Begum. When Akbar became padshah at only thirteen years of age, a group of 'milk mothers' or foster-mothers, became powerful, including Jiji Anaga and Maham Anaga. Then, as the padshahs settled into their growing empire, their wives gained in influence and so there was Harkha Bai, Salima Sultan Begum and, much more famously, Noor Jahan and Mumtaz Mahal. Finally, as the empire became truly luminescent, unmarried daughters became powerful and there is the astounding legacy of Jahanara Begum and Roshanara Begum. Under the last of the great Mughals, Aurangzeb, there are the waning stars of his daughters Zeb-un-Nisa Begum and Zeenat-un-Nisa Begum.

The ambition of the Mughals of India, from the time of Babur himself, was to found an empire worthy of their glorious ancestors. Hindustan, for them, was never a plunderous foray. It was a homeland to be created and claimed, at a time when anything less than blistering confidence meant instant death. And so, to bolster their claims, they carefully nurtured the old Perso-Chigizid symbology of the sun. In the genealogy created by Abu'l-Fazl for Akbar, the Mughals traced their lineage through Timur and Chinghiz Khan to Princess Alanquwa of Mughalistan who was impregnated by the divine light of the sun. The imagery of this powerful radiance was burnished by each successive emperor and used to stake their claims and mitigate their status as recent parvenus. In the interludes between battles, for example, Humayun liked to portray himself as the solar emperor in the centre of an elaborately constructed cosmic heaven. But Hindustan was a diverse land with its own venerable legacy of sun worship. There was the Parsi fire-worship and the Hindu veneration of the sun god. And so,

Akbar, in an affable, chimeric adoption of all these symbols, became 'His Majesty the Sun', who recited the 1,001 names of the sun and worshipped at the fire altar. Jahangir, who took the regnal name 'Light of the Faith', was often depicted with a divine solar light shining around his head like a nimbus. Shah Jahan took the enigmatic title Sahib-e-Qiran (Lord of the Auspicious Conjunction), thereby stating clearly his aim of lighting the 'Timurid Lamp'. But it was not only the Mughal emperors who so assiduously courted the divine glory of the sun. Many of the Mughal women—wives, daughters and mothers—all carefully placed themselves within the warm orbit of the sun. In some cases, the women consciously evoked the symbol of the sun, as when Mehr-un-Nisa Begum took the title Noor Jahan, or Light of the World and when Mumtaz Mahal came to be known as the 'Sun of Modesty'. But in many cases, it was the old Timurid ideal that the women aspired to. When Jahanara wrote her Sufi treatises and discovered a Shining Truth, it was the Timurid Lamp, once again, that shone through her. In their roles as ambassadors, peacekeepers, rulers in absentia and even as guardians of memory, it was the Timurid-Chingizid ideal that these Mughal women were claiming. They were equally invested in the fabric of myth-making and empire-building as the emperors, and were proud and ardent daughters of the sun.

The term I use for the space reserved for women is zenana, which is more Indian in its origin than harem, the term the Europeans used to speak of a general 'oriental' secluded space, whether they were referring to the Ottomans in Central Asia or the Mughals of India. When the Central Asian semi-nomadic warlord Babur rode into Hindustan, he did not only bring his warriors with him. He brought his 'haraman' or household, which included elderly matrons, young wives, children, servants, widowed relatives, divorced sisters and unmarried royal relatives. The women of the haraman lived in tents and spent most of their life on horseback, riding with the men and travelling great distances. These early Mughals, Babur and Humayun, had enormous respect for the matriarchs of the clan, their mothers and grandmothers, whose advice often helped keep warring brothers together and empires intact. One of the earliest women to travel into Hindustan on horseback was Khanzada, Babur's elder sister. Babur, and then his son Humayun, revered Khanzada because of the sacrifice she was required to make early in her life, when she was left behind with the Uzbek warlord Shaybani Khan, to secure Babur's safety. The Mughals were tenacious in their gratitude towards the matriarchs of their clan, who were robust, physically inured to hardship, and willing to suffer their menfolk's privations alongside them. They were pragmatic about women who 'fell' to an enemy, unlike their contemporaries, the Rajputs, who invested so heavily in their women's sexual chastity that death, through sati, was preferred to 'loss of honour' to an enemy.

In this early haraman, there was no fixed, cloistered space which was designated only for the women, as the very concept of home and homeland was still being formed. As the scholar Ruby Lal, in her ground-breaking work *Domesticity and Power in the Early Mughal World*, has shown, there was no clear separation of 'public' and 'private' space at all for these early Mughals. The women created a home on the move—travelling while pregnant, delivering babies, arranging marriages and parlaying with errant sons and brothers. When Khanzada left on her arduous, lonely mission from Kandahar across the icy passes as ambassador to Kamran Mirza's court at Kabul at the very advanced age of sixty-five, it is also the 'harem' that she represented. She carried with her the harem's ardent desire for reconciliation while also performing her duty as the padshah's ambassador. Maham Begum, Dildar Begum and Gulrukh Begum, Babur's principal wives, along with Gulnar Agacha and Nargul Agacha, Babur's concubines, bore Babur's children even as they were constantly on the move, harried by enemies. They helped to create a sense of a settled Timurid homeland even when, in the early years, this was just a mirage. Later on, when the thirteen-year-old Akbar was first declared Padshah Ghazi, he had to send for the haraman from Kabul so that his grizzled warriors, veterans of Central Asian wars, were persuaded to remain beside him and fight for Hindustan.

The resources to piece together a life of the Mughal women are available but they are sometimes unaccountably ignored. An extraordinary document exists, discovered and translated from Persian into English in the early twentieth century, though it is almost never used. Gulbadan Begum, sister of Humayun and daughter of Babur, arrived in Hindustan at the age of five. She was asked many decades later by her grandnephew, Akbar, to write a biography of Babur and Humayun. It is this document, Gulbadan's

Humayun-nama (History of Humayun), that I have used extensively to recreate the lives of many of the early Mughal women in Part I of this book. In Gulbadan's spontaneous, vivid and unselfconscious prose is a unique document, a first-hand account of the sixteenth-century haraman. Through Gulbadan's account we are given tantalizing fragments that are never referred to in the men's biographies. We hear of Babur's preference for Maham Begum over his other wives, we understand the close-knit and layered relationships in the haraman, and we are able to visualize Humayun's tempestuous and intricate relationship with his wives and womenfolk. The few details we know about Bega Begum, Humayun's first wife, come from Gulbadan's frank account of Humayun's opium habit and the turbulent yet intimate relationship he shared with this woman, who was sometimes quick to take offence and occasionally berated him with an acid tongue. Despite the sometimes volatile nature of her relationship with Humayun, Bega was a loyal custodian of Humayun's legacy, overseeing the building of his magnificent mausoleum in Delhi. Because of Gulbadan's close friendship with her sister-in-law Hamida Banu, we learn of this young woman's determined courtship by Humayun. Hamida Banu's feisty and spirited nature comes through clearly in Gulbadan's account, and we are told many details about her sojourn in Persia while in exile with Humayun. It is through Gulbadan's account, and that of Humayun's attendant Jauhar, that a very different sort of haraman becomes visible. This is a mobile, rugged space in which the purdah of the women is cursory and frequently porous. There are no rigid limitations to the women's freedom, and the matriarchs, especially, are constantly called upon to fulfil public roles. It is a raucous place filled with camaraderie, disagreements, hurt feelings, song and laughter.

In Gulbadan's biography we also come across more tender lives, more likely to be overlooked by male biographers writing the glory of an emperor. So there is the six-year-old daughter of Humayun, Aqiqa, who was lost at a famous battle, presumed drowned. I name her not only for the terrible pathos of a little girl dying in the middle of a massacre (so beloved that her father mourned her for a very long time and reproached himself constantly for having brought her to that dreadful place) but for the aberrant fact of a six-year-old girl being present at such a scene at all. For

Humayun took his haraman with him wherever he went, into battle, on desperate escapes and also on pleasure excursions and sightseeing. This is how we understand that there was truly no separation between private and public lives, that both were one, the life of the padshah and his family.

It was during the long reign of Akbar, accompanied by his ardent friend and supremely enthusiastic biographer Abu'l-Fazl, that the notion of a separate, sequestered space for the women of the royal haraman first appears. It is this new zenana, an idealized world, and the women who nevertheless resolutely manage to be 'seen', that I explore in Part II of this book. Akbar married many women, Rajput rajkumaris among others, to secure his claim, and the Mughal zenana grew huge as these women brought their retinue and dependents, as well as ambitious brothers, with them. So a walled palace in sandstone was built for the first time in Fatehpur Sikri and then in Agra to try and maintain the 'good and proper order' that Akbar and Abu'l-Fazl desired above all things. It was also at this time that it was decreed indecorous to mention the royal Mughal women by name and so they became further hidden behind the anonymity of grandiose titles: Maryam Makani (of Mary's Stature) for Hamida Banu, Akbar's mother and Maryam-uz-Zamani (Mary of the World) for Jahangir's mother, Harkha Bai. They were all further sanitized and erased by being described as 'pillars of chastity' or 'cupolas of chastity' by Abu'l-Fazl who would resolutely always refer to them as 'the chaste ladies' of the zenana, young or ancient. Wherever possible, I have tried to discover the names of these women and create an identity for them from the clues that escaped the censor's vigil. The identity of Jahangir's mother was so shrouded in myth that in all the profusion of lines written by contemporary biographers about Akbar, a veritable landslide of words, there is only one single line that states that Harkha Bai is indeed the mother of Salim, the future Jahangir. Hidden behind her official title of Maryam-uz-Zamani, this Rajput rajkumari became a formidable and independently wealthy matron, trading through her own ships in the dangerous, pirate-infested waters of the sixteenth century.

To try and understand these disappeared women better, it is necessary to look at alternative histories and biographies, and for this we have, amongst others, the brilliant but tortured scholar and historian Abd-al-Qadir Badauni. Badauni's great misfortune was to be a contemporary and biographer of such a liberal, curious and inquisitive padshah as Akbar. For this orthodox scholar, nothing could have been more grating and horrifying than the slow spreading of Hindu Rajput influence at Akbar's court. Through Badauni's consistently appalled commentary, we realize that the Rajput women that Akbar married, and in particular Harkha Bai, brought with them their Vedic fires, their sun worship, their vegetarianism, their marriage rituals, their fasts and their Rajasthani clothes. Badauni allows us to see beyond the opaque 'pillars of chastity' and high walls, to the living, breathing women that formed part of that boisterous community of women.

When Hamida Banu and Humayun were forced into exile by Sher Shah Suri, they left behind the infant Akbar, who was just over a year old. But as Humayun struggled to regain the lost throne of Hindustan over the next few years, Akbar was not left bereft. He was entrusted to a company of women who would ceaselessly watch over his life and his happiness, for the life of a child in the sixteenth century was as evanescent as summer snow. These women, many of whom also nursed him through his infancy, were his 'anagas' or milk mothers. Even after the throne was regained, chaos quickly returned when Humayun died, making Akbar the Padshah of Hindustan at the age of thirteen. Through these years of Akbar's childhood and adolescence, he depended completely on the support, loyalty and guidance of his milk mothers and their families. One of these women, Maham Anaga, became extremely powerful through the implicit faith Akbar had in her judgement and ability. She was politically astute and ambitious and at one point was considered the effective 'vakil', or vice-regent, of the empire. Maham Anaga would also become one of the first of the Mughal women to patronise architecture in Delhi through her Khair-ul-Manazil Mosque.

As Akbar grew older, he became less dependent on the support of his milk mothers, but he was always deeply attached to all the Timurid women of his haraman. In addition to Hamida Banu, his mother, there were his aunts, Gulbadan and Bega, and also Salima Sultan, widow of Bairam Khan. Salima Sultan was a granddaughter of Babur who was taken into the household of the nineteen-year-old Akbar when she was widowed at the age of twenty-two. Though Akbar married Salima Sultan, they never had any children together, so the alliance may have only been one of propriety. For the zenana of Akbar was certainly not only for wives. It was for the widows of his generals, relatives who sought asylum from other countries, elderly mothers and grandmothers, widowed stepmothers, unmarried relatives, servants, the entourage of Rajput rajkumaris, children, attendants and tradeswomen of all sorts. It was, in fact, a place of sanctuary which conformed to the real meaning of the word 'harem' as being 'a place of worship, the sanctum sanctorum, where the committing of any sin is forbidden (haram)'. While Akbar's Rajput wives were more opaque behind their grandiose titles and high walls, the older Timurid relations continued to lead lives of startling freedom. Salima Sultan accompanied Gulbadan on a Hajj pilgrimage which lasted for seven long and turbulent years. She was instrumental in rehabilitating Akbar's son Jahangir after he committed a crime so heinous it seemed his father would never forgive him. A favourite prince or nobleman of the zenana women could get away with riotous bad behaviour, as Aziz Koka did, and even murder, as Jahangir did. The women would shout out their opinions from behind the jaalis during the durbar, and set off unexpectedly to visit a son or a Sufi saint, causing sudden chaos within the 'good order' of things Abu'l-Fazl so desired.

And so the zenana was constantly evolving and changing, buffeted by the influence of various groups of women. Over the years the older Turki speaking matriarchs of the Timurids died out, venerated figures of love and respect till their last breath. They were replaced by other women, Rajput and Persian, no longer Chagatai Turkish ones, and the zenana changed once again.

Through most of the 200 years of the great Mughals, one woman at a time was given the title 'Padshah Begum', which she usually retained till she died. The title was always given to a woman of enormous prestige and respect, and the surprising thing was that this was very rarely the wife of the emperor. In the early decades, royal mothers and elder sisters held this title. Widowed second wives would become padshah begums as would sisters and unmarried daughters. This astonishing range is a reflection of the changing zenana, and also of the easy insouciance with which the

Mughals accepted power in whichever woman was talented, charismatic and ambitious enough to claim it. One of the few Mughal wives to hold the title Padshah Begum, most controversially, was Noor Jahan.

In this book, I have tried to bring to life the stories of those Mughal women who have been forgotten—women whose influence was more subtle and fragile, or who have been subject to the casual erasure of time. Some are not royal women at all. There are foster mothers and Persian refugee women, women whom readers might be discovering for the first time, or at least in a guise not previously known to them. Noor Jahan and Mumtaz Mahal are the most famous of the Mughal women, and a great deal has already been written about them. In Noor Jahan's case, I have written about a few specific areas of her contribution in an attempt to redress some common misperceptions about Jahangir's wife. For many of the Europeans who wrote about the court of Jahangir, the visible and overreaching influence of Noor Jahan was baffling and frustrating. For example, to conduct trade in Hindustan, the English ambassador Thomas Roe found that he would have to interact with Noor Jahan, and offer her suitably unusual and magnificent gifts. Englishwomen of the same period were expected to be meek and subservient. Inevitably, dealing with powerful Hindustani women caused resentment and bitterness in the European commentators. Later Indian biographers of Noor Jahan, writing under the patronage of Shah Jahan, who had suffered at her hands, were not much more forgiving. And so an idea of a 'junta' was proposed with all its Mafiosi connotation of an evil stranglehold over Jahangir by Noor Jahan's family. Or, not much more flattering, a 'petticoat government', with the smirking implication that Jahangir was in sexual thrall of his wife, helpless and debased. I also hope to have shown that Noor Jahan was not an isolated example of a powerful and talented woman, but that she followed in the example of many similarly talented women and, in turn, inspired her grandnieces. Thus, these powerful women were not so much unexpected cyclones, falling out of a clear sky, as waves building up momentum, steadily and gradually, over decades of influence.

In the case of Noor Jahan's niece, Mumtaz Mahal, the personality of the living, breathing human woman has been hopelessly subsumed by the great, obsessive love she is supposed to have inspired in Shah

Jahan, culminating in the building of the Taj Mahal. Of all the Mughal women in this book, Mumtaz Mahal is the most elusive, hidden behind the excess of her children, the luminous, glorious legacy of her husband, and the flawless perfection of the 'greatest monument to love' ever built. Mumtaz Mahal's memory is wrought by the ambition of her children and husband, and the living woman is lost. Even if it is almost impossible to ever know much about the real Mumtaz Mahal, I hope to have helped explore the nuances behind the building of the Taj Mahal.

In writing this history of the Mughal women, I have tried consciously to swing the narrative arc away from the Eurocentric vision we often encounter in Mughal histories. Since the Europeans wrote so much about the Mughals, works which are readily available, moreover, in English, it is naturally easy to fall into the seductive game of reading Mughal history from a European point of view. Paradoxically, trying to access contemporary Mughal history written by Indians has proved much harder, many of the documents being in Persian and Urdu, still untranslated. In writing from the Mughal men and women's point of view, I hope to have brought out what the Europeans were to the Mughals—a footnote. Many of the emperors did not even mention the Europeans who were clustering at the margins of the court, slightly contemptible 'firangis' who were unclean and rather grasping, with mean and paltry gifts. Indeed, Jahangir wrote only one line about the Europeans in his marvellously evocative autobiography, the *Tuzuk-e-Jahangiri*. The Europeans, meanwhile, wrote entire treatises about the Mughals, fairly panting in their descriptions of the magnificent court and all the wealth on display. Naturally, this very negligence by the Mughals would have a disastrous result later on, but this, too, is part of Indian history.

When I first started writing this book, I did not realize that the idea of a constantly evolving and dynamic zenana would become so central a concept in this work. In most books that deal with the life of the Mughals, the 'royal harem' is usually a single chapter, sandwiched arbitrarily between ornamentation at the Mughal court and the royal kitchens, for example. Two hundred years of women in Mughal history are crunched up into a single way of being. Noor Jahan is described as an aberration, scheming and manipulative. There is little in the way of the subtle yet all-pervasive manner in which these women exerted influence and the textured lives they led. Most of the women of the Mughal haraman were, in fact, not wives at all; they were mothers, like Hamida Banu and Harkha Bai, unmarried sisters, like Jahanara and Roshanara, divorced women, like Khanzada, single daughters, like Zeb-un-Nisa and Zeenat-un-Nisa, aunts, like Gulbadan, distant relatives, like Salima Sultan, elderly dependents, etc. They were not sexually available women at all. And yet they all had a role to play, a duty to perform, and they were respected, and paid, for these crucial jobs. The lives they led and the influence they exerted, changed in ways both subtle and significant over 200 years.

That Mughal women wrote quite extensively is remarkable and their works, wherever available, are extraordinary. Other Mughal women apart from Gulbadan left writings. Jahanara wrote two Sufi treatises as well as poetry. She corresponded extensively, not only with kings wanting her patronage but also with her brothers, Aurangzeb and Dara Shikoh, and she became the vortex of the succession struggle between the two princes, both brothers seeking her support. Many of the women, including Aurangzeb's daughter Zeb-un-Nisa, wrote poetry. The women wrote farmans, or orders, and had seals in their names, which can be as eloquent as an entire biography. Noor Jahan's seal reads 'By the light of the sun of the emperor Jahangir, the bezel of the seal of Noor Jahan, the Empress of the age has become resplendent like the moon'—this is surely as powerful a testimony to her own ambition and glory than any biographer's praise. Wherever I could, I have quoted from these women's works, for if women's images are denied us, we at least have their words.

There are other sources of information too, apart from writings. There are the miniatures of the Mughals, and the way in which they depict, or erase, women from the stories. And, of course, there are the objects and buildings, strewn casually across India's landscape like so much precious, sparkling gold. The women of the great Mughals began sponsoring building works very early on. One of the earliest such examples in Delhi is the Khair-ul-Manazil Mosque built not by a royal woman, but a milk mother of Akbar's, Maham Anaga. Through the two centuries of Mughal rule, women continued to sponsor building works which reflected their aesthetic sense, their desire for pious works and the message they wished to transmit in terms of a visual legacy for posterity. One of the most splendid examples of just such a woman who wished to be remembered for the glory of her works was Jahanara.

In Part III of this book, I have talked about the zenana when the Mughal empire was at its most gloriously opulent and wealthy. The women, the wives and the elder daughters, were independently and fabulously wealthy, and some chose to spend that wealth to further their own legacies and that of the emperor's. When Shah Jahan shifted his capital to Delhi and built the brand-new city of Shahjahanabad, he was enthusiastically joined in his efforts by his daughters and wives. Fully half the royal buildings of Shahjahanabad were built by women. These wives and unmarried royal daughters had unimaginable wealth at their disposal which they used to create a vision of an imperial city which would be nothing less than paradise on earth. For in their projects, and through their many achievements, the women were not only indulging in personal projects, they were contributing to a Timurid vision of glory shared by the emperor himself. Many of the Mughal emperors pointedly chose a specific aspect of Timurid legacy and then used it to further legitimize their claims to a fabled and divine grandeur. Some chose the Sufi way, some chose painting or architecture or a refined Persian aesthetic or writing. And many of the women, when they joined in this enterprise, had the very same ambition—to claim the luminescent Timurid legacy.

Jahanara was extraordinary in that she accomplished a great many of these things. She was a Sufi scholar and a peer-murid (Sufi-devout). She was a writer, a poet and a patron of writers and saints. She was a builder of enormous ambition, and a great swathe of Shahjahanabad was shaped by her wealth and design. Unfortunately today, almost nothing remains of Jahanara's buildings in Delhi, having been destroyed by the British in the violent and brutal reprisals post the 1857 Uprising. The huge building works that Jahanara and many other Mughal women were involved in were only possible because of the enormous wealth these women had at their disposal. It is often forgotten that as the Mughal empire grew in size and splendour, the women involved in its formation also grew in wealth. This increased wealth and the desire to patronise architecture was not only limited to royal women. The wives of influential Mughal noblemen, like Qudsiya Begum, and even single women, like the eighteenth-century singer Noor Bai, had the means and the ambition to leave a legacy. Lady Mary Wortley Montagu, an Englishwoman accompanying her husband to the Ottoman empire in the eighteenth century was amazed to learn that Muslim women, even married ones, had financial control over their own wealth, quite unlike their sisters in the Christian world. In India, meanwhile, Mughal women earned an income through cash and the revenue from jagirs, or land grants. Others, like Noor Jahan, Maryam-uz-Zamani and Jahanara, also actively took part in international trade, thereby greatly increasing their wealth. This wealth was then theirs to spend, according to their inclination and ambition. And when they died, they could leave their wealth to persons of their choice. Jahanara left her property and her gems to her nieces, both married and unmarried women, thereby extending her patronage of women beyond her death. Jahanara herself had received half of her mother's wealth when Mumtaz Mahal died, making her fabulously wealthy at the age of seventeen.

By the second half of the seventeenth century, the Mughal empire was one of the greatest, the largest and the most wealthy in the world. The women no longer had the sort of physical freedom that the earlier women like Maham, Gulbadan, Hamida Banu and Bega had. Their purdah was now more intransigent but, because the Mughals ruled over a diverse population, of Hindus and Christians and Parsis and other faiths as well as Muslims, the Mughals were never committed to the sequestration of their women with the same unflinching fervour as their contemporary Muslim empires, the Ottoman and the Safavids. The honour of Mughal men was not as irretrievably bound to the sexual chastity of their women. The Mughals, moreover, were always faithful to their nomadic Timurid ancestors for whom divorce and remarriage was a pragmatic way of life in a land intermittently ravaged by war. Widows were encouraged to remarry. There was never any stigma attached to a divorced woman, or one who had been 'taken' by the enemy. And this indulgent, stout acceptance also became part of Mughal culture. These Timurid ancestors, moreover, readily accepted the power and influence of respected women. And so the Mughal women increasingly contributed to the Timurid legacy and took part in that ancient but increasingly dangerous and volatile game—succession politics.

Because the Mughals did not follow a system of primogeniture, any Mughal prince, sufficiently ambitious and talented, could hope to ascend the throne one day. This naturally led to turbulent times, and many of the women of the Mughal zenana were actively involved in supporting one party or the other. In some cases, especially in the early years, the zenana acted as one body, united in their desire to protect the still vulnerable, nascent empire. But as the empire grew wealthier, the stakes higher, the posturing became more serious and the consequences bloodier. Now when the women supported a prince in his succession struggles, this was an individual choice and the outcome was uncertain. This dangerous game erupted spectacularly in the mid-seventeenth century in the succession struggle between Aurangzeb and Dara Shikoh. The entire empire, it is said, waited in terror while the future of the dynasty hung in the balance. The clash between the two brothers involved their two sisters, Jahanara and Roshanara, and the fury of this tussle caused shock waves far into the future. The sisters would stake all they had in this battle, their wealth and their liberty, and would bring about the most unexpected reversal of fortunes. The zenana had changed once again, more fractured and partisan now, the stakes immeasurably higher.

During the fifty years of Aurangzeb's rule, the Mughal empire sloped into the last phase of its grandeur. Outwardly massive but increasingly bankrupt and austere, the zenana also reflected this new reality. The glorious capitals of the earlier padshahs—Delhi, Agra and Lahore—were abandoned, and Aurangzeb spent most of his reign in the Deccan, where his daughter Zeenat-un-Nisa was padshah begum. Too potentially powerful because of their Timurid bloodline, Aurangzeb's older daughters remained unmarried, their ambitions frugal and their achievements less exalted than their predecessors. Zeenat-un-Nisa remained in the Deccan as head of Aurangzeb's zenana and Zeb-un-Nisa, caught on the wrong side of succession politics, was incarcerated in Salimgarh jail in Shahjahanabad for more than twenty years. In the 200 years since the first great matriarchs of the Timurid haraman, Qutlugh Nigar Khanum and Khanzada, rode beside the young Babur, bolstering his resolve and guarding his legacy, the zenana of the Mughals had changed irrevocably. Zeb-un-Nisa especially,

physically immobilized and written out of the Mughals' biographies due
to Aurangzeb's fury at her rebellion, is a disappeared woman. From her
prison on the Yamuna she wrote poetry while Shahjahanbad, abandoned,
gathered dust and an unassailable nostalgia for the glories of the past.

This book is not a history of the Mughals. I have not studied the great
wars that shaped the age of the Mughals or the administrative systems
they created in India, the agrarian reforms or the taxation system. It is
the story of some of the Mughal women who shaped the history of India
through 200 years, in ways sometimes subtle, sometimes dangerous, always
extraordinary. The reader may be surprised also at how little I deal with
the 'love life' of these Mughal women. What usually fascinates a modern
reader is a twentieth-century construct—the idea of romantic love. For
these medieval Muslim women, their relationships were based on a number
of mundane, pragmatic realities—expediency, practicality and complicated
genealogical calculations. Babur, most articulate of emperors on all possible
subjects, is strangely laconic and matter-of-fact when speaking of his
wives. Indeed, he writes with more passion about an erotic longing for a
young man than about any of his wives. Humayun, though smitten by
Hamida Banu, is usually more concerned with keeping all his relations,
wives and aunts and sisters, equally happy. Even Jahangir, who is famously
believed to have been overwhelmed by his love for Noor Jahan, writes
almost negligently about her in his autobiography. We are blindsided by
our search for an exclusive love in these lives, whereas the reality was a
shared goal and a mutual dependence. We are dazzled by the perfection
of the Taj Mahal, but do we really know if this was only a monument to
love and not also the expression of a blistering ambition and ego which
would be followed by the building of an entire city? As for the women,
there is not even a sliver of an expression of exclusive love. The most
haunting writings on love were Jahanara's expression of her love for her
brother, Dara Shikoh, whom she speaks of in terms of a soulmate, and
the erotic longing she describes when writing of her ecstatic Sufi visions.

In the background of the stories, I have also acknowledged the presence
of the Europeans, who were carrying on a parallel struggle in India for
spice and cloth and indigo. This juxtaposition helps to better understand
the place of the Mughals within world history. It helps to appreciate how

truly magnificent the Mughals were for their time, and how influential, wealthy and respected their women. I have tried to show that the reason some of the Europeans always wrote about the Mughals with unwavering criticism was because of ancient ties of hate and loathing. This makes it easier to understand how these attitudes became encrusted in the narrative. I have interspersed the stories of the women quite liberally with that of the personalities of the different emperors. These magnificent Mughals are, after all, the storm-lit skies against which the women are clearly defined. And, finally, I hope this book will draw these Mughal women out of the deep well of misremembrance they lie in, in the cold waters of prejudice and endlessly biased recordings, to walk once more in the sunlit glory they once so confidently, and foolishly, believed would always be theirs.

Part I

Peripatetic Queens from Persia to Hindustan

1494–1569

THE TIMURIDS, THE UZBEKS AND
KHANZADA'S SACRIFICE

When Umar Shaikh Mirza, the Timurid ruler of Ferghana, dies in 1494, falling through the dovecote of his fortress at the top of a ravine in modern-day Uzbekistan, he is only thirty-nine years old and his eldest son and heir, Babur, is just twelve. As befits a man who would profoundly love gardens and whose endless quest for a suitable garden site in the arid wastes of northern Hindustan, even in the midst of precarious empire-building, would drive him to distraction, the young Babur is in a charbagh in neighbouring Andizhan when he hears of his father's death. Almost the first thought the young mirza has on learning this calamitous news is that if his uncle, Sultan Ahmad Mirza, 'were to come with a large army, the begs would turn both me and the province over to him'. The prosaic reality of succession politics in the region known as Mawarannahr, as scholar Lisa Balabanlilar has noted, is that 'it was not outsiders but Babur's rapacious Timurid-Mongol uncles who posed the first and most immediate threat to the boy's inheritance'. Indeed in this volatile and fractious situation, the only unconditional support Babur can count on is that of his female relatives—his grandmother, mother and sister.

When Babur's great ancestor Timur came to power in Central Asia in 1370, some 150 years after the death of Chinghiz Khan, the enduring charisma of the Great Khan still lingered, though none of Chinghiz Khan's descendants were strong enough to wield effective power. Timur himself was a tribal nobleman but could not claim direct descent from Chinghiz Khan and, in recognition of that, never took the imperial title of khan, but called himself amir, commander. He did, however, carefully cultivate a Chingizid connection by marrying powerful Chingizid women. From then on, Timur added the title guregen, son-in-law, as an implacable addendum to his power, and also married all his sons and grandsons to Chingi women. But by the fourteenth century in Central Asia, Timur also had to incorporate a powerful new symbol of legitimacy into his mantle—Islam. In an audacious balancing act between his old Turco-Mongol yasa, and the new Islamic Shari'a, he wrought together the allegiance of a diverse group of followers and had in his army 'Turks that worshipped idols and men who worshipped fire, Persian magi, soothsayers and wicked enchanters and unbelievers'. So successful was Timur's strategy of catastrophic acts of violence and conquest combined with a careful nurturing of cultural symbols that, for his successors, there was no longer any need to invoke the Chingizid charisma at all. The Timurid legacy, for all its guregen humility, was incandescent enough.

By the time Babur's father dies, the sprawling empire of Timur has long since splintered into semi-autonomous provinces ruled by Timurid mirzas, ever more numerous and volatile. Which is why when Babur rushes to Ferghana to consolidate his inheritance, according to writer Amitav Ghosh, he is hardly alone, for 'the valleys and steppes of Central Asia teemed with Timurid princes in search of realms to rule'.

Babur's immediate strategy at this time of precarious reckoning is to meet with his close advisers and his grandmother, Aisan Daulat Begum. 'For tactics and strategy', Babur famously declares in his *Baburnama*, 'there were few women like my grandmother', before adding, 'she was intelligent and a good planner. Most affairs were settled with her counsel.' In contrast, when Babur talks about his father in his extraordinarily frank and evocative biography, though he acknowledges his ability to rule, he is not particularly tender. 'He was short in stature', Babur writes unsentimentally, 'had a round beard and a fleshy face, and was fat'. We are also told that 'he used to drink a lot', and that 'he grew rather fond of ma'jun and under its influence would lose his head'. In talking about his mother, grandmother and his sisters, however, Babur is never anything other than deferential and loving. Babur's clear reverence for his grandmother Aisan Daulat Begum is not surprising, for even in a land of strong and independent women, she was extraordinary. Earlier in her peregrinations with her husband, Yunus Khan, the two were taken captive by a certain Sheikh Jamal-ud-din Khan. Aisan Daulat was then handed over as prize to one of the sheikh's officers, Khwaja Kalan. According to the sixteenth-century general and chronicler Mirza Muhammad Haidar Dughlat, 'she made no objections, but appeared pleased'. However, when Khwaja Kalan went to Aisan Daulat's rooms in the evening, hoping to enjoy his new 'gift', he found the door precipitously locked behind him and the begum's servants 'laid hold of him and put him to death, by stabbing him with knives'. This plan had been masterminded by the begum and 'when day broke, they threw his body outside'. When the horrified Sheikh Jamal went to the begum for an explanation, she replied with matchless self-possession and pride: 'I am the wife of Sultan Yunus Khan; Shaikh Jamal gave me to some one else; this is not allowed by Muhammaden law, so I killed the man, and Shaikh Jamal Khan may kill me also if he likes.' But the sheikh, recognizing an indomitable adversary, sent her back with honour to her husband.

This, then, is the flinty and uncompromising woman who immediately stepped beside her young grandson upon the death of his father, guiding his next crucial steps and leading him to a place of safety. With the begum is her daughter and Babur's mother, Qutlugh Nigar Khanum, who, Babur says, 'was with me during most of my guerilla engagements and interregna'. With them also is his oldest sibling, Khanzada, elder to him by five years. The next few years are indeed a time of untethered wanderings, full of dangers and betrayals and physical hardships. Babur lays siege to Samarkand, ancient capital of Timur, several times, and spends restless years as an exile, a prince without a kingdom. The women wander with him in these grim conditions, consoling and supportive, even in the stark midwinter of Mawarannahr.

And yet life goes on, even in this unlikeliest of households, and in 1500, when Babur is seventeen, he marries for the first time. The bride is Ayisha Sultan Begum and Babur admits with painful honesty that 'although my affection for her was not lacking, since it was my first marriage and I was bashful, I went to her only once every ten, fifteen or twenty days'. Things only get worse for Babur in his amorous plans and 'I lost my fondness for her altogether', he admits sadly. It requires the intervention of his mother, who 'drove me to her with all the severity of a quartermaster'. Meanwhile the haraman, Babur's entourage of wives, children, family retainers and other dependents, are driven through these unstable lands like flotsam in a stormy sea. Notwithstanding Babur's reluctance, Ayisha Sultan finds herself eventually pregnant and travels in difficult conditions to Samarkand. Babur's firstborn child is a daughter, Fakhr-un-Nisa, but she dies within forty days and Babur is now confronted with his most relentless enemy. This enemy, in mercilessly evicting Babur and his family forever from their beloved homeland of Samarkand, will create a hopeless nostalgia in Babur for the lands of his childhood.

By 1500, Babur's greatest foes are no longer his own family, but his hereditary enemies, the Uzbeks, who have a premonition that the age of the Timurids is coming to an end in Central Asia and have stepped in to stake their own claim to these fabled lands. 'For nearly 140 years the capital Samarkand had been in our family', writes Babur bitterly. 'Then came the Uzbeks, the foreign foe from God knows where, and took over.' For six months, the Uzbek chief Shaybani Khan lays siege to Babur and his entourage at Samarkand. Babur's many uncles and cousins desert the young mirza and refuse to send him any help. Babur 'decided to make the Samarkand fortress fast and defend it to the last', and moreover '[his] mother and sisters stayed in the fortress'. As the siege wears on, however, conditions grow desperate and 'the poor and unfortunate began to eat dogs and donkeys'. Now, as hopes of any sort of honourable victory fade for Babur, he makes a decision which will irrevocably alter the fate of a beloved member of his family. It is a decision so compromised and shameful that he will never admit to it, even in his searingly honest autobiography.

As the eighteen-year-old Babur waits in febrile despair for the help that will never come from his uncles, Shaybani Khan sends a message to Babur. 'If you would marry your sister Khanzada Begam to me,' he writes to the young man, 'there might be peace and a lasting alliance between us.' And so Khanzada, at twenty-three years of age, is left behind with Shaybani Khan as ransom and war conquest because 'at length it had to be done'. Deserted by old retainers and soldiers, abandoned by his family, Babur 'gave the Begam to the khan, and came out himself (from Samarqand). With 200 followers on foot, wearing long frocks on their shoulders and peasants' brogues on their feet...in this plight, unarmed, and relying on God, he went towards the lands of Badakhshan and Kabul.'

Babur himself in his *Baburnama* stutters unconvincingly around the episode of his escape from Shaybani Khan. 'Wormwood Khan [Shaybani] initiated truce talks', Babur claims. 'There was nothing to be done. We made peace...I took my mother the khanim with me.... My elder sister Khanzada Begim fell into Wormwood Khan's hands while we were leaving.' This truncated, staccato account is revealing. Shaybani Khan had decisively starved and surrounded Babur and his people for over six months. There was no reason for him to offer an unconditional truce. Had there been a truce, there would have been no need for Babur to escape at night and for Khanzada to 'fall' into Shaybani's hands. 'Babar Padishah gave up Khanzada Begum in exchange for his own life', writes Mirza Haidar succinctly, 'and escaped'. Babur shifts and slides around the issue of Khanzada's fate because it was an outrageous violation of her dignity and demonstrated his inability to protect her. In fact, with the rise of the Uzbek confederacy, the number of forced marriages between Uzbek warriors and Timurid noblewomen became astonishingly high. Though the Uzbeks are direct descendants of Chinghiz Khan themselves, by the end of the fifteenth century they recognize the equally luminous allure of the Timurid name, and resolve to cleave it to themselves.

Khanzada now joins Shaybani's haraman and eventually bears him a son, Khurram, who dies in childhood. Shaybani divorces Khanzada after a few years, accusing her of remaining partisan to the cause of Babur and her Timurid family, an accusation that bears testimony to her undaunted spirit and pride in her own Timurid family. He then gives her in marriage to a lower ranked man, a certain Sayyid Hada. Altogether, Khanzada lives in enforced exile for more than ten years. Finally in 1510 Shah Ismail, a Shi'a religious leader and the founder of the Safavid dynasty, brings together all of modern Iran through a succession of conquests and then turns his attention to the Sunni Uzbek tribes. At the battle of Merv in 1510 he kills both Sayyid Hada and Shaybani Khan and in a gesture worthy of any Mongol excess, converts Shaybani Khan's skull into a jewelled drinking goblet. After the battle, when Shah Ismail realizes that Khanzada is Babur Mirza's sister, he has her returned to Babur, 600 kilometres south at Kunduz, with an escort of soldiers. Khanzada is now thirty-three years old and has lived for ten years a life in abeyance, safeguarding the honour and the future of her brother. Babur, we are told by Mirza Haidar, 'is overjoyed' and there is no reason to disbelieve him. It is a testament to Khanzada's resilience and the Timurids' gruff pragmatism that no stigma is ever attached to Khanzada, nor indeed to any other Timurid woman who 'falls' to an enemy. On the contrary, Khanzada reintegrated into Babur's household as a woman whose sacrifice for the safety of the padshah will be celebrated not only by Babur and his entire haraman, but by his son Humayun and into future generations. When Humayun becomes Padshah Ghazi of Hindustan, Khanzada, along with some of the other older women of the haraman, becomes a living repository of the memory of Babur and the Timurid dream. She is the guardian of those threshold stories that the early Mughals told themselves as they wandered ever further away from Samarkand in search of consolation. As a testament to the value of those dreams, she will become the most revered and respected member of Humayun's haraman. Long after Babur himself is dead, Khanzada will become the most powerful woman of the Mughals when she is named 'Padshah Begum of Hindustan'. There are times in the 200 years of the great Mughal empire that no padshah begum is named at all, so it is not an obligatory position. It is, instead, a mark of respect given to truly remarkable women who command enormous authority. In 1535 it is Khanzada, childless and twice-widowed, un-bolstered by son or husband, who holds this title in recognition of the valour of her sacrifice and the legitimacy of her memories.

HINDUSTAN AND THE COMING OF THE
BEGUMS AND THE KHANUMS

After the ignominious exit from Samarkand and the abandoning of Khanzada in 1501, Babur and his small band of followers and women scramble for survival and a secure home for the next few months and years, constantly harried by the Uzbeks. Apart from his mother, Qutlugh Khanum, Babur mentions the presence of two other women at this bleak time—serving woman Khalifa Bichka and foster-mother Menglig Kukaldash. Later, in Tashkent, Babur and his diminished group 'endured much poverty and humiliation. No country or hope of one... This uncertainty and want of house and home', laments Babur, 'drove me at last to despair'. In these conditions, 'the little band of homeless fugitives, surrounded by enemies, passed about twelve months in the hills of present-day Uzbekistan in great poverty, owing their survival solely to the loyalty or compassion of the wild nomads of that region'. Babur's mother is always by his side, travelling with him and sharing his every privation. 'So destitute were we,' admits Babur, 'that we had but two tents among us; my own used to be pitched for my mother and they set an alachuq [a felt covering with flexible poles] at each stage for me to sit in.' They are then joined by Babur's grandmother, Aisan Daulat Begum, who had remained behind in Samarkand when Babur fled. 'The hungry and lean family members who had stayed in Samarkand', also arrived with Aisan Daulat. Soon it is midwinter, harsh and unforgiving and 'there is a terrible cold snap' writes Babur. 'In this region,' he adds, 'the wind from Ha Darwesh never ceases and always blows hard.' Whatever water they find is almost completely frozen over and 'it was so bad', admits Babur, 'that within two or three days two or three men died'. In addition to the stark conditions, Babur and his party are attacked by marauding tribes. Once when separated from Babur, 'my lady mother and the uruq [family]...passed through great danger' writes Babur, rather tersely. The entire uruq 'having suffered plunder and seizure, escaped...and joined us at the Aba field'.

At last, 'at the beginning of my twenty-third year [when] I first put a razor to my face', Babur writes, they arrive at Kabul, where he is met with surprisingly little resistance, and captures the city almost as an afterthought. After some lackadaisical punishments—'I rode there and had four or five people shot and one or two dismembered'—Babur and his family settle in Kabul which he will rule for more than twenty years, taking the title Padshah. At first, Babur is thoroughly unimpressed by Kabul, calling it 'a trifling place', but he finds the resilience, nonetheless, to make it the base for a much more grandiose conquest.

In all the years that he is in Kabul, Babur will never stop dreaming of the fabled Timurid cities of Samarkand and Herat. But Uzbek ferocity scythes through his ambition and he will never reclaim what he always considered his own Timurid birthright. In Kabul, however, he finds a solace of sorts, even if it lacks the perfection of those other ancient capitals. 'The province of Kabul', writes Babur evocatively, 'lies in the midst of mountains that look like rows of clover'. He is appreciative of the fruits—'grapes, pomegranates, apricots, apples, quinces, pears, peaches, plums, jujubes, almonds and nuts'—and pragmatic about the people—'The people drink wine, do not pray, are fearless and act like infidels'. And always, relentlessly, he tries to improve and reshape and redefine: 'The stream used to run higgledy-piggledy until I ordered it to be straightened. Now it is a beautiful place.' But the Kabul years are still, for Babur, years of strife and constant battles. His attempts to reclaim lands from the Uzbeks are always thwarted and so, to consolidate his legitimacy and strengthen his vulnerable hold on this land, the two decades of his rule in Kabul becomes the time of the wives.

For someone who was to write an autobiography of astonishing detail, Babur is bafflingly circumspect about the women he marries. The scholar and colonial agent S. M. Edwardes argues that 'considering that the days of his youth and manhood were spent in constant warfare and in expeditions and wanderings, which demanded the utmost physical endurance, it is hardly surprising that amorous dalliance played little part in Babur's life.' While it is certainly true that Babur spends a very large part of his life on horseback, this never seems to stop him from composing the occasional quatrain or from noting in detail the effect of a particular wine on his behaviour and on that of his companions. It is perhaps that Babur is, after all, most comfortable in the gregarious rabble of this brotherhood of equals, his tribesmen and his warriors. It is with his men that Babur creates the intense bonds of camaraderie through his famous drinking parties, the majlis-e-sharaab, and it is the men who entertain him and who fight by his side. The women, meanwhile, create their universe in parallel, and the two intersect only occasionally.

By 1503, not surprisingly, Ayisha Sultan, the bride of Babur's teenage years, abandons her reluctant husband after the death of her daughter and no more is ever heard of her. Babur's next marriage, to Zainab Sultan Begum, a daughter of his paternal uncle, takes place around 1504 or 1505 through 'the good offices of my mother', as Babur has it. He adds, however, that 'she [Zainab Sultan] was not very congenial, and two or three years later,' somewhat conveniently, 'she dies of small-pox.' Around the same time, Babur is afflicted by a loss that affects him far more than that of his unloved wife. His intrepid mother Qutlugh Nigar, faithful companion of his lonely years, dies after a short illness. Babur carries the beloved body to a garden on a mountainside and 'entrusted her to the earth'. While still in mourning for his mother, he learns of the death of another fiery old lady, his grandmother Aisan Daulat. He is joined in Kabul by his mother's sister, Mihir Nigar Khanum, and 'grieving was renewed; the pain of separation', admits Babur, 'was unbearable.' Almost as a means to shake off his paralysing torpor, Babur gets an army together and sets off to attack Kandahar.

While away in Khurasan, in 1506, Babur marries Maham Begum, perhaps the most cherished of his wives, who will bear him five children, four of whom will die in infancy. One son survives, the future Padshah Humayun. Another marriage occurs when a young woman somewhat forthrightly decides to act upon an attraction she feels for Babur. When Babur is visiting his paternal uncle and aunt in Heri, their daughter Ma'sumah Begum is also present with her mother and, 'upon first seeing me', writes Babur candidly, 'she felt a great inclination towards me.' Ma'sumah marries Babur but dies bearing him a daughter, soon after. In the next few years, Babur marries two more women, Dildar Begum and Gulrukh Begum, who bear him five children each. In all, eighteen children are born to Babur during his years in Kabul. Maham, as mother of Babur's first surviving son, Humayun, is declared padshah begum of his court, and she is the first padshah begum of the great Mughals. It is around this time also, as this huddle of women and children begins to consolidate around Babur, that Khanzada is returned to him, escorted by troops sent by the Persian Shah Ismail. 'We had been apart for some ten years,' writes Babur 'when Muhammadi Kukuldash and I went to see her, neither she nor those about her knew us, although I spoke.' That Khanzada struggles to recognize her brother, whom she has last seen as 'a beardless youth' of seventeen, is hardly surprising. He is now a battle-hardened warrior of twenty-seven, with a long, drooping moustache. 'They recognized us after some time,' Babur assures the reader. Despite the laconic description, it is easy to imagine the effervescent joy and emotion of this important reunion. Babur has just recently lost the women who had tethered him to his Timurid inheritance—his mother and his grandmother. Now Khanzada will hold that exalted position, guardian of their family's luminous claims. The importance of this meeting is reflected in the fact that it was to be depicted in miniatures painted at Akbar's court, some eighty years later, and used to illustrate Babur's biography. In one such painting illustrated by the miniaturist Mansur, the siblings are depicted under the awning of a simple crimson tent, while a wall of red cloth keeps out the eager courtiers and soldiers. Khanzada is seated in front of an attentive and respectful Babur, raising a commanding hand while speaking to the men. She is wearing the classic Turkish tall pointed hat, her face is unveiled and she is the only woman in the composition who is as large as the seated men. The camels and the horses in the stony countryside outside the tents and the hustle of gesticulating men suggest movement and noise and a life spent travelling in the bruising, inhospitable countryside.

Khanzada returns to Kabul with Babur, bringing with her stories of resistance and sacrifice and fierce valour. In Babur's slowly forming haraman, she will meet his new wives, Maham, Dildar and Gulrukh. She will be given the easy respect and love which is the prerogative of older women, for at thirty-three, Khanzada is already middle-aged. She will have stories, also, for all the children who will grow up under her vigilant care—Humayun, Hindal, Kamran, Gulbadan and all the children who will shape the future of Hindustan once they are banished forever from Central Asia. Gulbadan, the daughter of Babur and Dildar, who will write a biography of Humayun decades after Khanzada's return, will only use the most affectionate and respectful terms for her aunt, aakaajanum (respected aunt).

The women that Babur marries during the years of his reign in Kabul are often daughters of powerful Timurid noblemen. For Babur, the Uzbek threat is a dominating, violent force that will never go away and, consequently, he increasingly distances himself from his Chingizid heritage, which the Uzbeks also claim, in favour of his Timurid one. His wives help burnish that lustre not just with their familial connections, but with the vigilance with which they contribute to its safeguarding. Babur spends a lifetime aspiring to the ideals of the great Timurid strongholds of Samarkand and Herat and his women will help him keep that 'Timurid flame' alive far into the following generations. Poetry, architecture, structured gardens, a glittering court, songs and the easy bonhomie of gilded companions were always close to Babur's heart. His Mongol cousins he abhors and considers brutish savages and would have been aghast to know that the Persianized word for Mongols was what his dynasty would be wrongly called—the Mughals. Babur's people always refer to themselves as Gurkani, the Persianized form of *guregen*, 'son-in-law', which was one of the titles of Amir Timur.

In the twenty years that Babur spends in Kabul, he conducts five raids on Hindustan. In 1519, on just such an expedition, Babur attacks the fortress of Bajaur, in modern-day Pakistan. The enemy is defeated and Bajaur is conquered, following which a grisly trophy is sent back to the anxious entourage and haraman at Kabul. 'Some of the sultans and rebels who had been taken prisoner were executed,' explains Babur. 'Their heads were sent to Kabul with news of the victory.' Babur makes another conquest at this time, in addition to Bajaur. While travelling through Afghanistan, he is approached by one of the Yusufzai chieftains, Malik Shah Mansur. The Yusufzai Afghan tribes are enemies of Babur and now a rapprochement is sought, for which a bride is offered. Babur marries Bibi Mubarika, daughter of Malik Shah Mansur, and 'confirm(s) his ties to the Yusufzai.' Bibi Mubarika, or Afghani Agacha as Gulbadan affectionately calls her in her *Humayun-nama*, will be a favourite and loyal wife of Babur. Some twenty years later she will stand alone before the forces of Sher Shah Suri, a subversive and frail hero, defending the body of her dead husband.

In Kabul, meanwhile, Dildar is pregnant. This news is sent to Babur, along with a letter from Maham in which she writes, astonishingly, 'whether it be a boy or a girl, I will take my chances. Give the child to me and I will raise it as my own.' Maham has already lost four of her children, only Humayun surviving, and this is quite possibly why Babur agrees to this adoption. The child that is born to Dildar is a son, Hindal, and when he is three days old, he is adopted by Maham. Four years later another child of Dildar's, the baby Gulbadan, will again be adopted by Maham. We are never told what Dildar's wishes are or whether she is distraught when her three-day-old infant is taken from her. It will have been a wrench, certainly, a visceral loss, but the baby will remain within the household and she has her two elder daughters to console her, and two more children will be born to Dildar. Certainly there is never any indication in Gulbadan's biography or in any other source of any bitterness or resentment between the women. The prosaic reality of the hierarchy between the wives and the harsh truth of infant mortality are enough to make this adoption a pragmatic necessity.

The Mughals of Hindustan would, in time, become the most roaming of dynasties anywhere in the world. They will travel constantly and change their capital cities on a whim. They will build great cities on the memory of a dream, just to abandon them immediately, and the most long-lived of them, Aurangzeb, will spend decades in self-imposed exile in a distant corner of his empire. But the first of their cities, the first capital of the Mughal empire is, in effect, the mountain kingdom of Kabul. Babur will be padshah of Kabul district for over twenty years, far longer than the time he will spend in Hindustan, in Agra. Though Babur is initially underwhelmed by Kabul, it is already a lively place, fizzing with movement and traders. Babur notes that up to twelve languages are spoken here and 'up from Hindustan come ten, fifteen, twenty thousand caravans bringing slaves, cotton cloth, refined and unrefined sugar and aromatic roots.' It is here, in Kabul, that a semblance of a court, a depth of household, slowly gathers. As the children are born to the wives of Babur, nurses and tutors and servants are added to their numbers. The children, both girls and boys, receive an education befitting their royal Timurid status. Turki is the language of the court but slowly the influence of Persian grows. Babur's daughter Gulbadan, who will write a biography of Babur and Humayun almost sixty years later, writes in robust, direct Persian with a smattering of Turki words and phrases. Aunts, retainers and obscure relations drift in; layer by layer the dense fabric of the Mughal tapestry emerges. The uruq gradually transforms into the haraman.

In 1520, the thirteen-year-old Humayun is given the province of Badakhshan by his father and is forced to leave Kabul and his home. Gulbadan tells us that 'his Majesty (Babur) and akam (Maham) followed and also went to Badakhshan, and there spent several days together. The Mirza (Humayun) remained and my royal father and my lady came back to Kabul.' It is only Gulbadan who notes in her memoir that both Maham and Babur travel with Humayun to settle their firstborn son and heir into his lonely outpost at Badakhshan. Maham's anxiety at the fate of her only surviving child, and his ability to thrive in the fractious borderlands as a Timurid prince, is easy to imagine.

In 1526, two further additions are made to Babur's haraman. Two Circassian slaves, Gulnar and Nargul, are gifted to him by Shah Tahmasp of Persia. These two women will later become valued and respected members of Babur's entourage, in a reflection of the fluid structure of the Mughal haraman. But at the end of 1525, Babur has once again gathered his army for an expedition, and this time the gains will be far greater than anything he has achieved so far and will, at last, be equal to his ambitions as Timur's worthy successor. Based on Timur's earlier successful raid into Hindustan, Babur now lays his gossamer-thin claim to the country. He sends a goshawk to Sultan Ibrahim in Delhi to ask for 'the country which from old had depended on the Turks.' Not unsurprisingly, Sultan Ibrahim is unimpressed. And so, 'with the sun in Sagittarius', writes Babur, 'we set out on an expedition to Hindustan'.

◆

Babur and all the fighting men will be gone from the lives of the women in Kabul for three years. This huge exodus of all the warriors is likely to have been one of the earliest memories of the children left behind in Kabul. The long, dancing procession of the horses carrying somewhere between 10,000 and 20,000 warriors. The glinting mail, the swirling dust and the fearsome double-curved bows of the cavalry. Gulbadan is just two years old when her father marches off to Hindustan, and for the next three years the women will wait anxiously for news from there. Humayun, now seventeen, is summoned from Badakhshan to join his father's forces, and it seems he makes his impatient father wait too long. 'Since Humayun was long overdue,' notes Babur angrily, 'I sent him some harshly worded letters.' Kamran, a young adolescent, is the oldest male child to remain in Kabul. Maham finds that she is pregnant and exactly nine months after Babur's departure delivers a baby boy on 2 August 1526. Two months after his birth a runner reaches Babur in faraway Hindustan to give him the news. However the child, Faruq, dies while still an infant and before Babur ever gets to see him. Messengers are constantly sent over the Hindu Kush through the Khyber Pass to Kabul, bearing news of the padshah's adventures and conquest. In 1526, news arrives of young Humayun's first victory in the town of Hisar-Firoza while Babur marches towards Panipat. As Babur gets ready for the first great battle for Hindustan, he is disappointed by the land itself. 'The cities and provinces of Hindustan are all unpleasant,' he writes witheringly. 'All cities, all locales are alike.' His greatest criticism is for the type of garden he finds here: 'the gardens have no walls, and most places are flat as boards'. Despite these reservations, Babur galvanizes his forces and Ibrahim Lodi, an Afghan Muslim of the Lodi Sultans, is killed along with some 15,000 of his troops at Panipat. When Humayun reaches Agra, the family of Ibrahim Lodi's ally, the Raja of Gwalior Bikramjit, offer him jewels and gems to safeguard their lives. Amongst these is a diamond whose worth is known to be 'the whole world's expenditure for half a day'. When Babur arrives in Agra, Humayun obediently presents the diamond to him but Babur, with a certain uncanny prescience, 'gave it right back to him'. This monstrous diamond, one of many with a bloody and secretive history in Hindustan, is said to be cursed. For now it is held in a silk purse which Humayun always keeps on him, where it clinks coldly against a growing collection of rubies and diamonds.

Babur has a long list of complaints about his brand new kingdom. He is horrified to find that the people appear scantily dressed and 'men and women for the most part go naked wearing only a cloth about the loins'. Babur himself, like his men, wears a heavy, long, kaftan-type coat called the chafan or a sheepskin coat called the posteen, derived from Turkish, Persian and Central Asian styles, appropriate for the cold weather they live in. The local residents of Hindustan, meanwhile, smirk at the thin drooping moustaches of Babur and his men, their sparse, scraggly beards and their shaved heads. 'Hindustan is a place of little charm,' Babur continues, scathingly. 'There is no beauty in its people...there are no good horses, meat, grapes, melons or other fruit. There is no ice, cold water, good food or bread in the markets. There are no baths and no madrasas.' The only fruit he is willing to consider somewhat positively is the mango. 'The mangoes when good are very good,' Babur concedes, 'but as many are eaten, few are first rate. Best made into condiments or preserved in syrup.' He is not, however, so blinkered as to ignore its obvious allure: 'The one nice aspect of Hindustan,' he admits, 'is that it is a large country with lots of gold and money.' It is also a fertile country, which the observant Babur would not have been unaware of, and farmers planted two crops of wheat a year and two crops of rice in the wetter regions. They also grew cotton, sugar, poppy and hemp.

Having discovered the 'treasures of five kings' in Agra, Babur arranges to have all of it distributed, sending presents back to all the members of his haraman in Kabul. This largesse towards the women of the haraman will continue into the future centuries, making the Mughal women of Hindustan amongst the most independently wealthy women in the world. Gulbadan, so many decades later, will make a meticulous record of all the presents received and she is the only one of Babur's chroniclers to do so. 'When you go,' Babur tells his oldest and most loyal follower Khwaja

Kalan, 'I shall send some of the valuable presents…to my elder relations and sisters and each person of the haram.' The household at Kabul, brittle with anticipation ever since news of the great victory at Panipat has reached them, are now amazed by the arrival of Khwaja Kalan and his magnificent gifts. Each begum is given 'one special dancing-girl of the dancing-girls of Sultan Ibrahim, with one gold plate full of jewels—ruby and pearl, cornelian and diamond, emerald and turquoise, topaz and cat's eye—and two small mother-o-pearl trays full of ashrafis.' There are gifts, specifically, for each of Babur's 'sisters and children and the harams and kinsmen, and to the begams and aghas and nurses and foster-brethren and ladies and to all who pray for me'. Gulbadan makes this careful record half a century later, and it is a loving testimony of the care and respect with which Babur surrounds the women and children of his haraman and all his kinsfolk.

Babur sends one final recommendation, along with the gifts. He wants all the begums to set up a temporary accommodation, within tents, in one of his favourite places in Kabul, the Garden of the Audience Hall. Here the begums are 'to make the prostration of thanks for the complete victory which has been brought about'. It is possible that Babur, who was never to return to Kabul, has a premonition that Hindustan will be the land of his destiny and that Kabul is a beloved past that he has to relinquish. 'Three happy days they remained together in the Audience Hall Garden,' writes Gulbadan, 'uplifted by pride and (they) recited the fateeha for the benediction and prosperity of his Majesty, and joyfully made the prostration of thanks.' From Khwaja Kalan the begums would have heard about this intriguing and unknown land, Hindustan, which has finally satisfied in Babur his vaulting ambitions for a great kingdom to rule. They will hear of Babur's devastating victory over Ibrahim Lodi, of the new gunpowder technology which he has acquired in Central Asia and which has been used with spectacular success against the Sultan's forces. The horses and elephants, in addition to the soldiers, had never heard anything like gunfire and the result had been pandemonium. Not long after the arrival of Khwaja Kalan, more sinister news reaches Kabul. Babur, ever curious about local customs had wanted to sample Hindustani food and had appropriated some of Ibrahim Lodi's cooks. Hearing of this, the dead Sultan's mother tried to murder Babur by having poison sprinkled on the meal the cooks had prepared—bread, hare, fried carrots and dried meat. 'Although it was a dreadful incident,' Babur writes to his haraman, 'thank God I have lived to see another day. Do not worry.' Babur is almost more shaken by the idea that Ibrahim Lodi's mother would want to poison him, since he feels he has treated her with courtesy and respect. He has underestimated the unsoundable depth of a mother's hatred for her son's killer.

Khwaja Kalan may have told them something of the ferocious heat, unlike anything he has ever experienced in Kabul. Babur is, at that very moment, growing dismayed at the sudden crumbling of his men's resolve. 'That year was extremely hot,' he admits. Grizzled steppe warriors are undone by the remorseless heat of Hindustan. 'Most of the begs and great warriors lost heart. They were unwilling to stay in Hindustan and began to leave.' But Babur is able to rally his troops, and most remain with him despite the many inclemencies of Hindustan. In 1527, Humayun returns to his post at Badakhshan and a marriage is arranged for him, his first, to his cousin Bega Begum. Humayun is still only nineteen and Bega will be the bride of his youth, the bride of his first forays into Hindustan and his early, erratic and aimless wanderings through Bengal. She will remain his chief wife, and will later be known by the sobriquet Haji Begum. And since she outlives him by fifty-two years, she will be the steadfast guardian of his legacy in Delhi. A year later, the young Kamran is also married to a cousin, Mihr Afroz Begum. But the year 1528 is a momentous one for the haraman in Kabul for another reason. A decree finally arrives from Babur in Agra three years after his departure asking all his haraman and kinsfolk to join him in Hindustan. 'He sent letters in all directions', said Gulbadan, letters in which Babur says he will 'take into full favour all who enter our service, and especially such as served our father and grandfather and ancestors'. It is not just the haraman which is in question now, but 'whoever there may be of the families of Sahib-Qiran [Timur] and Chinghiz Khan, let them turn towards our court. The most High has given us sovereignty in Hindustan; let them come that we may see prosperity together.' This, then, is more than just a royal summons to his family. This is an anointing of his dreams of empire. This is an invocation that is part battle cry and part prayer. Babur has realized that in 'unpleasant and inharmonious India', he will need his kinsfolk as bulwark against the chaos and strangeness of Hindustan. He needs his haraman's intricate memories to create an irrefutable history of Timurid splendour. He also needs the royal blood of every Timurid in exile to establish a court which will be a perfect Timurid-Hindustani chimera, an unassailable identity. And so, in the next few years, 'all the begums and khanums went, ninety-six persons in all, and all received houses and lands and gifts to their heart's desire'.

The Mughals of Hindustan, as proud and direct inheritors of Timurid nomadic aristocracy, will display an extraordinarily peripatetic lifestyle, whether they travel for battle, for a change of climate or for religious reasons, to seek the blessings of Sufi saints. In all these wanderings, in increasingly flamboyant tented mobile encampments, the women will accompany the padshahs, or will set off on their own or in groups of caravans. 'He was not a town dweller affected by dirty habits, as was the case with many rulers of Khurasan, Fars and Kerman', noted the fifteenth-century biographer of another Turkman tribe, the White Sheep, though he could quite easily have been writing of the Timurid-Mughals of India. '[He] followed the seasons wandering in open spaces going from summer quarters to winter quarters.' And of all the Mughals of Hindustan, there was none more restless, more wandering and more untethered than the founder of the dynasty, Babur. In his wake he gathered his haraman and trailed them across continents, and this legion of women and children, sun-blasted and rain blessed, will write poetry and stories, build tombs and create voyages that will be soaked with the nostalgia of these wanderings.

KHANZADA BEGUM
AND THE MYSTIC FEAST

The royal summons that arrives in Kabul in 1528 is straightforward. 'Kabul was royal demesne,' writes Babur, reserving for himself the right to Kabul, 'none of my sons should have any designs on it. My wives and household should come to me.' In a letter to Humayun, Babur reinforces this point unequivocally: 'I consider Kabul my lucky piece and have made it royal demesne. Let none of you covet it.' In a separate letter to Khwaja Kalan, Babur talks of 'the disarray of affairs in Kabul' and the presence of 'seven or eight rulers in one province'. This is a puzzling phrase, for all of Babur's fighting men are with him in Hindustan, none remaining in Kabul. The disarray he talks of can only have come from the volatile ambitions of the young mirzas, Humayun, Kamran and even young Hindal, and the women who keep a wary lookout for their interests, their mothers and wives. These women and sons are the 'rulers' that Babur is struggling to control, now that he is so far away. 'For this reason,' he adds in his letter, 'I have summoned my sister and wives to Hindustan.' In the Timurid system of inheritance, there is no law of primogeniture, so any talented and ambitious son can stake a claim to rule. Ruling is practically a family vocation amongst the Timurids and all they are trained to do from a very young age, so it is hardly surprising that Babur is now startled to find that his own sons, supported by their mothers, are leerily vying for his own beloved Kabul. Babur himself is already flayed by nostalgia for his homeland. 'How can one forget the pleasures of that country?' he writes to Khwaja Kalan, his old companion, talking of Kabul. 'Especially when abstaining from drinking, how can one allow oneself to forget a licit pleasure like melons and grapes?' Now the begums and the khanums are summoned to control the scattering chaos in Kabul and travel preparations are made for the long and uncertain voyage that will take them more than 1,000 kilometres away from the land that they have called home for more than twenty years. They leave in groups and in stages, the wives and sisters on horseback, the accompanying retinue sometimes on foot. The women are warmly dressed in the Turkish style, with long gowns in coarse, wool fabric, loose trousers, a kartiji, which is a short bodice worn under the gown, and a long outer jacket, similar to a vest. The women also wear the tall, conical Turkish hat, some adorned with a feather or a veil. Gulbadan, at six years of age is one of the youngest of the party and at fifty, Khanzada is one of the oldest. For them, as for the other women, this is a final departure from the lands of Central Asia, the stark mountains, the cedar pines and the snow in the winter. They know from Babur's runners and from Khwaja Kalan that the land they are travelling to, the Al-Hind, is altogether very different. It is also a land of extravagant wealth and mysterious creatures. What they do not know, at this stage, is that many of them will be making the reverse journey only twelve years later, in considerably altered circumstances, when Humayun loses the throne of Hindustan. Gulbadan, Khanzada, Dildar, Gulrukh, Bega and countless more women will be driven away from the fertile plains, back through the icy splendour of the Hindu Kush in a headlong rush away from Sher Shah Suri's Afghan hordes. But for now, they pack their felt tents and what dried fruits and food they can for the journey to a new future.

It is not only Babur's household and kinsfolk who travel to Hindustan. He has sent summons, after all, to all who would support his Timurid claim to rule. 'Babur is now,' writes a Timurid refugee, 'by the grace of God, senior-most among the progeny of Timur and it is only becoming that he should so extend his patronage to all living Timurids...that the lamp of the Timurid family may once again shine forth.' Thus the ninety-six women that Gulbadan mentions are all members of the extended Timurid royal family. 'Within the next five years,' writes scholar Lisa Balabanlilar, 'a steady flow of desperate women, some fleeing forced Uzbek marriages, accompanied by children and family retainers, arrived at the Timurid-Mughal court to join their male relatives in Agra.'

A year after Babur's summons, one of the first group to arrive in

Hindustan is Maham Begum and the six-year-old Gulbadan. After their long journey, begun in bitter midwinter in Kabul, they arrive six months later near Agra, trailing an impressive cavalcade: 'nine troopers, with two sets of nine horses and about a hundred of my lady's Mughal servants, mounted on fine horses, all elegance and beauty.' While Babur is at evening prayers, 'some one came and said to him: "I have just passed her Highness (Maham Begum) on the road, four miles out." My royal father did not wait for a horse to be saddled but set out on foot.' Gulbadan captures the eagerness of Babur to meet his wife and child, after a separation of almost four years. His impetuous haste, his rushing out on foot to meet them, speaks as much of Babur's impulsive nature as his desire to be finally reunited with beloved members of his haraman. Gulbadan has her first meal in Hindustan, which in the imagination of a six-year-old takes on epicurean proportions: 'The meal drew out to almost fifty roast sheep, and bread and sherbet and much fruit.' Finally she is able to meet her father and 'fell at his feet; he asked me many questions, and took me for a time in his arms, and then this insignificant person felt such happiness that greater could not be imagined'. Gulbadan's visceral joy and the tender candour of this scene is vibrant though she writes about it more than half a century later. It is through Gulbadan's account, and only hers, that we can see Babur as a loving father, a tempestuous family man and a devoted husband. The fiery warrior or the marauding opportunist is for the other biographers.

Babur's initial attempts at settling Agra are disheartening. Babur believes that 'everywhere that was habitable it should be possible to...create running water, and make planned geometric spaces'. But Agra defies even Babur's glum expectations and 'because the place was so ugly and disagreeable I abandoned my dream of making a charbagh'. But after his initial disgust and disappointment, Babur sets himself the task of transforming this inhospitable landscape. Babur brings seeds and gardeners from Central Asia and Persia and grows melons, peaches, apricots walnuts and almonds. He builds pools, bathhouses and gardens and 'thus in unpleasant and inharmonious India, marvelously regular and geometric gardens were introduced'. Babur's example is immediately emulated by all his Timurid noblemen. 'All who had acquired lands on the (Jamuna) river', Babur writes, 'also built geometric and beautifully planned gardens and pools'. These gardens are the very first examples in Hindustan of the Persianized enclosed garden with walkways, and Babur notes how amazed the people of Hindustan are when they see these structures. 'Since the people of India had never seen such planned or regular spaces, they nicknamed the side of the Jamuna on which those structures stood, Kabul'.

By the time the first of the begums arrive in Hindustan, they find a city already showing flickers of its future magnificent opulence. Babur has 'commanded buildings to be put up...on the other side of the river, and a stone palace to be built for himself between the haram and the garden'. Babur has other improvements made at this time, some with prosaic adjustments to suit his recent vow to be abstemious. 'He ordered a tank made in Dholpur...out of a single mass of rock, and used to say, "When it is finished, I will fill it with wine." But as he had given up wine before the fight with Rana Sanga, he filled it with lemonade.' Maham and Gulbadan are taken to visit the Dholpur tank, and then to Sikri garden where Babur 'used to sit and write his book', as Gulbadan, still just a child, remembers. That Gulbadan sees her father writing a book in the middle of the convulsion of empire formation, must have affected her deeply. She herself grows up to be a highly educated woman, writing in both Persian and Turki. She owns an impressive library and is considered a scholar. It is because of her reputation as a learned woman that her grandson Akbar, many years later, will ask her to write down her memories of Babur and Humayun. That biography will be a unique document. The first biography by a Muslim woman in India, with an insight into the lives of the first generation of the women of the great Mughals. Gulbadan's example is one that will inspire many future generations of Mughal women and there will be women writers, theologians and poets who will have as lustrous example this one Timurid woman, who was amongst the very first to cross the Khyber Pass into Hindustan.

Next to arrive in Hindustan is Khanzada and with her comes the rest of the household. 'Word was brought that the begums were on the way from Kabul,' writes Gulbadan. 'My royal father went as far as Naugram to give honourable reception to aakaa-janum, who was my oldest paternal aunt and my royal father's eldest sister. All the begums who had come with her paid their duty to the Emperor in her quarters.' Slowly Agra begins to swirl and glitter with the presence of all these Timurid women and refugee noblemen. The women are all given houses to settle in, which they will now own, and they bring with them their stories of exile and a lost homeland. Babur is very aware of his enormous responsibility towards these women as guardians of the Timurid legacy. 'All through the four years that (my father) was in Agra he used to go on Fridays to see his paternal aunts,' writes Gulbadan. So unflinching is Babur's routine that one day Maham asks that he not go. 'The wind is very hot indeed,' said Maham to Babur. 'How would it be if you did not go this one Friday? The begums would not be vexed.' But Babur knows the high price the women have paid in making the journey to Hindustan and will not hear of failing them. 'Maham! It is astonishing that you should say such things!' Babur says to his wife. 'The daughters of Abu-sa'id Sultan Mirza, who have been deprived of fathers and brothers! If I do not cheer them, how will it be done?' And so Babur visits his aunts and they, in turn, keep alive the memory of their shared Timurid ancestry. They speak the old language, Turki, they burnish the old stories with their constant retellings and they keep vigil over all they have lost and all that they hope to recreate one day. Gulbadan is careful to write down the extent of Babur's care and concern for his female companions. 'To the architect Khwaja Qasim, his Majesty gave the following order: "We command a piece of good service from you. It is this; whatever work, even if it be on a great scale, our paternal aunts may order done in their palace, give it precedence, and carry it out with might and main."'

Not long after all the refugee women and the haraman have been settled in Agra, Babur is overcome by an uncharacteristic lethargy and nostalgia. Perhaps having at last established a kingdom in Hindustan worthy of his great forbears, he realizes that Kabul is now forever relinquished. One of the last entries in the *Baburnama* is of his pleasure at growing typically Kabuli fruits in Agra. 'I was particularly happy that melons and grapes could turn out so well in Hindustan,' writes Babur, when his gardener brings him some fruit to sample. He makes a small trip to a favourite garden where, according to Gulbadan, Babur says, 'My heart is bowed down by ruling and reigning; I will retire to this garden. I will make over the kingdom to Humayun.' Babur's family are naturally upset and 'akam and all his children broke down and said with tears: "God keep you in His own peace upon the throne many, many years"...' But a few days later it is the little Alwar Mirza, last child of Dildar, who falls sick and dies after a short illness. 'His majesty was very sad,' writes Gulbadan, 'and Alwar's mother, Dildar Begum, was wild with grief for the child.' Dildar still has four surviving children but two have been adopted by Maham—Alwar was her only remaining son. 'Her lamentations passed due bounds,' writes Gulbadan, chastened, and to distract Dildar from her grief, Babur, man of action, proposes an outing for the haraman. 'Come, let us make an excursion to Dholpur,' he tells them. But now, unexpectedly and calamitously, a summons comes for Maham concerning Humayun's health: 'Her highness the Begam should come at once to Dihli, for the Mirza is much prostrated.' The distraught Maham sets off immediately to visit her son and they meet at Mathura where 'he seemed ten times weaker and more alarmingly ill than she had heard he was'. They reach Agra together and all the while Humayun appears to grow weaker and more disorientated by the day. Babur arrives at Agra too and seeing his firstborn son brought so low, 'at once became sad and pitiful, and he began more and more to show signs of dread'. For Maham, this is a particularly cruel and random act of fate. Humayun is her only surviving child and she has already buried four children. Humayun, at twenty-two, is finally poised for plenitude as a prince of substance after years of skirmishes in the outposts of Babur's lands. He is still the golden child and beloved heir, and he has not yet displayed all the incertitudes and irresolute fears and addictions that will thwart his talent. 'Do not be troubled about my son,' Maham tells Babur through her own tears. 'You are a king; what griefs have you? You have other sons. I sorrow because I have only this one.' In Gulbadan's account, Maham articulates the prosaic pragmatism of kingship, in which Babur has a comfortable excess of sons to choose from. But Babur will not have this. 'Maham! Although I have other sons, I love none as I love your Humayun. I crave that this cherished child may have his heart's desire and live long, and I desire the kingdom for him and not for the others, because he has not his equal in distinction.' In Gulbadan's account, Babur's love for Humayun and his articulation of this attachment is evident. Apparent also is his preference for Maham over his other wives as is his distress at her great grief. But the implacable will of Babur is not subdued even by the inevitability of death. He prays beside the sickbed of his son and offers his own life in lieu of Humayun's. 'O God! If a life may be exchanged for a life, I who am Babar, I give my life and my being for Humayun.' From that day on, Humayun recovers and returns to his post at Kalinjar while Babur begins to sicken. As Babur lies dying, one of his last wishes is to have his eldest daughters married, so he tells Maham and Khanzada. Having settled his worldly affairs, Babur dies a few months after Humayun's recovery, effectively anchoring his mythology within the great Hindustani tradition of superhuman acts.

Babur's death is devastating for his kinsfolk. The women and children are brought into the palace to be near Babur's body and the mood is bleak. 'Black fell the day for children and kinsfolk and all. They bewailed and lamented; voices were uplifted in weeping; there was utter dejection. Each passed that ill-fated day in a hidden corner.' In her own dark corner will have been the author of these lines, Gulbadan, only eight years old at the time of her loss from the father she has only recently rediscovered. In addition to the grief at Babur's death, there are oblique insinuations of poison and the fear of unknown, hidden enemies. The doctors attending Babur have hinted that he was showing the same signs of poisoning as he had done at an earlier time, when the mother of the defeated Ibrahim Lodi had been accused of poisoning the new padshah. But the business of empire has to continue and Humayun is crowned Padshah Ghazi of Hindustan. He is solicitous of all his female relatives and visits them and comforts them in this time of uncertainty. 'He came to visit his mothers and sisters and his own people,' writes Gulbadan 'and he made inquiry after their health and offered sympathy, and spoke with kindness and commiseration.'

Life slowly regains its momentum in Agra and Bega Begum, Humayun's faraway bride in Kabul, is finally brought to the imperial city now that her husband has been crowned padshah. She is pregnant, and the haraman eagerly waits for the birth of an heir for Humayun. Bega Begum's first child, a son, died in infancy. All we have of his short life is Babur's written disapproval of Humayun's choice of a name for him,

Al-Aman. 'You have not considered the fact that frequently the common people will say either "Alaman" or "Ilaman,"' wrote Babur pedantically. 'Moreover,' he adds, 'names with "al-" are rare.'

Meanwhile, Maham Begum, 'who had a great longing and desire to see a son of Humayun,' seems to encourage him to marry any likely-looking girl around. 'Whenever there was a good-looking and nice girl,' admits Gulbadan, 'she used to bring her into [Humayun's] service.' With admittedly obscene haste, only one day after Babur's death, Maham encourages Humayun to marry the daughter of the chamberlain, a certain Maywa-Jan. 'Humayun, Maywa-Jan is not bad,' Maham tells Humayun with rather faint praise. 'Why do you not take her into your service? So at her word, Humayun married and took her that very night.' It would seem that with Babur gone, dead at forty-seven from a mysterious illness, the haraman is gripped with a certain dread, a malaise that reflects how vulnerable they still feel in a kingdom which, for all its grand ambition, is still only five years old. Humayun has himself only recently been very ill and he still has no sons, so Maham, especially, would have worried for the future of her son's line. Kamran, Hindal and Askari, Humayun's brothers, are all fighting men by now, trained since adolescence for battle and leadership. They are already gauging Humayun's ability to rule and it is certain that they would not have hesitated to seize the crown for themselves had Humayun faltered at any point.

When the chamberlain's daughter announces that she is pregnant, Maham is overjoyed and prepares two sets of weapons and tells Bega Begum and Maywa-Jan that 'whichever of you bears a son, I will give him good arms.' Bega Begum in due course gives birth to a girl, the ill-fated Aqiqa, who will die later at an infamous battle at Chausa, and now Maham waits for the birth of Maywa-Jan's child. Under the intense scrutiny of the haraman and the febrile anticipation of the padshah begum, it is perhaps hardly surprising that Maywa-Jan's 'pregnancy' lasts endlessly. After twelve months, the haraman finally despairs of this fictitious pregnancy, no doubt brought on by hysterical expectation, and the chamberlain's daughter returns to her earlier obscurity.

Maham's world now resolves around the memory of her husband and the glory of her son, the padshah. She celebrates Humayun's victory against

Sher Khan at Chunar with 'an excellent and splendid feast'. Gulbadan describes the beautiful tents which are set up: 'The covering of the pavilions and of the large audience tent was, inside, European brocade, and outside Portuguese cloth. The tent poles were gilded; that was very ornamental... [My lady] had prepared a tent-lining...of Gujarati cloth of gold.' The bazaars of Agra are illuminated and all the common people and soldiers are also asked to decorate their houses and quarters. She accompanies Humayun to Gwalior when he goes on a military expedition, along with all the haraman, Babur's aunts and daughters.

But just a few years after Babur's death, Maham sickens and dies. 'The stamp of orphanhood,' writes Gulbadan sadly, 'was set anew on my royal father's children, and especially on me, for whom she herself had cared.' Gulbadan is twelve years old and has spent the last decade in the companionship and care of Maham, doted upon and cherished by a woman who found to her dismay that her own children kept dying. 'I felt lonely and helpless and in great affliction,' adds Gulbadan, who seldom writes so frankly about her own feelings in her memoirs of Babur. 'Day and night I wept and mourned and grieved.' Humayun, always compassionate towards his family members, 'came several times to comfort me', says Gulbadan, 'and showed me sympathy and kindness'. For the twenty-seven-year-old Humayun also, this is a time of reckoning. Babur's kingdom is still under threat, from warring chieftains, tempestuous Afghans and his own ambitious brothers. With the death of his mother, Humayun needs a respected and commanding presence in the haraman to help him strengthen his claim to Hindustan and it is Khanzada, now close to sixty years of age, who is made padshah begum.

A year after Humayun's accession to the throne, in 1531, a grand feast is organized by Khanzada to celebrate the kingdom they have wrought, against all odds, in this new and intemperate land. The Mystic Feast, as it will be known, will include all the Timurid and Chingizid refugees who now form the Timurid-Mughal elite of Hindustan. Gulbadan records the names of thirty-six of the ninety-six women who attend the Mystic Feast and they are all members of the erstwhile great ruling families of Central Asia.

On the banks of the Yamuna in Agra, in an octagonal shaped palace, all the objects proclaiming the grandeur of the Timurid-Mughals have been laid out. There are 'jeweled scimitar and gilded armour, broad daggers and a curved dagger…and a gold-embroidered over-mantle'. There are books and gilded pen-cases and 'entertaining picture-books written in beautiful character'. And there are objects of beauty and decoration, furniture and linen and fruits and beverages. Indeed 'everything for merriment and comfort and pleasure' had been meticulously prepared and recorded. In the middle of the octagonal room is a tank with a platform upon which 'young men and pretty girls and elegant women and musicians and sweet-voiced reciters' are getting ready for the evening's entertainment. A jewelled throne is placed in the courtyard on which preside Humayun and Khanzada. To Khanzada's right are cushions for all her paternal aunts and on another set of cushions are the sisters of Babur. Two of the guests at the feast are given a more detailed description by Gulbadan who is clearly intrigued by them. The two women, Shad Begum and Mihrangaz Begum, are both granddaughters of Sultan Husayn Bayqara, the last great Timurid leader of Khurasan. The women are unaccompanied by husbands and 'had a great friendship for one another', writes Gulbadan. 'They used to wear men's clothes and were adorned by varied accomplishments, such as the making of thumb-rings and arrows, playing polo, and shooting with the bow and arrow.' Lisa Balabanlilar has noted that these two women, dressed in men's clothes and with more traditionally manly interests, are clearly an unconventional, unusual couple because Gulbadan speaks of no other women in such wondering detail. And yet they are not ostracized in any way. Instead, along with every other female member of that feast, they are honoured and celebrated. These Timurid noblewomen, in permanent exile from a homeland which will never again be recovered, have retained their independence and the untouchable charisma of their Timurid lineage. In the turbulence of relocation to a new land, the women of the Mystic Feast lose none of their nomadic freedom and their accepted role in the public participation in social and political activities. Indeed, Humayun will actively seek and encourage the participation of Timurid women as a cuirass in these vulnerable times. In the balmy nights of Agra, as the breeze blows from the Yamuna, this unusual and exotic collection of women will host feasts and interact freely with men in the most perfunctory of purdah.

While the music of the flute, the lute and the harp floats over the densely flowing river and the embroidered brocade cloth of the tents ripple in the wind, these women will help consolidate the vaulting dreams of the Timurid-Mughal dynasty in Hindustan. Scholar Ruby Lal has noted that in the reign of Humayun, like Babur before him, there seemed 'to have been no distinction between the public and the private—in the sense of the physical separation of the court and the harem'. Too much time is spent on the move, on military expeditions, on excursions and in flight for the building of a cloistered space for women.

Gulbadan herself, as a chronicler of Babur and Humayun fifty years later, is part of the legitimizing process. Mughal padshahs will always be intensely interested in the creation of the imperial image. Babur wrote his own biography to justify his claims and lay out his legitimacy as a Timurid prince. Humayun will invite the famous historian Ghiyas-al-Din Khwandamir to write a history of his rule and Akbar, many years later asks Gulbadan, amongst others, to write what she can remember of her father and brother's reigns.

Now as she writes of the Mystic Feast, she is careful to describe the opulence of the occasion and this resplendence thus enhances the glory of Humayun. She writes of strings of pearls hung over the throne and 'gilded bed-steads and paan-dishes and water-vessels and jeweled drinking-vessels and utensils of pure gold and silver'. Gifts and coins are distributed and robes of honour are worn. Boats are set up with shop pavilions and a women's bazaar is organized. Many of these elements will be present, morphed and magnified, in the future courts of the Mughals. Khanzada is responsible for the minutiae of the feast, the hierarchy that must be observed and the protocol that is established. Khanzada's remarkable prestige at Humayun's court is solely based on her own individual merit as a respected older Timurid noblewoman. One who, moreover, made a supreme sacrifice for the safety of the Mirza of Ferghana, Babur. Khanzada is remarried a third time, at some point after her return to Babur in 1511, to a nobleman and companion of Babur's, Mohammad Mahdi Khwaja. However, this appears to have been a marriage of propriety and convenience, as Khanzada is already an older woman, in her thirties, and no child is ever born to the couple. Khanzada adopts Mahdi Khwaja's two-year-old sister, Sultanam, and brings her up as her own child.

Not long after the Mystic Feast, Khanzada organizes yet another lavish feast, this time for the celebration of the marriage of her adopted daughter Sultanam to Hindal, Humayun's younger brother. Magnificent gifts are given to the royal couple including 'Turki and Habshi and Hindi slaves'. Hindal's marriage, the first of the Mughal mirzas to be married in Hindustan, begins a tradition of opulent marriage feasts organized by women and will result in the most spectacular festivities ever witnessed in the world. Through all these numerous feasts, always organized by senior women, the glory of the nascent Mughal empire is burnished and elaborated. Traditions are brought in from Central Asia and given a new expression in a fledgling kingdom. New customs are created, adapting to local conditions, and a shimmering new court is born.

The Mystic Feast is set amidst riverside gardens along the Yamuna, most of which have been constructed by Humayun and his noblemen. But interspersed amongst the buildings and gardens, adding lustre and magnificence, is an element that has come straight from the wandering lives of these Mughals, from the Central Asian steppes and their past as semi-nomadic tribesmen—the tent. The circular Turki 'yurt' had already transformed itself into a more ceremonial structure even by the time of Timur. Babur, having spent most of his life in military campaigns and excursions, lived more of his life in tents than he did in stone buildings. But by Humayun's time, 'the yurt-type tent with its heavy outer layer largely vanished in the warmer climate and was supplanted by the marquee'. Elaborate embroideries and expensive cloths now add to the magnificence of the tents, which are often set in gardens and other beautiful locations. As a practical solution to their constant movement and a visual reminder of their nomadic Timurid past, the tents of Central Asia have come to stay in Hindustan.

After the feasts have been celebrated, Humayun sets about consolidating his kingdom. There is work to be done as the Lodi warlords are as yet unrepentant and a dangerous new player, Sher Khan, is quietly strengthening his position from his stronghold in Chunar in present-day Uttar Pradesh. Before setting off for war, Humayun spends a month in the 'gold-scattering' garden outside Agra. Elaborate tents and offices and audience tents are set up which Humayun comes personally to inspect. The begums and the many members of the haraman are also installed in tents and Gulbadan is careful to note the hierarchy in which they are placed. Ma'suma Sultan Begum, Babur's daughter, has her tent 'at the top of the row' and when Humayun visits the tented ladies, he dismounts first outside his aunt Ma'suma's tent. Next is the tent of another daughter of Babur, Gulrang Begum, followed by Dildar Begum, Babur's widow, and then Humayun's wives Gulbarg Begum and Bega Begum and others. It is clear that the older ladies, Babur's daughters and his widows, have precedence over Humayun's own family. 'When he went to any begum's or sister's quarters', writes Gulbadan, 'all the begums and my sisters were in his society'. So Humayun does not go alone to visit the women but the entire group of ladies, sisters, daughters and wives goes along with him. The women of the haraman spend all their time with Humayun, enjoying the entertainment laid out for them. So late does one evening's entertainment last that Humayun and all the ladies, sisters, wives and other ladies of rank, settle down on mattresses in a single tent to spend the night together. Unlike his father, who spent most of his life in the company of his brothers-in-arms and companions of war and adventure, Humayun takes his haraman wherever he goes and it is a mixed and varied group. It would seem that the hierarchy amongst the women is a somewhat delicate matter and can sometimes provoke hurt and resentment. Gulbadan recounts the time Humayun's main wife, Bega Begum, has a complaint for her husband. 'For several days now you have been paying visits in this garden, and on no one day have you been to our house,' complains Bega Begum to Humayun in front of all the other ladies. 'Thorns have not been planted in the way to it,' she adds, rather tartly, 'we hope you will deign to visit our quarters also, and to have a party and a sociable gathering there, too.' Bega Begum is in full flow now and will not be stopped. 'We too have hearts. Three times you have honoured other places by visits and you have run day and night into one in amusement and conversation.' Humayun goes away without answering but returns after the morning prayers and sends for his sisters, his wives and his father's widows and all the nurses. 'He said not a word, so everyone knew he was angry,' writes Gulbadan, about the usually easy-going Humayun. He then explains to Bega Begum that it is his duty to visit his elder relations. 'It is a necessity laid on me to make them happy,' he says, in an exact echo of his father's words years before. 'Nevertheless, I am ashamed before them because I see them so rarely.' Now, as punishment, he asks his wives, Bega Begum and Gulbarg Begum, to make him a written apology. His explanation for his sometimes erratic visits is unusual—'I am an opium-eater', Humayun tells them rather frankly. 'If there should be delay in my comings and goings, do not be angry with me. Rather write me a letter...' Bega Begum, fiery and tempestuous, is not so easily placated. 'Your majesty has carried the matter to this point! What remedy have we? You are Emperor.' Bega taunts Humayun, further grumbling that 'the excuse looked worse than the fault'. Eventually even Bega is won over and 'he made it up with her also'.

This, then, is an altogether different harem from that of popular imagining. It is a raucous, vibrant place constantly moving and formed and re-formed around the emperor with the addition of innumerable women, children and attendants who cluster to the court. The most venerated members of this haraman are the older women. They hold their exalted positions less due to the men they marry or the children they have than for their own precious Timurid bloodline and the force of their personality. They arrange marriages and feasts, they watch over the continuation of the royal line and they are the guardians of the Timurid legacy. The haraman, as much as the emperor, spend their lives in tents and mobile encampments in addition to stone buildings. Because they do not remain behind in cloistered security and instead accompany the emperor in his uncertain quests, they are also constantly vulnerable and no single incident is as clear a reflection of the haraman's scandalous insecurity as the infamous rout of Humayun and his encampment at Chausa.

ROUT AT THE BATTLE OF CHAUSA AND
THE AFGHAN MENACE

On a sweltering day in June 1539, as monsoon clouds scud across from the Bay of Bengal, two armies face each other across the Karmanasa River, near Chausa in Bihar. It has been three months since these armies have been camped beside the river, just a stone's throw from the slow-moving gharial swimming in the turbid depths of the gently-rising Ganga. As the storm clouds gather over the warm waters of Bengal, these two armies are about to decide the fate of northern Hindustan.

The two armies, encamped in uneasy proximity, are led by two vastly different men. On the one hand is the fifty-three-year-old Pashtun Afghan leader Sher Khan, later to become Sher Shah Suri. He has risen from inauspicious beginnings as the son of a horse-breeder and jagirdar in Bihar, through talent and ambition, to become the ruler of Bihar and Bengal. He has spent four scrappy decades demonstrating the bravery, skill, intelligence and patience that have brought him to this riverfront, facing a younger and decidedly less resolute leader. Across from Sher Khan is the thirty-year-old Padshah Ghazi of Hindustan, Humayun. Humayun has spent the last nine years since the death of his father trying to retain, if not consolidate, the empire his father founded in Hindustan almost as a consolation for having lost his beloved homeland of Samarkand. Humayun has faced the fractious ambitions of his own half-brothers, as well as the local Afghan and Hindustani chieftains, who are gauging this vulnerable new pretender and making their own periodic and violent attempts to rule. Conscious almost to a fault of Babur's advice to him to 'conduct yourself well with your younger brother', because 'elder brothers need to have restraint', Humayun is conciliatory where he should show strength. As he waits now for Sher Khan to agree to a truce, Humayun is about to be betrayed by these brothers. Erudite, impulsive, generous and superstitious, Humayun, despite personal bravery, is also shackled by his inability to decisively conclude a military action. Addicted to opium and the easy companionship of his women and followers, Humayun is given to 'very unaccountably shut[ting] himself up for a considerable time in his Haram, and abandon[ing] himself to every kind of indulgence and luxury' after successfully subduing an area.

Now as the rain begins to fall, with the sudden violence of tropical thunderstorms, the Mughal army realizes the terrible mistake it has made. Cut off from the safety of the Agra route by Sher Khan's army, they have camped on low ground between the Ganga and the Karmanasa, which is immediately flooded. Bridges collapse under the driving rain and the ground shifts and dissolves under the stampeding armoured war horses. Having waited for this exact moment and with ferocious precision, Sher Khan conducts a three-pronged attack against the Mughals and the effect is instantaneous and devastating. In this watery dawn, the Mughal forces are crushed between the explosive Afghan army and the roiling water of the flooding rivers, and there is pandemonium. 'They made a dreadful uproar', admits Jauhar, Humayun's personal attendant, 'and caused the greatest confusion both among the troops and followers'. Humayun beats his drums of war and tries to rally his forces but only 300 followers answer his call. The vast majority, some 8,000 of his best Turki troops, die trying to escape the Afghans or drown in the fast-flowing rivers. The air is filled with the cries of dying men and the screams of terrified women. For in Humayun's camp there is also his haraman, in this place of uncertainty and violence. And now before Humayun can ride off to war, there is one last, bleak order he must give. He calls four of his bravest and most loyal men, Tardi Beg, Baba Beg, Koch Beg and Mir Bachka Bahadur and 'bade them go quickly and bring away the noble lady Haji Begum'. These men rush to the tents of Bega Begum. They surround Bega Begum's tent and in the sliding rain, attempt valiantly to defend their queen from the Afghan troops. They die gallantly, says Akbar's chronicler and friend Abu'l-Fazl ibn Mubarak in his more florid description, and 'drank the wholesome sherbet of martyrdom at the door of honour's enclosure'. Only Tardi Beg survives and Bega Begum is captured, but despite the terrible predictions of the Mughal chroniclers, Sher Khan treats her with great courtesy and respect. 'Wicked thoughts did not find their way into the hearts of those wretches,' admits even Abu'l-Fazl. Indeed Sher Khan gives orders 'forbidding the killing or enslavement of any Mughal women or children', therein exhibiting a chivalry far ahead of his times. All the women and children captured by the Afghans are sent to Bega Begum's tent for safety and will be returned later, unscathed, to Humayun.

The presence of women at this tumultuous scene is disquieting. For the padshah it has been a time of endless journeying and sudden skirmishes. Only thirteen years after his father's great victory at Panipat, Humayun's prevarications have exposed his weakness and his kingship is uncertain. But everywhere he goes, even into the very borderlands of his fluid kingdom, his haraman will follow. Not so for the careful and pragmatic Sher Khan, who has transferred all his women, children and treasure to the sombre hill fort of Rohtas in Bihar before his campaign against Humayun, entrusting them to the protection of the Hindu raja there, noblesse oblige. But for the Mughal women, there is no such concept of a settled and permanent home. There is no walled city, or even a stone city at all. There are gardens and tented dwellings and the court is often just a motley collection of Timurid refugees. Especially in the reigns of these early Mughal padshahs, the women of the haraman will go wherever the padshah goes.

At the debacle of Chausa the women pay a very high price for their constant proximity to the king. 'A terrible blank was made in the royal household by the loss of several women', writes Beveridge, translator of Gulbadan's biography of Humayun, of the battle at Chausa. 'Of many who were in that rout', writes Gulbadan starkly, speaking of the missing women, 'there was never heard, in any way soever, news or sign'. Bega Begum's six-year-old daughter, Aqiqa, disappears at Chausa, presumably drowned. 'I have been consumed by a hundred thousand regrets,' writes the inconsolable Humayun later. 'Why did I take her with the army?'

Another illustrious woman lost at Chausa is Ayesha Sultan Begum Bayqara, daughter of the last great Timurid ruler of Herat, Sultan Husayn Mirza Bayqara. Having been forcibly married twice to Uzbek noblemen, the feared and hated enemies of the Timurids, she came to India in 1531 after Babur had created an area of safety for all the displaced Timurids. Also lost are two minor wives of Humayun, Shad Bibi as well as Chand Bibi, who was seven months pregnant at the time. Bichka Khalifa, an old woman-servant of Babur's household who, along with Babur's mother is one of only two women to have escaped Samarqand as the Uzbeks advanced and routed Babur in 1501, also dies at Chausa. Of all these women, old and young, and children, they 'never even heard a word as to whether they were drowned or what became of them'. Gulbadan is waiting at Agra for the royal party to return. 'In spite of all possible inquiry and search,' she grieves, 'what had become of them was never found out.'

Humayun himself barely escapes with his life at the ignominious routing at Chausa. Forced off the battlefield, his horse drowns while crossing the river and Humayun is saved by a water carrier, Shams-ud-Din Atga of Ghazna, buoyed up by Shams-ud-Din's inflatable leather water pouch. In this wretched and inglorious fashion, the Padshah of Hindustan makes his way back to Agra, followed by his decimated cortège and haraman.

In Agra, Humayun's situation is precarious and he is undone by his brothers' many betrayals. His nineteen-year-old brother Hindal, impressionable and often in the thrall of advisers, has rebelled against his padshah and brother and has had the khutba (sermon) read in his own name, thus declaring himself Padshah Ghazi. Having done this, according to Abu'l-Fazl, he then goes to see his mother, Dildar Begum, who is wearing blue, the colour of mourning in Islam. When he angrily questions her about the inauspicious colour she is wearing, she rebukes him. 'I am wearing mourning for you,' Dildar Begum tells him bleakly. 'You are young and have...lost the true way; you have girded your loins for your own destruction.' Dildar Begum's disapproval is eloquent and clear. The rules of kingship are above filial bonds and maternal incertitudes, and it is her duty to show her son the mortal danger of his ways.

Unsure about his brothers, Humayun turns instead to the women at the court in Agra. He meets his younger sister Gulbadan after a gap of several years. She is seventeen years old and married now; it is clear that he has missed her companionship during his ceaseless wandering and battles. 'My Gulbadan, I used very often to think of you, and I was sometimes sorry, and said: "I do wish I had brought her!"' A few days later, Humayun meets with the senior-most women at his court. Apart from Gulbadan and her mother Dildar Begum, there are also three other widows of Babur and a foster-mother. It is indispensable for Humayun to bring the young Hindal back over to his side at this time of uncertain loyalties. To show the women he means Hindal, always beloved with the haraman, no harm, he swears upon the Quran that 'now there is no anger in my heart against Hindal'. When they have been reassured, he asks Gulbadan to go and bring back Hindal, who has since gone back to his fief in Alwar. Dildar Begum objects, since Gulbadan is still very young, and goes herself to Alwar to bring back the rebellious younger brother.

Also present at Agra is Humayun's other half-brother, Kamran, younger to him by only one year. Ambitious and endlessly restless, Kamran has been allotted the fiefdom of Kabul and Kandahar by Humayun; however, sensing his brother's vulnerability, Kamran will constantly try and claim the kingdom. For now, the three brothers are watchful and uneasy with ill-controlled impatience as Sher Khan unfurls the full scope of his ambitions. He has had the Friday khutba read in his name in Bengal and has now become Sher Shah, first of the Sur clan, and is gathering his forces to decimate, once and for all, Mughal pretensions. After several months of fatal indecision, Humayun finally rides out to meet his Afghan rival with a large Mughal army and is quite decisively routed at Kanauj, by a much smaller Afghan cavalry.

While Humayun and Hindal are losing the bulk of the Mughal forces to the savage precision and skill of Sher Shah's Afghan troops, Kamran abandons Agra, which had been left to his charge, and flees north to Lahore with all his soldiers. Before leaving Agra, he orders Gulbadan to accompany him: 'You are commanded to go with me to Lahore.' Kamran tells Gulbadan peremptorily. 'Then he took me by main force,' Gulbadan complains, and leads her 'with a hundred weepings and complaints and laments, away from my mothers, and my own mother and sisters, and my father's people, and my brothers, and parted us who had all grown up together from infancy.' Gulbadan is clearly distressed at leaving everything that is familiar to her, but Kamran is determined to have the presence of a young but influential member of the haraman with him. Gulbadan writes a beseeching letter to Humayun and asks him to keep her with him. 'I had no heart to part with you,' Humayun assures Gulbadan, 'but the Mirza persisted, and was miserable, and begged very hard, and I was obliged to trust you to him,' writes the ever-accommodating Humayun. So Gulbadan must leave the great tribe of her family, all that anchors and consoles her in a country she has lived in for barely a decade. She will not see Humayun, or her mother and foster mothers and all her sisters, for a very long time. When she next returns to Hindustan, Humayun will be dead, having finally recovered his throne and his kingdom only to die in an accident, falling down a flight of stairs in his library. For now she must leave with Kamran, along with the wives and families of a number of other Mughal officers and retainers who have sensed the tremors of the approaching Afghan storm. Though she rails and weeps, Gulbadan is leaving for a safer haven. Those who have stayed in Agra face a grim and dangerous future. The defeated Humayun returns with his obliterated troops and they are all 'broken and dispirited, in a state heart-rending to tell'. Humayun is scalded by the memory of the women and children lost in these battles. 'Why did I not kill her in my own presence?' he asks Hindal in despair, mourning the disappearance of his daughter Aqiqa. 'Now again, it is difficult to convey women with us.' What Humayun is dreading now is that the remaining women and children of the haraman need to move yet again, this time with the Afghan menace harrying them on one side and at the other end the oblique ambitions of Kamran. But Hindal reassures Humayun: 'So long as there is life in me,' he gallantly tells Humayun, 'I have hope…that…I may pour out my life's blood for my mother and my sisters.'

Hindal now leaves with his mother, Dildar Begum, his young bride Sultanam, and the remaining members of the haraman. Humayun follows close behind and on the long journey across Punjab and towards Lahore, this vulnerable group of refugees is harried and attacked intermittently. The padshah's hold on the throne of Hindustan was a mirage, easily blown away, and now local chieftains and disgruntled groups are increasingly volatile and attack the royal party whenever they can.

In Lahore the four brothers, including Askari, are briefly reunited and they gauge each other's ambitions uneasily. Kamran is increasingly hostile, laying claim to the historically important city of Kabul, while Sher Shah continues his inexorable advance towards Lahore. There is no longer any pretence from Sher Shah that he means to submit to his padshah, or even accommodate Mughal ambitions in any way. He refuses to even allow Humayun the insubstantial fiefdom of Lahore. 'I have left you Kabul,' declares Sher Shah to Humayun, with the arrogance of a new king. 'You should go there.' When it becomes clear that Sher Shah means to attack Humayun even unto his last, desperate refuge, 'it was like the Day of Resurrection', writes Gulbadan. The entire tribe of the Timurids, the women and children, the followers, the amirs and their families now all leave Lahore in such catastrophic haste that 'people left their decorated places and furniture just as they were'. Taking only 'whatever money they had', this disparate group of refugees, perhaps up to 200,000 strong, now begins a long and calamitous journey that will lead them out of Hindustan altogether. Starting with the rout at Chausa sixteen months previously, Mughal aspirations have been effectively destroyed and they have been made homeless once again. Humayun is advised to have Kamran killed, because his loyalty has proven to be illusory and he now blocks Humayun's passage to Kabul. But 'never, for the vanities of this perishable world, will I imbrue my hands in the blood of a brother', announces this decidedly sentimental padshah before heading south, instead, towards Bikaner. Only Babur's Afghan widow, Bibi Mubarika, remains alone in Agra to bravely defend the grave of Babur from defilement at the hands of the conquering Afghan forces. Sher Shah the Lion King, no stranger to matters of gallantry himself, is so impressed by the valour of this one lone woman that he not only leaves the grave unmolested but sends an escort with Bibi Mubarika and has Babur's remains transported to Kabul, where they lie today in the Bagh-e-Babur.

The rest of the haraman leaves Lahore with the fleeing cortège. They abandon all their possessions and their fragile claims on the great cities of Hindustan. All of northern Hindustan, from the Indus River in the west to Bihar in the east and south to Gwalior to the south, is lost. Their home now is the dusty road and the tents snapping in the cold autumn breeze. They leave on foot, if they are lowly attendants, or on litters on horseback for the more exalted, but their fate is always uncertain and dangerous. They cross the mighty rivers of the Punjab and climb the crumbling mountainsides of the Salt Range. One of the lesser wives of Humayun, Bibi Gunwar, is heavily pregnant and delivers a baby girl on the way. Having crossed the Jhelum River in Punjab, there is a splitting away of the great Timurid caravan. One section creaks north, under Kamran and Askari, almost 700 kilometres to Kabul. Gulbadan is amongst the large number of women who are led by Kamran towards Babur's old stronghold. The other section takes the southern route towards Sind. Hindal and his mother, Dildar Begum, go to Multan where there is a sizeable Persian community already established while Humayun drifts towards Bhakkar district. Conditions are dire for the Mughal padshah, and food and hospitality are hard to come by in these badlands of his kingdom. 'The soldiers killed and ate their horses and camels,' writes Gulbadan. 'Sometimes there was corn to be had,' she adds, 'and sometimes not.' In the next few years of incertitude, Humayun's soldiers and followers will abandon him, disappearing into the arid countryside. For the next six months, meanwhile, Humayun and his small band of followers and haraman wearily drift through Sind, uncomfortably aware of the watchful and often hostile presence of the ruler of that province, Shah Husain Mirza. Dispirited and unmoored, Humayun finally decides to head towards Hindal and his entourage who have settled in Paat, in western Sind. Though his fortunes are at their lowest ever yet, Humayun is about to have an encounter that will change not only his life, but indeed the very future of Hindustan.

DILDAR BEGUM AND
A MARRIAGE PROPOSAL

When Humayun reaches the ancient town of Paat, Hindal's mother Dildar Begum arranges for a 'grand entertainment' in which all the members of this fractured court are able to come and greet their dispossessed padshah. Included in this party is a fourteen-year-old girl, native to the town of Paat, Hamida Banu Begum. She is the daughter of Hindal's preceptor, Shaikh Ali Akbar Jami, who is himself a descendant of a Shi'a sage known by the awe-inspiring sobriquet of His Reverence the Terrible Elephant. 'Who is this?' asks Humayun when he sees the young girl, clearly smitten by her beauty and grace. Hamida Banu is often to be found visiting Hindal's haraman in Dildar Begum's company, and it is not long before Humayun indicates to his stepmother his desire to marry the young Hamida Banu. But the thirty-two year-old, battle-scarred and already much married Mughal pretender is probably an underwhelming proposition for the very young Hamida Banu and she initially refuses to consider Humayun's proposal. Even Hindal is angry at Humayun's behaviour, quite probably believing that with Sher Shah Suri and Shah Husain Mirza as immediate dangers, it was hardly the time for Humayun to be considering matrimony. 'I look on this girl as a sister and child of my own,' says Hindal angrily to Humayun, now reminding him of his impoverished condition and the need to produce a suitable mahr or bride gift. 'You are a king. Heaven forbid there should not be a proper alimony.' But Humayun is annoyed at these objections and asks Dildar Begum to intercede on his behalf. 'As for what they have written about alimony,' he pleads with her, desperately and somewhat unrealistically, given his circumstances, 'please Heaven, what they ask will be done.' Dildar Begum acknowledges the patience and tact required in such a situation and advises Humayun to stay calm. 'It is astonishing that you should go away in anger over a few words', she tells him. Dildar must also handle her son Hindal's objections and, according to Jauhar, she rebukes Hindal: 'you are speaking very improperly to his Majesty, whom you ought to consider the representative of your late father.'

To Hamida Banu herself, Dildar is gentle and pragmatic. 'After all you will marry someone,' Dildar tells the young girl. 'Better than a king, who is there?' And this is the prosaic reality of a girl's choices which Dildar wants Hamida Banu to understand. It is an eloquent testimony of Hamida Banu's wit and spirit that she is said to have replied: 'Oh yes, I shall marry someone,' she admits to Dildar, with bracing candour, 'but he shall be a man whose collar my hand can touch and not one whose skirt it does not reach.' If Humayun is a king, Hamida Banu argues, then he is too exalted a person for her and she would rather marry someone closer to her own standing in society. Humayun persists, and asks Dildar to send Hamida Banu to see him. But the young girl refuses, questioning Humayun's motive and invoking propriety: 'If it is to pay my respects, I was exalted by paying my respects the other day,' she tells Humayun tartly, before adding, 'why should I come again?' But after forty days, with the sympathetic Dildar's efforts, Hamida Banu finally agrees to the proposal and she is married to Humayun. A mahr of two lakhs is given to the bride. Hamida Banu could never have imagined, as a young fourteen-year-old, how irrevocable her decision would be and how precipitous the changes that it would bring to her life.

The many intimate details we know of Hamida Banu's brusque courtship by Humayun is because the two young sisters-in-law, Gulbadan and Hamida Banu, will become very close friends later in life. When Gulbadan writes her biography more than forty years later, many of the incidents will have been told to her by Hamida Banu herself, still sharp in the women's minds almost half a century later and long after Humayun himself is dead. It is in the audacious memory of Gulbadan's biography that we have an intermittent view into the many human emotions and the domestic politics that lay behind the grander scope of the Mughals' canvas. The small fallibilities and unexpected weaknesses and through it all the complex network of female influence that allowed life to carry on in the most desperate and unusual of circumstances. This particular incident, with its irresolute bride and harried groom will, of course, have particularly far-reaching consequences as it will result in the birth of Akbar, the greatest of the great Mughals.

The immediate future for Humayun and Hamida Banu, however, is decidedly more prosaic and holds only uncertainty and betrayals. The newly-wed couple travels to Bhakkar along with Humayun's much depleted and battered army, hoping to gain a foothold in the district of Sehwana. Shah Husain Mirza continues to pursue Humayun through Sind with deadly intent, and all the while Humayun's few remaining officers surreptitiously desert the increasingly frayed Mughal camp whenever they can. So piteous is Humayun's situation that at one point he stays up all night to physically prevent any potential deserters from leaving him. In the morning, his great amirs Tardi Beg and Munim Beg, somewhat farcically, try and run towards their horses to make a getaway while Humayun is bathing, and the Padshah Ghazi of Hindustan has to run after them himself, admonishing and pleading, till they have no choice but to remain with their padshah, albeit with bad grace.

For Humayun and Hamida Banu, meanwhile, the erratic and hopeless wandering continues. They lack basic supplies, sometimes foraging for wild berries or seizing supplies of grain and provisions from errant caravans like common thieves. Finally, and by this time Hamida Banu is seven months pregnant, Raja Maldeo of Jodhpur invites them to Rajasthan where they are relieved to find at least some grain and water. But the onward march through the desert of Rajasthan is gruelling and it is a 'horrid journey' in which 'many of our people died, and all suffered exceedingly', writes Jauhar grimly. Upon reaching the territory of Maldeo, moreover, Humayun finds that there is 'no act of hospitality being shown us or any comfort given to the distressed monarch'. The raja, 'that ravening demon' as the ever bombastic Abu'l-Fazl has it, instead makes 'idle excuses' and sends a rather derisory present of fruit. All this while, Humayun's retainers continue to desert him and the mood in the Mughal camp is one of anxiety and bleak despondency. 'If you leave me, whither will you go?' the unhappy Humayun asks his retainers. 'You have no other refuge.' But while Humayun's followers continue to leave him for better prospects, the ones who truly have no other refuge, and must follow him through this landscape of the damned, are his haraman, and the diminished party now disconsolately marches on into the desert. Hamida Banu, now a heavily pregnant fifteen-year-old, rides on horseback in the unforgiving desert heat while the other women manage as best they can, on foot or on camel. 'Many women and men were on foot,' admits Jauhar. They head towards Umerkot, in heat so fierce the 'horses and other quadrupeds kept sinking to the knees in the sand'.

The Mughal party proceeds westwards, harried not only by the heat, the thirst and the hunger, but also by querulous chieftains and Rajput rajas who sense the increasing vulnerability of Humayun and attack him whenever they get a chance. Humayun sends his great amirs onwards, to divert the attention of the marauders, and himself remains with his female companions and servants. His amirs are attacked and resolve to 'sell our lives as dearly as possible' but in the end, Humayun's officer Shaikh Ali Beg is able to hustle the attacking soldiers and decapitates two of their chiefs, bringing the heads as macabre trophies to bolster Humayun's faltering resolve. The few wells Humayun's party are able to find are filled up with sand, apparently on Raja Maldeo's orders, so that when water is found at last, the soldiers and servants and animals are desperate with thirst. 'The misery we suffered at this stage,' admits Jauhar, 'was intolerable.'

When water is found at last in these wells, buckets are lowered and 'people flung themselves on it; the ropes broke, and five or six persons fell into the wells with the buckets. Many perished from thirst.' Humayun passes around his own water bottle to try and control his retainers and appeals to his amir Tardi Beg 'in the Turky language', with considerable grace, given the circumstances, to 'be so good as draw off your people for a short time from the well till mine are served, which will prevent disputes'. By this stage, there are hardly any horses left with the Mughal party, only a few sturdy mules and camels. Not far from Umerkot, finding himself short of a horse, one of Humayun's officers unchivalrously demands his horse back from Hamida Banu. Humayun, now only accompanied by seven horsemen, then gives his own horse to his wife and mounts a camel belonging to a water carrier.

In these miserly circumstances, the bedraggled party arrive at Umerkot to be given a civil reception by Raja Rana Prasad. 'The day was not a fortunate one,' says the raja with courteous understatement, hoping that 'on the following day he would mount the throne.' The raja assigns Humayun 'excellent quarters' inside the fort while the amirs pitch their tents in the pleasant surroundings of the fort amidst greenery and water tanks. So reduced is Humayun's situation that he only has the clothes on his back. When he gives his clothes to be washed, he must wait in his dressing gown till they are ready to be worn. Hamida Banu's situation, now in the final months of her pregnancy, can hardly have been much better. While Humayun is waiting in his tent in his dressing gown, a beautiful bird becomes trapped inside the tent. Humayun captures the bird, snips off a feather before releasing it, and then has the feather painted by an artist in his entourage. It is hardly an unremarkable fact that even in his depleted, meagre following, Humayun has a painter accompanying him. There is a glitter, already, of the later magnificence of the Mughal's miniature painters. Hamida Banu, meanwhile, finds that provisions can at last be bought, however, and goats are found to be very cheap, only one rupee for four goats. 'Several days,' says Gulbadan, clearly echoing Hamida Banu's satisfaction, 'were spent in peace and comfort.' For a few weeks, at least, Hamida Banu is able to rest in relative comfort and security for these last months of her pregnancy.

After seven weeks, Humayun prepares to leave for Jun, near the Rann of Kutch. Hamida Banu remains at Umerkot with the rest of Humayun's haraman, under the care of her brother Khwaja Muazzam. Three days later, on 15 October 1542, a son is born to Hamida Banu. When the news is conveyed to Humayun, he is overjoyed and breaks a pod of musk which he distributes amongst his chiefs and amirs saying, 'This is all the present I can afford to make you on the birth of my son, whose fame will I trust be one day expanded all over the world, as the perfume of the musk now fills this apartment.' This son he now gives the name he had once heard in his dream—Jalaluddin Muhammad Akbar.

When Akbar is five weeks old, Hamida Banu leaves the comfort of Umerkot and travels with the haraman and her baby to reach Humayun's camp at Jun, where tents have been pitched in a garden surrounded by deep trenches. For a while their fortunes seems to improve as several local 'zemindars' and chieftains join Humayun. Then there is the usual squabbling, and the Rana of Umerkot leaves with his followers, muttering damningly that 'any attempt to assist the Moghuls was a loss of labour and time'. Several amirs also desert, including the long-wavering Munim Beg. A matter of some consolation for Humayun is the 'joyful news' that Bairam Khan, his veteran general who was captured by the Afghans at Kanauj, has come to join Humayun's party.

Hindal is dispatched to Kandahar, responding to a letter from the governor of Kandahar, Qaracheh Khan, who has news regarding the duplicity of Shah Husain Mirza. Once Hindal arrives in Kandahar, however, Kamran plots with his brother Askari to have Qaracheh Khan removed and to take Kandahar for himself. For Humayun, this is disastrous news. Now faced with the possible loss of both Kandahar and his brother Hindal, Humayun turns to someone whose loyalty is above reproach and whose influence is always undisputed with the padshah as with all the pretenders in this fractious tribe. Khanzada is an old woman now, sixty-four years old, and it is to her that Humayun entrusts the delicate and physically arduous mission of travelling to Kandahar to urge Hindal and Kamran to work together against their common enemies. At this advanced age, Khanzada travels from Jun to Kandahar on horseback, more than 750 kilometres of unforgiving terrain, fording rivers and crossing gorges and mountains. Kamran, meanwhile, travels from Kabul to meet with her. Kamran, most ambitious and duplicitous of all Humayun's brothers, now urges Khanzada to have the khutba read in his name. He had already written to Dildar Begum with a similar request. 'Be a mother to me as you are to Mirza Hindal,' Kamran writes to Dildar, trying to manipulate the women in their maternal instincts. But all the begums are unequivocal and defer to the greater authority of the padshah begum. Dildar stoutly replies that he best ask Khanzada Begum, his 'elder kinswoman, and oldest and highest' of all of them 'the truth about the khutba'. The hierarchy amongst the women is clear, the deference they owe Khanzada unquestioned. Khanzada then tells Kamran 'as his Majesty Firdaus-Makani (Babur) decided it and gave his throne to the Emperor Humayun, and as you, all of you, have read the khutba in his name till now, so now regard him as your superior and remain in obedience to him.'

Meanwhile the royal party finally decides on a plan to leave the province of Sind where Shah Husain Mirza is a constant menace. Shah Husain Mirza, on being informed of this plan, is understandably suitably supportive and agrees to send '2000 loads of grain and 300 camels' which are distributed amongst Humayun's followers. Humayun then 'went on board boats, with kinsfolk and family, army and the rest and travelled for three days on the great river' and the Mughal camp is on the move once again. The camels are not as impressive a gift as they first appeared, as they 'were such that one might say they had not known city, or load, or man for seven or rather seventy, generations'. Since there are not many horses, Humayun's followers must nonetheless ride the camels and there are scenes of outright farcical momentum as 'every camel which was mounted at once flung its rider to the ground, and took its way to the jungle.'

It is late in the year of 1543 by the time the Mughal party begins the march that will lead them now into Afghanistan. Akbar is just over a year old and Hamida Banu begins her wearying march with the rest of the retinue. From the arid desert of Rajasthan they now journey to the foothills of the Afghan mountains and reach an open plain where 'in the hot season the *Semun* blows with such violence, that the very limbs of a man are melted, and he dies; but in the winter the cold is so severe, that if a person takes his soup out of the pot and pours it into a plate, it becomes instantly a piece of ice'. All the people 'who were without warm clothing, suffered very severely'. The destination of the party is still uncertain and Humayun is shackled by doubt and the wavering loyalties of his brothers and the local chieftains. He is, indeed, 'stupefied and bewildered' and asks piteously 'what is to be done? Where am I to go?'

Humayun finally decides to head towards Kandahar, hoping to find the support of his brother Askari and the other Afghan peoples and on the way they stop in a village where 'it had snowed and rained, and was extremely cold'. But Askari has treason on his mind and had an informant not come upon the Mughal camp just in time, it is quite possible they would have all been massacred by Askari's troops. There is a sudden commotion and 'Mount, your Majesty!' shouts an 'Uzbeg youth' galloping towards the royal party on 'a sorry and tired-out pony.' 'There is no time

Daughters of the Sun

to talk.' In the frenzied haste with which Humayun and his followers now leave, 'there was not a chink of time in which to take the Emperor Jalalu-d-din Muhammad Akbar'. Humayun sends Khwaja Muazzam and Bairam Khan to fetch Hamida Banu and she quickly mounts a horse to follow Humayun but she must abandon her infant son. The total number of people with Humayun now is a paltry thirty or forty, including two women, Hamida Banu and the wife of Hasan Ali, the chamberlain. All the servants, and the remaining haraman, are left behind with the infant Akbar, and the royal couple now gallop away into the frigid wastes of Afghanistan, leaving behind Hindustan and their dreams of an empire.

At the end of 1543, Babur's dream of a homeland and kingdom in Hindustan, a place of safety and refuge for the lost Timurids of Samarkand, is in ruins. These Timurids, the Mughals of Hindustan, are scattered like detritus across the span of the continent. Bega Begum is somewhere with Sher Shah Suri, along with all the other captured member of the haraman. Bibi Mubarika is in Agra, about to make her lonely way across to Kabul with Babur's remains. Dildar Begum and Gulbadan Begum are in Kabul, anxiously waiting for news of Humayun and the haraman. Khanzada is in Kandahar, trying to control the tempestuous claims of her nephews, and Hamida Banu is about to cross into Persia with Humayun, racing away to an unknown destiny. These are the first of the women of the great Mughals. Many of them will long outlive Humayun and some will live through the reigns of three separate Mughal padshahs. They will have extraordinary destinies and will achieve remarkable feats. They will build mausoleums, write memoirs, rule in the padshah's absence and travel to foreign lands, sometimes by sea, on their own, and for many years. They will often travel constantly, in all kinds of conditions, and their travels, put end-to-end, will circumnavigate the globe. The haraman, with these women in it, will create a sense of identity and home for Babur, Humayun and even Akbar. Very often, in the padshahs' endless wanderings and ruinous search for a meaningful space, these women *are* the Timurid homeland.

HAMIDA BANU AND
THE PERSIAN ESCAPADE

In the winter of 1543, Humayun and Hamida abandon their kingdom, their inheritance and their son, and head for Persia. The royal party is much reduced and numbers, according to Hamida, only 'as many as thirty people'. Accompanying the royal couple are, amongst others, the great general Bairam Khan, Hamida's brother Khwaja Muazzam, the eunuch Ambar, and Humayun's foster-brother Nadim Kuka, whose wife Maham Anaga remains behind with the infant Akbar in Kandahar. Left with Akbar is another foster-mother, Jiji Anaga, and both these 'milk mothers' will have spectacular, intertwined and bloody destinies linked to this early role they play in the care of the young Akbar. The royal party, meanwhile, make their miserable way, hounded by 'that unjust creature, Mirza Askari', through the frigid mountains. They labour through the snow and so scarce are the rations that a precious horse is killed for food. 'There was no cooking-pot,' writes Gulbadan, aghast, 'so they boiled some of the flesh in a helmet, and some they roasted.' The people of the mountains are as inhospitable as the arid countryside and Gulbadan writes that they saw 'a few savage Biluchis whose speech is the tongue of the ghouls of the waste'. In bitter midwinter cold so intense that Humayun would complain that 'my very head was frozen by the intense cold', Hamida and Humayun and their paltry entourage make their way to Khorasan and then on to Sistan, a province of Persia.

In Sistan, the governor Ahmad Sultan Shamlu welcomes the royal party to his province and according to Jauhar, 'made an offering of a celebrated horse called Leilet al Kudder (the Night of Power), after which he conducted the padshah to his own habitation and performed all the rights of hospitality,' including sending his mother and his wives to wait on Hamida Banu. The Shah of Persia is now Shah Tahmasp, son of Shah Ismail who had converted the loathed Shaybani Khan's skull into a drinking cup in an earlier time. A formal representation is now made to Shah Tahmasp, the gist of which is 'we are arrived in your country, and await your royal orders'. At the court of Shah Tahmasp, the news that the descendant of the great Timur himself was seeking the hospitality of Persia 'was hailed with delight' and 'the kettle-drum was beat for three days at the royal residence at Kazvin'. Farmans are sent to the different governors, ordering them to give Humayun an honourable welcome. Shah Tahmasp's orders to his governors are meticulous and detailed and he specifies that 'upon his auspicious arrival let him drink fine sherbets of lemon and rosewater, cooled with snow; then serve him preserves of watermelon, grapes and other fruits with white bread just as I have ordered. For this royal guest prepare each drink with sweet attars and ambergris; and each day prepare a banquet of five hundred rare and delicious and colourful dishes.' This is a fine reversal of fortune for Hamida and Humayun. The contrast between the delicate sherbets and fresh fruit with the fibrous horse-meat cooked in a helmet could not be starker. But there will be a price to pay.

Shah Tahmasp is the twenty-seven-year-old son of the founder of the Safavid dynasty, Shah Ismail. Pronounced king at the age of ten when his father died, Tahmasp is an enthusiastic patron of Persian adaab (etiquette) and cultural life, and has in his ateliers all manners of artists, miniaturists, calligraphers, historians and poets. A talented painter himself, the influence of Persian culture as promoted by Tahmasp on the conquered cities of Khorasan, Marv and Herat is unprecedented. Between the years 1541 and 1555, the cities of the Safavid empire, enthusiastically supported by the royal family, show a singular degree of cultural sophistication. Tahmasp's royal ateliers are now producing illustrated books of spectacular brilliance and these are indeed the most magnificent works created in the Islamic world at the time. And it is to Herat that the royal Timurid-Mughal couple now proceed. As they approach Herat, the royal couple finds that there are people lining the streets of the villages and towns, as orders have been sent 'that every person of the city from seven years of age to seventy should advance to meet his Majesty'. Farmans have been sent to the governors of the cities on their route commanding them 'to receive and entertain the imperial guest with every mark of honour, and to furnish him and his retinue with provisions, wines, fruits, and whatever else would contribute to their comfort'. In Herat, the governor is ordered to present 'five hundred trays of meat of different kinds besides sweetmeats' and 1,000 men on horseback were always to attend him. Outside Herat the hills and plains are a mass of gesticulating, waving people acclaiming the arrival of the padshah and the queen. They are conducted to an encampment in the Murad Bagh (Garden of Desire) outside the town of Herat itself.

For Hamida Banu, the complete alteration of her circumstances is almost unimaginable. Her wildering years are over and the jagged fear of life as a haunted exile will never return. In Persia, Humayun and Hamida are always treated as royalty and are consistently feted as glorious inheritors of a fabled line. The splendour and opulence of Hamida's life now is extravagant. As one example, the presents sent by Tahmasp for the royal couple include horses, daggers, ornamented swords, housings of cloth of gold, and brocades. White bread, baked with milk and butter is served on spotless table linen accompanied by sherbets cooled in ice. The days of gleaning for seeds and berries and scrambling for muddy water are truly over. Costumes and clothes are offered to them and they are supplied with utensils of all kinds. Hamida is attended upon by the very cultured ladies of a most refined court and she is still only nineteen years old. For the next two years Hamida will be able to admire the finest miniature paintings anywhere in the world. She will visit monuments and cities of ancient magnificence. She will admire the gorgeous elegance of the people at the court, their layered, long robes in contrasting colours of lapis blue, emerald green and blood red all enhanced with silk and gold brocade.

Humayun and Hamida spend several months between the great cities of Persia, visiting shrines, forts, fountains and monuments along the way while they await a summons from the Shah. A message finally arrives from Tahmasp, first requesting the presence of Humayun's ambassador Bairam Khan at the court at Kazvin. Bairam Khan is a Turkic tribesman originally from Persia who had fought alongside Babur before joining his son Humayun. Now, accompanied by ten horsemen, he presents himself before Shah Tahmasp where he is faced with a delicate and potentially incendiary situation.

After a relatively carefree and even somewhat libertine youth, Shah Tahmasp has undergone a spiritual awakening of sorts, rejecting his earlier sinful ways and bringing back Twelver Shi'ite orthodoxy to Persia. Tahmasp has outlawed irreligious behaviour and taverns and brothels have been closed. This expression of Twelver Shi'ism is visibly demonstrated by the wearing of the Taj-e-Safavid, or Taj Haidari, which is a white turban with twelve folds wrapped over a red felt cap, a creation of Tahmasp's grandfather, Shah Haidar. When Bairam Khan arrives at the Persian court, Tahmasp brusquely asks him to cut his hair and wear the Taj-e-Safavid but Bairam Khan is able to diplomatically side-step the issue by declaring that as a servant of another prince, he can do nothing but obey his own master. Tahmasp does not insist, but in a fit of pique and certainly in an attempt to impress Bairam Khan with his power, has a few heretics of the Ismalia sects brought into his presence and beheaded. After this awkward and bloody meeting between Tahmasp and Bairam Khan, relations are, not surprisingly, somewhat strained between the Shah and Humayun for a while. There are a number of minor incidents in which the Persians seem to be testing the Hindustani padshah, grazing the limits of arrogance and posturing. At last Humayun and his entourage are received by Tahmasp himself at his summer palace in the mountains. 'The Persian monarch placed Humayun to his right,' writes Jauhar approvingly, 'and they sat down on the same cushion.' But soon enough, Tahmasp asks Humayun to wear the Taj-e-Safavid and thereby demonstrate his conversion from Sunni to Shi'ite. The pragmatic Humayun, who has clearly known what would be expected of him, courteously tells Tahmasp that 'a Taj (crown) is an emblem of greatness; I will with pleasure wear it.' Humayun wears the Taj, without much fuss, and honour is saved. Tahmasp is enormously mollified and 'they passed the night in feasting and carousing'. Despite further excursions and amusements, however, Tahmasp is relentless about Humayun's conversion to Shi'a Islam. Humayun understands the true heft of his helplessness, at the mercy of Tahmasp's uncertain moods and so, one day, after visiting the ruins of Persepolis, Humayun 'ordered his diamonds and rubies to be brought to him; and having selected the largest diamond, placed it in a mother-of-pearl box; he then added several other diamonds and rubies; and having placed them on a tray gave them in charge of Bairam Beg to present them to the Persian monarch, with a message, "that they were brought from Hindustan purposely for his majesty."' The large diamond is the same magnificent one which Humayun has obtained from the family of Bikramjit, Raja of Gwalior. Some believe it to be the famous, and cursed, Koh-i-Noor, which eventually made its way back to the Deccan.

'His majesty's time in Iraq,' writes Gulbadan, quite without guile, 'was (now) spent happily. In various ways the Shah showed good feeling, and every day sent presents of rare and strange things.' Gulbadan herself, at this point, is in Kabul under duress with Kamran. She is raising her young family and anxious for news from her exiled brother Humayun. The details she is able to write about of the life the royal couple are leading in Persia are known to her through Hamida. It is from Hamida herself that Gulbadan hears of the adventures they go through in Persia and it is often forgotten that we have the remarkable presence of a sixteenth-century Muslim woman's voice, vibrant, textured and alive with observations unique to that woman and to that time.

Gulbadan writes of the hunting parties that were organized for Humayun and his entourage. 'There was hunting eight times while he was in Iraq, and each time trouble was taken for him also.' We are also informed that 'Hamida Banu Begam used to enjoy the sight from a distance in either a camel or a horse litter.' But another woman, Tahmasp's sister Sultanam takes a more active interest in the men's hunting. 'Shahzada Sultanam, the Shah's sister, used to ride on horseback, and take her stand behind her brother.' Humayun notices Sultanam's presence and mentions it to Hamida later. 'There was a woman riding behind the Shah at the hunt,' he tells her, impressed. 'People told me it was Shahzada Sultanam the Shah's sister.' Sultanam is especially solicitous of Hamida and visits her regularly. One day she arranges for a feast outside the city precincts, in a beautiful meadow. Large tents are set up and the Shah's 'kinswomen and his paternal aunt were there, and his sisters and the ladies of his haram and the wives of the khans and sultans and amirs, about 1000 women in all splendour and adornment.' It must have been a very splendid sight. The women all in their best silk brocade garments, the swaying tents with their bright colours and the famous Persian rugs in geometric, scarlet magnificence on the ground. Sultanam and Hamida stand together and watch this sumptuous tented arrangement and Sultanam asks the younger woman: 'Are such chatr and taq met with in Hindustan?' To which Hamida replies, with impeccable pride in her own country, 'They say two dang with respect to Khurasan and four dang with respect to Hindustan. When a thing is found in two dang, it is clear it will be found better in four.' Even surrounded by Persian opulence, Hamida is aware of the superior size and greater scope of Hindustan, its boundless lands and great wealth. Hamida Banu is, after all, of Persian extraction herself. Her father is Shaikh Ali Akbar Jami, an Iranian Shi'ite Muslim originally from Khorasan. She would have been familiar with the language, Persian, and some of the customs of the country and from her wit and vivacity it is clear that she felt comfortable in the company of all the grand ladies of the Persian court. 'They passed the whole day very well in sociable activity' writes Gulbadan, echoing Hamida's satisfaction at the day. 'At the time of eating, all the Amirs' wives stood and served, and the Shah's ladies placed food before Shahzada Sultanam.'

Hamida Banu has her second child, a daughter, while she is in Persia. Though she is now an exile, the circumstances of her second pregnancy are vastly different from her first one. In Persia, though she still travels constantly, it is for the pleasure of visiting charming and legendary sights. She is now preceded by horsemen and drummers and trumpeters. The road ahead is swept and sprinkled with water. Her retinue includes elaborate tents and mobile kitchens. Hamida and Humayun will no longer have to depend on the volatile loyalty of local chieftains and the erratic produce of parched lands. She is also, remarkably for the age and the place, the only woman in Humayun's life in Persia. Through the circumstances of their precipitous exile from Hindustan, Humayun and Hamida's two years in Persian will perforce be years of rare intimacy and shared discovery.

Though Gulbadan, and the ever tactful Abu'l-Fazl do not mention it in their biographies of Humayun, relations between the Hindustani Padshah Ghazi and Shah Tahmasp are often frayed. Tahmasp's behaviour is sometimes arbitrary and negligent, aimed at wounding the more forgiving and sentimental Humayun. Apart from their religious differences, Tahmasp also seems to be critical of Humayun's lack of ruthlessness and resolve, which allowed him to lose his kingdom to his ambitious brothers and enemies. According to the forthright Jauhar, Tahmasp derides Humayun saying, 'It was a consequence of your foolish vanity, that you could not properly govern those extensive dominions; you were therefore driven away by the villagers, and left your wife and family captives.' The wife in question here is Humayun's senior consort, Bega Begum, whose fate at this stage is unknown, since no biographer mentions the date at which she is returned to Humayun.

Notwithstanding these occasionally withering criticisms, Tahmasp is unfailingly hospitable. He arranges a final banquet for his Hindustani guests, for which '300 tents had been fetched...and twelve bands of military music stationed in different places, all of which struck up when his Majesty advanced; and the whole of the ground was covered with the imperial carpets. On the first day there was a great profusion of every kind of eatables and dresses of honour were conferred on the King, and on all the guests.' The elaborate banquet prepared for the royal guests must have been of intense interest to Hamida, and it is certain that she would have returned to her court and family, in Kabul and then in Agra, with elaborate details of the foods served. As per the traditions of the Turko-Islamic cuisines of the time, there would have been 'flat, lightly raised breads, lamb, mutton, and chicken soups and stews, skewered and grilled meats, meat dumplings or pastries, ground meat with spices, meats marinated in yogurt, sugar confections...and sherbets and yogurt drinks.' Tahmasp then tells Humayun that the 300 tents, and all the attending staff and equipment, were his to take back to Hindustan in addition to 12,000 cavalry to help him reconquer his lost lands. But before leaving, Tahmasp has a final request. He wants Humayun to arrange for a farewell banquet a-la-Hindustani so that he may sample the cuisine of that land.

After two years of impeccable hospitality by the Persians, the Hindustani party would have been keen to prepare as sumptuous a feast for Tahmasp as possible. Ghee, which was used in Hindustan as opposed to the fat of the fat-tailed sheep which was what the Persians used, would have been one of the discoveries for the Persian guests at the banquet in

Tabriz. Musicians are summoned and the feast is begun by the ceremonial slicing of a fruit, after which the banquet begins. Dishes such as khichdi are cooked with an amount of ghee equal in weight to the rice and legumes fill the tented halls with a rich, buttery fragrance. Despite all the meat on offer, Tahmasp is most impressed with a vegetarian dish. 'Various kinds of food and drink were presented, 'writes Jauhar, 'and everybody heartily participated; but Shah Tahmasp was more pleased with the dish of rice and peas (daal khuske) than any of the others, it being a mode of cookery unknown in Persia.' Another ingredient the Persian diners would have tasted for the first time would have been turmeric, the golden, slightly pungent spice used in Hindustan since Vedic times.

Finally the Hindustani party is ready to leave, but apart from the flavours of the food, the brocade robes, the voluminous tents and cavalry, there is another element that they take with them which will alter the trajectory of art in Hindustan forever. After his years of enthusiastic patronage of the arts in his ateliers, Tahmasp has wearied of painting by the 1540s and the artists of his ateliers have begun dispersing. Tahmasp allows two of his younger artists, Mir Sayyid Ali and Abd al-Samad, to leave Persia for Humayun's court. After Humayun's return to Hindustan, and then under the patronage of his son Akbar, the imperial Safavid style becomes established as the basic element of Mughal miniature painting and most of this influence can be directly attributed to the two artists from Tahmasp's atelier. Under their tutelage, the fine draughtsmanship and finely calibrated use of colour famous in Persia fuses with Hindustani energy and vibrancy and creates a new and resplendent style which will result in the jewels of the *Hamzanama*, the Shah Jahan album, and the Dara Shikoh album.

Humayun is accompanied out of Tabriz by Shahzada Bahram, Tahmasp's son. While leaving him, Humayun gives him a diamond ring which had belonged to Maham Begum telling the prince, 'such is my friendship for you, that I would willingly remain with you all my life'. These are no ordinary words of politesse, however, for instead of heading straight towards Hindustan, as requested by Tahmasp, Humayun turns his entourage around, unbeknownst to Tahmasp, and goes back to visit the city of Tabrez. 'We remained there five days,' admits Jauhar, 'during which time his Majesty visited the bazaar of Caesarea and the dome of Syria.' The royal party are already more than 2,000 kilometres away from Kabul but they now move on to Ardabil, itinerant tourists, to visit the famous shrine complex of the Sufi leader Sheikh Safial-Din Khanegah. They would have seen, at the mosque of Ardabil, the famous Persian rugs, made of silk, and gold and silver threads, which were offered to the shrine. After a week in Ardabil, the wandering guests now go to visit the nearby Caspian Sea, 'over which there is constantly a thick fog or mist'. After further peregrinations and stops, the royal party finally reach Kazvin. Shah Tahmasp, having thought Humayun long gone, is shocked to come upon his tents outside Kazvin. 'What!' he exclaims, according to Jauhar. 'Has he not yet left this country?' Thoroughly unimpressed by Humayun's delays, Tahmasp demands that the Hindustani party leave immediately, double quick, and cover at least twelve leagues the very same day. And so Humayun and his entourage leave Persia, reluctantly but enormously strengthened, with a total of 14,000 horsemen, and march towards Hindustan.

When Kamran hears, in 1545, of Humayun marching back towards Kabul backed by the Shah of Persia, he realizes that the stakes have changed. He sends back the child Akbar along with his elder sister Bakshi Banu, the five-year-old daughter of another wife of Humayun's, Gunwar Begum, from Kandahar to Kabul. The children travel through swirling winter snow and when they finally reach Kabul, the elderly Khanzada, stationed at Kabul, sees Akbar for the first time and according to Gulbadan, 'she was very fond of him and used to kiss his hands and feet, and say "they are the very hands and feet of my brother the Emperor Babur, and he is like him altogether"'. But Khanzada does not have the pleasure of her little grandnephew's company for a long time. Kamran, increasingly scared for his life, sends Khanzada on a peace mission to Humayun and the old woman now makes the last journey of her life through the mountains of Central Asia. 'At Qabal-Chak', writes Gulbadan, 'she had three days of fever...and on the fourth day of her illness she passed to the mercy of God'. And so Khanzada dies, as she lived, bravely serving the honour of the family through diplomacy and love and impossible hardship.

Humayun marches in triumph into Kabul and the haraman are finally reunited with their padshah. 'For five years,' writes Gulbadan with still vivid sorrow, 'we had been shut out and cut off from this pleasure, so now when we were freed from the moil and pain of separation, we were lifted up by our happiness.' There was rejoicing and celebration and 'many festive gatherings and people sat from evening to dawn'. One final reunion remains, however, as Hamida has been left behind in Kandahar. Now she arrives in Kabul and Akbar is brought to her. Hamida has last seen her son almost two years previously, when he was just over a year old. Wanting to see if Akbar would recognize his mother, Humayun has him taken into a room where a number of ladies are waiting for him, all similarly attired. Akbar recognizes his mother, who must have been overwhelmed herself, having abandoned him in such precarious circumstances. A feast is now organized for Akbar's circumcision and Hamida is introduced at last to Humayun's extended haraman in Kabul. 'People dressed in green,' writes Gulbadan, and 'they went out to the Hill of the Seven Brothers and there passed many days in ease and enjoyment and happiness.' Hamida would have had much to say about her adventures in Persia, especially to Gulbadan, who is a young woman of her own age. The haraman would have heard with raucous enjoyment the stories of the Persian extravagance, the impeccable adab of the court, the strange and wonderful foods filled with dried fruit and nuts and the rich brocades. They will observe with wonder Humayun's new custom of choosing daily the colour of his royal robes in accordance with the movements of the planets, a habit picked up in Persia. The effervescence of the feast spreads to the entire city of Kabul and all the princes, the amirs, and the sultans 'decorated their quarters beautifully'. As for the haraman, they gather in Bega Begum's quarters where 'the begams and ladies made their own [quarters] quite wonderful in a new fashion'. This is the first mention we have of Bega Begum since her capture by Sher Shah, so she is returned, at least by 1545, to Humayun's haraman.

For the next ten years, Humayun is intermittently involved in battles and skirmishes with his three brothers, Kamran, Askari and Hindal. The haraman often follow him on horseback, on expeditions or on excursions. They visit waterfalls and meadows and pitch tents wherever they find a place of beauty. Humayun's patience is sometimes sorely tried when his haraman are not able to comply with his superstitious regard for the proper timing of a journey. 'All of you go on', he tells them wearily, when his new bride Mah Chuchak has delayed a departure by falling off a horse into a stream. 'I will follow when I have taken some opium and got over my annoyance.' The reconquering of empire seems to be a whimsical dream. But there is a violent underbelly to these fraught ambitions and tragedy strikes when Hindal is killed, in an arbitrary encounter, after coming over to Humayun's camp. The haraman and Hindal's sisters are devastated and Gulbadan writes of it with clear and broken pain, so many years later. 'Would to Heaven that merciless sword had touched my heart and eyes, or Saadatyar, my son's, or Khizr Khwaja Khan's! Alas! A thousand times alas!' Kamran is eventually defeated, blinded, and exiled to Mecca. Sher Shah dies, after a short but brilliant career, and Humayun can at last march back into Hindustan in 1555.

The haraman remain in Kabul while Humayun marches away into Hindustan with his Persian troops and the thirteen-year-old Akbar. The haraman wait for news of Humayun and for a summons to the reconquered court. But these women will never see Humayun alive again. He dies within six months of arriving in Hindustan, falling down a flight of stairs at his library in Delhi, and Akbar is crowned Padshah Ghazi. Hamida is now dowager queen mother, at only thirty-one years of age. She is reborn, after her arrival at Akbar's court in 1557, as Maryam Makani (of Mary's Stature), the chaste and quasi-holy mother of a divine king. Akbar's favourite chronicler, his friend and ardent admirer Abu'l-Fazl, is an altogether different biographer from Gulbadan. Gulbadan's manuscript stops abruptly after the death of Hindal, and the remaining missing document has never been found. Without Gulbadan's unaffected and textured narrative, we lose the sense of warm immediacy and easy companionship that the haraman shared with the padshah, and with each other. Gone are the recollections of endless stories in the gloaming of a perfect autumn evening or of falling asleep at the break of dawn after a night spent in songs and laughter. Hamida is now, by Abu'l-Fazl's much more rigid standards, the 'veil of chastity' or 'the pillar of purity', the faultless mother of a perfect king. During Akbar's long reign, as the institutions of empire are slowly consolidated around the glorious figure of the emperor, the women slowly disappear from the biographies of the time. Nevertheless, even the distilled memory of the women in Abu'l-Fazl's *Akbarnama* allows us to see that perhaps something remains of the Hamida of old, who had escaped murderous troops on horseback as a young girl, who had spent years on the road, on icy mountainsides and arid deserts. Even Abu'l-Fazl mentions in the *Akbarnama* that she has a startling habit of setting off, unexpectedly, and travelling great distances when possessed suddenly by 'the desire to behold' her son Akbar. She once arrives in Delhi, following Akbar but unknown to him, to visit Bega Begum. On another occasion when Akbar was in Afghanistan, Hamida travels to Kashmir, along with her old friend Gulbadan. Finding that Akbar had moved on to Kabul, they then followed him there. On each occasion it is noted that her son greets her with great joy and reverence though it is clear that her arrival is unexpected and always creates a minor flurry. For Hamida, as for Gulbadan and the older members of the haraman, the court is where the emperor is and it is a discordant absence to be away from that imperial presence.

There is a painting in the *Tuzuk-e-Jahangiri*, the official history of Padshah Jahangir's reign, entitled *Birth of a Prince*. The painter is Bishan Das, one of the favourite painters of Jahangir, an expert in capturing the expression and essence of the person depicted. The prince whose birth the painting is celebrating is Jahangir, son of Akbar. The effulgence of the painting is striking, all warm colours and ochre tones. There is movement and vibrancy and fizzing excitement. There are Hindustani fortune tellers and eunuchs and Persian robes and Central Asian faces. This is the court of Akbar the Great, in which dusky Rajasthani women in short blouses mingle with fair-skinned Turkish and Persian women with their high, conical Persian caps. In the middle of it all is an older woman, the only one on a chair, ornately decorated, sitting by her reclining Rajasthani daughter-in-law. The older woman wears a tall Turki hat, a veil on her hair, and simple, elegant robes and her feet rest on a richly decorated carpet very much like the Persian rugs she would have admired at Ardabil. The very miniature painting she figures in is a fortuitous result of the artists that came back in her train after her return from Persia. After a lifetime of restless wandering, Hamida Banu Begum is home.

BEGA BEGUM AND HUMAYUN'S TOMB

At the end of 1556, a macabre and grisly message arrives from Delhi to Kabul, where Humayun's widows and sisters and household have been waiting anxiously for news of Mughal fortunes now that Humayun has died. It is a severed head, bloodied and sightless, and it is hung from an iron gate where it is a gruesome but eloquent invitation, informing Humayun's household that it is safe now to join the new Padshah Ghazi, Akbar, in Hindustan. The head, whose body now hangs from a tower at Dinpanah in Delhi, is that of an independent Hindu chieftain called Hemu, styling himself as the more Kshatriya sounding Raja Vikramaditya, last in a long series of challengers. 'The drums of joy beat high,' proclaims Abu'l-Fazl, describing the Kabul party's reaction 'and after thanksgiving and rejoicing, the expedition set out in a propitious hour.'

Akbar has had a precipitous year since the death of his father made him padshah at the age of thirteen. Assisted by his regent, Bairam Khan, he has spent the last year quelling all the challenges to his claim to the throne of Hindustan. But his ambition, the scope and the certitude of it, is blistering. Akbar is no refugee prince and Hindustan is his birthright and for this he needs to create a homeland. 'He remembered the highnesses the Begums,' we are told, and 'for the quieting of the devoted heroes who had recently come to India,' he now sends for 'their highnesses the Begums, and, secondly, the families of the servants of the household into the delightsome and extensive lands of India, so that men might become settled and be restrained in some measure from departing to a country to which they were accustomed.' The women, it is acknowledged, are needed to tether the men to this land of Hindustan. And so the women of the haraman leave Kabul for Hindustan in a large cortege, as they had done twelve years before when Babur had summoned them, though for some of the women the circumstances are sadly altered. Hamida Banu and Bega Begum are widows now and there have been signs of a shearing and reforming of old alliances in the Mughal camp. Tardi Beg, an old nobleman from Babur's entourage who had also fought, though admittedly sometimes less than enthusiastically, beside Humayun, has been killed by the ambitious general Bairam Khan and it is Akbar's foster-mother Maham Anaga who is sent to great the party from Kabul when they arrive at Mankot. 'There were mutual rejoicings' at the arrival of the haraman and 'the army which had become straitened by the long siege were greatly rejoiced at the arrival of their highnesses and…increased their efforts.'

Akbar, though now still only fourteen years old, is already showing signs of the force of nature he will become. 'He was of medium stature but inclining to be tall,' writes his son, Jahangir, much later. 'His complexion was wheaten or nut coloured, rather dark than fair, his eyes and eyebrows dark black and the latter running across into each other; with a handsome person, he had a lion's strength which was indicated by an extraordinary breadth of chest.' Undeterred by the fraught nature of his claim, Akbar has already had the khutba read in his name in Delhi and now goes by the title Shahanshah. The women of the haraman, as they ride into Hindustan, are dressed in the layered style of Central Asia, with long loose jama-like robes with long sleeves, ankle-length vests and a veil covering the hair.

Bega Begum, now, is standing in the headwind of an unsettling storm. She has always been very close to her nephew, whom she helped raise for ten years in Kabul after the early deaths of her own children. Akbar, who has a strong bond with all the older women of his family, is always indebted to the care she lavished on him as a child. 'The kindness and affection she showed me', Akbar tells Abu'l-Fazl, 'and my love for her are beyond expression'. When he suffered from toothache as a child in Kabul, Bega Begum brought a medicine for him but Hamida Banu, fearful of poison in a court still violent and unsettled, was reluctant to let Akbar have any. 'As she knew what the state of feeling was', explains Akbar, 'she, in her love to me swallowed some of it without there being any order to that effect, and then rubbed the medicine on my teeth'. Hamida Banu's concerns were allayed, as was Akbar's toothache. 'Everyone who did not know the real facts', 'said Akbar, meaning that those who did not know she was his stepmother, 'thought that she was my own mother'.

But Akbar is now Shahanshah of Hindustan and is on the threshold of a grand destiny. Bega Begum has no children and no husband. She has the tenacious memory, however, of her husband with whom she shared a clearly intimate and unusually feisty relationship. 'Jinnat Ashiyani [Humayun]', agrees Abu'l-Fazl, 'had a great respect and regard for her'. Humayun, initially buried at the Dinpanah (later renamed Purana Qila), then removed to Kalainur in Punjab when Hemu Vikramaditya threatened Delhi, has now been re-buried at Dinpanah. With Akbar occupied with consolidating his empire, no attempt is initially made to build a fitting mausoleum for Humayun. When Akbar and the haraman move to Agra, Bega Begum remains in Delhi. This, after all, was the last residence of Humayun. This was where he had brought his painters, Abd al-Samad and Mir Sayyid Ali back from Persia, and where he had installed his precious books. It is also the resting place of the great Chishti Sufi saint, Nizamuddin Auliya, and the sacred power of that magnetic presence draws both kings and ordinary pilgrims.

At some point during the next few years, probably around 1563, Bega Begum performs a Hajj pilgrimage. Nothing is known of the details of her trip for no biographer thought it necessary to record it. She was away from Hindustan for three years and 'after she had returned from the holy places [Mecca and Medina], she had, in spite of her ties of love between her and His Majesty (Akbar), chosen Delhi as her place of abode'. In her wake, she brings back masons and scholars from Arabia and begins the supervision of what would become the first truly magnificent example of a Mughal Persianate garden tomb as a mausoleum for Humayun.

The site for the tomb is chosen carefully, in close proximity to Nizamuddin's Durgah and with the Yamuna flowing beside it, making access to the tomb easier. The chief architect of the tomb is Mirak Mirza Ghiyas, a Persian craftsman, who has worked previously in Herat and Bukhara. The tomb will combine, for the first time in Hindustan, certain elements of Central Asian architecture which till now had never been found together. They include a massive onion-shaped Timurid dome, a radial geometry and symmetry and the use of red sandstone along with white marble structures. The tomb's double-shell dome construction is especially reminiscent of the domes in Timurid Central Asia, which Humayun and Hamida Banu were familiar with. The materials and the craftsmen's skills, however, are local. The red sandstone is quarried from Rajasthan and the white marble from Makrana. The Persians build in brick and the Indian masons use stone, which is easily available in Hindustan, so the local craftsmen have to transform the architect's vision through marble and stone. The mausoleum is set in a classic walled charbagh with a central pavilion which, in this case, is the tomb itself. There are water channels and walkways and the gardens, too, reflect an early fusion of Timurid and Hindustani elements. The charbagh plan is Timurid, but the plants used would have been the local flowering shrubs that Babur had so admired—oleander, hibiscus and semi-tropical fruit trees. Tomb gardens had existed in Hindustan before the Mughals, after all the Lodis are buried in gardens a short distance from Humayun's tomb. There was nothing, however, of the planned symmetrical perfection and, most importantly for Babur, the consoling stream of clear, flowing waterways. Here we have, for the first time in Hindustan, paradise on earth.

Akbar, meanwhile, once the political turmoil of his early years has been subdued, begins building the Agra fort in 1565 and then Fatehpur Sikri in 1571. These buildings, in Fatehpur Sikri especially, show considerably more Hindustani features than Humayun's tomb does. As for Bega Begum, she remains in Delhi, supervising the work on Humayun's mausoleum and staying behind when it is completed. 'One of his wives had loved Emaumus [Humayun] so faithfully that she had had a small house built close by the tomb and had watched there till the day of her death', narrates the Jesuit priest Father Antoine de Monserrate in 1591. 'Throughout her widowhood she devoted herself to prayer and to alms-giving. Indeed she maintained 500 poor people by her alms. Had she only been a Christian', he further bemoans, 'hers would have been the life of a heroine.' Even the stringent Abu'l-Fazl agrees; 'She had taken up her residence in the neighbourhood of the tomb of HM Jahanbani Jinnat Ashiyani [Humayun] and devoted herself to works of charity.' She is visited by Akbar and by Hamida Banu, and herself travels to Agra to congratulate her beloved stepson on his successful conquest of Gujarat in 1573. 'One of the joyful occurrences of this glorious year', writes Abu'l-Fazl, 'was the auspicious arrival of the secluded lady of the Court of Chastity, the noble dame Haji Begum'. 'There were great feasts', we are told, and 'His Majesty went out to welcome her'. But despite Abu'l-Fazl's careful hyperbole, Bega Begum leads a startlingly un-sequestered and adventurous life. From Kabul to Agra and back again, she finally made Delhi her home. Empress of Hindustan once, then losing everything, including her young daughter Aqiqa in that scathing dawn at Chausa, she refuses the constrained splendour of Akbar's court, preferring the company of artisans and craftsmen in Delhi. She travels to Mecca, one of the first Mughal women to do so, and dedicates her life to the memory of Humayun and to the care of the poor. In stark contrast to what Akbar and Abu'l-Fazl are trying to create in the royal court, Bega Begum is sole guardian of her own honour. These Timurid-Mughal women—Bega, Gulbadan, Hamida and Khanzada—the matriarchs of the first Mughals, would never be constrained tidily within the definition of the chaste and ordered 'harem', invisible to all and beyond reproach. That destiny would be reserved for the next generation of women.

Part II
Disappeared Wives and Imperial Splendour
1556-1631

MAHAM ANAGA AND THE RIVER OF MILK

There is a premonition, on a leaden day in May 1562, of murder and blood and a catastrophic reversal of fortunes. Heat crackles across the city of Agra where Akbar, twenty years old, rests in the zenana of the royal residence. This is still the old, dilapidated brick-built Badalgarh fort and Agra is an unpretentious town yet, with little claim to magnificence and splendour. But the river Yamuna flows dense and cool through the city and noblemen from the time of Babur, dreaming of Kabul, have been building mansions and gardens on the riverbank. The young Akbar has started construction on the first major fort of the Mughals and grainy red sandstone arrives in huge quantities every year from quarries in Rajasthan. But on this derisory day in May, Akbar is asleep in the afternoon in the zenana when a young man, richly dressed in a fine muslin jama, strides into the ruined fort with murder on his mind.

The man, thirty-year-old Adham Khan, a general and a foster-brother of Akbar, walks into the palace, his hands on his dagger, and enters a hall where a number of ministers are sitting on creamy white takhts on the floor attending to court matters. Shams-ud-Din Atga Khan, the elderly vakil, and the other ministers, all get up to greet the visitor but Adham Khan signals to one of his men who then stabs the old vakil in the chest, never uttering a word. The dying man backs out of the room, bleeding, and stumbles into the courtyard where he is hacked to death by Adham Khan's men. All the men assembled, the ministers with their jewelled turbans, the servants in their patterned coats, the guards and the drummers and the lute players, are paralysed, struck dumb by the violence unleashed on this terrible, torpid day. Adham Khan is a favoured member of the young emperor's inner circle and 'on account of his nearness to the emperor, had no equal owing to the pride of his youth and the insolence of his rank and riches'. The acts he is carrying out, murder and treason, are beyond their imagining. Adham Khan climbs the steps to the inner apartments, towards the zenana, where Akbar is sleeping. The eunuch Ni'mat, guarding the door to the zenana, is suddenly shocked into action. He bolts the door and gallantly throws his body across it and prevents Adham Khan from entering the room. Akbar, meanwhile, has woken up to an ominous commotion and a persistent banging on his door. An old servant, Rafiq, shows him the mangled corpse of Shams-ud-Din and Akbar is convulsed with rage. Wrapping a simple cloth around his body, 'from a divine inspiration he [Akbar] did not come out by the door where that demented wretch was standing and meditating evil, but by another way'. Wordlessly, anticipating the only action possible, a servant holds out one of Akbar's special scimitars. Akbar grabs the sword and strides onto the blazing courtyard, where the sun has leached all colour from the sky. Adham Khan is standing there, with 'great hauteur and pride and entire confidence in the favour of the emperor'. But this time, he has gone too far. 'Son of a fool!' shouts Akbar, as he confronts Adham Khan bare-chested, his long hair loose around his shoulder, 'why have you killed our Atga?' Adham Khan reaches out to Akbar, either to attack him or to placate him, but Akbar is furious, beyond placation and even beyond fear. He 'struck him such a blow on the face that that wicked monster turned a somersault and fell down insensible'. Akbar orders his servants to bind Adham Khan and throw him from the terrace, a height of some eight feet. When Adham Khan survives the fall, Akbar orders him dragged up and thrown down again and this time he is flung head first, 'so that his neck was broken, and his brains destroyed'.

There have been acts of violence in the emerging Mughal empire in the seven years since Akbar has become padshah. There have been mounds of skulls of the defeated, there have been rivers of blood. But this is a desecration at the very heart of the empire. Moreover, despite the bruising, killing men, the guards, the ministers and the old retainers, it is a woman who is at the epicentre of this bizarre and unnecessary violence. It is a woman who has gambled, and lost. After the death of Adham Khan, there is a fracture in the structure of empire, a loosening of old and once essential ties. The drama on this blighted afternoon has involved a community of foster brothers, foster fathers and foster mothers, and they will never again be as powerful as they once were. The twenty-year-old Akbar, standing on the terrace of the zenana and looking down at the wrecked body of his vakil and the blood spreading out from the skull of Adham Khan, understands that the things of his childhood, the hunts and the appalling tests of strength, must now cease. For the next forty years of his reign, Akbar will be regent of his own fate. The audacious community of foster mothers will never recover.

◆

When Humayun and Hamida made their precipitous journey away from Hindustan and into Persia in 1543, they left behind the one-year-old infant Akbar with trusted servants and retainers. There are wet nurses amongst this party, for it is customary in noble families for infants to be fed by loyal and deserving women, as a mark of honour. Akbar, therefore, temporarily loses his parents at the age of one but he gains an entire foster-family, one that will cherish and dote on him with proprietary and complete devotion, and anchor their destinies to his uncertain fortunes. There are at least eleven women appointed as wet nurses to Akbar and chief amongst them is Maham Anaga, mother of a ten-year-old son, Adham. The position of wet nurse is a keenly desired one for it confers a great honour on the entire family of the foster-mother. The mothers, too, are carefully selected for it is believed that they transmit not only milk to the infant, but also some of their central traits of character. The women, therefore, need to be 'even-tempered, spiritually-minded' women from whose breasts Akbar's 'mouth was sweetened by the life-giving fluid'. While Maham Anaga is the superintendent of the wet nurses, she does not feed Akbar herself. The principal wet nurse is Jiji Anaga, who has an infant son too, Aziz Koka. 'Maham Anaga, Jiji Anaga and Atka Khan were made fortunate by serving him' is Abu'l-Fazl's assessment. Most of Akbar's wet nurses are attached to Humayun in some form. Jiji Anaga is married to Shams-ud-Din of Ghazni, now known as Atga Khan, who saved Humayun's life at the battle of Chausa during the scandalous routing by Sher Shah. Some are wives of trusted servants and retainers. Loyalty to the infant prince is a ferocious certainty and they guard his life and his future with vigilant love. There is bitter jealousy, at times, over who will suckle the infant and it is often Jiji Anaga who is targeted by the other women. Abu'l-Fazl notes that at one time, Jiji Anaga is distressed to learn that the other nurses have told Humayun that she 'was practicing incantations', or black magic, so that Akbar would accept only her milk, and no one else's. These women, their children and husbands, form a cross-hatch of watchful relationships which will stand guard over Akbar and last well into the coming generations.

Even after Humayun and Hamida's triumphant return from Persia, Akbar's fate, at age three, remains highly uncertain. He is held hostage by his uncle Kamran several times in Kabul but even in the most fraught circumstances, he has his foster-family around him. Maham Anaga especially is a stout and loyal presence through all these years of dangerous turmoil, as are some of the other royal ladies, Gulbadan and Bega in particular. Maham Anaga, Abu'l-Fazl admits, 'was always in charge of the nursling of fortune'. At one point, the desperate Kamran even uses the three–year-old Akbar as a shield, placing him upon the battlements so that Humayun doesn't use heavy cannons against him. By some accounts, it is Maham Anaga herself who rushes to Akbar's side to keep him out of harm's way. 'For the sake of his wives and children and the begums and the household etc.', Gulbadan writes, 'the Emperor [Humayun] did not have the canon fired.'

Akbar finally rides into Hindustan alongside Humayun, to reconquer the Mughal empire, when he is thirteen years old. The royal ladies all remain behind in Kabul but Maham Anaga accompanies Akbar into Hindustan. Akbar is a turbulent, boisterous adolescent, physically brave and endlessly distracted. Unlike his studious father, fascinated by the occult, Akbar can never be made to sit and study, preferring by far the company of his racing pigeons, dogs, horses and companions in arms. He never will learn to read and will remain effectively illiterate, the only Mughal padshah to be so, possibly due to his hyperactive nature exacerbated by extreme dyslexia. When Humayun's court astrologer had painstakingly chosen a propitious hour to begin the education of the young mirza, they found that 'he had attired himself for sport and had disappeared'. But Akbar will compensate by developing a prodigious memory and excellent visual skills. So when Humayun dies barely a year later, Akbar is already a skilled and supremely brave warrior but he is far from ready to rule. Akbar is in the Punjab, when his father dies, under the charge of Bairam Khan, the Turki general who had attended the awkward, unexpectedly violent interview with Shah Tahmasp in Persia during Humayun's exile. The young boy is proclaimed Padshah Ghazi in a garden at Kalanaur, on a makeshift throne placed on a simple brick platform, and Bairam Khan is now Vakil-e-Sultanat.

The first challenge to the young padshah comes from an unlikely hero. Hemu Vikramaditya is a lower caste Hindu who, despite 'a wretchedly puny physique' and a less than distinguished background, becomes an inspired commander and routs the Mughal army at Delhi and re-conquers the city. Bairam Khan, the fifty-five-year-old seasoned general stands firm, however, and chance is on his side, for a stray arrow finds its mark and pierces Hemu's eye while he is mounted on his war elephant. Hemu's collapse leads to disarray amongst his troops and this valiant leader is beheaded and his head is dispatched to Kabul, a grisly summons to the household. Hamida Banu, Gulbadan, Bega Begum and all the families and retainers get ready to leave Kabul under the guardianship of Munim Khan, an old and trusted confidant of Humayun's. But news now arrives in Kabul of a much more discordant murder. One that announces the arrival of a new kingmaker and challenges all the old contenders from Humayun's entourage. Bairam Khan has had Tardi Beg, lieutenant of Humayun and survivor of the Chausa rout, murdered. Munim Khan is sufficiently worried by this disquieting news to turn back to Kabul, leaving the haraman under the care of Shams-ud-Din Atga Khan.

When the Kabul party reaches Hindustan, a delighted Akbar sends Maham Anaga to greet them, 'who, on account of her abundant sense and loyalty, held a high place in the esteem of the Shahenshah, and who had been in his service from the time of the cradle till his adornment of the throne, and who trod the path of good service with the acme of affection.' The household is finally reunited at Mankot with Akbar, who left Kabul an unruly twelve-year-old and who is now Padshah Ghazi. The stakes have changed. There is a quickening of intent around the young padshah and the women of the zenana waste no time. An alliance is arranged between Akbar and a granddaughter of Munim Khan and now loyalties have been proclaimed. Suddenly it is Bairam Khan's turn to be unnerved by the arrival of the household from Kabul and the loyalty of the zenana to Humayun's old retainers. The clear ambition of Maham Anaga, in particular, leads him to believe that Akbar himself had been turned against him. During an elephant fight arranged by Akbar, the royal elephants, still fighting, happen to stray close to the tent where Bairam Khan is resting. He is convinced that this is an assassination attempt organized by Akbar himself and sends a trusted servant to Maham Anaga complaining; 'I am not conscious of having committed any offence… and I have not displayed anything except well-wishing respect. Why then have mischief makers imputed some mischief to me and caused such unkindness as that furious elephants should have been let loose against my tent?' Maham Anaga, we are told, 'by soothing expressions quieted his disturbed mind'.

Bairam Khan is further placated by his marriage with Salima Sultan Begum, a niece of Humayun and therefore a Timurid herself. 'All the court ladies', we are told, 'and especially Maham Anaga showed great alacrity in furthering the marriage.' But Bairam is still unsettled by the incident with the rampaging elephants and now accuses another foster parent, Jiji Anaga's husband, Shams-ud-Din Atga of complotting against him and rages: 'I know that these unkindnesses which have appeared from his Majesty are the result of your unkindness towards me'. Shams-ud-Din has to appear before Bairam Khan with all his sons beside him and swear allegiance on the Quran before the regent is appeased. But it is clear that Bairam Khan is disconcerted by the influence of Akbar's many foster parents and brothers. Despite his own considerable prestige and rank, there is a persistent, acknowledged belief that Akbar's foster-family have a prior, and often infallible, claim on his loyalty.

Bairam Khan is increasingly isolated in the next two years not only by Akbar's foster-family, but also by the Timurid noblemen who have returned to court and who resent the Turki regent's imperious high-handedness. Badauni, Akbar's much more critical biographer, even claims that Akbar's servants are kept in miserly conditions, and that the adolescent Akbar himself has a limited privy purse, while Bairam Khan's servants enjoy rich fiefdoms. Maham Anaga and her son Adham Khan especially have an unquestioned access to the young emperor. 'At every opportunity they said to His Majesty…words which might produce disfavour in his mind [towards Bairam Khan]', complains the disapproving biographer Ahmad Shah Nizamuddin. 'Especially Adham Khan, who on account of being the son of Maham Anka, had precedence over all who were specially favoured, and always in concert with his mother followed the path of envy.' Bairam Khan himself is arbitrary in his decisions, sometimes violent and vengeful, and the atmosphere at court seethes with suspicious rumours and uncertain brinkmanship.

Finally on a day in March 1560, following another capricious killing of Akbar's mahouts by Bairam Khan, 'Maham Anka thought in her mind that here was no better course, than that she should persuade his Majesty and take him to Delhi and in concert with Shahab-ud-Din Ahmad Khan, who was in those days in Delhi, they might attempt to do whatever might be proper'. This 'proper' thing that Nizamuddin rather preciously refers to is nothing less than a coup against Bairam Khan. Akbar suddenly leaves Agra for Delhi, professing a need to meet his mother, Hamida Banu. In Delhi, 'Shahab-ud-din and Maham Anka made mountains of mole-hills and prejudiced the emperor's mind against the Khan Khanan' complains Badauni bitterly. But Maham Anaga, 'who was a marvel of sense, resource and loyalty', is scathing about Bairam Khan's desire for absolute power. 'As long as Bairam Khan would remain', Maham Anaga explains to Akbar, 'he would not allow His Majesty any authority in the affairs of the empire' because 'in reality the imperial power was in his hands'. Hamida Banu, and Maham Anaga strengthen Akbar's uncertain resolve and the hold that Bairam Khan has had on Akbar disappears and the padshah is emboldened. Akbar decides he will 'inflict suitable punishment on Bairam Khan and his assemblage of flatterers, so that they should awake from their sleep of neglect…' Maham Anaga is aware of the dangerous game she has just played, and that the powerful Bairam Khan will turn his incendiary gaze on her. 'The Khan Khana would know,' she warns Akbar,' that your coming to Delhi was due to our representation, and would suspect us of this offence and we have no power of withstanding his hostility, it would be kindness to us, if your Majesty would grant us the honour of your permission to go to Mecca.' But Akbar will not hear of it, as he has 'great affection for Maham Anka, on account of her assiduous attention and service' and will not allow her to leave his court. He will 'ask the Khan Khanam to excuse her fault', he assures her, and so Maham Anaga remains in Delhi as no doubt she has always intended to do. She hasn't come so far, with real power only a breath away now, to give it all away and go to Mecca. Shahab-ud-Din Ahmad Khan, who is Maham Anaga's son-in-law, now takes over charge of state affairs and 'in concert with Maham Anka, publishes the fact of the change of the emperor's disposition towards the Khan Khana'. The nobles from all over the country read the portent in these proclamations, desert Bairam Khan and ride towards Delhi. Reassured, Munim Khan arrives from Kabul as does Shams-ud-Din Atga Khan from the Punjab. Shahab-ud-Din Ahmad Khan, 'in consultation with Maham Anka, gave everyone who came to the threshold...hopes of rank and jagir commensurate with his circumstances'. Largesse is shown, and the recipients are all faithful loyalists of Maham Anaga. Bairam Khan himself, after a half-hearted revolt, submits to Akbar and is then exiled to Mecca.

There are two families now around Akbar, neither related to him by blood, who gauge the rapidly evolving political scenario and aim for the highest posts. The first is Maham Anaga's family; her son Adham Khan, her son-in-law Shahab-ud-Din and her husband, Nadim Koka. The other is Jiji Anaga's family; her husband Shams-ud-Din Atga Khan and their sons, including Aziz Koka. So powerful and numerous are Jiji Anaga's family that they are known by the collective sobriquet—Atka Khail. Both these families owe the honour and power accorded to them to the foster mothers who bind them to Akbar—Maham and Jiji. There is a quick succession of contenders to the important posts in this rapacious court where the eighteen-year-old Akbar searches for a balance between these different factions. At one point, both Shahab-ud-Din Khan and Maham Anaga are given vakalats in tandem. Maham Anaga, 'in her great loyalty, took charge of affairs and made Shihabuddin Ahmad Khan and Khwaja Jahan her tools.' As Akbar trusts Maham Anaga and values her judgement, her ambition and intelligence allow her considerable power in this nascent Mughal court. 'In those days,' writes Abu'l-Fazl, referring to a vakalat (vice-regency) with Bahadur Khan, 'Bahadur Khan had the name of vakil, yet in reality, the business was transacted by Maham Anaga... For this noble work, wisdom and courage was necessary, and in truth, Maham Anaga possessed these two qualities in perfection. Many a woman treads manfully wisdom's path.'

The Mughal empire, in these early days, is still turbulent and heaving and many fractious warlords and chieftains must be subdued. While Akbar sends Adham Khan, now a commander in his army, to invade Malwa, two women at the court in Delhi begin construction on architectural projects which will be amongst the first in what will become the glorious heritage of the Mughal empire. Bega Begum is building the Arab Sarai in Delhi, a guesthouse for travellers going to Agra along the Grand Trunk Road. Maham Anaga, meanwhile, begins work on the mosque and madrasa complex called the Khair-ul-Manazil. It is built at an auspicious and clearly ambitious spot, directly opposite the entrance to Humayun's Dinpanah fort, and right next to the Lal Darwaza of the last emperor, Sher Shah Suri. It has a fine gateway with a Persian inscription exalting the builder of the mosque—Maham Anaga;

> In the time of Jalal ud-Din Muhammad, who is the greatest of just kings, when Maham Beg, the protector of chastity erected this building for the virtuous, Sahabuddin Ahmad Khan, the generous, assisted in the erection of this good house.

The mosque has an unusual upper story of classrooms, which encloses the courtyard within a high screen which suggests that the school is for girls, and the mosque for women only. Behind the mosque are the large mansions of the nobility and lining the mosque are bustling shops. It is, at the time, one of the finest mosques of Delhi.

There is glorious news, meanwhile, for Maham Anaga from the battlefields of Malwa, for Adham Khan has successfully defeated Sultan Baz Bahadur. This ruler, an ethnic Pathan, was always more interested in music and dance than in ruling and the particular object of his poetry and romance is his favourite, Roopmati. Roopmati was 'renowned throughout the world for her beauty and charm', admits even the usually austere Abu'l-Fazl. '[Baz Bahadur] had a great passion', agrees Nizamuddin, 'for the society of women and the company of musicians'. But Baz Bahadur is defeated and flees, while his zenana and his treasure fall to Adham Khan and his generals. Roopmati drinks poison, and 'carried her honour to the hidden chambers of annihilation', but there are still many beautiful dancing girls and great treasure which Adham Khan seizes. Instead of sending everything as tribute to Akbar, which is the custom, Adham Khan only sends a few elephants back to Delhi, keeping treasure and 'the dancing girls, and nautch-girls, belonging to Baz Bahadur, and all his precious things'. Adham Khan is complacent and supremely confident after his recent victories as general, safe in the knowledge that Akbar considers him a brother and certain of his mother's very great influence over the emperor. But Akbar, though still only nineteen, is starting to chafe at this constant belittling of his supremacy. Hearing of the spoils Adham Khan has kept for himself, especially the dancing girls, Akbar rides for Malwa so suddenly that Maham Anaga is not able to send riders in advance to warn her son. Maham Anaga is terribly wary of her tempestuous and hot-headed son and the very next day she 'brought the zenana which had remained behind and arranged a great entertainment' in Malwa. Maham Anaga is implacable with the arrogant Adham who wants to keep away some of Baz Bahadur's possessions. Finally all the spoils and 'wives, dancing girls and courtesans' are presented to Akbar and four days are spent in triumph and celebration. Adham Khan, however, is smitten by two 'special beauties' of Baz Bahadur's and with 'folly and blindness' in his heart he intrigues 'with his mother's servants who waited in the royal harem', quite clearly with the knowledge of Maham Anaga and despite her better judgement, and brings away the two beautiful women. Akbar hears of this further betrayal and orders a search. Maham Anaga is appalled, knowing that if the two girls are found, 'the veil over her acts would be raised, and her son's treachery be revealed'. Knowing, also, that if the girls are captured, they will expose Adham Khan's dangerous indiscretion, she orders the girls to be killed for 'a severed head makes no sound'. Out of love and respect for his foster-mother, Akbar chooses to overlook Adham Khan's excess yet again, but it is a precarious balance now between loyalty to his foster-brother and an increasing awareness of his imperial prerogative.

Five months after the killing of Baz Bahadur's dancing girls, Adham

Khan is recalled to Delhi to be 'distinguished by the honour of rendering service' but in effect, it is a disgrace of sorts for Maham Anaga's clan because Munim Khan is removed from office and Shams-ud-Din Atga Khan, Jiji Anaga's husband, is made vakil in his stead. Maham Anaga had, in fact, 'regarded herself as substantive prime minister' of the land and was necessarily unhappy at this clear change of guard. The fault line in the relations between the Atka Khail and Maham Anaga's family now splits wide open and it is an inevitable and lurching twist of destiny that brings Adham Khan to kill Shams-ud-Din Atga Khan on that hot day in May, in what he considers just retribution for his family's fall from grace.

After Adham Khan has been killed, Akbar goes to inform Maham Anaga and gently tells her: 'Adham killed our Ataga, we have inflicted retaliation upon him'. It was all Maham Anaga could do to whisper back, 'you did well'. 'She did not complain or lament', Abu'l-Fazl recounts admiringly, 'but she became inwardly wounded by a thousand fatal blows.' Forty days after the death of her beloved but tempestuous and ultimately uncontrollable son, Maham Anaga dies too. Akbar has a mausoleum built for his foster-brother and foster-mother, in Mehrauli in Delhi, near the sainted presence of Qutbuddin Bakhtiyar Kaki. It is one of the first tombs of the Mughal empire and is stark and massive, almost regal, but shorn of external decorative elements. Atga Khan, meanwhile, will be buried near the dargah of Nizamuddin Auliya and his is a small, but elaborately decorated tomb.

Despite the ruinous violence of Adham Khan's actions, Akbar retains his organic, intimate closeness with his foster families. Mirza Aziz Koka, Jiji Anaga's son, has a particularly long, illustrious, but rambunctious career as a nobleman at Akbar's court. He is often 'openly critical and even defiant of the emperor' but Akbar always forgives him his faults. 'Between me and Aziz', says Akbar with poetic tenderness, 'there is a river of milk that I cannot cross'. This debt of milk remains close to Akbar's heart and gives enormous leverage to his foster-family. Two of Akbar's daughters are later married to sons of Mirza Aziz Koka and there are other wet nurses whose sons have honourable careers at court. When Jiji Anaga dies, Akbar is devastated and he shaves his head and chin in mourning, only the second time in his life he was to do so.

In the end, Maham Anaga is undone by both her sons, her foster son and her own, because of the essential vulnerability of the foster families. Her success and her power were always dependent on the good favour of Akbar. No matter her shrewd intelligence, political skills, loyalty and ambition, from the time her interests diverge from Akbar's, she is forsaken. Adham Khan, counting on the affection Akbar has for his mother, believing himself invincible because of the 'river of milk', forgets the ultimately tenuous hold of this relationship. For the foster relationships are outside the scope of imperial Timurid ambitions. They are sustained-and encouraged as long as they promote the imperial legacy, but no further. Maham Anaga would never have tested Akbar in this manner but Adham Khan did and Maham is ruined. But despite the fact that she gambled and lost, Maham Anaga is unconstrained by Abu'l-Fazl's description of her as a 'protector of chastity'. We see clearly the glinting shards and fragments of her broken ambition in the Khair-ul-Manazil mosque, in the vaulting arc of her son's career, in her own considerable power at court. These mothers and foster mothers remain resolutely outside the confines of the imperial harem and their individuality, and human failings, shine true.

DISAPPEARED WIVES AND THE MYSTERY
OF JAHANGIR'S MOTHER

In 1564, two years after Maham Anaga's death, Akbar's general Asaf Khan is returning from his successful campaign against Gondwana. He carries with him almost unimaginable wealth as spoils of war. The huge amount of plunder includes 'coined and uncoined gold, decorated utensils, jewels, pearls, figures, pictures, jewelled and decorated idols, figures of animals made wholly of gold and other rarities'. There are 1,000 war elephants and jars full of Khilji-era gold coins. Included in the plunder are two women, aberrant sole survivors of a monstrous collective massacre. Asaf Khan's soldiers also bring back to Akbar stories of desperate and ferocious valour and incendiary destruction. In fact Asaf Khan himself has temporarily absconded, having 'strewed the dust of ruin on the head of his own honour' by disappearing with the bulk of the wealth due to the 'sense-robbing intoxication' of all the gold. The two women, however, are sent to Akbar's court where they join the zenana and 'obtained honour by being sent to kiss the threshold of the Shahinshah'. Within Akbar's zenana they bring into the innermost sanctum of Mughal life their stories of chivalry and sacrifice, and pride beyond all reckoning. They, and the other Rajput rajkumaris who will join the zenana, will add their own very particular notions of honour and chastity to the gossamer threads that will form the texture of the new zenana under Akbar. The territory that has now been brought under Mughal rule after the battles of Gondwana might be modest, though the currently absconding plunder is surprisingly vast, but the sacrifice and the gallantry displayed before it was won was immense and shockingly disproportionate to the value of the lands fought over.

The ruler of Gondwana that Asaf Khan attacks is a Rajput woman, Rani Durgavati. She has been ruling Gondwana for sixteen years, wisely and well, since the death of her husband. She is a beloved and benevolent leader who is also a fierce warrior, always quick to defend her territory herself, on elephant or on horseback. 'She was distinguished for courage, counsel and munificence,' agrees Abu'l-Fazl, and 'was a good shot with gun and arrow, and continually went a hunting.' Rani Durgavati defeated Baz Bahadur, the famously musically inclined paramour of Roopmati, but now when the Mughal army thunders up to the outskirts of Gondwana, the chain-mail armour of the endless soldiers glinting in the sun, it is a new dawn being proclaimed over the serene forests of Gondwana. Rani Durgavati fights gallantly, on elephant-back, and appears initially to be holding her own, but many of her soldiers now desert her, hearing of Mughal victories in the neighbouring countryside. Her own advisers inform Rani Durgavati about the deserting soldiers but ''twas better to die with glory than to live with ignominy', says the Rani dismissively, thus forging a place of immortality for herself. In the end, Rani Durgavati leads 300 men against 10,000 Mughal cavalry. She 'put armour on her breast and a helmet on her head', and headed into battle. 'There was no weakening of the Rani's resolution and she continued to wage hot war alongside of her own gallant followers.' Finally, when heroism alone would not suffice, the Rani is fatally wounded and preferring death to dishonour, 'she drew her dagger, and herself inflicted the blow, and died in virile fashion'. Asaf Khan then attacks the main Gondwana stronghold, the nearby fortress of Chauragarh, defended by Durgavati's young son, Raja Bir Narayan. As Bir Narayan fights a last, desperate battle, another, more sinister conflagration is taking place within the lofty stone chambers of the fort. The raja, anticipating his death in battle, has appointed two trusted men, Bhoj Kaith and Miyan Bhikari Rumi to supervise the jauhar of the women of the house. 'It is the custom of Indian rajas under such circumstances', the appalled Mughal general is told, 'to collect wood, cotton, grass, ghee and such like into one place, and to bring the women and burn them, willing or unwilling'. The two attendants have a further, more macabre, role for those women who find themselves unable to confront the monstrous flames. 'Whoever out of feebleness of soul was backward (to sacrifice herself) was, in accordance with their custom, put to death by the Bhoj aforesaid.' And so the chastity of the women is preserved, either by fire or by sword, and all the women burn. However on this day, 'a wonderful thing' occurs. 'Four days after they had set fire to that circular pile, and all that harvest of roses had been reduced to ashes, those who opened the door found two women alive.' Two women have indeed survived this terrible carnage, saved because 'a large piece of timber had screened them and protected them from the fire'. One of the women is Rani Durgavati's sister, Kamlavati, who will have heard the stories of her sister's magnificent heroism and sacrifice on the battlefield. The other is a young woman who had been betrothed to Rani Durgavati's son. These are the two women who will be taken back to Akbar's zenana in Agra and they will bring with them, into Akbar's inner sanctum, these stories and their impossible ideals of female honour and chastity.

Akbar has a further similar encounter with extreme valour when he confronts the Rajputs, and these will only reinforce this notion of chivalry and sacrifice almost beyond endurance. While most of the Rajput fiefdoms submit to Akbar's imperial ambitions, the Rana of Chittor resists. Incensed by the rana's dogged resistance, Akbar joins the assault himself in 1568 against the great fortress of the Sisodiyas of Chittor. Rana Udai Singh abandons Chittor, earning the abiding, visceral disapproval of the chronicler James Todd, and retreats to the Aravalli forests where he will later found a new capital, Udaipur. But he leaves Chittor in the valorous care of the young rajkumars Jai Mal and Patta. Akbar leads the siege of Chittor, which drags on for months. Finally the Mughal war elephants are brought in, some 300 imperial animals trained for battle, encased in metal armour with slicing blades tied to their tusks and their ferocity and courage become part of Mughal legend. It is when Akbar sees the huge black billowing plumes of smoke arising over the destroyed battlements of Chittor that the Mughals realize the battle is won. Three separate gargantuan pyres have been lit within the city walls for the women of the clans of the Sisodiyas, Rathors and Chauhans. 'Nine queens, five princesses, their daughters, as well as two infant sons and all the chieftains families who happened not to be away on their estates perished either in the flames or in the assault', retaining clan purity even unto death. Abu'l-Fazl estimates the loss at 300 women. No longer bound by their duty to protect their womenfolk, the Rajput men now commit the dreadful

Saka ritual. Dressed in saffron, and sometimes semi-naked in a simple loin cloth, their suicidal courage amplified by opium, they charge into their enemies, determined to die in battle to the last man. In Chittor, some 8,000 men die in a desperate last stand against Akbar's forces and many are trampled and gored to death by the rampaging elephants. The Mughals are astounded by this almost insane violence, the anarchy and apparent senselessness of it. The shocked Babur had noted during his interlude in Hindustan that 'in a short time the pagan, in a state of complete nudity, rushed out to attack us'. Hundred years later Akbar's great-grandson Aurangzeb will be torn between disdain and respect for 'the crass stupidity of the Hindustanis, who would part with their heads but not leave their positions (in battle)'.

After Chittor, Akbar moves on to the neighbouring great fortress of Ranthambhore but the resistance, as well as the ensuing massacre, is much less determined. Akbar has begun to understand something of the Rajput temperament. He has gauged their prickly sense of honour, their plundering violence combined with fierce loyalty. Himself a pragmatic tactician, Akbar realizes that for these Kshatriyas, death on the battlefield is a perfect victory, both over the enemy and over death itself. Now as long as they recognize Akbar's suzerainty, the Rajput noblemen are recruited into Mughal imperial service where they become the second-tier ruling elite, raising armies for the padshah yet retaining control over their homelands and customs. Part of Akbar's strategy of binding the Rajputs to the cause of empire while consolidating his own position, especially in the early decade of his reign when he is young and his grasp is uncertain, is to marry Rajput rajkumaris.

One of the first such alliances with a Hindu woman occurs in 1562, when Akbar is twenty years old. A courtier, Chagatai Khan, informs Akbar of the staunch loyalty of Raja Bihari Mal of the relatively insignificant Rajput Kachhawaha clan of Jaipur. Akbar summons Bihari Mal to court and his 'discerning glance read devotion and sincerity in the behaviour of the Rajah and his relatives'. The raja further offers his daughter in marriage to Akbar and Bihari Mal's daughter, the twenty-year-old Hira Kunwar Sahiba Harkha Bai is placed 'among the ladies of the harem'. Harkha Bai arrives at Akbar's court resplendent in the sensuous and excessively feminine style of the Rajput nobility. She wears a heavy, swinging and gathered ghagra which stops well above the ankle and a tightly fitting choli, tied at the back with tasselled strings. Her head and shoulders are covered with an odhani but so translucent and fine is the shimmering cloth that her bare midriff and arms are clearly visible. Light flickers off the heavy gold jewellery she wears—the swaying earrings and nose-ring, the clinking bracelets and the girdle of gold. In just a few years, this Rajasthani style will irrevocably influence Mughal court dress and etiquette. Tight jackets and tunics in diaphanous materials, elaborately printed, will replace the more pragmatic, flowing qabas of the Mughal women. Hindustani materials and textiles used will also subtly enter the court. The wild silks of Hindustan, gathered from silkworms living on mulberry trees and castor oil plants in the Himalayas have been known for almost a 1,000 years before the Mughals are smitten by it. But the wearing of silk next to the skin is sometimes forbidden by Islamic laws and so a special fabric, known as the mashru, is developed so that a layer of cotton cloth lines the forbidden silken face of the cloth. Hairstyles will change too and the Turkish ladies, instead of wearing their hair loose, start to twist it 'into a flat pad at the back from which a few curls rolled on'.

Akbar had already married, in 1552 at the age of fourteen, the daughter of an important Delhi zamindar, Jamal Khan. Now, after marrying Bihari Mal's daughter, Akbar conducts a number of further alliances, with some of the leading Muslim families of Delhi. 'Qawwals and eunuchs,' Badauni writes, 'were sent into the harems for the purpose of selecting daughters of the nobles, and of investigating their condition.' But these qawwals and eunuchs, professional intermediaries between Akbar and the noble Delhi families, lack finesse and cause resentment and 'a great terror fell upon the city'. Akbar abandons his project of acquiring brides from these Muslim families but he continues to make alliances, especially within the Rajput clans. In 1570-71, he marries the rajkumaris of Bikaner and of Jaisalmer, and northern Hindustan is increasingly soldered to his cause.

Akbar is now almost thirty years old and has 'a type of countenance well-fitted to his royal dignity'. He is no longer the restless adolescent of his early years in Hindustan and has 'broad shoulders, somewhat bandy legs well-suited for horsemanship, and a light brown complexion. He shaves his beard, but wears a moustache.' Following the Hindustani custom, 'he does not cut his hair; nor does he wear a hat, but a turban, into which he gathers up his hair.' Like his grandfather Babur, Akbar loves the gregarious company of his men and 'it is hard to exaggerate how accessible he makes himself to all those who wish audience with him', writes Monserrate. 'He is especially remarkable for his love of keeping great crowds of people around him and in his sight.' Other, more punctilious ambassadors to the Mughal court, are less amused by the boisterous throng around Akbar. 'Is the custom of showing respect not observed at this court?' thunders Shirazi, the ambassador of Iran, who is further shaken by the sight of the youthful Mughal padshah flying a kite one day from the roof of his palace wearing just a lungi, his head uncovered. Even while engaged in numerous campaigns to expand his empire, Akbar uses his endless vitality and energy to create a dwelling worthy of his ambition and his expanding zenana. The old Badalgarh fort of Agra is transformed into an enormous city complex of red sandstone which Akbar's Hindustani craftsmen embellish with white marble detailing and exquisite stone carvings. When it is completed, after eight years of work, the nearly 100 acres of land inside the walls contain endless, intricate buildings. Now, for the first time in the history of the eternally travelling Timurid-Mughals of Hindustan, there is a self-contained, settled city space which adequately reflects the growing lustre of Mughal imperial ambitions. Apart from Bega Begum, who remains in Delhi, and indeed who leaves for the Hajj at this time, the other women of the zenana gather in Agra. Gulbadan, Hamida Banu, the household from Kabul as well as all the new wives of Akbar. The Muslim begums as well as the Hindu rajkumaris, with their retinues and relatives, add to the ever-increasing clamour of the zenana. Children are born to Akbar at this time, a girl and twin boys, but they all die very young.

For Akbar, now approaching thirty, the birth of an heir is indispensable. He seeks the blessings of Sheikh Salim Chishti, a Sufi mystic who lives in the village of Sikri, sixty-five miles from Agra. Sheikh Salim promises him three sons and Harkha Bai is shifted to the hospice of the sheikh to be near his blessed presence. She gives birth to a son in 1569, the young Prince Salim, and Akbar appoints Sheikh Salim's daughters and daughters-in-law as Salim's wet nurses. Two more sons are born to Akbar from different wives over the next few years, Murad Mirza and Danyal

Mirza, and slowly the future of the Mughal empire is secured. As northern Hindustan is brought firmly within the empire, Akbar temporarily suspends his battle plans and turns his attention to building the first planned city of the Mughals at the small village at Sikri.

Fatehpur Sikri, as it comes to be known, is a testament in red sandstone to Akbar's implacable vision of his majesty and the order he craves in the world. All the aspects of imperial life are clearly marked out and separated; there are administrative, residential and religious buildings. Outside the main complex there are bazaars and caravanserais and individual palaces. Within the main complex there are mosques and courtyards and ponds. The zenana is separated by a wall from the rest of the complex and it contains the second largest palace after that of the padshah's. This is the first time that a completely separate, enclosed space has been built for the women of the Mughals, whose numbers now exceed that of any of the previous padshahs'. Within a few years, a young liberal Muslim scholar will join Akbar's court, along with his poet brother, and together the three men will use their considerable skills to create an image in stone, in literature and in painting that will reflect, to their satisfaction, the immutable glory of the Mughal padshah.

In 1567, a brilliant young poet, Abu'l-Faiz, joins the court of Akbar, and later becomes a tutor to the three young Mughal mirzas. Faizi, as he later becomes known, is an erudite scholar and a liberal theologian who soon earns the abiding distrust of the orthodox Ulema in Agra. In 1574, Faizi introduces his younger brother, Abu'l-Fazl to Akbar. Fazl is equally brilliant and equally liberal and becomes Akbar's ardent admirer, chronicler and lifelong friend. Badauni, a strict and firmly orthodox Sunni, joins Akbar's court at the same time as Faizi's younger brother but the two men are catastrophically opposed in their views. Badauni is sarcastically and bitterly critical when he writes of Faizi that 'all Jews, Christians, Hindus and fire-worshippers, not to speak of Nizaris, and Sabahis, held him in the very highest honour for his heresy, his enmity to the followers of Islam, his reviling of the very fundamental doctrines of our faith, his contemptuous abuse of the noble companions (of the Prophet) and those who came after them'. In Fatehpur Sikri, as the women are increasingly immured within the high sandstone walls, Akbar simultaneously invites a cauldron of men of different faiths and beliefs to create a 'veritable bazaar' of thinkers and religious ideologues including the mystical Sufis, Jains, and other bhakts. Abu'l-Fazl, as much of a liberal freethinker in religion as Akbar, will write an unabashedly flattering history of Akbar, whom he regards with complete devotion as the ideal monarch with the divine right to rule. Through the *Akbarnama*, his biography of Akbar, Abu'l-Fazl will not only record the history of Akbar but will create the glittering scaffolding of a perfect empire. While in the ibadat khana, behind the mosque at Fatehpur Sikri, holy men of different faiths gather to 'draw the sword of the tongue on the battle-field of mutual contradiction and opposition', as the horrified Badauni notes, in the *Ain-i-Akbari* Abu'l-Fazl describes an impeccably ordered world in which even the women are hustled away into a rigorous and contained anonymity.

In his chapter on the organization of the imperial zenana, wedged between chapters on the composition of minerals and the mobile imperial camp set-up, Abu'l-Fazl admits that the very large number of women now in Akbar's zenana has brought up 'a vexatious question even for a great statesman' such as Akbar. This troublesome question is that though it is only 'through order [that] the world becomes a meadow of truth and reality', this order, yearningly aspired to by Abu'l-Fazl for Akbar, is hard to maintain in the raucous community of women, children, staff, relatives, guards, tutors and assorted entourage that Akbar's zenana has become. 'His Majesty has made a large enclosure with fine buildings inside', Abu'l-Fazl assures posterity, 'where he reposes. Though there are more than 5,000 women, he has given to each a separate apartment. He has also divided them into sections, and keeps them attentive to their duties.' Making sure the women are indeed sufficiently 'attentive to their duties' are 'chaste women' who have been appointed as superintendents, or darogahs, over each section, with written reports required of the women's activities. Within the hierarchy of the harem administration, the most important woman is the mahaldaar, who is 'like a female major dome [acting] as a spy in the interest of the Emperor'. The mahaldaar is appointed personally by the padshah and is a woman from a good family, intelligent and discerning. Even Niccolao Manucci, a Venetian adventurer and chronicler, agrees that 'they have much wit and judgement, and know all that is passing in the empire'. This is a delicate and demanding job for the mahaldaar must keep the padshah informed about the smooth running of all the affairs within the zenana. For this purpose, she has numerous darogahs, women who supervise different sections of the zenana—the dancing and singing girls, the tutors, the concubines, the conduct of the mirzas within the zenana and then report back to the mahaldaar. The mahaldaar also reads out the weekly reports of the Waqia-Nawis (public news writer) and the Khufyan-Nawis (secret news writer) to the padshah.

All the women of the harem are paid a salary, with the highest ranking ones earning up to Rs 1,610 per month. Akbar is extravagantly generous with the women's allowances and the 'best and most costly' of all items are reserved for the king, the queens and the princesses. 'The inside of the harem', we are reassured by Abu'l-Fazl, 'is guarded by sober and active women; the most trustworthy of them are placed about the apartments of his Majesty'. This succinct description by Abu'l-Fazl coyly sidesteps the issue of what these 'sober and active' women are like. Possibly slaves of diverse ethnic backgrounds, Ethiopians, Turks, Tartars from Central Asia and Kashmiris, they combine 'the roles of personal attendants and well-armed (and presumably well-trained) bodyguards of sufficient physical strength to protect the ruler's person, to ensure the safety of the harem, and perhaps to serve as enforcers'. They are 'large and robust women', physically intimidating and skilled and strong warriors. Essentially slaves, they are bought from merchants who bring them to the Mughal court from Central Asia. These women are armed with bows and arrows and short daggers and are collectively known by the Chagatai-Turkish word—urdubegis. Within the zenana they often guard the bedchamber of the padshah himself. Some impression of their appearance can be inferred from the description of the urdubegis of Ghiyath Shah's zenana, in the previous century:

> Five hundred beautiful young Turki females in men's clothes, and uniformly clad, armed with bows and arrows, stood on his right hand, and were called the Turki guard. On his left were five hundred Abyssinian females also dressed uniformly, armed with fire-arms.

And finally, in that dangerous space between the zenana and the outside world there is the eunuch, neither fully male nor female. Eunuchs are prized and bought from the slave markets of Bengal, and it has become customary for a family in Bengal to have at least one son castrated so as to be able to join the service of the padshah. Eunuchs guard the zenana from outside the enclosure of the apartments and beyond the eunuchs is a guard of loyal Rajput soldiers. Porters patrol the palace gates and beyond them, on all four sides of the palace are further guards of noblemen including the famous quiver-bearing Ahadis, arranged according to rank. At sunset, as dusk quickens into night with the carefree haste of tropical nights, smoking torches are lit and the massive doors of the zenana are slammed shut. From this time onwards, the women of the zenana are now officially designated as 'pardeh-gyan', the veiled ones. Physically as well as metaphorically, the women are disappearing from the narrative.

When Akbar's first son Salim, the future Jahangir, is born, the event is so extraordinary as to be almost miraculous. Until then, no child of Akbar's had survived beyond a few months and the padshah has become increasingly desperate, finally seeking the blessings of Sheikh Salim Chishti. The birth of Salim Mirza, not long after the saint's blessing, is a momentous event in the life of Akbar and in the formation of the Mughal empire. Abu'l-Fazl confirms that the birth of 'the unique pearl of the Caliphate' was a cause for 'great joyousness and celebration'. In this lustrous new empire, led by its invincible young padshah, the birth of Salim is celebrated with all the requisite flamboyance of a new parvenu. 'The prisoners of the imperial domains were released, horoscopes were cast, and poets composed congratulatory odes' of sufficient flattery and exaggeration. The miniature later painted to depict this event swirls with energy and unrestrained joy. There are drummers and buglers and female dancers in their tall Turkish hats and long robes. Gold coins are being flung from the palace walls to the thronging crowds below. But for the first time in the history of the Mughal empire, there is no record, whatsoever, of the name of the mother of this much-desired child. While Akbar is feted in a fulsome manner for the birth of his son, his wife, the mother of the child, is never named. The time when Maham Begum and Dildar Begum's pregnancies and subsequent sad losses were openly discussed is long gone. The queen mother is now more than just a mortal woman who suffers and gives birth. She is a sacrosanct symbol of a resplendent institution. Her irreproachable chastity is hidden behind not just a veil, and high walls, but a title—Maryam-uz-Zamani, Mary of the World.

In Abu'l-Fazl's biographies, unlike Gulbadan's touchingly human *Humayun-nama*, there is no longer any space for tender terms of endearment and evocative sobriquets. The biographer of Akbar's grandson Shah Jahan will note that 'ever since the reign of Akbar, it had been ordained that the names of the seraglio should not be mentioned in public, but that they should be designated by some epithet derived either from the place of their birth or the country or the city in which they might have first been regarded by the monarch with the eye of affection.' The royal women are glorified and exalted; Hamida Banu is now Maryam Makhani and Harkha Bai is Maryam-uz-Zamani, but they are also sanctified almost beyond any recognizable human identity. The female body, as described by Abu'l-Fazl, becomes a repository of sexual chastity. Whenever he refers to a group of royal women, they are now invariably 'the chaste ladies'. Maham Anaga is now the 'cupola of chastity', as is Haji Begum, Hamida Banu is the 'veil of chastity' or the 'pillar of purity', and Akbar's step-sisters are similarly 'chaste' connections of the royal family. All the females of the zenana are now resolutely 'chaste', whether they be newborn babies or toothless grandmothers. These royal women, as extensions of Akbar's imperial grandeur, are now required to be so untouchable in their pristine purity that 'even the sight or the thought of anything implicating the female body was considered a dilution of the purity of her self'. The only way to maintain the illusion of this increasing sanctity is to veil, to sequester and to hide the women behind the anonymity of the high walls of Fatehpur Sikri and the grandeur of their titles.

When Harkha Bai joins Akbar's zenana in 1562, she is allowed to bring her traditions and her beliefs with her. When her son, the young Salim Mirza, marries her niece, the daughter of Raja Bhagwant Das, Badauni notes that Akbar participates fully in all the Hindu ceremonies at the bride's home. 'And they performed all the ceremonies, which are customary among the Hindus', writes Badauni, 'such as lighting the fires etc. and over the litter of the princess the Emperor ordered gold to be scattered all the way from [the bride's] to the palace...people's hands were weary of picking them up.' Similarly Harkha Bai brings her own entourage with her, as well as her customs and religious rituals. Her brother and heir to Bihari Mal's title, Bhagwant Das, also joins Akbar's court as does his eleven-year-old grandson and the future ruler of Amber, Man Singh. Man Singh goes on to have an illustrious career at the Mughal court and the Kachhawaha clan prospers. Even physically, Harkha Bai has not had to travel very far from her maternal home to her married one. The distance from Amber to Agra is just over 200 kilometres and the wrench is not so great as it might have been, and Harkha Bai travels often to her hometown. In addition to Harkha Bai, Akbar marries a number of other Rajput brides, possibly another ten or more. His three sons also marry Rajput women and each time a new bride and her male relatives enter Akbar's palace, a sliver of Rajasthani Rajput culture infiltrates the Timurid-Persianate one of the imperial court.

The eternally anguished and tormented recorder of the Hindu practices that enter Akbar's court is Badauni, yet again. 'Another (order) was the prohibition to eat beef', Badauni darkly notes. 'The origin of this embargo was this, that from his tender years onwards, the emperor had been much in company with rascally Hindus, and thence a reverence for the cow (which in their opinion is the cause of the stability of the world) became firmly fixed in his mind.' Badauni is quite clear about the provenance of this subtle indoctrination; '[Akbar] had introduced a whole host of the daughters of the eminent Hindu rajas into his haram, and they had influenced his mind against the eating of beef and garlic and onions, and association with people who wore beards—and such things he then avoided and still does avoid.' Another unusual habit Akbar develops is vegetarianism which Abu'l-Fazl describes, approvingly: 'His Majesty cares very little for meat, and often expresses himself to that effect. It is indeed from ignorance and cruelty that, although various kinds of foods are obtainable, men are bent upon injuring living creatures.' The padshah drinks only gangajal and will have it fetched from Soron (in present-day Uttar Pradesh) wherever he may be residing. Akbar also 'fasted regularly and gradually increased the number of days on which he did so'. And so the influence of the Rajput brides, who are often vegetarian themselves, even when their menfolk are not, spreads even into the kitchens of the Mughal empire.

Akbar, always curious about religious and philosophical practices, easily adopts some of the Rajput traditions. 'From his early youth in compliment to his wives, the daughters of rajahs of Hind,' Badauni continues to lament, 'he had within the female apartments continued to offer the hom, which is a ceremony derived from sun worship; but on the new year of the 25th year after his accession he prostrated himself both before the sun and before the fire in public, and in the evening the whole court had to rise up respectfully when the lamps and candles were lighted.' In this way does the Vedic fire altar also find its place behind the high walls of the women's zenana. In another instance Badauni also notes that 'his majesty had also one thousand and one Sanskrit names for the sun collected and read them daily at noon, devoutly turning himself towards the sun'. It is perhaps no coincidence that the emblem of the Kachhawaha clan that Harkha Bai comes from is the sun god Surya. In another of his orders, Akbar seems to be strictly adhering to the iron patriarchal will of the Rajput system when he ordains that 'if a Hindu woman fell in love with a Musulman and entered the Muslim religion she should be taken by force from her husband and restored to her family'.

There are elements of this Rajput culture which will be incorporated within the Mughal zenana, precipitating the disappearance of the royal Mughal women. Married Rajput women do not retain their own names, going by either their paternal name or the name of their clan. The Rajputs sequester their women jealously and for the Rajputs, too, their honour as a clan is deeply invested in their women's sexual chastity, leading to the horrific excesses of the sati and jauhar fires. When Harkha Bai marries Akbar, it has been only a dozen years since another Rajput rajkumari, Meerabai, disappears at the Krishna temple at Dwarka, preferring to die rather than return to her marital Rajput home and a life of insufferable restrictions. Meerabai spent a lifetime wandering the dusty trails of the Gangetic plains, while Humayun and Hamida were journeying out of Hindustan, discarding her gold jewellery and her fine silks as hated symbols of a cloistered suhaagan's (married woman) life. 'Like the casting off of the veil,' sang Meerabai, 'honour, shame, family pride are disavowed.' Meerabai's songs are hummed by the Rajput women, and in the years to come her haunting lyrics will create a maelstrom of divine longing in a legion of followers, but the noblewomen are loath to follow her example. For these women, and their male kin, Rajput sacrifice and honour and chastity are irreducible truths. Akbar himself is appalled at the ritual of sati, and bemoans 'the strange determination of the men that they should seek their salvation through the repression of their wives'. He also disapproves of the stark fate of widows, so unlike that of his Timurid womenfolk, and laments the fact that 'here in India among the modest, a woman once married cannot go [again] to anyone else'.

And yet, for all his personal misgivings, Akbar's zenana becomes increasingly guarded and the fine-grained lives of the earlier Mughal women fade as the individuality of Akbar's wives is scuffed out to present a smooth, impossibly lustrous surface. But as the number of women in the zenana increases, it is evident that the cascading tumult these complicated lives present is a challenge to the 'proper order' that Abu'l-Fazl and Akbar desire. A less than subtle message is contained in the very first document that is illustrated in the fledgling atelier of Akbar's court—the *Tutinama* (Tales of a Parrot). While Akbar never reads himself, he is fascinated by books and the knowledge they contain and assiduously studies from an expanding library by having books read out to him. Akbar is particularly keen on having manuscripts illustrated and the hundreds of painters he will eventually employ will create a stupendous body of work. These illustrations are not only important for Akbar himself, since he does not read the accompanying text, but also serve to spread a required message to those who are not familiar with the Persian script, notably the Hindu women of the zenana. The *Tutinama* is a collection of fifty-two stories annotated by a Persian-language writer in the fourteenth century. The central figure is a married woman whose husband has gone away for a long time and who wants to meet up with her lover. To prevent her from doing so, and to force her to maintain her sexual chastity, her pet parrot tells her an intriguing, different story every night for fifty-two nights. As part of the royal library is kept in the zenana and is accessible to the women, servants, children and extended female kin, it is very likely that the *Tutinama*, as pointed out by historian Bonnie C. Wade, 'was a pleasant sort of control, but control nevertheless, with the point about correct behaviour of a woman being made fifty-two times'.

Akbar also translates more unusual subject matter for a Muslim ruler: the great Indian epics, the Mahabharata and the Ramayana. Indeed with his natural insouciance, Akbar asks the narrow-minded Badauni to translate the Mahabharat, a job which will require four years of laborious work and in which the long-suffering Badauni naturally found only 'puerile absurdities of which the 18,000 creations may well be amazed...but such is my fate, to be employed on such works'. But however tormented Badauni may have been, these beloved illustrated epics will offer comfort and familiarity to the Hindu wives of Akbar's zenana.

As for Harkha Bai, safe behind the fathomless deep of the zenana's walls, she is as elusive as the silver carp that swims in the turbid waters of the Yamuna. She has the familiar comfort of her maternal family, her brother and her nephew, the countless serving girls and the eternally smoking Vedic fire. She has the certainty of her own glorious tradition as a veiled woman, and the example of all the women who have burned in sooty underground chambers to preserve their honour. In memory of the arid lands of her birth, she has a stepwell built in Bayana, in the district of Bharatpur. She is implacable behind her title, Maryam-uz-Zamani, and so ceaseless is the vigilance that there is only one contemporary written record hinting at her identity. In the imperial records, there is a hukm, or edict, written in the name of the queen mother, Maryam-uz-Zamani. In this hukm, the legend reads: 'Wali Nimat Begam Walidah i Jahangir Badhshah.' In this first and only instance, Maryam-uz-Zamani is clearly mentioned as the mother of Jahangir, the first padshah born of a Hindu mother. But despite all the efforts at concealing the mother of the future ruler, an image of Harkha Bai does exist. In the miniature painting made by Bishen Das for the *Akbarnama*, in which Hamida Banu Begum sits on a chair beside her daughter-in-law who has just had a baby, it is Harkha Bai and the infant Salim that are being depicted. Through Bishen Das's remarkably realistic drawing, Harkha Bai's fine, strong profile is clearly visible. She is darker than her mother-in-law and her complexion glows warmly against the gold of her headband. She has the contented expression of a new mother and her odhani is the most magnificent of any woman in the painting. In this one miniature, at least, the opaque veil of the Mughal queen is lifted.

GULBADAN AND THE MUGHAL HAJJ

It is September 1576, and the port of Surat in Gujarat is a lurching, heaving maelstrom of noise and movement. The monsoon has departed, leaving only a fetid, clinging heat that covers the labouring men with sweat and an organic, briny smell. The men are dressed in the most cursory of clothing, white lungis and tight turbans, and they curse and shout out occasional terse warnings as they carry and stack huge bales of goods coming off a ship: olive oil, wine, pottery, pewter and copper wares. On the opaque sea, ships jostle in companionable proximity. Coir ropes groan and shear, straining to hold cloth sails which snap and flap in the warm breeze. A hustle of men is hurrying to unload a huge ship, a Portuguese India naus, a 500-ton monster with three masts, slashed across with gigantic red crosses, which has reached the shores of Hindustan after a journey of eight months. The ship is ominously armed with heavy cannons and is clearly a warship doubling up as a goods ship. The European crew of the Portuguese ship are gaunt, their limbs twisted and broken by scurvy, but their eyes are bright with fever as they stare at the promised land full of riches for which they have gambled their lives and their sanity. Luckily for the people of Surat, the wind blows away the stench coming off the Portuguese naus, for that foul and acrid miasma is an abomination. With no fresh water available on board for hot, endless months, filth and sickness have created a noxious atmosphere and, despite the sea breeze, the labourers tie cloths around their faces to stop from retching.

A small group of women stands on a hillock overlooking the Tapti River and the ships docked nearby. One of them is Gulbadan, now a respectable fifty-two-year-old but with a timeless vigour in her sturdy frame. There is also Salima Sultan Begum, an older wife of Akbar's as well as Sultanam, widow of Hindal, now a member of Akbar's huge zenana.

The women are accompanied by the governor of the port of Surat, Quliz Khan Andijani, and it is clear from Gulbadan's agitated expression that something is worrying the women. It has been a year since this large group of royal women, led by Gulbadan, left the court at Fatehpur Sikri bearing magnificent gifts and 6,000 rupees in donation for the holy places of Mecca. For Gulbadan had decided to perform the Hajj, the sacred pilgrimage to Mecca, because she had 'long ago made a vow to visit the holy places'. The Hajj has been performed by royal women previously; Gulbadan's sister-in-law Bega Begum now went by the sobriquet 'Haji Begum', possibly because she has performed it more than once, but this was the first time that a royal party of such magnificence, organized and composed of only women, was to travel to Mecca. There were a few men accompanying the women, naturally, because for women to travel unchaperoned in the medieval Muslim world is inconceivable, but it is clear that Gulbadan is very much in charge of the decisions and the arrangements. Having decided not to take the dangerous overland route through Shi'a Iraq, the women have reached Surat, the Bab-ul-Mecca or blessed port, for it is the gateway to the sea route to Mecca. Now in Surat, the women are confronted by another problem, one that all the Mughal emperors were to ignore, at their detriment, until it was too late.

By 1576, Surat has been under Mughal control for three years but Akbar, as indeed all his successors, always looks inland towards the deserts, the grasslands, the marshes and the forests of Hindustan. The Mughal empire is an agrarian entity, one in which more than 90 per cent of the population is involved in agricultural and related activities and each successive padshah steadfastly refuses to look outward towards the open ocean. And yet danger arrived almost a century earlier, when Vasco da Gama had discovered the maritime route to Hindustan in 1498. Since then the Portuguese have settled along the Coromandel coast, building fortresses and an insatiable appetite for the spices, the gems and the cloths of Hindustan. By the mid-sixteenth century, the Portuguese are the greatest naval power of the region, warships bristling with firepower, and have effectively seized control of the Asian trade from the Muslim merchants. The Dutch and then the English are not long in discovering the lucrative trade of the India route and, by the second half of the sixteenth century, are ready to defend their interests with violence and excess. Piracy is rampant and the seas are unsafe for the Hajj ships which regularly carry goods and traders as well as pilgrims across the Red Sea.

As the group of women watches the Portuguese naus, they are surprised to see a number of sleek, well-fed men walk onto the gangplank and off the boat. Unlike the crew, who are emaciated and bearded, and caricatures of human beings, these men have pink and plump cheeks and the satisfied air of those who have lived well. There are businessmen and a few noblemen and then a group of individuals in long, black flapping robes. To Gulbadan Begum, the Jesuit missionaries look like malevolent black crows in their shapeless robes and their ridiculous large-brimmed round hats. These men have spent most of the past few months indulging in meals of gargantuan proportions to stave off the craven boredom of the endless days in cramped conditions on the ship. The Jesuit priests have brought fresh pork, smoked ham, sausages, dried fish, wine, olive oil and even fresh fruits and figs and cheeses. They loaded live animals to be eaten as the journey progressed: chickens, turkeys, geese, rabbits and lambs. Each meal was rounded off with sweets, jellies and jams of cherries, pears, apples, lemons and peaches. The crew meanwhile survived, barely, on hard bread, some salted meat, beans, rice or lentils.

It is the presence of ships like this Portuguese naus and the fervour of these Jesuit missionaries that has caused Gulbadan and her party to delay their departure from Surat for almost a year. For the Portuguese vessels use any means possible to harass and hinder all other ships in these seas, including the pilgrim ships destined for the Hajj. They attack and sink ships, blockade important ports and threaten sea pathways near the Red Sea and the pilgrimage routes to Mecca. And if Gulbadan hesitates to set sail with her family it is with reason, for the Portuguese have long had a history of sudden and insane acts of violence. In 1502, an anonymous Dutch voyager who travelled with Vasco da Gama to Calicut said that they captured a pilgrim ship and having seized all the goods then 'burnt the ship and all the people on board with gun-powder'. The missionaries and their radiating rage add to the volatile situation. In 1567, just a few years before Gulbadan arrives in Surat, the Archbishop of Goa, Gaspar de Leão Pereira thunders against the 'many Muslims and other infidels' who 'come to our ports with books of their sects, and their false relics that they bring from the House of Mecca'. These relics, he clarifies, are to be seized and burned. The Archbishop despises all manner of 'pagans' and believe them to be 'sensualists' who 'do not have souls because they have converted it into flesh'.

Despite the fiery rhetoric, the main concern of the Portuguese is to defend their commercial interests, for the most important source of revenue in Portugal during the whole of the sixteenth century is commerce with Hindustan. Every year a fleet of sixteen to eighteen ships sets sail for Hindustan and the most valuable item of that trade is peppercorn, followed by ginger, cinnamon, clove and mace. On the return journey to Portugal, the India naus currently unloading at the Surat dock will be filled with bales of cotton, silks, gems, perfumes, dyes, betel nut, opium and spices. The holds in the lower deck will be filled with peppercorn and then caulked and closed for the duration of the journey. In Portugal, the pepper will be used to salt and preserve meat and to disguise the flavour of rancid foods and will make the fortunes of the King of Portugal.

Now finally, after months of negotiations, Gulbadan and Quliz Khan have accepted an official cartaz, or pass, from the Portuguese authorities safeguarding the passage of their pilgrim ship. For this, Gulbadan has even gifted the Portuguese the town of Buxar, 'to ensure friendly treatment in case she fell in with the Portuguese fleet on the voyage'. For the devout Gulbadan, carrying the cartaz is itself a desecration of sorts for it 'bore the idolatrous stamp of the heads of the Virgin Mary and of Jesus Christ'. Akbar, thirty-four years old now, is said 'to have raged against the Portuguese verbally' when he hears of their cavalier treatment of his aunt's party, but does little else. Akbar, at this stage, is entering the full resplendence of his magnificent court. 'Its splendour', we are told, 'is unsurpassed in Europe'. Twenty vassal kings are in attendance at all times and Akbar, we are further informed approvingly, is 'almost as fair as southern Europeans... His dress consisted of a robe of cloth of gold, embroidered with leaves and flowers... Instead of Moslem trousers, he wore the Hindu dhoti of the finest and most delicate silk.' Scribes write down whatever he utters and foot soldiers stand nearby with bows and arrows and other arms. And yet for all the riches of the Mughal court, Akbar, like the padshahs who follow him, will not give the Portuguese menace the weight that it deserves and will make the catastrophic error of never maintaining a navy. And in the slipstream of the Portuguese presence the Dutch and the English and the French will arrive and, unlike the Portuguese, they will not content themselves with trade.

But on 17 October 1576, Gulbadan and her party of women is finally ready to set sail. They have hired two large Turkish vessels, the *Salimi* and the *Ilahi*, and when they leave now it is with the acceptance, as with all Hajj pilgrims, that they may never return. A crowd gathers at the port to watch this royal party of women board their ship. Apart from Gulbadan, Salima Sultan and Sultanam, there were also two stepnieces of Gulbadan—Haji Begum and Gulizar Begum. There is also a granddaughter of Gulbadan, Umm-kulsum, and Salima Khanum, a daughter of Khizr Khwaja Khan. A number of these women are related to disgraced men, Humayun's rebellious brothers Askari and Kamran, as well as Bairam Khan, who were all sent to Mecca as punishment through exile, but these women travel with honour. In addition to these royal ladies there are a number of lesser women also, from the households of Babur and Humayun, elderly servants. There are no young women on this Hajj; it is a company of matriarchs and older women, the most respected members of Akbar's court. Hamida Banu Begum remains in Agra, with her son the emperor, standing in lieu of the imperial presence when Akbar absents himself from court, and Bega Begum is in Delhi, overseeing the construction of her husband's tomb. The matriarchs of the Mughal empire in this third quarter of the sixteenth century have lavish ambitions and have spread their influence far and wide. Though none of the Mughal emperors are permitted to abandon the empire to perform the Hajj, they support the Hajj 'at great public expense, with gold and goods, and rich presents'. Apart from the enormous sum in cash, the Mir Hajj of the party, Sultan Khwaja, loads 12,000 robes of honour to give away as presents at Mecca. The people of Surat gather in huge numbers for Surat 'is very populous, as all other cities and places are in India, which everywhere abounds with people'. There are both Hindu and Muslim onlookers for 'they live all mixt together, and peaceably, because the Gran Moghel, to whom Guzarat is now subject, although he be a Mahometan, makes no difference in his dominions between the one sort and the other'. So there are Hindu and Muslim men in white linen shirts and loose pants and slippers, and Hindu women in short red waistcoats, long colourful skirts and clinking, voluble jewellery. They wear huge pendants on their ears, 'very disproportionate' to the traveller Pietro della Valle's foreign eyes and no veils, so that they may be 'freely seen by everyone both at home and abroad'.

It is a sombre moment for all the Hajjis, as they murmur prayers and board the *Salimi*. After a year of impatient waiting at Surat, they are thrumming with excitement at the audacious scope of their enterprise. Yet they must know, as they look one last time at the fertile fields of Hindustan, the turgid and silty waters of the Tapti, that the voyage that leads to the arid deserts of Arabia is full of dangers. They will have heard, from other travellers, of the threat of shipwrecks, of drowning, of piracy, of Bedouin attacks on land, of disease and of accidents. But the holy pilgrimage to Mecca is also the fifth pillar of Islam, and a religious duty that all good Muslims should undertake at least once in their lives. Gulbadan and her party are conducting the Hajj not only for their own immortal souls but also on behalf of the padshah. So the mood will be contained, certainly, but also lit through with joy and divine fervour.

For the next few weeks, through the winter of 1576, Gulbadan's ship sails across the Arabian Sea, following the monsoon winds as the Hajj ships have done for centuries. This is a long way to come for Gulbadan, child of Kabul and indomitable traveller through the Hindu Kush. The open seas offer an altogether different sort of challenge and there are sudden, gusting winds and crashing, lurching waves. Fear scrabbles in the hearts of the women occasionally when storms rock the ship and the dense blackness of the nights makes the sea appear endless and opaque with hidden monsters. There are coral reefs, especially in the Sea of Berbera, which can eviscerate a sewn-plank ship like the *Salimi*. The Sea of Berbera, later renamed the Red Sea, is a monstrous stretch, infamous for its gigantic waves and hidden coral reefs. Pilgrims recite the Litany of the Sea feverishly and chant prayers for the calming of the ocean. It is well known that there are mischievous sea djinns skulking at the bottom of the sea and 'in order to ward off evil, merchants would throw their rice or other food into the sea'. But apart from the often pervasive seasickness and occasional boredom, the women travel in comfort, through Akbar's largesse, in separate quarters lavishly appointed for them. The poorer pilgrims sleep on top of the merchandise or in the hold of the ship, in the pungent company of the rats and the livestock—the sheep, goats and camels.

When finally the women disembark near Mecca, they are disorientated, after the torpor of the weeks at sea, by the blazing colours and the tumult of the pilgrims pouring into the holy city. Because the Hajj is a time-bound ritual, to be conducted at a specified time of the year, all aspirants converge upon Mecca in the same week. There are enormous pilgrim caravans from Egypt, Syria and Iraq, several miles long, with combined numbers of some 200,000 persons and 300,000 cattle. There are hundreds of soldiers to protect the unarmed pilgrims, Mamluk warriors on horseback, archers, elite bodyguards, cavalry and cannon. There are camels loaded with water barrels for pilgrims who are too poor to arrange for their own transport. For Gulbadan and the other Hindustani ladies, even though they are now used to the splendour of Akbar's court, the pilgrim caravans and the Ottoman's regalia will have been a magnificent sight. They will have been conscious, also, of the need to maintain their own unquestioned opulence, ambassadors as they are of Akbar's Mughal court. But first, there is the Hajj to perform.

When the women arrive at Mecca, they find it arid and barren. 'In my opinion,' thunders the damning Swiss traveller, Johann Ludwig Burckhardt, 'the curse of God has been laid upon the said city, for the country produces neither grass nor trees, nor any one thing'. The people, nonetheless, seem prosperous and Ibn Battuta, the notoriously intrepid fourteenth-century Moroccan voyager is impressed by their good looks: 'The Meccans are elegant and clean in their dress, and as they mostly wear white their garments always appear spotless and snowy. They use perfume freely, paint their eyes with kuhl, and are constantly picking their teeth with slips of green arak-wood. The Meccan women are of rare and surpassing beauty, pious and chaste.'

As Mecca and the moment of the sacred Hajj approaches, Gulbadan and all the women prepare to enter the state of complete mindfulness and surrender required. The women physically prepare themselves as well, performing the first of the prescribed rituals connected with the Hajj, the Ihram, in which all old clothes are removed and a special white cloth is worn. A lock of hair is symbolically cut off, jewellery and perfume are forbidden, and the face must remain uncovered. The women in this state of ritual purity, now all indistinguishable in their white, seamless robes and flat sandals, may not 'kill either flea or louse with their hands'. At last, in a great heaving mass of white-robed bodies, the women approach the Haram area of Mecca, shouting out the traditional greeting: Here I am, O God, at Thy command! Under the arches of the circular Haram are thousands of persons selling all kinds of odoriferous things. 'Truly it would not be possible to describe the sweetness and the odours which are smelt within this temple. It appears like a spicery full of musk, and of other most delicious odours.' But the women will not be distracted now because their entire being strains towards the square building of black stone covered in black embroidered cloth which stands in the centre of the Haram, and is the mystical and holy vortex towards which they have directed their prayers all their lives—the Ka'ba. The Hajjis swarm towards the Ka'ba, their collective longing and ecstasy swirling to form just one formless emotion: Bismillah! The pilgrims circumambulate the Ka'ba seven times, touching and kissing the stone as they walk, and they are all overcome by the mystery and power of this most sacred place. 'I profess, I could not choose but admire to see those poor Creatures so extraordinary devout and affectionate', writes Joseph Pitts, who participates in the Hajj himself, adding, 'with what Awe and Trembling, they were possess'd'. It is essential, during this sacred moment, to keep the genders separate for even a glancing touch by a member of the opposite sex would invalidate the entire ritual purity of the moment. So Hajj officials employ eunuchs to direct and control the crowds and to gather the women in a separate group. It is understood that the women have a deep and visceral need for contact with the holy Ka'ba and the men accept that 'when the women are at the stone, that its esteem'd a very rude and abominable thing to go near them, respecting the time and place'.

Having travelled so far, in such perilous circumstances, the Hindustani ladies will have been determined to conduct all the rituals of the great Hajj in as faultless a manner as possible. So for the next ten days, always wearing the same white seamless garb, Gulbadan and her family join the immense company of Hajjis as they make their way around the sacred sites of the Hajj. This includes going to the plains of Arafat where most Hajjis are deeply overwhelmed by this contemplative mood and 'it is a sight, indeed, able to pierce one's Heart, to behold so many Thousands in their Garments of Humility and Mortification with their naked Heads and Cheeks watered with Tears'. Pitts, a captured English slave temporarily travelling as a Muslim, is moved to admit that 'it is a matter of sorrowful reflection to compare the Indifference of many Christians, with this Zeal of those…Mahometans'.

Having performed the sacred aspect of the Hajj, the women are now free to participate in the communal aspect of this great Islamic medieval gathering. The entire region of the holy sites is gaudy with celebration and in Mecca 'all that night there is nothing to be heard nor seen but gunshot and fireworkes of sundry sortes, with such singing, sounding, shouting, hallowing, rumours, feasting and triumphing as is wonderful'. Women participate in music and dance and as the veil is not allowed, it is observed that 'the women of the place are courteous, jocund and lovely, faire, with alluring eyes'. Now at last, the Hindustani ladies can appear in the full, sparkling glory of their Mughal legacy. Only fifty years after her father conducted his blistering battle at Panipat, Gulbadan has journeyed far into the heart of Islam to give thanks for the unimagined success of his grandson Akbar. The women now wear their most exquisite garments and jewellery and distribute all the robes of honour and the lavish gifts and money they have brought with them from Agra. Flocks of destitute visitors from across the Muslim world, eager to benefit from some of this largesse, converge around Mecca. Indeed the donations by the Mughal party are so extravagant, and lead to so many rumours of their extreme piety and wealth, and put so much strain on the infrastructure, that the Ottoman authorities are 'somewhat alarmed by their ostentatious distributions of alms'. The Ottoman authorities, custodians of the holy cities of Mecca and Medina and guardians of the faith, are unnerved enough by Gulbadan and her lavish donations to suggest that the Mughal subjects should return home directly after performing the Hajj.

But Gulbadan and her Mughal party stay for almost four years in the holy cities. Quite apart from the sacred aspect of the voyage, and we know she completed all four Hajjs and some of the minor Umrahs too, there is the great freedom and the glittering, boisterous company that make up the social aspect of the trip. 'After they are return'd from Meena to Mecca', explains Pitts, 'there is a great Fair held where are sold all manner of East India goods and abundance of fine stones for rings, and bracelets etc. brought from Yeamane, also of china ware and musk and variety of other curiosities.' There are travellers from distant West Africa, from Egypt and Damascus but also Uzbeks from Central Asia, and Turks and Moroccans. Now, at last, Gulbadan can buy interesting and unusual specimens which she will take back with her to Hindustan for 'they do not think it lawful to buy a thing till they have received the title of Hagge'.

According to Badauni, the Mughal women also visit Karbala, Qom and Mashad, all holy sites of Islam. The women travel for months, on opulent litters placed on camels. In the hot season, they travel at night, beginning at two in the morning and stopping at noon. They travel in a huge convoy, with soldiers and supplies of food and fruit for these are scarce in the arid lands between towns. There is also the ever-present threat of raids by the Bedouin Arabs who lie in wait for these wealthy pilgrims at the time of the Hajj. Ludovico de Varthema, the fifteenth-century Italian adventurer describes these rapacious Arabs, startlingly, as 'very small men, and of a dark tawny colour...feminine voice, and long stiff, and black hair', who wait for the guileless pilgrim and then 'fly like falcons' to attack them with lances. The roads through the desert are littered with 'the fresh carcasses of asses, ponies and camels' that have been abandoned to die for lack of water. The water, wherever it can be found, is 'brackish' according to Ibn Jubayr and the heat can become so unbearable he describes it as 'flaming air'. In these demanding circumstances, Gulbadan rallies her large group of women and journeys more than 8,000 kilometres through foreign lands while in Fatehpur Sikri, Akbar has raised the walls around an increasingly sequestered, inviolable zenana.

Finally, after nearly four years spent in Arabia, Gulbadan is ready to return to Hindustan under the guidance of a new Mir Hajj, Khwaja Yahya. But the Mughal party do not get very far down the Red Sea before they are shipwrecked, off Aden, the southernmost port in modern-day Yemen. The Red Sea was always an extremely dangerous stretch because of the presence of treacherous underwater rocks, corals and submerged islands. There is also the dangerous north wind and the whole region 'is subject to very thick fogs, and to violent gales of wind'. But the most fearful event for the pilgrims is the unleashing of the fierce northern winds which create 'waves like towering and immovable mountains'. Drowning is a deep, nameless fear, for most cannot swim. The pilgrims huddle together and pray, 'each one of us was silently praying that we would be released from the danger of these reefs. Every now and again the coral would stick out and appear fortress-like around us.' Despite their prayers, and their immutable belief in divine protection as newly-minted Hajjis, Gulbadan and the zenana women are shipwrecked, and left stranded at Aden for almost a year. Gulbadan has to wait a long time to find a ship that will take them back home and when finally they land at Surat, they will have been away from Hindustan for almost seven years. At Surat, delayed again for some months, Gulbadan reasons that 'no longer requiring to be on good terms with the Portuguese', the town of Buxar should be reclaimed and 'told the people of Surat to demand that Butzaris [Buxar] should be given back again'. But the Portuguese are impatient and increasingly irascible and the Mughal cavalry 'are routed by the Portuguese with considerable loss'.

Gulbadan finally leaves for Fatehpur Sikri and the beloved young prince Sultan Salim is sent to Ajmer to greet the triumphant returning Hajj party. Despite their long absence from Agra, they are in no hurry to get home. They make detours wherever they can and 'they pay a gratuitous visit to the shrine of the saint Muin-ud din, and left their gifts there'. At every stage of Gulbadan's journey, an amir is sent with greetings from the padshah, who finally meets the party at Khanwa. 'The night of reunion,' we are told 'was kept awake by questions and entrancing stories; gifts were shown and happiness brimmed over.' 'When his aunt returned from Mekka,' added Monseratte, 'the king had the street-pavement covered with silken shawls, and conducted her himself to her palace in a gorgeous litter, scattering largess meanwhile to the crowds.' For Akbar, it is not just the return of a beloved aunt, but also a validation, through her pious acts, of his claim to rule Hindustan as a defender of the faith.

Back at the court of Akbar, Gulbadan's greatest regret will be to learn that her old friend and companion in exile, Bega Begum, has just recently died. She will not be able to compare her own stories of the Hajj with Bega Begum, who had already performed the pilgrimage, though in less ostentatious style than Gulbadan. She will also, certainly, be startled to find a group of Jesuit priests in attendance on the padshah. For Akbar, ever affably inquisitive about theological matters, has invited a group of Jesuit missionaries to stay at his court at Fatehpur Sikri. The Jesuit Father Rudolf Acquaviva, 'a man of much learning and eloquence' according to Abu'l-Fazl, and also a fierce proselytiser, is convinced he will be able to convert 'the great Mogul' to Christianity. 'Mahomet is everything here,' laments Acquaviva, 'Antichrist reigns.' The Jesuits seem to be unaware that in Islam, too, the figure of Maryam, or Mary, is greatly revered. Gulbadan will certainly have added her scathing disapproval to Hamida Banu's and the rest of the zenana for 'whether it was the murmurs of the mullahs, the outspoken complaints of the queen mother, Hamida Begam and of the ladies of the harem…the emperor began to be weary of the father's teachings'.

The zenana at Fatehpur Sikri that Gulbadan returns to in 1582 is very different to the haraman of her wandering with Humayun. The great tented mobile cities have disappeared, replaced by the sandstone and marble walls and palaces of Akbar's zenana. Within a few years, Akbar shifts his capital once again, this time to Lahore. During the relative stability of the second half of Akbar's long reign, there are no headlong rushes away from enemies, no crackling escapes on horseback through strange lands. Instead, Akbar has made alliances to stabilize his empire further and 'his Majesty has made a large enclosure with fine buildings inside'. But the older women of the court, irrepressible and untouchable, continue to abandon the 'proper order' of the court and leave on extended trips to follow the emperor, unannounced but always welcomed. The women are also busy with more scholarly pursuits and it is around this time that Gulbadan is asked by Akbar to write her memoirs of Babur and Humayun. Gulbadan sits for days with Hamida Banu, researching her stories of her escape with Humayun into Persia. In the fastness and splendour of Lahore, these women's memories of their earlier, more precarious adventures, are as blisteringly sharp as ever.

Gulbadan lives the next twenty years of her life at Akbar's court, performing celebrated acts of charity and greatly cherished by her nephew. She dies in 1603, at the age of eighty, with Hamida Banu Begum by her side. Hamida Banu, trying to revive the dying woman, calls out to her by her term of endearment, 'Begam Jio'. Gulbadan, opens her eyes one last time, long enough to look at the queen mother and her old friend to say, 'I am dying, may you live long.' Akbar is inconsolable and carries Gulbadan's bier himself part of the way to her grave and for the two years that he survives her, constantly complains that he misses his beloved aunt. Hamida Banu does not long survive Gulbadan and dies the following year, in 1604. Akbar shaves his head and his chin in mourning, the first of only two times in his life that he does so. With Bega Begum also long gone, the age of the matriarchs has finally passed.

SALIMA SULTAN BEGUM AND
THE PRODIGAL SON

A decade passes at Fatehpur Sikri. The Hindu rajkumaris live their lives, with their sun worship and regular fasts, in the increasing opulence of the court. Akbar, the first of the Mughal padshahs to be born on Indian soil, adopts a large number of Hindustani and Hindu practices so as to integrate the varied peoples of Hindustan into his empire. His whimsical curiosity and endless energy extends even to the court garments. He recognizes the unsuitability of the earlier thick cloaks and coats worn by Babur and Humayun and introduces the 'chakdar jama', the first truly Hindustani garment, to the Mughal court. This is a cross-over long tunic, made of very fine cloth, often transparent, styled with a rounded hemline and a full skirt. This versatile garment can be made of silk, embroidered with gold, or of fine woollen cloth, of which Akbar is particularly fond. The long sleeves are close fitting and below the jama the courtiers wear pajamas which are full at the waist but tight in the lower half in the churidar style. The pajamas are often made of brocade and silk, in contrasting colours. All the courtiers, Hindu and Muslim, wear turbans in the Rajasthani pugri style. The Hindu chakdar jama fastens on the left-hand side of the body with a string, while the Muslim courtiers fasten it on the right. In this way, Akbar masterfully unifies the disparate members of his court while maintaining a necessary distinction.

The sons and daughters of Akbar, regardless of the religion of their mothers, are given a thorough education and brought up as Timurid shahzaadas and shahzaadis. About the shahzaadis it is noted that '[Akbar] gives very great care and attention to the education of the princesses, who are kept rigorously secluded from the sight of men. They are taught to read and write, and are trained in other ways by matrons.' In this they differ radically from the Rajput tradition in which boys are given a cursory, mainly martial, education, and the girls none at all. Indeed, the Mughal women will be better educated than most of their contemporaries anywhere in the world. Three hundred years later, in the nineteenth century, an Englishwoman will marvel that Mughal women have the same education as the men. 'In Europe,' she will complain, 'men have so greatly the advantage of women from receiving a superior education... The women are kept under and have not fair play.'

Meanwhile in Agra, the children add to the clamour and the chaos of the zenana which is alluded to later by Salim, after he has become Jahangir; 'After my birth they gave me the name of Sultan Salim,' Jahangir writes in his memoirs, 'but I never heard my father, whether in his cups or in his sober moments, call me Muhammad Salim or Sultan Salim, but always Shaikhu Baba.' Thus the young Shaikhu Baba is brought up by his Hindu mother, his Persian tutors, his Turkish foster mothers and his occasionally inebriated father in a bustling and constantly changing world that has not yet reached the state of perfect splendour and immutability that Abu'l-Fazl writes about. Akbar is now in early middle age and 'his expression is tranquil, serene and open, full also of dignity, and when he is angry, of awful majesty'. It is clear, however, that through these decades the zenana remains much more porous, visible and influential than the one which is described in the *Akbarnama*. Now, in the gloaming of what will become the most magnificent empire on earth, one woman—a young childless widow, that most insubstantial of creatures—becomes a quietly powerful presence at court.

When Bairam Khan left Akbar's court in disgrace in 1561, heading for exile in Mecca, he never got beyond the shores of Hindustan. He was murdered in Gujarat, on the shores of the Sahasralinga Talaab in a bizarre, and apparently quite random, act of revenge. He was stabbed by Mubarak Khan, an Afghan youth whose father was killed at the battle of Machhiwara, a battle which Bairam Khan had commanded. The terrified survivors of Bairam Khan's murder include the disgraced Khan Khana's first wife, the daughter of the nobleman Jamal Khan of Mewat, her four-year-old son, Abdur Rahim, and Bairam Khan's second wife, Salima Sultan Begum. The twenty-two-year-old Salima Sultan Begum is no ordinary woman. She is a Timurid of impeccable lineage—granddaughter of Babur and a niece of Humayun and Gulbadan. When news reaches the then nineteen-year-old Akbar of the murder of his old Khan Khana, he immediately takes in the young Abdur Rahim and marries Salima Sultan Begum himself. For Akbar, this is a chance for him to demonstrate his generosity and protection, faced with what must necessarily be residual guilt for the fall from grace of Bairam Khan. It is also, in these early years of empire-building, an additional association with the powerful Timurid name. Of Abdur Rahim's Mewati mother, no more is heard.

In Akbar's household at Agra, Salima Sultan finds much that is familiar and beloved to her. She has the company of her cousin, Ruqayya Begum, first wife of Akbar and daughter of Hindal, as well as of her aunts, Gulbadan, Hamida Banu and the many other members of the extended Timurid family from Kabul. She is a cultivated, educated woman and shares much in common with her aunt Gulbadan. Salima Sultan now has access to the enormous imperial library, part of which is kept within the zenana. There are 'prose books, poetical works, Hindi, Persian, Greek, Kashmirian, Arabic' works and also translations of famous Hindustani works. Her interest in Hindustani books is noted when it inadvertently brings misfortune, once again, to the decidedly ill-fated Badauni. Badauni has translated an ancient Sanskrit work, *Simhaasana Dvaatrimshika* (*Singhasan Battiti*), tales of the life and adventures of Vikramaditya, into Persian, and has named it the *Khirad Afza*. Salima Sultan has been reading this work occasionally when it disappears from the imperial library. Suspicion immediately falls on the unfortunate Badauni, who is away on leave. Akbar himself becomes involved and, already annoyed at Badauni's frequent absences from court, orders his translator's yearly allowance to be annulled.

◆

When Gulbadan organizes the Hajj voyage in 1575, Salima Sultan is the only one of Akbar's wives, and one of the youngest women, to be part of the Hajj party to Mecca. Akbar personally funds the travel expenses of all the imminent Hajjis, and he 'poured into the lap of each the money that they wanted and so made the burden of their desire light'. None of the Hindu wives of Akbar accompany Gulbadan on the Hajj and it appears that these women are free to remain true to their own beliefs and the purdah is more ferociously applied to these young women than to the older, Timurid connections of Akbar. Salima Sultan is away from the court for seven exciting and tumultuous years, including a year spent shipwrecked at Aden before finally returning to Fatehpur Sikri in 1582.

The town of Fatehpur Sikri, like Agra, is now 'a very great citie and populous, built with stone, having fair and large streets, with a fair river running by it'. An incredulous English traveller to Akbar's court at this time notes that there are '1000 elephants, thirty thousand horses, 1400 tame deer, 800 concubines; such store of Ounces, tigers, buffaloes, cocks and hawks that is very strange to see'. This first-time traveller to Hindustan is moved to comment that 'Agra and Fatepore are two very great cities, either of them much greater than London and very populous'. Adding to the splendour of Salima Sultan's homecoming are pavements covered in silk shawls and the coins distributed by Akbar to the waiting crowds as he welcomes back the Hajj party.

Salima Sultan and her co-travellers bring back stories from their exotic adventure across the turbulent seas, of the effervescent Hajj pilgrimages and the shipwreck and all their other travails. They will have brought back, no doubt, mementos and gifts for the other ladies of the zenana. In the past, Hajj pilgrims have brought back Arab horses, Abyssinian slaves and holy relics from Mecca. But the returning women will also hear confounding stories from Hamida Banu and the other zenana women. They will learn that the previous year for many months the chief commander at Fatehpur Sikri was not Akbar, but Hamida Banu herself. Akbar has a step-brother, the blustery Mirza Hakim, son of Humayun and Mah Chuchak Begum, who has been causing friction and unrest in Kabul for many years. He has, in the past, made alliances with Akbar's enemies and has had the khutba read in his name. Finally Akbar decides to settle matters once and for all with this recalcitrant half-sibling and marches to Kabul with his army, carrying the 'black standards, the sign of war to the death, which Timur the Lame—ancestor of the Mongol kings—had been wont to employ in his wars'. Before he leaves, Akbar arranges for the governing of the empire in his absence; Aziz Koka, Jiji Anaga's son, is made viceroy of Bengal and Qutub-al-Din Khan, also of the Atga Khail, is made viceroy of Gujarat. But Hamida Banu remains in charge at Fatehpur Sikri with her youngest grandson, Danyal, and 'the king's mother was to be superior to both of these, and was to have charge of the province of Indicum or Delinum (Delhi)'. While Qutub al-Din is given 10,000 cavalry as garrison, Hamida Banu is given 12,000, and Akbar's infant daughter is also left in her charge. Salim, Murad and 'a few of [Akbar's] principal wives, and his older daughters' leave for Kabul, and war, with Akbar. The day Akbar leaves for Kabul, Hamida Banu also leaves Fatehpur Sikri with him and spends two days in his company in his 'immense white pavilion' in the Mughal mobile tented camp.

There are other, more baffling changes at Fatehpur Sikri, too, which will remind Salima Sultan and the Hajj party of their uncomfortable encounter with the high-handed Portuguese authorities at Surat. The Hajj party return to find Jesuit priests lecturing Akbar on the merits of the Gospel and overseeing the education of Murad Mirza. 'Learned monks also from Europe', bemoans Badauni, 'brought the Gospel and advanced proofs for the Trinity'. The Portuguese have, by now, established thriving trading posts along the Malabar Coast. Goa, the capital of the Estado da India with a population of 225,000, is larger than Madrid or Lisbon. The Portuguese have been forcibly converting the inhabitants of Goa to Christianity, and are quite uninterested in anything the local culture can offer. They persecute converts for following 'heretical' customs such as 'refusing to eat pork or beef, cooking rice without salt and wearing their traditional clothing'. A couple of years before the return of the Hajj party, Akbar grants the Portuguese a charter to settle a village near present-day Kolkata. Now there are more than 20,000 Portuguese and their descendants living there, where they 'dressed in the style of the local nawabs, and made merry with dancing slave girls, seamstresses, cooks and confectioners'. Along with potatoes, chilies, okra, papayas, pineapples, cashews, peanuts, custard apples, guavas and tobacco, which the Portuguese are able to bring into Hindustan from their conquests in the Americas through the Columbian Exchange, the Portuguese also bring with them priests and a fervent desire to save 'heathen' souls, and are delighted to find a generous and hospitable Akbar willing to converse with them, deferential and respectful of their religious beliefs, despite their own narrow, religious bigotry. In Fatehpur

Sikri, the priests are amazed when Akbar prostrates himself before an image of Jesus. He is also willing to wear Portuguese clothes—'a scarlet cloak with gold fastenings...together with Portuguese hats'. For a while the Jesuit priests are convinced that Akbar's interest in Christianity will give them a resplendent convert in the Padshah of Hindustan himself. But Akbar is equally interested in Hinduism, Judaism, Zoroastrianism and Sufi mystics. As the ever-tortured Badauni laments, Akbar is just as likely to prohibit the 'slaughter of cows, and the eating of their flesh because the Hindus devoutly worship them and esteem their dung as pure'. Akbar is interested in a syncretic faith, which contains the best of all religions, and this is what drives his passionate interest in all sorts of holy men. The Jesuit Father Monserrate comes closest to Akbar's true state of mind when he says 'it may be suspected that Jalal ud-Din [Akbar] was moved to summon the Christian priests, not by any divine inspiration but by a certain curiosity, and excessive eagerness to hear some new thing'. In the next few years there are other intriguing foreign visitors to the court. In 1581 Queen Elizabeth of England grants a charter to a small mission company entitled the Company of Merchants to the Levant. Travelling under the auspices of this company, John Newberry, William Leedes and Ralph Fitch arrive at the capital of the 'Great Mogor'. Leedes will settle at the court of Akbar as court jeweller and Ralph Fitch will leave the first documented account of an Englishman's visit to the Mughal court. So inconsequential, however, is the English presence to the Hindustanis that there exists no contemporary record of them in the Mughal texts.

But if Akbar delights in the churn and curdle of philosophical arguments, the women of the zenana are less than impressed. Neither the Hindu rajkumaris nor the Timurid-Mughal women are at all tolerant of 'these strange-looking, unarmed men...with their long black robes, their curious caps, their shaven faces, and their tonsured heads'. 'Akbar's numerous wives', we are told, 'afraid of being repudiated, adopted an attitude of hostility toward the Christian religion'. The Jesuit priests are in equal measure horrified and confounded by the many women Akbar has in his zenana. While they are tempted to conjure a lascivious and debauched sanctum sanctorum, they are surprised at the very modest number of children that Akbar has. '[Akbar] had only three sons and two daughters,' writes Monserrate musingly, despite what appears to be a disproportionately large number of women. What the priests fail to understand is the large number of attendants and auxiliary staff and also bereft women and relatives to whom Akbar has extended his protection, without there ever being a sexual connection. Salima Sultan herself will never have any children. Now when the Hajj party and its powerful senior women return to Fatehpur Sikri, they put enough pressure on Akbar to make the priests feel unwelcome at the Mughal court. 'The opposition of this party (harem) stiffened after the return, early in 1582, of Hamida Bano Bagum, and Gulbadan Begum from Mecca. These two causes produced a state of tension that soon broke into open hostility.' By 1583 all the priests have been recalled to Goa.

Not long after the return of the Hajj party, the entire Mughal court is in a state of upheaval again. In 1585, Akbar decides to move the court to Lahore. Not being near a river bank, Fatehpur Sikri does not have an adequate water supply and what little water the town has is 'brackish and fretting'. There are, moreover, serious uprisings in the northwest of the empire which Akbar wants to monitor closely. So Fatehpur Sikri is abandoned, never to be reclaimed, and slowly becomes a ghost town. The vaulting red sandstone retains in its dark shadows the memories of the Rajput rajkumaris' Vedic fires and the ibadat khana is forlorn without the furious philosophical exchanges that used to rage through the dense, still, tropical nights.

In Lahore, the zenana is kept busy arranging for the marriages of the Mughal princes. Shaikhu Baba, now Salim Mirza, marries the daughter of Raja Bhagwan Das of Amber as well as rajkumaris from Jodhpur and Bikaner. Murad is married to a daughter of Aziz Mirza Koka, and the tensile connection to Akbar's foster-family is renewed. The women of the court and the Muslim brides wear a peshwaz for these celebrations. This is a long dress of coloured muslin which reaches down to the ankle. The upper part of the dress is fitted closely to the body, like a choli, and the lower, front opening portion 'being as much frilled as the waist-band will carry' is attached to the top. The lower part of the skirt 'is trimmed with bands and flounces of gold lace, and silver and gold tissue'. The imperial kitchens are also producing increasingly refined and elaborate cuisines.

The best ingredients from the four corners of the empire—rice, butter, duck, waterfowl—are brought to the court. The chickens of the palace are 'fed by hand with pellets flavoured with saffron and rosewater, and massaged daily with musk oil and sandalwood'. Carefully planted trees and plants, watered personally by Akbar with rose water to improve the flavour of their vegetables, supply fresh vegetables and fruit. Dishes are created which will carry the glory of the Mughals much beyond the shores of Hindustan—naan, poultry cooked with finely ground onions known as 'do piaza', a Turkic dish called the sanbusa, later samosa, dampukhta and harissa.

The old Timurid nomadic habit, to never stay long settled in a single city, also remains a constant trait of the Mughal family. In 1586 Kashmir becomes incorporated into the Mughal empire and in the following decades, it becomes the summer retreat for the Mughal imperial family. The journey from Lahore to Kashmir is a gruelling two-week-long expedition which involves enormous planning and suitable fanfare. Drummers and trumpeters, mounted on elephants, ride in front of the retinue, a single drummer sounding his drum at short, regular intervals. Scouts have already ridden off ahead to drive away anyone on the roads, so as not to further impede the royal party. 'Queens ride on female elephants, hidden from view in gaily decorated howdahs. They are guarded and escorted by 500 old men of very dignified and venerable appearance'. These men keep away any loiterers who might be trying to get a glimpse of the zenana women and 'the higher the rank and dignity of these old men, the more careful they are in fulfilling their functions'. There are also 'the ladies in waiting of the queens', who do not ride imperial elephants but 'follow their mistresses on camels, under white sun-shades'. As they leave the heaving, roiling plains of Hindustan and climb into the hills of Kashmir, they cross rivers and cliffs and meadows and the air is suddenly crisp and fragrant in the deep blue skies. It is a dangerous journey, for the hills are crumbling and steep and when it rains, the rivers become suddenly huge and ravenous. Horses fall over embankments and are lost, as are many soldiers, and passes are blocked by snow. They walk over snow, when animals cannot pass, and for the Rajput women, daughters of the hard-scrabble lands of Rajasthan, and all the other Hindustani party, this is their very first experience of snow. The Timurid women, Hamida Banu, Gulbadan, and Salima Sultan, will remember the frigid winters of Kabul and Hamida Banu has her long-ago memories of the desolate and icy mountains where Humayun cooked horse-meat in his helmet. But the desert-born are shaken by these unfamiliar conditions. 'Shall I describe the severity of the cold?' muses Abul-Fazl, '[o]r shall I tell of the depth of the snow, and the bewilderment of the natives of India?' And yet there is beauty also, and stark splendour: 'Shall I write of the fountains, the trees, the flowers?' Akbar assigns officers to station themselves along the route with 'tents, fuel forage and food' so that 'the ladies should not suffer any inconvenience'. Finally a high plateau is reached, where 'the groves, the blossoming flowers, the glorious air, the melody of the waterfalls' delight all the weary travellers. The zenana ladies, who have been travelling at a slower pace than Akbar, are a few stages behind and Salim is sent to escort them to the royal camp. But conditions remain dangerous and Salim prefers to leave the women at an earlier stage and returns to Akbar's camp alone. Akbar, who 'was looking for the arrival of the ladies' is incensed by Salim's decision and refuses to allow the mirza to pay him his respects. 'In his wrath', recounts Abu'l-Fazl, quite discountenanced, Akbar orders 'in the midst of the rain, and the slipperiness of the ridges that his horse should be brought. His whole thought was that he should go in person and bring the ladies.' Akbar leaves with a small party to bring the zenana ladies himself and Abu'l-Fazl is unnerved by Akbar's sudden, seething anger, and his tempestuous decision. Salim, unsurprisingly, is humiliated and 'shut himself up in his tent, and abstained from food and sleep'.

This episode in Kashmir is symptomatic of two of Akbar's traits—his sudden, savage temper and his volatile relationship with Salim. When the mirza is still the infant Shaikhu Baba, born after so many fervent prayers and hopes, he is cherished and nurtured by a veritable coterie of women—his grandmother Hamida Banu, his grand-aunt Gulbadan, his foster-mother Salima Sultan and his milk mother, the daughter of Sheikh Salim Chishti. 'Indeed she is kinder than a mother', says Salim of his milk mother, 'and I had been raised from infancy in her care'. Of the doting and erudite Salima Sultan, Salim says: 'She possessed all good qualities.

Amongst women, such combination of talent and capability is rare.' Akbar, too, is very fond of his young children but as they grow older, his love is brusque and demanding. 'The King's nature,' admits Monserrate, 'was such that though he loved his children very dearly, he used to give them orders rather roughly whenever he wanted anything done; and he sometimes punished them with blows as well as harsh words.' Indeed the Jesuit priests who are entrusted with Danyal's education for a few years are surprised to find him 'so submissive that he sometimes did not even dare to raise his eyes to his teacher's face'. The boys have grown up under the very long shadow of their magnificent father and his impossible achievements. The two younger boys, Murad and Danyal, are not able to withstand the unforgiving gaze of Akbar's expectations, becoming alcoholics and drug addicts early on. Intoxicants have always been a part of Timurid culture and Babur himself wrote frankly of his own encounters with drink. At his parties, guests drank 'chaghir', a cider like alcohol made from apples, pears or grapes imported from Kabul. Ma'jum, a paste of poppy seeds (opium), hashish seeds, mixed with walnuts, pistachios, cardamoms, milk and honey, was very popular with the aristocracy at Babur's court. Akbar himself drinks 'post', an intoxicant made from poppy seeds, after which, the Jesuit priests have noted, 'he sinks back stupefied and shaking'. Akbar has even tried smoking tobacco from a hookah, introduced into the Mughal court for the first time by a courtier called Asad Beg, who found it in the Deccan, where it has just been imported by the Portuguese. Out of curiosity, Akbar agrees to try the hookah and 'taking the mouth piece into his sacred mouth, drew two or three breaths'. But the young mirzas lack their father's iron will and blistering ambition and will succumb completely to the intoxication of drugs and drink. Murad will die, in 1599, before his thirtieth birthday, in a state of delirium tremens brought on by his addiction to opium. Danyal will survive Murad by only a few years, a hopeless addict who weeps when his servants are ordered by Akbar to hide all the alcohol in his house.

Salim survives, but as Akbar's reign stretches on endlessly into the waning years of the sixteenth century, Salim, now thirty, worries that he may never succeed to the throne at all. Akbar is fifty-eight years old and still as vigorous and energetic as he ever was. Once the Uzbek threat to

Hindustan has been removed by 1598, he shifts the capital back to Agra. His authority is completely unquestioned and his grandeur is supreme. Akbar is disappointed in his sons, their weakness and their lack of resolve and Salim reacts by being furtive, deceitful and unreliable. It will make of him an undecided man, a man of extremes 'sometimes barbarously cruel and at other times...exceeding fair and gentle'. Salim's own son, Khusrau, the son of Man Bai, Harkha Bai's niece, is now a teenager, popular with the nobles at the court. He has 'a pleasing presence and excellent carriage, was exceedingly beloved of the common people, their love and delight'. Khusrau has the support, moreover, of the now-powerful Kachhawaha Rajput clan and the Atka Khail because he is married to a daughter of Aziz Koka. Salim, by the early years of the seventeenth century, is a desperate man, convinced he will be thwarted of his rightful place on the Mughal throne. But he has an invaluable source of support—the senior women of the zenana. For Hamida Banu, Salima Sultan, Gulbadan and his milk mother, he will always remain their beloved Shaikhu Baba and when he sputters into a series of revolts against his father, these women will condense around the cause of his rehabilitation. For these older women, survivors of those uncertain and dispossessed early years between Kabul and Hindustan, these fractious relations between father and son are untenable, and dangerous to the future of the Timurid-Mughal empire in Hindustan. For them, Salim is the one true heir of Akbar.

In 1600, Salim goes to Allahabad and sets himself up as an independent king, issuing farmans from his court there. In 1602, Akbar resolves to send the trusted Abu'l-Fazl to bring Salim to his senses, when the mirza seems to be heading towards open rebellion, striking coins in his own name. But Salim knows that Abu'l-Fazl despises him, deeming him an unworthy son to a great king. 'He both publicly and privately spoke against me', complains Salim. So Salim arranges to have Abu'l-Fazl assassinated by Bir Singh, the Bundela chief of Orchha, who beheads Akbar's old and steadfast friend, and sends his head to Salim. When Abu'l-Fazl's deputy arrives before Akbar bearing this terrible news, wearing a blue handkerchief around his wrist as an unspoken signal of what has happened, Akbar is utterly devastated. Akbar 'uttered a cry and became insensible' and so undone is the great padshah by the murder of his closest confidant that all reconciliation between father and son appears doomed. But it is at this point that the senior women of the zenana, and Salima Sultan especially, resolve to bring back the errant son to court before it is too late.

Hamida Banu, Gulbadan Begum and Salima Sultan plead with Akbar to forgive their beloved Shaikhu Baba despite his very grievous violence. Akbar finally agrees to their wishes and then asks Salima Sultan to bring Salim back to court. Knowing that the guilty mirza will be terrified of the retribution his furious father is likely to visit on him, and suspicious of any attempt to lure him to court, Salima Sultan 'in order to soothe the prince's apprehensions', takes Akbar's favourite imperial elephant, Fath Lashkar, a special horse, and a robe of honour when she goes to Allahabad where Salim is ensconced. 'When she arrived within two stages of Allahabad', we are told, 'His Highness [Salim] went out to greet her, meeting her with the greatest of respect, humbling himself immeasurably before His Majesty Arsh-Ashyani's [Akbar's] representative, and returning to the city with the begum in great pomp.' Salima Sultan has to convince the terrified Salim that Akbar means him no harm, despite the horrific crime of Abu'l-Fazl's murder and all his attempts to stage a rebellion. She spends a long time with Salim at Allahabad, reassuring him and trying to bolster his buckling resolve. Matters are delayed unexpectedly by the grievous news of the death of the formidable old lady, Gulbadan, on 7 February 1603. A month later, Salim issues an edict calling himself Abu'l Muzaffar Sultan Salim Badhshah Ghazi but by the following month, Salima Sultan is able to write to Akbar that she has 'cleaned the stain of savagery and suspicion from the heart of the prince' and that she will bring him to the court. 'When she had promised the prince all sorts of imperial favours and removed all traces of apprehension from his mind, His Highness accompanied the lady to court.' Before appearing in court, Salim pays one final visit to another, beloved and senior, woman, Hamida Banu.

Salim is finally brought back and rehabilitated, but for the next few years, until Akbar's death in 1605, the court simmers with tension between the camps of Salim and his son Khusrau. Man Bai, Salim's proud Rajput wife, is so distressed by the fighting between her husband and her son that, unable to bear the shame, she commits suicide by taking an overdose of opium. Supported by the senior women of the zenana, Salim finally becomes Nur-ud-Din Mohammed Jahangir, Padshah Ghazi of Hindustan, soon after Akbar's death in 1605. Khusrau is imprisoned and another, more craven and catastrophic crime is committed against the fifth Sikh Guru, Arjan Singh. Arjan Singh gave Khusrau hospitality when the young prince begged for sanctuary during his fugue but for Jahangir, this is an act of treason. He has Arjan Singh tortured and killed, making him the first of the Sikh martyrs. The Sikhs will never forget this abomination, and it will come back to haunt the Mughals many centuries later. Meanwhile, in 1606, Khusrau escapes from his jailers and mounts another rebellion, supported by Mirza Aziz Koka, his father-in-law. Jahangir is furious and discusses the role of Aziz Koka at court and it seems increasingly likely that he will be executed by the new monarch. But Aziz Koka is a favourite of the senior women of the zenana, who remember with fondness and love his mother, Jiji Anaga, and his own special place in Akbar's heart. They remember the 'river of milk' that Akbar himself never crossed. Salima Sultan, representing a coterie of senior women, calls out to Jahangir at court from behind a jaali saying: 'Your Majesty, all of the Begims are assembled in the harem for the purpose of interceding for Mirza Aziz Koka. It would be better if you come there,' she carefully advises, 'otherwise they will come to you.' Suitably warned, Jahangir goes to the zenana and, hustled by the women, is forced to pardon Mirza Aziz Koka.

For Salima Sultan Begum, now old, twice-widowed, and childless, there is respect and a final, incandescent title. At the dawn of the seventeenth century, for the first decade of Jahangir's reign, she is Padshah Begum of the Mughal empire.

MARYAM-UZ-ZAMANI, THE *RAHIMI* AND THE PERFIDIOUS PORTUGUESE

The town of Bayana in Rajasthan is a grim and crumbling place that once 'hath beene great and faire', but was now 'ruinate'. There remain two sarais, or inns, and a bazaar, from an earlier, more glorious time. There are 'a few straggling houses, many faire ones being fallen, and many others not inhabited (except by rogues and thieves) so that many streets are quite desolate.' On the outskirts of this wasteland there are still tombs, and ruined monuments and an ancient, whimsical sense of decay where cattle-keeping Gujjars roam. But Bayana, despite appearances, has a hidden treasure. It is here that the best indigo grows and it is this precious dye that has attracted, on a cool December day in 1610, the London merchant William Finch who is determined to make his fortune here.

After the lucrative trade in spices that the Portuguese have been conducting in Hindustan, it is the turn of the Dutch and the English, in the early years of the seventeenth century, to become smitten by the great fortune of Hindustan. By the time of Akbar's death in 1605, the Mughal empire extends from the Sindh to Lahore and then through the fertile and immense Gangetic plains up to Bengal. Hindustan contributes almost a quarter of the world's economy and to the unabashed astonishment of the Europeans, Hindustan is entirely self-sufficient 'in all necessaries for the use of man'. There is wheat, rice, barley and other grains from which they make bread which the Indians then eat with butter and cheese made from the milk of 'Kine, Sheepe, and goats'. There is meat, from buffaloes, cattle, sheep, venison, hares as well as fish and poultry. There is a bewildering amount of fruits, which the Mughal court consumes in huge quantities: muskmelons, watermelons, pomegranates, 'pome-citrons', lemons, oranges, dates, figs, grapes, plantains or bananas, mangoes, pineapples, apples and pears. But the adventurers, traders and merchants who arrive in India in the early seventeenth century are not as interested in the diet of the locals as they are in the produce that has made the Mughal empire the most extravagantly wealthy empire in the world: cotton, cotton goods and indigo.

In 1600, piqued by the success of the Portuguese in the spice trade with India, the English form the chartered English East India Company and send a few reconnaissance voyages to India before dispatching, in 1607, an unusually accomplished ambassador in William Hawkins, along with his agent, William Finch. Hawkins arrives at Jahangir's court at Agra 'very richly clad', wearing apparel of 'scarlet and violet', his cloak 'lined with taffeta and embroidered with silver lace', a suitably high idea of his own importance and carrying a letter of introduction from King James, rather perplexingly written in Spanish. But Hawkins has an advantage over the other pretenders to Jahangir's favour, far more effective than his rich robes; he is a fluent Turki speaker and Jahangir is delighted to be able to converse with a foreigner in the old language. He greets Hawkins warmly and invites him to come daily to the palace for talks and drinks, and even bestows on him the very generous post in the imperial service of 400 horse. Finding his name unaccountably difficult to pronounce, Jahangir offers Hawkins the much more suitable title of Khan, and Hawkins Khan settles into courtly life at Agra, dressing in the 'Mohameddan manner' of the Mughal noblemen and even marrying Mariam, an Armenian Christian woman who has been living as Jahangir's ward in his immense zenana and who Jahangir chooses for him for a wife.

The Portuguese, who have been trading on Hindustani shores for almost a century, are extremely leery of these new English interlopers who seek trading rights from the padshah. As for the Catholic Jesuit priests, who have again been sent to Jahangir's court on mission, the protestant Hawkins is the devil in disguise. 'Religion was the first subject they discussed,' mutter the Jesuits about Jahangir and Hawkins, with the padshah 'enquiring especially about the most holy sacrament.' To the Jesuits' horror, Hawkins, 'like the heretic he was, told him much that was contrary to the truth and to the catholic doctrine of this mystery.' After this they grumble bitterly to Jahangir, even gracelessly criticizing the wording of the Spanish letter which Hawkins has brought as introduction.

Hawkins, on the other hand, is furious to find that the Jesuits are plotting against him and rails that they 'were like madde Dogges, labouring to work my passage out of the World'. Hawkins himself, despite his fluency in Turki and his perseverance, is arrogant and rash, refusing to play by the rules of the Mughal court, where nuance and finesse is preferred to intransigence. The amirs of Jahangir's court, meanwhile, barely notice the presence of these grasping 'firangis', endlessly manoeuvring at the periphery of the Mughal court. For the Mughal noblemen, it is 'a kind of uncleanness to mingle with us', admits an Englishman, while another one specifies that 'Mahometans in general think us Christians so unclean they will not eate with us, nor yet of any thing dressed in our vessels'. Even so, Hawkins may have been able to secure some farmans from the ever-generous Jahangir had his agent, William Finch, not made a grave error in judgement in crossing Harkha Bai's path.

When Finch reaches the outskirts of Bayana, he sees fields of cultivated indigo, or neel (from the Sanskrit neela, meaning 'blue'). The indigo shrub is a small, crouching plant not more than one yard high, which is pulled out after the rainy season and soaked in water, weighed down with stones and allowed to steep for a few days. When the shrubs are thoroughly rotted, the juice is removed, the decaying shrubs are rolled into rough, fibrous balls and allowed to dry. These nondescript dried balls are the indigo of commerce, used to dye the fine cotton cloth that the empire produces. There are some 300 dye-yielding plants in India, which are used by the dyers in a secret and complex technique to create fabrics and designs of such beauty, brilliance and colour that they are the envy of the world. The most popular colours are burgundy, gold, mustard and indigo while recently, a subtler palette has been created to cater to the tastes of the Persianate Mughal court. Thus pistachio green has been created using pomegranate dye while vibrant yellow is derived from the priceless saffron. Black and red are particularly valued dyes but the most expensive and sought-after colour, by far, is indigo. Faced, in December 1610, with this unprepossessing looking treasure, Finch makes a rash decision and one which will have catastrophic consequences for the immediate future of the EIC at Jahangir's court. Surveying the harvest of indigo at Bayana is another agent, one sent by Maryam-uz-Zamani, with orders to buy all the indigo and load it onto the queen mother's ship which is bound for Mocha, near Mecca. Maryam-uz-Zamani is particularly interested in the harvest of Bayana and has even had a garden and stepwell built here at a cost of 20,000 rupees to guarantee the availability of water for the cultivation of this precious plant. The agent bids for the indigo, and secures a price for it after which Finch foolishly outbids the royal agent and offers 'a small matter more than she [Maryam-uz-Zamani] should have given' and thus buys the entire indigo harvest. This is something a local merchant would never have had the temerity to do and the queen's merchant is rightly incensed and complains that it is Hawkins who has encouraged his factor to behave in this outrageously disrespectful way. When the agent appears before the queen mother empty-handed, Maryam-uz-Zamani is furious and complains to her son, the padshah. Already shackled by the Jesuits and the Portuguese, who have undermined his every effort, Hawkins now faces endless prevarication from Jahangir after Maryam-uz-Zamani's complaint. Hawkins' fate is further sealed by the curious complaint that his men are 'bibbers of wine, that before they came to the courte daylie they filled their heads with strong drinke'. Undone, Hawkins finally leaves Agra in 1611 and dies a couple of years later, on his way back to England, as does Finch, at Babylon, also in 1611. The Armenian Mariam arrives in England a young widow, one of the first women from Mughal India to ever reach England.

If the consequences of undermining Harkha Bai are particularly grave for these English factors, then the Indian merchants and traders are no less wary of the respect and deference owed to this extraordinarily powerful woman. In 1612, the local traders are so anxious of royal disfavour after the indigo debacle of 1611 that an English captain, John Jourdain, notes that since the queen's ship, the *Rahimi*, is bound for Mocha, 'the local merchants wouldn't lade their goods aboard until wee (Europeans) are gone from the country'. What the Hindustani traders know and what Finch failed to sufficiently acknowledge, is that Harkha Bai, now Maryam-uz-Zamani and queen mother of the empire, is a prodigiously wealthy woman with her own ship, who controls her finances and trades under her own name. Indeed, many of the Mughal noblewomen, since the time of Akbar, have become independently wealthy as the Mughal empire has flourished. In addition

Khanzada Begum is returned to Babur's court after ten years in exile.
Khanzada is seated in front of an attentive and respectful Babur, raising a
commanding hand while speaking to the men.

In a few years tight jackets and tunics in diaphanous materials will replace the more pragmatic, flowing qabas of the Mughal women.

As a Timurid woman and the daughter of Babur, Gulbadan Begum enjoyed enormous respect at the courts of Humayun and Akbar.

Mughal women accompanied the emperor, travelling on horseback, on camels, on elephants and in palanquins. Here, Hamida Banu travels by boat on the Yamuna from Delhi to Agra.

In the court of Akbar the Great, dusky Rajasthani women in short blouses mingle with fair-skinned Turkish and Persian women with their high, conical Persian caps. Hamida Banu sits on a chair by her reclining daughter-in-law, Harkha Bai, who has just given birth to the future Jahangir.

The women wear long jamas of exquisitely fine muslin, so sought after that they have names of their own—running water, night dew, woven air.

Akbar introduces the 'chakdar jama'—the first truly Hindustani garment—to the Mughal court. The Hindu chakdar jama fastens on the left-hand side of the body, while the Muslim courtiers fasten it on the right.

اين مجلس دل افروز مرد زبلطافى خاصرمه بیشه وموادجت وذرى خاصه عام مهیابیگشت

Maham Anaga, Akbar's milk mother, 'was a marvel of sense, resource and loyalty'. Her high status at Akbar's court is visibly demonstrated by her prominent position, seated next to the emperor himself.

محمد امین جو یانه و بابای زنورو خواجه ملک عبدالرحیم راکه خلف صدق بهرام خاست و دران
منکام جهارساله بود و بابا الده و بعضی خدمتکاران ازان عاد نیرگ بربد به محمد ایا درویان شدند

After the murder of Bairam Khan, Akbar marries his widow, Salima Sultan
Begum, granddaughter of Babur, as 'this is an additional association with
the powerful Timurid name'. Salima Sultan travels to Agra in a palanquin
while Bairam Khan's son, Abdur Rahim, is carried by a horseman.

Women have their own entertainment in the zenana. Groups of dancers, called the Kanchani (the blooming), are allowed into the zenana and 'they are trained singers and dancers and dance with wonderful agility'.

Top: The Qila-e-Mubaarak is a city unto itself, with wide corridors, open skies, shaded gardens, great beauty, waterfalls, canals and fountains.

Bottom: Mughal women are better educated than any of their contemporaries anywhere in the world. Many will become writers and famous poets.

Top: Jahangir, first of the Mughal padshahs born of a Hindu mother, has no beard, but a neat moustache that drops at the edges and curls outwards. He is a flamboyant emperor, who wears a different set of jewels every single day. 'All his clothes are designed expressly for him and he wears them just once.'

Bottom: Harkha Bai, better known by her title Maryam-uz-Zamani, was a prodigiously wealthy woman who was actively involved in trade at the court of her son, Jahangir. She is buried in Lahore in the Maryam Zamani Begum Mosque that Jahangir built.

'Noor Jahan cares for Jahangir as one would a child, with gentle charm and coddling but also with firm guidance.' For the last sixteen years of his life, Jahangir will marry no further women after Noor Jahan.

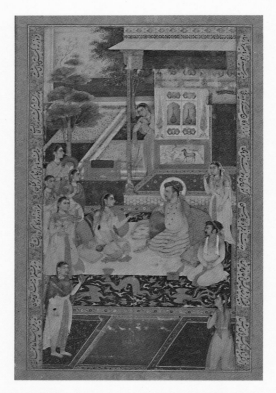

In 1621, Noor Jahan remodelled the Bagh-i-Noor Afshan, also known as the Ram Bagh, most probably the garden depicted in this miniature. Pleasure gardens increased the uncensored space allowed to Noor Jahan and the other Mughal women to enact their lives.

Noor Jahan had gold and silver coins struck in her name and was allowed to issue farmans, both of which were kingly prerogatives. When Shah Jahan became emperor, he had all of Noor Jahan's coins melted, making them extremely rare today.

Top: The marriage of Mumtaz to Shah Jahan will give rise to one of the most
expensive and glorious monuments to love the world has ever seen,
the Taj Mahal in Agra.

Bottom: The Europeans at the court of Shah Jahan were equally fascinated and
mystified by the visible opulence and power of Jahanara Begum. 'She was loved by
all,' marvelled Manucci, 'and lived in state and magnificence.'

Organized by Jahanara Begum in 1633, Dara Shikoh's 'wedding is the most expensive ceremony ever staged in Mughal history and costs thirty-two lakh rupees'. When she becomes padshah begum at seventeen, Jahanara must organize the weddings of all the royal princes.

Dara Shikoh wears a sehra of pearls on his turban and his hands are stained with henna, in the Hindu tradition. The fireworks in the background are spectacular, with artificial trees, rockets and elaborate puppets.

This portrait is thought to be of Dara Shikoh's wife, Princess Nadira Banu Begum, daughter of Sultan Parviz. She is seen here wearing a patka, odhani and magnificent jewels reflecting her status.

to their monthly allowances, Mughal noblewomen are given expensive gifts by courtiers, own property, and further increase their wealth through trade. Of all the Mughal nobles who conduct trade, fully half of the names documented are that of women. Akbar had prodigiously increased the wealth of the Mughal empire and the Mughal noblewomen became consequently immeasurably wealthy. When Akbar dies, according to a Flemish visitor's calculations, his gemstones alone, 'his diamonds, rubies, emeralds, sapphires, pearls and other jewels' will be valued at 60,520,521 rupees.

Jahangir is a famously generous padshah and when he comes to the throne in 1605 he is proud to claim that he 'increased the allowances of all the veiled ladies of [his] father's harem from 20% to 100% according to their condition and relationship'. Half of this allowance comes to the women directly from the royal treasury and the other half is in the form of a grant, or jagir, of a district of land whose yield is theirs. In addition there are magnificent gifts for the women for different occasions: birthdays, hunts, military victories as well as occasional, more eccentric, celebrations. Not long before the indigo fiasco Jahangir gifts a string of pearls to his mother-in-law for having invented the itr (attar) of roses. Other gifts include elephants, costly dresses, cavalry horses and perfumes. For the most influential women at court, there are gifts from courtiers and foreign ambassadors and merchants who want to win their favour and who are aware of where the real decision-making powers often lie. In the coming years the English agents at Jahangir's court will hunt for ever more exotic and exquisite presents for the powerful women of the zenana. There will be musical instruments, feathered hats, gilded carriages and European oil paintings. All these presents add to the wealth of the women, which is theirs to control and spend as they wish and now Harkha Bai, senior-most woman of the zenana after the death of Salima Sultan in 1612, and Rajput rajkumari from the erstwhile obscure province of Kachhawaha, is one of the wealthiest women in the world.

Maryam-uz-Zamani's favoured status at Jahangir's court is reflected in the fact that she is one of only four members of the court (one of whom is Jahangir himself) and the only woman to have the high rank of 12,000 cavalry, and she is known to receive a jewel from every single nobleman at court 'according to his estate' every year on the occasion of the new year's festival. But what Maryam-uz-Zamani is most interested in, what she invests her money in and actively participates in, is trade.

Surat, one of the main ports and commercial centres, is now a large and thrumming town, through which pass all the goods exchanged between Central Hindustan and the Deccan and the rest of the trading world. As for the quantities of fine cotton cloth traded, it is said that 'everyone from the Cape of Good Hope to China, man and woman, was clothed from head to foot in material made in Gujarat', most of which passes through Surat. Muslims hold the key administrative posts but the majority of the population, and almost all of the traders, are Hindus. 'Its Hindu majority ruled by Muslim Moghuls,' writes an admiring Pietro della Valle, 'lives peaceably and freely with all the other groups in this mixed society and many of its members are admitted to high government and military posts.' There are also Parsis, who work as weavers and most of the silks and cloths made at Surat are made by them. But it is the Hindus, of the 'Bania' caste, who are the throbbing heart of the trade at Surat. Every year when the ships arrive, following the monsoon winds, and dock at the port of Suwali, 'the Banias pitch tents and erect booths and straw huts in great numbers all along the coast'. At the market they thus create overnight they sell 'calicoes, china satin, porcelains, scrutores (writing desks) of mother-of-pearl, ebony, ivory, agates, turquoises, heliotropes, cornelians; as also rice, sugar, plantains, arrack etc. Many little boys work here of a pittance running errands, doing odd jobs, or acting as interpreters.' It is commonly known to all visiting merchants to beware of 'the sugared words' used by the Banias which 'make many simple men lose themselves'. The tawny Banias are lean of body with long hair and are notoriously quick at numbers and well versed in the various currencies in common use. These dark-skinned Indians, moreover, do not admire white or fair-skinned people because they look like lepers to them. There are women, too, 'who are lighter than the men, rouge their faces and load themselves with bracelets and fetters of brass, gold and ivory. Over their long and disheveled hair they throw a piece of fine white lawn (linen), through whose transparency it seems more lovely.' Adding to the boisterous melee of this trading town are Europeans, who arrive in ever-increasing numbers. 'Life is made pleasant for Europeans as well as for Indians of means,' we are assured, 'by the great number of available servants and slaves.' All these people, whatever be their religion and class, wear clothes of the fine white cotton which is the pride of Surat.

It is from the hustling, garrulous town of Surat, where a scattershot of languages ricochets off the lanes while the merchants work, that Harkha Bai trades through the enormous ship that sails under her colours, the *Rahimi*. Harkha Bai, like the other Mughal noblewomen, cannot trade directly with the merchants and so the zenana employs a huge number of agents, middlemen and financial advisers, 'mirroring in miniature the emperor's own finance ministry'. The women send out their personal servants to bargain and negotiate with the Europeans at the court and gifts and favours are exchanged. The *Rahimi* is one of the largest vessels of any kind to sail the Indian seas. Her capacity is upwards of 1,500 tons and the ship has room for a load of 1,500 passengers. In 1613, the *Rahimi* is transporting goods worth 100,000 pounds equivalent to, in today's currency, half a billion rupees. But the *Rahimi*, like Gulbadan's *Salimi* and *Ilahi* thirty years previously, is also a Hajj ship. The *Rahimi* trades in Hindustan's major exports—indigo, cotton and silks, but also leather, metal, carpets, spices, opium and jewels. In return, it brings back goods of particular interest to the noblewomen—gold, silver, ivory, pearls, amber, perfumes, wines, brocade, cutlery and glassware. But it also carries passengers to and from Mecca, for the sacred Hajj pilgrimage. Indeed the *Rahimi* is famous amongst the Europeans for being 'the great pilgrimage ship'. Which is why the outrageous and scandalous piratical attacks by the Portuguese against the *Rahimi* in 1612 and 1613 will be considered so grave as to bring about a complete reversal of fortunes, both for the Portuguese and, incidentally, for the newly arrived English.

There has been trade, and piracy, carried out from India's western shores for a very long while by the time the Portuguese enter the fray in the sixteenth century. The hereditary title of Calicut's rulers, Samudri Raja, or Lord of the Seas, which is later mispronounced by the English as Zamorin, is a whimsical indicator of India's long association with the ocean. Marco Polo himself comments on the large numbers of Indian pirates and warns travellers. 'You must know,' he clarifies, 'that from this kingdom of Melibar, and from another near it called Gozurat, there go forth every year more than a hundred corsair vessels on cruise…These pirates,' he adds, 'take with them their wives and children and stay out the whole summer', describing a piracy which is almost a family enterprise. The light and small country craft which the Indian pirates use, described in Portuguese sources as 'paraos', are ideally suited to surprise attacks on more cumbersome merchant craft, sliding away to hide in the many backwater canals after their sudden, explosive attacks.

The Portuguese, meanwhile, have had a long history of violent encounters with Muslim conquerors. For the Portuguese, ever since the bloody conflicts between Muslims and Christians in the fifteenth and sixteenth centuries in the Iberian peninsula, all Muslims are 'Moors,' whether they be Arab or Berber or, later, Mughal. Their unassailable belief in their own moral superiority is reflected when Pedro Alvares Cabral, Portuguese commander of a large fleet sent to the East in 1500 is told: 'If you encounter ships belonging to the aforesaid Moors of Mecca at sea, you must endeavour as much as you can to take possession of them, and of their merchandise and property and also of the Moors who are in the ships, to your profit as best you can and to make war on them and do them as much damage as possible as a people with whom we have so great and so ancient an enmity.' And so, inflexible faith is linked with endless greed and leads to a convenient, and widely encouraged, rapacity.

By the sixteenth century, this Portuguese bloodlust is combined inexorably with increasingly superior naval power. The heavily armed carracks and highly manoeuvrable caravels make the Portuguese a deadly menace. This has made the Hajj traffic between Hindustan and Mecca a veritable nightmare. Of all the Europeans who are drawn to Hindustan's shores by the spices and the cloth and the gold, it is the Portuguese who are the most thoroughly detested. They are the most enthusiastically violent proselytisers to reach Indian shores and have been since Albuquerque himself made clear his agenda in 1509:

> The King of Portugal commands me to render honour and willing service to all Gentile kings of his land…but i am to destroy the Moors, with whom i wage incessant war… And so we shall drive out of Calicut the Moors, who are the people that furnish him

(a local Hindu king) with all the revenue that he requires for the expense of the war.

Called the 'Portuguese menace', these Europeans are the most paltry in their gifts to Indian kings and the most plundering in their violence towards all competitors. In the early seventeenth century, they react with bullying force to English efforts to set up a trading base at Surat. They decimate Arab trade and control the type and the quantity of goods traded by Indians overseas. This control is enforced by the humiliating and arbitrary 'cartaz' system which Gulbadan had to contend with as well. But in 1613, the entire Mughal court, as well as the city of Surat, is in an uproar when the Portuguese seize the *Rahimi*, a ship that is owned by a Hindu woman with a 'Moorish' title who happens to belong to the most powerful empire in the world.

When the *Rahimi* is seized by the Portuguese in the autumn of 1613, just after the end of the monsoon season, and carried off to Goa, the tumult and outcry at the Mughal court is unprecedented. Everyone knows the *Rahimi* is Maryam-uz-Zamani's ship, and she carries the requisite and loathed Portuguese pass, with its sacrilegious image of the Virgin Mary. The English are aghast at this action and describe the *Rahimi* as being 'verye richly laden', and even more provocatively, not only do the Portuguese seize the ship and its goods 'but took also 700 persons of all sorts with them to Goa; which deeds of theirs is now grown so odious that it is like to bee the utter undoing of the Portungales in their parts'. So the Portuguese, in seizing the goods and passengers of a Hajj pilgrim ship filled with pilgrims, have carefully gauged the freight of their action and this is not only an act of piracy, but an act of religious persecution against the Mughal empire. It is clearly intended to be both a rebuke and a scathing warning to Jahangir, to dissuade any further contact and trade with the recently arrived English adventurers. But the Portuguese have miscalculated their hand. Jahangir is furious.

When it becomes clear to Jahangir and the court that the Portuguese are not going to return the *Rahimi* immediately, the emperor acts with crackling speed. Jahangir orders the halt of all traffic through Surat and this immediately paralyses the lucrative trade which has made the fortune of this city. He further shuts down the Jesuit church in Agra, which had been built under Akbar, and suspends all allowances to Portuguese priests living in Mughal India. Jahangir also sends his agent, Mukarrab Khan, to lay siege to the Portuguese town of Daman. These extreme actions taken by Jahangir are unusual, for the Mughal court has become used to the rapacious brutality of the Portuguese and has usually reacted by ignoring it or accommodating it if possible. But this is the *Rahimi* which has been seized by the Portuguese, Maryam-uz-Zamani's flagship pilgrim ship, and the queen mother demands retribution. This is an altogether unusual situation, demonstrating the great cultural upheavals and the tectonic changes that are shaping the Mughal empire—this is a Hindu queen's Muslim ship, carrying Hajj pilgrims in Christian waters patrolled by the Portuguese armada. This fraught situation lasts a long time, with neither side willing to concede defeat. But the age of Portuguese dominance in Indian waters has effectively been ended. 'The Great Mogul's mother was a great adventurer,' writes an English agent succinctly, 'which caused the Great Mogul to drive the Portingals out of the place.'

The capture of the *Rahimi*, and the insult it is perceived to be to the queen mother of the Mughal empire, precipitates the decline of Portuguese fortunes. Already in 1612, an EIC fleet under Captain Thomas Best had decisively defeated a Goa armada off Surat and had shown the Portuguese to be less than invincible. Jahangir even writes about the 'good news' of Portugal's defeat at English hands with satisfaction in his *Jahangirnama*. 'Battle had taken place', he writes, between the English and the Portuguese, 'most of whose ships were burned up by English fire'. This is the only incident involving the 'firangis' that Jahangir ever writes about in the *Jahangirnama*. Now, after the perfidious actions of the Portuguese, Jahangir is increasingly inclined to negotiate trade agreements with the English and in the next few years the English will slowly replace the Portuguese as the primary foreign power at the Mughal court. Harkha Bai lives another ten years, dying at the very respectable age of eighty-one in 1623. She never will get back the *Rahimi*, but this daughter of the desert, who has never seen the ocean, will have the satisfaction of knowing that she has been part of the process that evicts the great naval force of the Portuguese from Indian shores.

NOOR JAHAN, AN ENGLISH AMBASSADOR AND THE POLITICS OF COLOUR

It is a cool October day in 1616 and twenty-four-year-old Khurram Mirza is resplendent in his long cloak of silver, exquisitely embroidered with pearls and diamonds. Accompanying him are 10,000 horsemen, wearing jackets of gold with feathers in their turbans, and 600 richly draped elephants. He presents himself before the durbar of his father, Padshah Jahangir. Jahangir embraces his favourite son with great affection and gives him a sword with a jewel-studded gold scabbard, a dagger, an elephant with the unlikely name of Bansi-badan (flute-bodied), two horses and instructions to add the title 'Shah' to his name. Khurram is now Shah Sultan Khurram, heir apparent to the Mughal throne. Jahangir also gives him an imitation English coach driven by an English coachman who takes Khurram to his tented camp outside Ajmer. All along the way, Khurram throws coins from the coach to the bustling crowds who follow him out of the city. Khurram is leaving the Mughal court to ride south with his army, to try and subdue the independent Muslim sultanates of the Deccan. Accompanying him is his young wife, Arjumand Begum, their two young children, Dara Shikoh and Jahanara Begum, and a newborn infant son.

The next day, Jahangir also leaves Ajmer since he has promised to accompany Khurram to the Deccan. Jahangir, first of the Mughal padshahs born of a Hindu woman, is now forty-seven years old. He is 'of a complexion neither white nor blacke, but of a middle betwixt them'. He has no beard, but a neat moustache that drops at the edges and curls outwards. Unlike his father, Akbar, who could often be found wearing a white linen dhoti and a simple string of pearls, Jahangir is exceedingly fond of jewellery and fine clothes. Diamonds, rubies, and pearls are wrought into necklaces, rings, armbands, waistbands and bracelets. He wears a different set of jewels every single day. His courtiers are equally flamboyant, and one wears a dagger in his cummerbund made in the kundan gold style with 2,400 separate gemstones on it. Before leaving the court at Ajmer, Jahangir distributes presents, which are let down from the terrace of the palace by silk strings. Included in the awe-struck crowd is the first official English ambassador to the Mughal court, the aristocrat Sir Thomas Roe. Roe is an educated and cultured man, on familiar terms with the English royal family and already a well-travelled adventurer. At thirty-five, he is 'in the prime of his life, of a pregnant understanding, well-spoken, learned, industrious, of a comely personage', and, moreover, prickly about his personal honour. He is tall and handsome, 'quite a dandy—his lovingly groomed moustache like the wings of a bird in flight'. Looking up at the palace, Roe notices a window covered with a bamboo screen. Two women are looking down at the festive scene below, peering through a small space they have made by pulling apart the bamboo. 'I saw first their fingers,' says Roe, 'and after laying their faces close now one eye, now another; sometime I could discern the full proportion. They were indifferently white, black hair smoothed up; but if I had had no other light,' Roe adds, 'their diamonds and pearls had sufficed to show them.' When they see Roe looking up at them, the women 'retired, and were so merry that I supposed they laughed at me.' One of these women is Noor Jahan, Jahangir's newest wife, wed only five years previously and now his chief queen.

Jahangir is finally ready to leave his court and when he descends the stairs of the palace, the people acclaim him with such loud shouts of 'Padshah Ghazi Salaamat' that the uproar resonates right through the palace. He is wearing a qaba of gold cloth with a sash around his waist woven around with a chain of huge pearls, rubies and diamonds. His turban is set with two enormous stones, a ruby and a diamond. Before leaving the palace, Jahangir anoints himself with a tilak, then climbs into another replica of the English carriage Roe has presented to him. Two eunuchs, carrying gold maces set with rubies, stand on each side of the padshah, and the royal carriage leaves the city, preceded by the riotous music of the drummers and the buglers. Noor Jahan rides behind, in the original English carriage, while the rest of the zenana ladies ride on canopied elephants, some fifty in all. Jahangir's noblemen follow on foot and this mobile city glitters and sways in the early winter sun. Pennants and insignia flutter in the breeze and rich cloths of satin, taffeta, gold and silver drape every elephant and horse while blood-red rubies sparkle in an excess of opulence on every furnishing. Jahangir stops at the door of a house near the outskirt of Ajmer and a young man comes out to salute him, his overgrown beard reaching the middle of his torso, his unadorned body a desecration before the fiery opulence of Jahangir. This is Khusrau Mirza, Jahangir's disgraced firstborn son, a prisoner these past ten years. Jahangir bids him sit on a spare elephant and father and son leave the city together to the great joy and applause of the population. The people of Ajmer are extremely fond of Khusrau, for the handsome and easy-going prince is 'a gentleman of a very lovely presence and fine carriage, so exceedingly beloved of the common people'. But Jahangir has never forgiven him his teenage rebellion and resents his popularity and so keeps him close by and guarded at all times.

Jahangir settles into his own tented camp, along with the women of his zenana, his amirs, and the huge retinue of followers, including the court dancers, artists, musicians, cooks, servants, merchants and soldiers. The tented camp itself is like an enormous movable city, walled-in, and in the shape of a fort. The layout of the different parts of the camp is meticulously prepared and each time the camp is dismantled and set up in a new location, it is rearranged in the same configuration, to minimize confusion. There are separate tented quarters for the women of the zenana and their entourage, the mirzas, and the noblemen. The tents are 'in excellent formes', admires Roe, 'some all white, some greene, some mingled, all encompassed as orderly as any house, one of the greatest rarities and magnificences I ever saw'. Jahangir's tents are red, the imperial colour, and the wall panels are made of red embroidered cloth or hand-painted chintz. The window of Noor Jahan's tent is screened with a gold medallion set with pearls and gems and golden chains. The Mughal tents have come a long way from Babur's yurts but in their splendid magnificence are a constant and visible proclamation of their nomadic Timurid legacy.

As Khurram leads his army towards the Deccan, the imperial entourage follows in a more leisurely fashion. There is time for sightseeing, and for that most favoured of Mughal pastimes, hunting. Jahangir is inordinately fond of hunting, and often takes the ladies of the zenana along with him. Noor Jahan is a particularly good markswoman and Jahangir is very proud when he describes how 'she shot two tigers with one shot each and knocked over two others with four shots'. The admiring Jahangir underlines that 'until now such shooting was never seen' and, much pleased by his wife's cool-headed skill, gifts her a pair of diamond bracelets worth 100,000 rupees and pours a tray full of gold coins over her head.

Meanwhile, Jahangir is further delighted to hear of the defeat of an aberrant thorn in his side—the Sultan of Bijapur, Malik Ambar. Malik Ambar has come a long way from his inauspicious birth as Chapu, in Ethiopia, where he was sold to an Arab slave runner before landing up in the Deccan in the early 1570s. In the Deccan, black Africans, or Habshis, are extremely valued, usually for their strength and courage, but Chapu is also talented, ambitious and a great military strategist and quickly rises to power as Malik Ambar, constantly thwarting Mughal attempts to conquer the Deccan. Jahangir is particularly vexed by Malik Ambar's bravado, though he recognizes his military skill. 'This black-faced, ill-starred, disastrous man Ambar of dark fate' he rails episodically in his biography, furious at the way Malik Ambar always evades defeat. The Deccan contains a prize especially attractive to Jahangir, the Golconda diamond mines. Since the medieval ages, Hindustan has produced diamonds for the entire world and Jahangir, of all the Mughal padshahs, has an endless, unquenchable lust for gemstones. For now, however, through Khurram's skill and persistence, Malik Ambar promises to remain 'quiet and loyal'.

When the victorious Khurram returns to his father's court in October 1617, the delighted Jahangir arranges for a glittering welcome. Jahangir now confers on Khurram the title Shah Jahan and amongst many other gifts, Jahangir pours a tray of jewels and gold coins over Shah Jahan's head and also over the head of the elephant Sarnak, who has been offered as tribute. The feast of victory for Shah Jahan, however, is organized and prepared by Noor Jahan. During the feast Noor Jahan offers Shah Jahan robes of honour speckled with gems, 'a turban with a fringe of pearls, a waistbelt studded with pearls', horses with jewelled saddles, and elephants. She also offers robes and cloths to his children and wives and even his servants are presented with horses and jewellery. Altogether, this entertainment costs Noor Jahan 300,000 rupees (15 crore rupees by today's standard) and is a lustrous symbol of the high prestige she now commands at the Mughal court. Nothing about the calamitous circumstances of Noor Jahan's birth, almost forty years previously, could have predicted the extraordinary and glorious career she was to have at the most glittering court of the world.

Noor Jahan is born in a caravan, outside the town of Kandahar, as her parents flee poverty and persecution in Tehran to seek their fortune in the rising Mughal court of Akbar in Hindustan. Her parents, Asmat Begum and Mirza Ghiyas Beg, are from a noble Persian family and the child Mehr-un-Nisa is given a thorough education in the Persian arts and letters. The educated, cultured Ghiyas Beg obtains a modest mansab of 300 horse at Akbar's court at Fatehpur Sikri, which already counts numerous other Persian immigrants in attendance. At seventeen, Mehr-un-Nisa is given in marriage to Ali Quli, a Persian mercenary, who obtains some measure of fame as an excellent shot at the court of Salim Mirza, the future Jahangir, and is given the title Sher Afghan, killer of tigers. Mehr-un-Nisa learns how to hunt and shoot with her husband and gives birth to a daughter, Ladli, in 1605. Three years later, at the age of thirty, Mehr-un-Nisa is widowed. Mehr-un-Nisa and Ladli are taken into the household of the Mughal court, where Jahangir is now padshah. Her father has been awarded the title Itimad-ud-Daulah, 'Pillar of Government', and is Jahangir's revenue minister while her brother, Asaf Khan, is an increasingly influential nobleman of the court. Mehr-un-Nisa is taken into the entourage of Ruqayya Begum, Akbar's senior-most surviving widow, a childless woman, to whom she is a steady and cherished companion. 'This Begam,' writes a Dutch cloth merchant, Van den Broecke, about Ruqayya, 'conceived a great affection for Mehr-un-Nisa; she loved her more than others and always kept her in her company.' It is an established custom at the Mughal court that the padshah must protect all the widows and dependent members of those who have served him, and this tradition adds to the ever-growing number of women, children, and retainers in the Mughal zenana. In the imperial zenana, Mehr-un-Nisa has the close companionship of her family, especially her beloved parents, and the enormous network of zenana women.

Jahangir, in 1605, is already a much married man with many grown children. His principal wives are Rajput rajkumaris, Man Bai of Amber and Jodh Bai of Marwar, daughter of the 'Mota Raja' Udai Singh. There is also Karamsi of the Rathore clan, Sahib Jamal, and various other concubines. His many wives, their attendants and all his extended household live within the zenana of the Agra red fort, as did the zenana under Akbar. Indeed for Jahangir, Agra, as the imperial city, has quasi-divine status as 'the centre of the state, the abode of the ladies of the holy harem, and the depository of the world's treasures'. While Mehr-un-Nisa spends the next few years living a retired life in the zenana under the care of Ruqayya Begum, Jahangir consolidates his rule and lobbies the various factions at court to isolate the Rajput supporters of his rebellious son Khusrau and finally imprisons and then partially blinds this charismatic but strangely obdurate son. In time, this leads to the weakening of the earlier Rajput-Chagatai clans and the rise of the Persian-Khurasani one. Jahangir's three other sons, Pervez, Khurram and Shahriyar, parse their ambitions and spend these dangerous years building up a network of supports, soldiers, and influence.

In 1611, preparations for the Navroz festival have overtaken the entire palace at Agra. This spring festival, celebrating the Persian solar year, was revived in Hindustan by Akbar and now under Jahangir it is an eighteen-day extravaganza meant to display the glory, generosity, and magnificence of the Mughal padshah. All around the courtyard are canopied awnings of gold cloth and the furnishings are an eclectic mix of European, Persian and Hindustani craft. On the walls of the enclosure are European paintings, which Jahangir is particularly fond of. Paintings of the King and Queen of England, the Countesses of Somerset and Salisbury, and a 'Citizen wife of London' flicker incongruously in the light of the candles and the smoke from the incense. On the floor of the courtyards are thick Persian carpets and all around the throne are unusual and magnificent gifts that all the noblemen are presenting to Jahangir. The women of the zenana can watch from behind the jaalis the audacious posturing of the noblemen who try to outdo each other in presenting as charming and unusual a gift as possible to their discerning and enthusiastic padshah. But the women have their own attractions in the zenana, for a meena bazaar has been set up as part of the Navroz celebrations. In the women's quarters, a long series of magnificent tented stalls has been set up where the wives of the noblemen as well as ordinary tradeswomen have set up their wares. Every evening, amongst the mansion gardens of the zenana, in the pale light of the moon and a thousand flickering candles, the women greet each other and marvel at the glittering treasures on offer from the distant reaches of the empire. It is a time of freedom and gregarious joy for the women who can chivvy each other and their customers away from the gaze of any man, for the only male allowed here is the padshah. Jahangir visits the meena bazaar and talks to all the tradeswomen, who are permitted to be as boisterous as they wish and these women, from all the corners of the Mughal empire, haggle with Jahangir, using their wit and charm to make him spend as much money as possible. The women are all unveiled, as there is no other man present, and it is in the meena bazaar in 1611 that Jahangir, now a respectable forty-two years old, sees Mehr-un-Nisa with Ruqayya Begum. Jahangir would have known who she was, since Mehr-un-Nisa's father and brother are already valued members of his entourage, so the circumstances of her family and widowhood are known to him. Speaking to her, Jahangir is now seduced by the beauty, grace and charm of this thirty-four-year-old widow and within two months Jahangir has married her and Mehr-un-Nisa has become Noor Mahal, 'Light of the Palace', in a mirroring of Noor-ud-Din, Jahangir's own title, 'Light of the Faith'.

Noor Mahal will be Jahangir's last legal wife and by 1616, she has become Noor Jahan, 'Light of the World'. They never have any children together and, indeed, by the standards of the day, Noor Jahan is a mature woman, but for the next sixteen years of his life Jahangir will never again search for distraction in a younger wife's charms. He has always been nurtured and cherished by a coterie of older women—Gulbadan, Haji Begum, Salima Sultan, Hamida Banu and his own milk mother—and in Noor Jahan Jahangir finds a felicitous blend of comforting, reassuring care and a woman with enormous talent, charisma and ability. Noor Jahan shares Jahangir's aesthetic sense and contributes in many ways to the expansion of his imperial vision and legacy. Within a few years, Noor Jahan is issuing royal farmans signed with her own seal, having gold coins struck in her name, engaging in trade and has a series of magnificent buildings constructed through the breadth of the empire. Exceptionally for a woman, drums are beaten before her advance and 'sometimes she would sit in the balcony of her palace, while the nobles would present themselves and listen to her dictates'. Noor Jahan's family, already influential, further prospers as she becomes more powerful. Itimad-ud-Daulah, temporarily disgraced because of charges of embezzlement, which a contemporary writer sarcastically notes when he says that 'in the taking of bribes he certainly was most uncompromising and fearless', is reinstated. Asaf Khan, Noor Jahan's brother, is honoured with the gift of one of Jahangir's special swords, the Sarandaz, 'Thrower of Head', and the atmosphere at the Mughal court becomes conducive to an increasing influx of Persian talent. Where once the Atka Khail and Chagatai reigned supreme, and then the Rajputs, the Persians now are increasingly powerful. But it is in conducting international trade that Noor Jahan is exceptionally successful and the quantum of wealth this creates for her gives Noor Jahan the financial reach to sponsor buildings, offer gifts, organize marriages and entertainments, and sponsor charity, on a scale rarely seen before in a Mughal woman. And a part of this trade is brought about by the persistent and often anguished efforts of Sir Thomas Roe.

Lured by the stories of the lustrous wealth of the Mughal empire, English factors are landing on Indian shores in tentative but doggedly increasing numbers in the early seventeenth century. Thomas Mitford, an English merchant, is breathlessly prescient when he writes to the EIC committee in 1614 that 'we could not have come in a more fit time, by reason of the wars betwixt the Portingals and the Indians', due to which, he adds, 'there had been very little or no commodities transported by sea'. Despite the skirmishing between the Indians and the Portuguese, however, the English merchants are treated shabbily when they first arrive. The often ragged adventurers and traders 'suffered blowes of the porters, base Peons, and beene thrust out by them with much scorne by head and shoulders without seeking satisfaction'. They are disregarded and bullied, and their insubstantial presents are derided and mocked and found wanting. And yet, they persist, for 'here is great store of goods in the country and at reasonable rates', is an English factor's admiring assessment. 'This is a very good country,' he insists, 'a very good air and a quiet sort of people. I should have been glad to spend my time in these parts.' Another merchant is dazzled because 'the country here is full of commodities' and when he writes to the Governor of the EIC, he struggles to think of goods from England which would find favour with the discerning locals. '[Y] our cloth [is] little respected', he mentions witheringly, 'your cases of looking glasses and knives are little enquired after in these parts... For the lead and iron I fear they will be forced to seek a new market for it.' It is only rare curiosities which may find favour he adds and 'vermilion, quicksilver and elephants' teeth are in great request and will prove good commodities in this place'. Instead, lacking goods that the Hindustanis may be interested in, it is silver that is exchanged at the Mughal court and silver bullion streams into the country. It is at this threshold moment, with the Portuguese star waning and immense riches awaiting, that the aristocratic Thomas Roe finds himself at the court of Jahangir in Ajmer in January 1616.

Roe discovers an atmosphere at court very different from the genial bonhomie of the earlier court of Akbar. At the durbar of Jahangir, where the padshah holds court between three and four in the afternoon, Roe notes the clear stratification of all the courtiers, everyone designated a place according to rank and function, like an elaborate theatre. Jahangir himself sits at an elevation, in the company of his grown sons, chief minister and fan bearers. On the wall behind him are pictures of Christ and the Virgin Mary. Ambassadors and men of high rank stand within a railed off canopied area below the padshah. Lower still, but still on a platform within a railed elevation are 'the meaner men, representing Gentry', while the common people are outside the railed sections altogether, standing at a distance. Everywhere there are rich carpets and canopies of velvet and silk and everyone gazes up at Jahangir and the great men of the empire, in an atmosphere of studied elegance and almost oppressive silence. Opposite the court are long golden bells which anyone seeking justice may ring to obtain Jahangir's attention.

Unlike the previous English visitors to the Mughal court, Roe is not a mere merchant but an official diplomat, perfectly familiar with the nuances of courtly etiquette. He has come armed with gifts, a letter from

King James, and an expense account for himself and his staff. Upon his vigorous refusal, Roe is excused the usual deferential full-body prostrations required at court, his firangi status offering him an immunity of sorts. Jahangir himself is genial and friendly and pleased to find a drinking companion. And yet, Roe is made quickly aware of his presents 'being too meane' and his presence at court supremely insubstantial. At the very same time as Roe's visit to the Mughal court, Jahangir is writing with satisfaction in his diary of a courtier, Dayanat Khan, who has offered him 'two pearl rosaries, two rubies, six large pearls, and one gold tray, to the value of 28,000 rupees'. Another courtier gives him a jewelled dagger with a yellow ruby (topaz), 'clear and bright', on its hilt half the size of a hen's egg. Jahangir in turn promotes the courtiers and also distributes enormous quantities of gifts himself—elephants, horses, cloths of gold, arms and jewels. This seamless offering of gifts to the padshah and his subsequent largesse are an essential ingredient of empire in Hindustan, a visible symbol of mutual dependence and honour. When Roe arrives at the court, the trade the English hanker for most desperately is in cotton textiles and indigo dye. Much to Roe's astonishment, he finds that noblewomen such as Maryam-uz-Zamani and Noor Jahan own ships and conduct their own trade with the Middle East and Africa. The influence of women is everywhere, Roe notes, from the women around Jahangir who 'guard him with manly weapons' to the more invisible ones who watch from within the zenana all the important goings-on of the court. They are also often present at the durbar, behind screens of marble jaalis, where they may listen to the proceedings and from where Noor Jahan does not hesitate to speak directly to the padshah. Roe realizes that it is Noor Jahan, more powerful than all the rest, who must first approve of his credentials before he is officially accepted at court. But Roe is hopelessly shackled by his need to be accepted as a serious contender and refuses to abide by the unavoidable custom of offering gifts to those in power. He realizes that his intransigence has disastrous consequences. 'The neglect of [Noor Jahan] these last years', he writes bitterly in a letter to the English merchant Thomas Kerridge, 'I have felt heavily'. Roe loathes this custom, which he equates to bribing, but nonetheless now scrambles for the most unusual and interesting objects that can be presented to

Noor Jahan. 'Fine needle work toys, fayre bone lace, cuttworke, and some handsome wrought wastcote, sweetbagges or cabinets will be most convenient', he urges Kerridge. 'I would add any faire china bedsteads or cabinets or trucks of Japan are here rich presents.' Roe discovers, to his dismay, that unless he has the favour of Noor Jahan, all his requests for trade concessions are summarily dismissed and ignored. In addition to the Portuguese and the Jesuits, who are consistent detractors, Roe also has to manoeuver against Asaf Khan, Noor Jahan's powerful brother, as well as Shah Khurram, whom Roe finds too 'proud', a touching underestimation of the man who would become the most magnificent of all the great Mughals of Hindustan.

Finally Roe is moved to observe that 'Noormahel fulfills the observation that in all actions of consequence in Court, a woman is not only always an ingredient, but commonly a principal drug of most virtue, and she shows that they are not incapable of conducting business, nor her self void of wit and subtlety.' Roe now assiduously courts Asaf Khan as a conduit to Noor Jahan's favours and finally, in October 1617, Roe is notified by a servant of the shahzaadi 'that she had moved the Prince [Khurram] for another farman that all her goods might be in her protection, and that she had obtained it, and was ready to send down her servant with that... that she would see that we should not be wronged.' In this manner, Noor Jahan becomes the 'Protectresse' of the English. Noor Jahan, naturally, never interacts with Roe directly, but through a network of servants and noblemen, including her brother Asaf Khan. She does, however, peer down through the bamboo screen in 1616 when the court prepares to move from Ajmer and Noor Jahan, delicate beauty and Persian aesthete, laughs at the sight of Roe, this curious Elizabethan gentleman with the strange whiskers, preposterous high collar and stockinged legs poking out from beneath his short, velvet cloak.

Roe is now tireless in his efforts to find gifts that might charm this discerning and powerful shahzaadi. Many of these items are hopelessly unsuitable to the climate and customs of Hindustan: there are steel knives that rust in the steamy monsoon, valuable horses and dogs that sicken and die, unsuitable and untouchable leather garments that develop mould, and woollen garments that are too rough and hot in a court that values exquisitely fine cottons and linens. But Roe does eventually find that European paintings, prints and drawings are most likely to find favour with Jahangir, who then asks his atelier to reproduce them, which they do with such finesse that Roe cannot make out the original from the copies. European art will thus seep into the artistic language of the Mughals, to be reproduced in miniatures, and embroidery and architecture. There will be a reverse trajectory to this artistic influence for within a couple of decades, a young Dutch draughtsman and painter by the name of Rembrandt will study the images brought back by the Jesuit priests and create remarkable Mughal-influenced drawings. For Noor Mahal, there are gems, embroidered cloths, beaver hats and English carriages. Noor Jahan's interest, or lack of it, for particular kinds of English goods substantially shapes the nature of English trade at this time, her interest lying solely in obtaining the most elegant luxury items for the Mughal court. While the English merchants are openly clamouring for Indian cottons and dyes, there is no reciprocal need from the Mughal court for English wares and Noor Jahan is aware of this. Jahangir, meanwhile, is most pleased with gifts of alcohol, unsurprisingly, and of two English mastiffs, who are given a palanquin and four servants to carry them around. Additions to the royal menagerie are particularly appreciated, for rare animals are prized by Jahangir. Included in this eclectic collection is an entire selection of albino animals including a North American turkey, an Abyssinian zebra, and a Sri Lankan orangutan. For Thomas Roe, however, though he is finally granted a farman to trade in 1618, and the first English factory is built in Surat, the exclusive trading rights that he has fought so hard for never materialize.

As for Noor Jahan, her trade with the English is only a small part of her commercial activity. She owns and rents trade ships and trades with the Dutch and the Portuguese, in addition to the English. She collects duties at Sikandarabad on goods coming from Bhutan and Bengal, raw silk, spikenard, borax, verdigris, ginger and fennel, and invests specifically in the commerce of indigo and embroidered cloths. 'The officers of Noor Jahan Begum, who built their Sarai there,' clarifies a Dutch merchant, Francisco Pelsaert, 'collect duties on all these goods before they can be shipped across the river, and also on innumerable kinds of grain, butter, and other provisions, which are produced in the eastern provinces.' She begins her construction activities as early as 1616, when she spends 200,000 rupees on the Noor Manzil gardens in Agra. She also invests in infrastructure which helps in the smooth functioning of her trade routes. In 1620, following a proclamation from Jahangir for mileage towers, kos minars, to be built along all major highways in a bid to ensure safe travel in the empire, Noor Jahan builds a monumental caravanserai outside Agra called the Serai Noor Mahal. While many caravanserai were built during the reign of Jahangir, the Serai Noor Mahal is particularly magnificent, reflecting the wealth and splendour of its patron. It has large carved gateways, compartments for travellers, a bathhouse and a mosque. Two thousand travellers at a time, along with their camels and horses, can camp inside the serai at no expense. In the serai there are 'servants, entrusted with the preparation of the food for guests, as well as doing all the other duties essential to comfort within the house, even to providing hot water for washing the feet'. All one has to do, specifies Manucci, is send for food from the nearby bazaar, since all other needs are met. 'If the guests have horses,' moreover, the servants 'are required also to cook mung or chick pea, which is given instead of the barley we feed such animals in Europe.' All this is done for just a small coin, which Manucci marvels at, admiring the servants' work ethic when he says that 'uncivilized and heathens though they are, they surpass our stable men and innkeepers of Europe' who apparently are much more voracious in their fees. At night, the huge gates to the serai are slammed shut and bolted, to guard against thieves and brigands. The guard shouts out a warning to all the travellers, to guard their belongings, picket their horses by the leg and stay vigilant against wild dogs 'for the dogs of Hindustan are very cunning and great thieves'. While most of the serais in the Punjab are relatively pedestrian, made from bricks, the Serai Noor Mahal is made from red sandstone, brought at great expense from the quarries at Fatehpur Sikri more than 300 miles away. The serai is decorated with traditional Islamic arabesques, but also with the Tree of Life and the flower pot of Persian iconography and elephants, peacocks and human figures reflecting the influence of Hindu art. There is also an inscription on the serai that proudly announces the name of the patron, the 'angel-like Noor Jahan

Begum' so that all the traders and travellers on this lucrative trade route between Agra and Lahore are reminded of the power and compassion of the Mughal shahzaadi.

The trade, revenues collected and exorbitant gifts offered to the queen make Noor Jahan an exceedingly wealthy woman. In 1622, upon the death of her father Itimad-ud-Daulah, Jahangir awards the entire estate of this fabulously wealthy man to Noor Jahan, completely bypassing the dead man's son, Asaf Khan. Noor Jahan is now the wealthiest woman in the Mughal empire and, arguably, in the world. Indeed Pieter van den Broecke, a Dutch cloth merchant, remarks that at the time of Jahangir's death in 1627, Noor Jahan had amassed wealth 'more than that left by the King' himself. Jahangir himself had dazzling amounts of wealth which Hawkins estimated at half a billion rupees, a clearly inflated figure, but nonetheless a reflection of the visible opulence of the Mughal empire.

The wealth that she creates allows Noor Jahan, as it does the other wealthy noblewomen, to buy the luxury items so prized by the court: perfumes, ornaments, rich costumes and paintings. But it also allows her to entertain lavishly, marking important occasions such as birthdays and seasonal holidays and also joyous occasions such as Shah Jahan's triumphant return from the Deccan. These feasts and entertainment are an extension of Jahangir's largesse and proclaim Noor Jahan's grandeur as a suitable reflection of the padshah's. Jahangir is particularly appreciative of his wife's exquisite, refined taste in all that she does. In 1621, in Kashmir, Jahangir is laid low by a severe attack of asthma. Desperate for relief he takes to drinking excessively, all through the day. Finally it is 'Noor Jahan Begum, whose skill and experience are greater than those of the physicians, especially as they are brought to bear through affection and sympathy', who manages to reduce Jahangir's dependence on wine. After he has recovered, Noor Jahan asks for a particular privilege, that of hosting the feast for Jahangir's solar weighing ceremony. This ceremony, a Hindu tradition introduced by Humayun, is carried out twice a year for the padshah's birthday. For his solar ceremony, the padshah is weighed against twelve articles: gold, quicksilver, silk, perfume, copper, mercury, drugs, ghee, rice-milk, seven kinds of grains, and salt. These articles are then distributed amongst the poor. The time of the weighing ceremony is precisely calculated by astrologers and as the padshah sits on the scales, the elderly men who hold up the scales recite prayers for him. Physicians check his health thoroughly and keep an account of their findings. Preparations for the ceremony begin two months in advance, as tents are erected and gifts organized, so for Noor Jahan to undertake this organization is a huge investment of money and a clear declaration of her supremacy. Earlier the solar weighings were held by Maryam-uz-Zamani, Jahangir's mother, but Noor Jahan is now padshah begum after the death of Salima Sultan, and her resplendence is unchallenged. 'In truth,' declares the admiring Jahangir, 'they prepared one (ceremony) which increased the astonishment of the beholders.' Though Noor Jahan has participated in these ceremonies before 'and knew what were the requirements of good fortune and prosperity', even so 'on this occasion she had paid greater attention than ever to adorn the assembly, and arrange the feast'. Jahangir has been sickly this past year, so Noor Jahan shows 'suitable kindnesses, such as dresses of honour, jeweled sword-belts, jeweled daggers, horses, elephants, and trays full of money', towards the servants who have attended to the sick padshah. And even though Jahangir grumbles that the physicians have 'not done good service', they also receive presents in jewels and cash. There is a muted hush amongst the courtiers when the padshah's weight is announced for it has gone down compared to the previous year and this is an unhappy fact. Jahangir notes that his weight in the past year, due to his illness, has gone down by ten kilograms, to sixty-six kilograms.

Jahangir will struggle for years with his ill-health, exacerbated by an unshakeable opium and wine habit. It is telling that his very first mention of Noor Jahan in his biography is of an incident following days of fever and debilitating headache. Not wanting to alarm the country with news of his health, he does not even consult the court hakims and tells no one of his illness. 'A few days pass in this manner,' he writes unhappily, 'and I only imparted this to Noor-Jahan Begam, than whom I did not think anyone was fonder of me.' In Noor Jahan, Jahangir finds the ideal companion. A mature woman who cares for him and understands his foibles and his uncertain moods, as the older women in his life have always done. With an experienced woman's intuitive tact and grace, she knows how to navigate his sudden violences, his inexplicable cruelty and his obdurate dependence on drugs. Jahangir himself is surprisingly candid about his drinking. He describes how his habit grew 'to twenty cups of doubly distilled-spirits, fourteen during the daytime and the remainder at night'. Such is the eventual decrepitude of his condition that 'in the crapulous state from the excessive rambling of my hand I could not drink from my own cup, but others had to give it me to drink'. Finally, Jahangir is able to reduce his drinking, down to six cups of a wine and spirit mixture. Drinking to excess is a veritable epidemic at the Mughal court at this time and the most common cause of death amongst the Mughal nobility, followed by stomach ailments. Francisco Pelsaert describes a corroborating scene in the audience hall when Jahangir is drinking with his noblemen his three permitted cups of evening drink. Once the courtiers have left, the 'Queen comes with the female slaves and they undress him, chafing and fondling him as if he were a little child; for his three cups have made him so "happy" that he is more disposed to rest than to keep awake'. Though Pelsaert writes with scathing judgement, Noor Jahan does indeed care for Jahangir as one would a child, with gentle charm and coddling, but also with firm guidance when required. In this vulnerable state, it is also essential for Jahangir to have someone by him whom he can trust implicitly. Khusrau is a fugitive but ceaseless presence at the periphery of Jahangir's life, a shadowy reminder of a challenge to his kingship and his own guilt at his treatment of his son. The Mughal court has become a place of ragged ambitions and plundering intrigue and Noor Jahan will always, with calm infallibility, have the padshah's best intentions at heart and his imperial legacy in sight.

In their assessment of Hindustan and the Mughal court, English memoirists often struggle between awe at the richness of the lifestyle and furnishings and a certain repugnance for what is considered 'foreign', especially in contrast with what is considered high good taste in late Elizabethan England. When faced with the cool, open and airy spaces of Mughal interiors, it is lamented that 'they have no furniture of the kind we delight in, such as tables, stools, benches, cupboards, bedsteads etc.' There is no furniture of the sort admired in England because it is not required, all Mughal private life being carried out on immaculate takhts laid on the floors, with elaborate bolsters and cushions. No doubt a Mughal observer of a classic Elizabethan home would find it oppressive, claustrophobic and dank, with its oak panelling, elaborately carved furniture and cluttered spaces. Roe is similarly torn between admiration and distaste when he visits a mahal, a woman's rooms, when the inhabitant is absent, and finds it 'so diverse...[and its pieces] so unstable that it was rather patched than glorious, as if it seemed to strive to show all, like a lady that with her plate sett on a Cupboard her embroidered slippers'. Pelsaert is more damning when he writes that 'their mahals are adorned internally with lascivious sensuality, wanton and reckless festivity, superfluous pomp, inflated pride, and ornamental daintiness'. In their harsh judgement, the men inadvertently expose their own fetid imaginings at the 'sensual and wanton' activities they suppose take place within.

But the Mughals, and most certainly their women, are supremely indifferent to the opinion of these bizarre, prancing foreigners, though they are occasionally delighted by occasional European novelties such as the pencil and the eraser. Noor Jahan continues to be a dominant player in court politics and is also capable of being a talented and constant companion to Jahangir in all his activities. She is by his side in Ajmer when he participates at the urs at Moinuddin Chishti's shrine. Jahangir has a large cauldron made in Agra and brought to Ajmer during the saint's death celebrations. The padshah 'ordered them to cook food for the poor in that pot, and collect together the poor of Amir to feed them whilst I was there', Thomas Coryat, an English traveller, is surprised to note. He also observes Jahangir 'kindling a fire with his own hands and his Normahal under that immense...brasse-pot, and made kitcherie for 5000 poor, taking out the first platter with his own hands and serving one; Normahal the second; and so his ladies all the rest'. Noor Jahan often accompanies him on the hunt, which Jahangir is very fond of, and excels at it. She understands his flamboyant need for entertainment as distraction from his many ills and occasional bad humour and organizes the most resplendent feasts. Even to the details of her involvement in embroidery design, clothing and jewellery, she demonstrates a fine taste which reflects Jahangir's. Noor Jahan loves the colour white, and favours clothes in paler colours, as opposed to the more riotous tastes of the Rajput and other Hindu wives. She invents the farsh-e-chandani, a spreading of snow-white sheets instead of carpets in a room. She also invents the dodamni, a light cloth weighing two dams, and the pachtoliya, a cloth weighing five tolas, as a head covering for women, the high Turkish hats having long disappeared from the Mughal court. Jahangir too is an aesthete and passionately interested in the clothes and jewellery worn at the court. All his clothes are designed expressly only for him, and he wears them just once. Certain textiles and garments are reserved solely for his use and no courtier may use them. He introduces the fashion of embroidery on the collar and the hems of the long sleeves of the qaba. He also starts the fashion for earrings for men when in 1615, after a recovery which he believes he owes to Moinuddin Chishti, he has pearl earrings made which signified that he was a slave of Moinuddin. All the nobles and courtiers immediately do the same and now it is de rigueur for the elegant men of the Mughal court to wear earrings. Even Asmat Begum, Noor Jahan's mother, contributes to the elegance of the courtly life by making perfumes. The Mughals love perfumes, having a visceral hate for the sweat that is provoked by the intolerably hot climate of Agra and Delhi. They bathe frequently and change their clothes every day, casting off their day-old clothes, handing them on to their servants. Incense is burned throughout the day through the rooms of the zenana and fresh flowers are brought in from the flower gardens to perfume the rooms. Chameli, mogra, champa, nargis, harsinghar gulab, kamal and malti are some of the flowers grown in the palace gardens and scent is also extracted from these flowers. One day, while Asmat Begum is making rose water, she finds that a scum is formed on the top of this hot concoction and that by collecting the scum bit by bit, she is able to gather a potent oil of such strength 'that if one drop be rubbed on the palm of the hand it scents a whole assembly and it appears as if many red rosebuds had bloomed at once'. Jahangir is delighted by this perfume, which Salima Sultan tactfully names Itr-e-Jahangiri. 'It restores hearts that have gone,' exclaims the jaded padshah, 'and brings back withered souls'. Noor Jahan and her talented family surround the emperor with beauty and elegance and it is not surprising that according to the eighteenth-century biographer Shah Nawaz Khan 'the emperor used to say that until she came to his house, he had not understood domestic pleasures or the spirituality of marriage'.

In the second decade of her marriage, Noor Jahan encourages and participates in another beloved activity of Jahangir's, one that leads to a more ephemeral and subtle legacy—the springtime migration of the Mughal court to Kashmir. Jahangir has detested the dry heat of Agra for a very long time, and now that he is getting older, over fifty years old, his intolerance has become chronic. 'The air of Agra is warm and dry,' he writes critically, 'physicians say that it depresses the spirits and induces weakness.' Pelsaert uncharitably attributes Jahangir's hankering for Kashmir to his opium addiction. 'The reason of the King's special preference for this country [Kashmir],' he writes, 'is that when the heat in India increases, his body burns like a furnace owing to his consumption of excessively strong drink and opium.' Agra has become a heavily populated town with narrow, crowded and dirty streets. The noble mansions along the riverside are magnificent, with carefully tended gardens, but the rest of the town is a chaotic warren. The common people build homes of mud and thatch 'which cause often and terrible fires'. In summer, the desert winds bring grazing, choking sand, adding to the misery of the season. The springtime exodus to Kashmir therefore becomes a joyful and regular part of Mughal courtly life from 1620 onwards. The journey up to Srinagar takes months, and is sometimes perilous. The weather is unpredictable and springtime thunderstorms are not rare. 'On that night a great wind blew and a black cloud hid the face of the sky,' writes Jahangir of one such occasion. 'The rain was of such violence... It turned to hail, and every hailstone was the size of a hen's egg.' The bridge across the Jhelum shatters from the violence of the wind and the rain and Jahangir 'with the inmates of the harem, crossed in a boat.' But Kashmir is a 'garden of eternal spring' and the streams, meadows and cool breezes are worth the effort for Jahangir and his zenana. There are wild roses, violets, narcissus and herbs. There are flowering almond and peach groves, saffron fields and tulips. Even the houses of Kashmir are organically feral, for the Kashmiris cover their roofs with earth and plant tulip bulbs which bloom in the spring. Jahangir is the first of the Mughals to staunchly prefer the Indian flowers and fruits above all others, even the Kabuli ones. 'From the excellence of its sweet scented flowers,' Jahangir writes, 'one may prefer the fragrances of India to those of the flowers of the whole world.' He further describes all the traditionally beloved Indian symbols such as the Indian water lily, the koel and the lotus loving bees. At the Dal lake in Srinagar Jahangir builds the Shalimar gardens, an evanescent dream made of cascading waterfalls, perfumed flowering trees and bushes and eternal pavilions. It is an elegy in flowers and stone to the old Timurid dream that Babur craved. An ordered and genteel garden in hostile Hindustan. Noor Jahan and her family enthusiastically join Jahangir in this imperial vision and, over the next few years, in an orgy of construction, they will build some of the most beautiful gardens of Hindustan. In Srinagar Asaf Khan builds the magnificent Nishat Bagh and Noor Jahan adds to the Noor Afza. She also builds the Pathar Masjid on the banks of the Jhelum in Srinagar. Unlike the other mosques in Srinagar, which are made of wood, the Pathar Masjid is made of polished limestone, altogether more durable, and Noor Jahan becomes the first Mughal woman to lay claim to Kashmir. In Agra she builds a riverfront garden, the Bagh-i-Noor Afshan, with a view of the gently flowing river where the moonlight is reflected in fractal geometry while the cool air rises off the water. These pleasure gardens increase the uncensored space allowed to Noor Jahan and the other Mughal women to enact their lives. In these cool and fragrant gardens they may entertain each other and receive guests. They live in these garden palaces for days at a time, holding poetry competitions, entertaining the padshah and organizing elaborate outdoor feasts. They may remain alone, to write poetry or read books. There are carpets and cushions beneath the flowering shrubs. Wine is drunk, paan and opium are eaten and the hookah is passed around. There are fruit trees, apple, apricots, pears, almond and cherry in Kashmir, mango, ber, guava and pomegranate in Agra. It is an area of unrestricted beauty and uninhibited enjoyment, a counterpart to the strict formality of the durbar.

Noor Jahan is now at the height of her power and influence at the Mughal court. Her family have also become immensely successful, marrying into the Persian nobility and gaining steady promotions under Jahangir, none more so than Itimad-ud-Daulah. As early as 1617, Jahangir honours him 'as an intimate friend by directing the ladies of the harem not to veil their faces before him'. There are very few men, apart from the padshah, his young sons and the eunuchs, who are allowed to visit the women of the zenana when they are without their veils so this is a high honour indeed. Itimad-ud-Daulah is appointed prime minister and granted a flag and a drum and, as a special favour, is permitted to sound his drums in the royal presence. In 1619, as part of elaborate Navroz celebrations, Itimad-ud-Daulah presents to Jahangir a magnificent throne, made by a Frenchman and erstwhile counterfeiter of precious stones. Augustin Hiriart is hired by Jahangir for his skill in making beautiful, jewelled objects, and at the Mughal court he is renamed Hunarmand from the Persian hunarmandi or skilful. The throne that Hunarmand has created takes three years to build and costs a staggering 450,000 rupees and Jahangir is well pleased. Jahangir is able to delegate most matters to his talented wife while he occupies himself with the matters that interest him the most: the beauty of the natural world, his ateliers with their painters of miniatures and the aggrandizement of the imperial image through the visual arts. Jahangir consults Noor Jahan, Itimad-ud-Daulah or Asaf Khan on most matters and the biographer Shah Nawaz Khan agrees that 'the disposal of the affairs of the kingdom were in her hands'. Such is her power that 'except for the khutba not having been read in her name, she exercised all the prerogatives of royalty'. The farmans she issues are wide ranging and numerous, similar in scope to Jahangir's edicts. Moreover, whereas the earlier Mughal women such as Hamida Banu and Harkha Bai had simply had their names written on their seals, Noor Jahan's seal on her farmans reads; 'By the light of the sun of the emperor Jahangir, the bezel of the seal of Noor Jahan the Empress of the age has become resplendent like the moon.'

In 1621, Asmat Begum, Noor Jahan's mother, dies and Itimad-ud-Daulah is devastated. Within three months of his wife's death, Itimad-ud-Daulah dies too and for Noor Jahan, this is a shattering loss. She inherits all of her father's riches and becomes fabulously wealthy but she acquires two powerful new enemies. In the next few years, as Jahangir becomes increasingly ill, his body faltering under the years of assault from wine and opium, various factions across the empire swirl and coalesce together to stake a claim for the Mughal throne. Asaf Khan's daughter, the young Arjumand Banu has been married for ten years to Khurram Mirza, now Shah Jahan. Disinherited from his own father's fortunes and wary of his sister's ambition for her daughter Ladli Begum, Asaf Khan aligns himself with his son-in-law. Noor Jahan, meanwhile, has married Ladli Begum to the youngest of Jahangir's sons, the handsome but imbecilic Shahriyar. The unfortunate Khusrau is given over to the uncertain care of Shah Jahan, who soon has him murdered, for the Mughal empire has now become worth killing for. The days when Babur encouraged his sons to get along with each other are long gone. There are betrayals and alliances and flickering violence. Noor Jahan enters the fray gallantly, at one point riding on elephant-back to rescue her beleaguered husband, who is practically being held prisoner by his erstwhile faithful retainer, Mahabat Khan, and his army of 5,000 Rajputs, because of the high-stakes intrigues surrounding Jahangir's sons. But Shah Jahan has gathered a huge following during his years on campaigns for his father and upon Jahangir's death, in 1627, he becomes Padshah Ghazi of the Mughal empire. Noor Jahan, vanquished, retires to Lahore with Ladli Begum, who is soon widowed when Shahriyar is murdered upon the orders of Shah Jahan. Mother and daughter live in quiet retirement and Shah Jahan decrees a generous yearly allowance of 200,000 rupees for Noor Jahan. All other signs of Noor Jahan's influence and power, however, are meticulously erased. He bans the use of Noor Jahan's gold coins, under pain of death, and has all her coins melted. Her royal drums fall silent and the imperial elephants are no longer hers to command. Noor Jahan displays the same grace and dignity in retirement as she did when she was Padshah Begum of Hindustan. She dies eighteen years later, and steps into immortality as the most charismatic and influential of the Mughal queens. But before her death, Noor Jahan creates one last piece of art—the ultimate reflection of her flawless aesthetics and her visionary and unique artistic expression. She builds a tomb, from her own funds, for her parents at Agra called Itimad-ud-Daulah's tomb, which is so beautiful it will be used as an inspiration for a later, more famous, monument to love.

When Noor Jahan begins the tomb for her parents in 1623, she has the wealth, the resources and the assurance to build a monument exactly to her specifications and aesthetic sensibility. The exact extent of her wealth is not known, but her brother, Asaf Khan, when he dies in 1641, leaves behind a fortune estimated at 2.5 crore rupees, or 12.5

billion rupees in today's money. Noor Jahan, as the richest woman in the land, would certainly have commanded an equal amount of wealth, if not more. The exquisite and jewel-like monument she creates with this wealth is both absolutely unique for its time, and also outstanding in its syncretic and seamless use of Persian, Mughal and Hindustani elements. This small and supremely gorgeous tomb is the very first of the Mughal tombs to be made entirely of white marble rather than the red sandstone favoured until now. White, Noor Jahan's favourite colour, gives the tomb an air of pristine purity, which is then further enhanced with the second unique innovation of this tomb: inlay work in the pietra dura technique that covers almost the entire surface of the marble facade. Meanwhile, the interior of the two-tiered mausoleum is completely covered with inlay decorations of astounding profusion and delicacy. The effect is that of a miniature jewel box which has been breathed upon by a careless djinn to attain monumental proportions. Even the floor is covered in a carpet-like geometric pattern and the space resembles a richly furnished and elegant room, in which light shimmers and floats gently, not a stark and cold mausoleum. Light and air are allowed in through the Gujarati-influenced intricately carved jaali panels that cover the windows of the upper pavilion. This light that glows against the sumptuous colours of the inlaid stones is a reminder of Noor Jahan's imperial and symbolic association with light since she is, after all, the 'light of the world', and also a resplendent invocation of the divine light of paradise.

The decorations in semi-precious stones inside the upper pavilion are bewildering in their variety and opulence. There are Persian-inspired wine vessels, water ewers, fruit trays with grapes and pomegranates, and cypress trees. But there are also animal representations, extremely rare in Mughal architecture. There are fish, birds, ducks and deer. And finally there are also, for the first time in Mughal art, single flowers accentuated by being placed against an empty white background. The exuberance of flowers that Jahangir and Noor Jahan saw in their springtime trips to Kashmir, the tulips, the narcissi, the roses and the violets, are famously reflected in the miniature paintings that Jahangir sponsors. But they are also present in the tomb of Itimad-ud-Daulah where Noor Jahan brings her beloved Kashmir valley into the Gangetic plains. Against the pure white panels of marble, these single flowers are a bright red colour. Red, in Noor Jahan's Persian culture is a symbol of suffering and death. But in her homeland of Hindustan, it is the imperial colour and only padshahs and their favoured heirs may have red tents. Perhaps it is Noor Jahan's final tribute to the eternal glory of her father, who overcame such inauspicious beginnings to walk by the side of the most powerful man in Hindustan.

Noor Jahan owed her meteoric rise to power to her status as the wife of the padshah. From the time that Jahangir dies, her powerful charisma vanishes, like dew on the misty mornings in her flower gardens at Agra. It is poignant that the most ephemerally beautiful and enduring monument Noor Jahan builds is not to the memory of Jahangir, but to her beloved parents, whose warm abiding presence was the bedrock upon which she built her legacy. Noor Jahan will spend eighteen years in charmless obscurity in Lahore, and it will be a galling reality to a woman who once commanded ships and ambassadors. As Shah Jahan settles into Agra and makes it the imperial capital, Noor Jahan may have taken some comfort from the fact that he was circled by a luminescent series of buildings, the Noormahal Serai, the Noor Afza gardens with their pleasure pavilion and, further away, Itimad-ud-Daulah's tomb, all built through the wealth and the grace of her patronage.

MUMTAZ MAHAL AND A LOVE SUPREME

When the fifteen-year-old Khurram Mirza, still known fondly to his father as Baba Khurram, becomes engaged to the fourteen-year-old Arjumand Banu Begum in Lahore in 1607, it is the most prosaic of arrangements between a talented Mughal prince and the most promising Persian family at Jahangir's court. The bride is the daughter of Abu-al-Hassan Yamin-al-Daulah and the niece of Mehr un-Nisa, soon to become Noor Jahan. She is also the granddaughter of Ghiyas Beg, who is now celebrated as Itimad-ud-Daulah, Pillar of the Government. This alliance thus solders the cause of a talented, hard-working and ambitious family of impeccable Persian lineage to the Mughal throne and romance is a desultory, irrelevant notion. And yet this marriage will give rise to the most intemperate assessments of this celebrated union, tethered by the building of the most expensive and glorious 'monument to love' the world has ever seen. But the journey to the building of the Taj Mahal is not straightforward. It involves monstrous egos, a flawless aesthetic vision, profligacy and also, fragile as the bulbul's song, love.

After Arjumand Banu and Khurram are engaged, five long years go by. While Jahangir's oldest son Khusrau Mirza rebels and is defeated by Jahangir, Khurram steadily gains in independence and authority. He is given the right to his own drums and standard, and a separate establishment at Agra and still Arjumand Banu waits. Even more provocatively for Arjumand Banu, Khurram is married to another woman in 1609, the daughter of Mirza Muzaffar Husayn Safavi, a direct descendant of Shah Ismail of Persia. No explanation is ever given for the excessively long engagement of Arjumand Banu. This young woman waits in Lahore, certainly dismayed by the passing years, as Khurram begins his implacable trajectory to glory. But in 1611, Mehr-un-Nisa marries Jahangir and becomes Noor Jahan,

Light of the World. Within six months, Noor Jahan has become one of the most powerful women of the empire and the fortunes of this émigré Persian family will be changed forever. All obstacles, astrological or otherwise, to Noor Jahan's niece's wedding are removed and Arjumand Banu, nineteen years old, is married to the prince, now Sultan Khurram, in a month-long celebration in March 1612 at Agra.

For the next nineteen years of her married life, Arjumand Banu will be the constant companion of a man who will be ceaselessly, restlessly, on the move. Sultan Khurram, only the third son, will not waver in his determination to inherit his father's throne, and will use his considerable energy, military acumen and relentless will to remove all possible impediments in his way. One of the first such obstructions the young mirza must attend to is the Rana of Mewar, Amar Singh, the grandson of the ruler who had evaded capture by Akbar in an earlier time by escaping into the hills and founding a capital at Udaipur. To deal with this decidedly evasive and irksome opponent, Khurram and his entire entourage and zenana shift to the fort at Ajmer. Khurram garrisons hills previously thought to be impervious and relentlessly harries the rana, taking hostage the most prominent of the Sisodia family until Amar Singh finally capitulates. Amar Singh presents himself to Khurram and this proud old rana asks that he never be required to pay obeisance to the padshah himself, offering his son Karan Singh instead. These conditions are accepted by the Mughals, who know only too well the prickly Rajput temperament and, indeed, Jahangir is delighted with this proposal and adopts it with gusto and writes that 'as it was necessary to win the heart of Karan, who was of a wild nature and had never seen assemblies and had lived amongst the hills, I every day showed him some fresh favour'.

While Khurram is busy bringing the whole of Rajasthan within the Mughal fold, Mumtaz Mahal, as Arjumand Banu is now known, has four children in four years in Ajmer, two daughters and two sons. Each birth is meticulously recorded by their grandfather Jahangir in his autobiography. These are gilded years for Mumtaz Mahal. Her young husband is invincible in everything he does and is beloved by Jahangir above all his brothers. When Khurram returns in triumph from his campaigns in Mewar, he is greeted with exceptional warmth by Jahangir and Khurram honours his earlier pledge to donate 1,000 gold mohurs to the Chishti shrine of the saint Moinuddin. Mumtaz Mahal's own family prospers every day, their fierce ambition a reservoir of strength and comfort for the young woman. During the Navroz festivities of 1609, Mumtaz Mahal's father is given an honorific title, Asaf Khan, which was the title given to the chief minister of Prophet Solomon himself. But in 1616, tragedy walks softly into the palace at Ajmer and Mumtaz Mahal loses her firstborn daughter, Hur-al-Nisa, to smallpox. Jahangir is so distraught by the death of this grandchild that he cannot even bring himself to write about the event in his biography, making Itimad-ud-Daulah, the great-grandfather, write it down instead. Jahangir is inconsolable for days, refusing to attend to his courtiers, but very soon after the tragedy, Mumtaz Mahal gives birth to her fourth child, the future Shah Shuja.

In the zenana at Ajmer, Mumtaz Mahal is surrounded by capable, distinguished women who help her raise her children and run the household of Shah Khurram. The children all have wet nurses, chosen for their merits and family name. Mumtaz Mahal's eldest surviving daughter, Jahanara, has for wet nurse Huri Khanum Begum, the wife of an accomplished courtier. Her education is also carefully supervised and entrusted to an exceptionally talented woman—Sati-un-Nisa Khanum. Sati-un-Nisa has been brought from Persia to the Mughal court by her brother, Abu Talib, poet laureate at Jahangir's court, after the death of her husband. Sati-un-Nisa is a talented woman from a highly accomplished family of physicians and scholars. She is acknowledged by all who know her to be an erudite, charming woman with a working knowledge of medicine. The ancestral homes of Sati-un-Nisa and Mumtaz Mahal, Amol and Qazvin, are just 200 kilometres apart in Persia and there would have been the intimacy of a shared language, a beloved homeland lost and remembered. Arriving in Hindustan, she is immediately taken in by Mumtaz Mahal, following the tradition of the imperial patronage of deserving, widowed women. She is 'adorned with an eloquent tongue, and knowledge of etiquette, and knows housekeeping and medicine', and so is quickly promoted over all the older servants. The more fulsome praise of the *Shahjahanama* says that she is 'chaste and innocent', and that it is due to her 'confidence, eloquent tongue, excellent service and noble etiquette' that she serves

Mumtaz Mahal. She is entrusted with Mumtaz Mahal's seal and as she can read Persian and recite the Quran, she becomes tutor to Jahanara.

Jahangir continues to take an intense, avid interest in Khurram's young family, especially Shah Shuja, who has been entrusted to Noor Jahan. The child, writes Jahangir, 'towards whom I have so much affection that he is dearer to me than life' suffers from infantile epilepsy. 'His insensibility,' writes the distraught grandfather, 'took away my senses.' When all other remedies fail, Jahangir, in utter desperation, makes a vow 'that I would thenceforward not harm any living thing with my own hand'. This is a momentous sacrifice for the padshah, who spends all his spare time in Ajmer hunting near the lakes and forests of Pushkar. Shah Shuja momentarily recovers, and Jahangir is true to his vow. Two years later Shah Shuja 'had an eruption so violent that water would not go down his throat and his life was despaired of'. Jahangir is once again desolate and calls for the royal astrologer, Jotik Ray. The astrologer assures Jahangir that the child would be spared, and that another child would die in his stead, because of 'the great affection for the child' that Jahangir has. Shah Shuja does, indeed, recover and another son of Khurram, Sultan Afroz, dies at Burhanpur. The delighted Jahangir has Jotik Ray weighed against money and rewarded with the cash.

The child whose life is so cavalierly traded for Shah Shuja's is born to the third wife of Khurram. In 1617, Khurram marries the daughter of Shahnawaz Khan. This is, once again, a political marriage, for Shahnawaz is the son of Abdur Rahim Khan-e-Khanan, one of the most influential noblemen of the court. It is evident that Khurram maintains the most cursory of relations with the two other women he marries, apart from Mumtaz Mahal, fathering just the one child with each. Mumtaz Mahal, on the other hand, will bear Khurram fourteen children in nineteen years of marriage. This in itself is not so very unusual for a woman in the seventeenth century. Mumtaz Mahal's exact contemporary, Henrietta Maria of France who is the consort of King Charles I of England, bears her husband nine children, till Charles I is executed. Noblewomen in Hindustan, moreover, do not nurse their own children so that natural form of contraception is unavailable to them and yearly pregnancies are quite the norm. What is unusual, for the polygamous Mughals, is this intense, intimate and erotic bond between a man and one wife, for the entire duration of their married life. The Mughals before Khurram have not distinguished themselves as being particularly amorous husbands. Babur is much more invested in the companionship of his men-at-arms and even Humayun, who shares a close relationship with Hamida Banu, marries a new wife on his return to Hindustan and lives with her, fathering six children in nine years with her, while Hamida Banu remains at Kabul. Akbar has few children and does not distinguish any one particular wife, no mention being made of the women in any way. Jahangir's love for Noor Jahan is based on a nurturing, rather than a passionate, relationship, and no children are ever born to them. But Mumtaz Mahal's seven surviving children, and only hers, will together shape the destiny of Hindustan. They will build cities and write poetry and fight battles that will resonate with their impossible dreams and their destructive longings. No other woman in Mughal history will so exclusively and so extravagantly capture a Mughal padshah's love, and influence the course of history through the ambition of her children.

There are other examples of an exclusive, mutually binding love in Mumtaz Mahal's family. Itimad-ud-Daulah and his wife, Asmat Begum, are so devoted to each other that upon the death of Asmat Begum, Jahangir's wazir gives up the will to live. 'From the day his companion (wife) attained to the mercy of God he cared no longer for himself,' agrees Jahangir, 'but melted away from day to day.' Jahangir tries to console the old man but 'in his heart he grieved at the separation, and at last, after three months and twenty days, he passed away'. For Mumtaz Mahal, caught in the weave and whirl of empire consolidation, it will mean uncompromising relocation every few years, so as to be close to Shah Khurram, always in the furthest reaches of the unfurling empire. From the end of 1616 onwards, equipped with the English carriage, Bansi-badan the elephant, and the title Shah Sultan Khurram, it will mean travelling to Burhanpur, to subdue the ever-recalcitrant Malik Ambar and the Sultans of the Deccan.

For the next decade, Burhanpur, in modern-day Madhya Pradesh and gateway city to the Deccan, is the capital of Shah Khurram's court. Mumtaz Mahal, her children and retinue, settle into the imposing Badshahi Qila, a fort built by the Faruqi dynasty by a bend in the river Tapti. Shah

Khurram renovates the fort, adding a Deewan-e-khaas, a Deewan-e-aam and an exquisitely decorated hammam for the women of the zenana. In 1617 Mumtaz Mahal's fifth child, Roshanara Begum, is born at Burhanpur amongst the secretive corridors and intricate courtyards of the Badshahi Qila. Under the patronage of the Mughals of Shah Khurram's court, Burhanpur becomes a lively centre of commerce. There are already many madrasas here and it is a city of scholarly excellence. Abdur Rahim Khan-e-Khanan, the young boy who was adopted by Akbar when his father Bairam Khan was murdered, now an old general in Jahangir's army, has lived in Burhanpur for many years, lending it gravitas and power. Now weavers from Sind and Thatta stream into Burhanpur and they provide beautiful printed cottons for the insatiable court. But Shah Khurram does not remain long in Burhanpur, returning to Jahangir's court at Mandu in triumph in 1617 and earning the title Shah Jahan. Mumtaz Mahal accompanies Shah Jahan everywhere, often pregnant. She gives birth to her sixth child, Aurangzeb, in Dohad, a small village en route from Gujarat to Ujjain, and three months later Mumtaz Mahal is pregnant again. In 1620 the entire Mughal court is on the move yet again, this time heading for Kashmir.

In 1620, Kashmir is ablaze with the delicate blossoms of the almond and peach trees. Mumtaz Mahal is surrounded by her family and children and these are pristine months, filled with beauty and peace. Itimad-ud-Daulah is Jahangir's trusted adviser and Mumtaz's father, Asaf Khan, is steadily gaining in influence. Noor Jahan is Mumtaz Mahal's constant companion and Jahangir tends to his frail health, noting the black tulips blooming on the roof of the Jami mosque. These powerful, volatile personalities hold their precarious ambitions in abeyance for now, and a shallow peace reigns. The only moment of sharp disquietude for Jahangir is when the four-year-old Shah Shuja suffers a fall from the palace window. Jahangir 'ran out in a state of bewilderment' when he hears this news and 'for a long time holding him in my affectionate embrace' he is amazed to find the child unhurt. He distributes alms in thanks for this divine favour and keeps a close, watchful guard on the small boy. 'His nurses', writes Jahangir with anger, 'must have been very careless', and one imagines the quaking terror of these unfortunate women under the wrathful gaze of this unforgiving and unpredictably violent padshah.

These months in Kashmir in 1620 are a mirage for the Mughal royal family. The subterranean currents of distrust, jealousy and spiking ambition are about to be exposed to the clear light of day. Jahangir is over fifty years old and now often ailing. This is respectable old age for the seventeenth century, further exacerbated by Jahangir's lifelong addiction to alcohol and opium. Shah Jahan, almost thirty and with decades of military experience, is watchful and vigilant about his right to the throne. When news arrives in Kashmir that Malik Ambar, yet again, now allied with the Sultans of the Deccan, is attacking Mughal forces in Burhanpur, Jahangir wants to send Shah Jahan to deal with the situation. But Shah Jahan is suddenly loath to travel so far from the Mughal court with his father ill and surrounded by potentially powerful claimants to the throne. Khusrau Mirza, though partially blinded, is still a potent symbol and, allied to Noor Jahan, could be indestructible. So Shah Jahan agrees to ride south to the Deccan, but on one condition. He gives up alcohol and has his store of wine thrown into the Chambal River and his gold and silver goblets broken and distributed to the poor, but he asks that Khusrau be handed over to him, supposedly to join in the campaign but really as assurance that he would not be used to make a claim for the throne. So Shah Jahan rides south, more than a thousand miles away, with Mumtaz Mahal once again pregnant. He will not see Jahangir alive again and his days of being the beloved heir and cherished son of his father are over. Shah Jahan has seen in Noor Jahan a perfect reflection of his own ambition and talent and is unnerved. Noor Jahan has never been coy about the power and wealth she commands, carving it into stone and coaxing it out of her flower gardens and stamping it onto her gold mohurs. For the man who will one day be Shahenshah Al-Sultan al'-Azam, King of the World, this untainted ambition in a woman whose aim is not perfectly aligned to the enhancement of his own glory is unacceptable.

Mumtaz Mahal is a very different sort of woman altogether. She is a cultured and refined woman, certainly, a beautiful one, most probably, and a charming and talented one, no doubt, to have captivated a man like Shah Jahan for so many years. But she is, essentially, a profoundly voiceless woman. Unlike many other Mughal women, and clearly unlike Noor Jahan, she leaves behind no poetry, no biography, no architecture, no garden, nor any daring deed in battle. What she leaves for posterity she cleaves out of her own flesh, and bones and blood. She leaves seven living children, Jahanara, Dara Shikoh, Shah Shuja, Roshanara, Aurangzeb, Murad Baksh and Gauhara. These children, their ecstatic visions and vicious battles, their supreme confidence and disastrous rivalries, will chart the course of Hindustani history.

Over the next few years, there are increasing signs of the different currents that eddy and foam around the ever more glittering throne of the Mughals. Noor Jahan marries her daughter, Ladli Begum, to the youngest and most inept of Jahangir's sons, Shahriyar Mirza. Far away in the Deccan, Shah Jahan reacts with violence to this realignment of loyalties and has the ill-fated Khusrau Mirza killed, and this is the first time that brother kills brother in the bloody fight for the Mughal throne. These are also brutal years for Mumtaz Mahal and four of her five next children do not survive more than a few years. Along with Sati-un-Nisa, she begins setting aside and collecting gems, cash, jewels and brocades for the marriages of the elder princes, Dara Shikoh and Shah Shuja. For Mumtaz Mahal is a wealthy woman with a yearly allowance of one million rupees. She must keep the elaborate and expensive business of Mughal life running while Shah Jahan leads his men into battle. And all the while Mumtaz Mahal travels with the zenana alongside her restless husband, in curtained howdahs on elephant-back or, when heavily pregnant, in brocaded and jewelled palkis carried between smooth-stepping men. In 1622, Shah Jahan mounts a tepid rebellion, proclaims himself Padshah of Hindustan and earns the abiding displeasure of Jahangir who will now only refer to his once beloved son as bi-daulat, 'that wretch', in his biography.

In 1624, while Shah Jahan continues to fight, attacking the governor of Bengal and Orissa, he sends his family to Rohtas fort where Mumtaz Mahal gives birth to Murad Baksh. In 1625, fearing for the safety of his family, Shah Jahan finally submits to his father but Jahangir now demands that Dara Shikoh and Aurangzeb be sent to court as hostages, to ensure the good behaviour of their father. The boys are only ten and eight years old, and Mumtaz would certainly have feared for their safety in a court where the lives of young mirzas have become fragile as hope. But at the end of 1627, Jahangir dies and Shah Jahan moves with ruthless speed and determination. In an orgy of royal blood-letting, Shahriyar Mirza, Khusrau's sons, Dawar Bakhsh and Garshasp, and the sons of Danyal Mirza, are all put to death. In 1628 Shah Jahan arrives at Agra and becomes Padshah Ghazi of Hindustan and Mumtaz Mahal is Padshah Begum.

Sati-un-Nisa has accompanied Mumtaz Mahal to Agra, where she heads the running of the royal zenana. One of Sati-un-Nisa's most demanding and unchanging duties is to meet destitute girls and women and to plead their cause every day to the padshah begum so that their requests may finally reach the padshah. Once that happens, they are 'assigned grants of land, daily allowances, or cash. Some unmarried girls who, owing to their poverty and indigence cannot afford the necessaries of marriage, receive according to their family and condition, ornaments, clothes, money and other things which are indispensable for the wedding ceremony, and are then married to their equals.' It is Noor Jahan who began this custom in a sustained manner, on one occasion arranging for the marriage of 500 destitute girls on one day. It is now continued by her niece, and it is a lifeline for women of merit fallen on hard times who would otherwise disappear into disgrace and squalor. Mumtaz Mahal also starts to plan Dara Shikoh's wedding. The mirza is fifteen years old and the wedding of Shah Jahan's oldest son, the first imperial wedding of Shah Jahan's reign, will be magnificent. But in 1631, Shah Jahan marches once again towards the Deccan in pursuit of a rebellious nobleman, Khan Jahan Lodi. Mumtaz Mahal, though pregnant for the fourteenth time, accompanies Shah Jahan as she has always done. They arrive in Burhanpur where Mumtaz Mahal dies in July 1631, giving birth to her last surviving child, Gauhara Begum.

By all contemporary accounts, Shah Jahan's grief at the death of his wife is extravagant. He sheds tears 'like rain water' and orders the court to remain in mourning. A more dramatic biographer claims that Shah Jahan's hair goes grey overnight, a claim which later miniatures of a black-haired padshah wordlessly contradict. But Shah Jahan is clearly distraught by the death of the woman who was by his side through nineteen turbulent and uncertain years. The trajectory of his life till now had always been true and straight, no obstacle being allowed to remain in his path. Brothers and nephews have been murdered by Shah Jahan with supreme assurance in the power of his own destiny. Now death, that unsolicited and unexpected guest, has come calling, and Shah Jahan is undone. Jahanara, seventeen years old now, weeps over the body of her beloved mother but she is named Padshah Begum of Hindustan and the affairs of empire must continue. Sati-un-Nisa is promoted to Sadr-e-Anas (superintendent) of Shah Jahan's zenana and she is a source of comfort and continuity to the young Jahanara. Mumtaz Mahal's body is temporarily buried in the Aahukhana, the deer garden built by an earlier prince, and Shah Jahan visits her grave every Friday to recite the fateeha.

After Mumtaz Mahal's death, Shah Jahan finally puts an end to almost two decades of constant battles and warfare. He is Padshah Ghazi of Hindustan now, Shadow of God on Earth, and it is time for him to start creating a legacy worthy of his ambition and glory. Six months after Mumtaz Mahal's death, on 1 December 1631, her body is exhumed and, accompanied by Shah Shuja and Sati-un-Nisa, transported to Agra. Burhanpur has never acquired the brilliance and wealth of the other imperial cities—Lahore and Agra—and so it is in Agra that Shah Jahan commissions the first of his great architectural monuments and one which will inexorably be bound to the legend of Mumtaz Mahal—the Taj Mahal.

That the Taj Mahal is also equally a testimony to Shah Jahan's ambition is made quite explicit by the padshah's own biographer, Abd al-Hamid Lahawri, when he writes that the building will be a 'memorial to the sky-reaching ambition of His Majesty...and its strength will represent the firmness of the intentions of its builder'. In Agra, land is bought from Raja Jai Singh by the river Yamuna. Work begins on the main platform of the structure and on the first urz, or death anniversary, of Mumtaz Mahal, a great feast is held and Shah Jahan returns to Agra from the Deccan. Work continues at a blistering pace, all resources, manpower and wealth diverted to Agra. The finest materials from around the world are procured for the mausoleum; marble from Makrana, transported by bullock cart, red sandstone from Fatehpur Sikri, turquoise from Tibet and lapis lazuli from Afghanistan. It is estimated that a total of fifty lakh rupees (2.5 billion rupees in today's money) is spent by Shah Jahan and it is a substantial fraction of the imperial revenue, which ten years later will be approximately twenty crore rupees. No force, earthly or divine, is able to subvert the work. In 1632, an almost countrywide famine decimates the empire but Shah Jahan diverts grain to Agra to feed his teeming workforce and the mausoleum emerges like a dream from the sandbanks along the Yamuna. By 1633, Peter Mundy, a visiting Englishman recounts that 'there is already about her Tomb a rail of gold. The building is begun and goes on with excessive labour and cost, prosecuted with extraordinary diligence'. Within six years the main structure of the tomb is complete and in 1643, for the twelfth urs of Mumtaz Mahal, the Rauza-i-munavvara, (the Illumined Tomb) as Shah Jahan calls it, is officially completed.

The Taj Mahal, as it is more popularly called, has a classic Timurid dome as seen earlier in Humayun's tomb. It has a Persian charbagh garden but it also has, more intriguingly, a pure white marble exterior with gorgeous mosaics in pietra dura. These are elements which were already seen in Itimad-ud-Daulah's tomb, completed four years earlier by Noor Jahan. It is interesting that Shah Jahan uses these very elements, unique for their time, to build something much more grand and awe-inspiring than Itimad-ud-Daulah's tomb. Since the day Shah Jahan became Padshah Ghazi, he uses his radiating energy to remove all traces of Noor Jahan's immense influence. He exiles her to Lahore, to pedestrian anonymity, and melts all the gold mohurs with her name on them. But Itimad-ud-Daulah's tomb is an exquisite and unique masterpiece and so when Shah Jahan builds the first of what will become a most glorious legacy in architecture, he creates something that is much grander in vision and scope but is still, nonetheless, an acknowledgement of Noor Jahan's peerless artistic vision.

When the Taj Mahal is only halfway constructed, Shah Jahan decides, in 1638, to build an entirely new capital city, in Delhi. Agra is already swarming with people and jostling mud huts. For Shah Jahan's imperial legacy, nothing other than a glorious, brand-new city which will bear his name will suffice and so Shahjahanabad is built, at a cost of sixty lakh rupees, considerably more than the cost of the Taj Mahal. The Peacock Throne which he then commissions for himself is the most expensive and opulent throne ever built, costing eighty-six lakh rupees. Five years after the Taj Mahal is completed, Shah Jahan moves the entire court to his new capital at Shahjahanabad and Agra slowly empties of its craftsmen and wealth.

For a building that is staunchly believed to be Shah Jahan's monument to love, it is surprising that the padshah then moves so far away from the city where the Taj Mahal is built, and that he almost never returns to visit it. There is only one recorded visit, in 1654, before Shah Jahan is brought back to Agra under duress as a prisoner. When Aurangzeb visits the mausoleum after the torrential monsoon of 1652 on his way to the Deccan, he is shocked to discover the beautiful building in a state of extensive damage and disrepair, leaking from the substandard cement used. 'What a pity,' exclaims Aurangzeb in a letter to Shah Jahan, 'that such magnificent buildings should have suffered such a great misfortune! Were the brilliance of your Majesty's careful attention to be directed towards restoring them,' he urges his father, 'how suitable that would be.' But Shah Jahan does not visit the Taj Mahal, which glows in solitary splendour beside the warmly forgiving Yamuna. When Shah Jahan does visit, in 1654, his shadow oblique across the marble floor, he is alone with his memories, for no one is allowed within the mausoleum. The noblemen in attendance must wait in the jamat khana (place of gathering) and even the murmuring priests must remain in the outer chambers. And if Shah Jahan does not return, it may be because he knows he will perforce return, one last and final time. No other mausoleum is ever built by Shah Jahan for himself and it is inconceivable that a man so obsessed with his own magnificence, his image, and sense of destiny would not have thought about his final resting place. The Rauza-i-munavvara will be Shah Jahan's first great architectural masterpiece and will also be the place where he will lie in eternity. Till then, Shah Jahan returns to Shahjahanabad, where he has created 'paradise on earth', while Mumtaz Mahal waits for him, as she has always done, silently.

Part III

Ambitious Siblings and a Shahzaadi's Dream

1631-1721

SHAHZAADI

It is a glittering spring day in Shahjahanabad in 1654 and the usually raucous crowds at the stalls lining the Chandni Chowk have fallen silent, beguiled by the magnificence of the procession moving down the wide, tree-lined street. In front of the slow-moving elephants, liveried men sprinkle water on the street so that no dust rises off the ground. Cavalry and infantry follow, the horses tripping and impatient, the soldiers fierce and sombre. Eunuchs walk behind the soldiers, surrounding the imperial elephant on all sides. 'Hoshiyaar!' they shout, and make a great show of keeping back the crowds. They raise their silver sticks, 'shouting out, pushing and assaulting everyone without the least respect of persons'. The Abyssinian eunuchs are particularly fearsome, their muscles rippling beneath their dark skin like a promise. The traders at the shops stand back respectfully and there are Armenians, Persians, Italians, Turks, Portuguese and French adventurers who will spread the stories of Mughal grandeur throughout the world. While the procession passes by, the merchants forget to haggle over the Chinese eye glasses, the jewellery, the perfumes, the gemstones, the slaves, the eunuchs and the caged cheetahs. The elegant white-robed men at the coffee houses drinking the dark brew made from imported beans from Persia set down their tumblers and stand to watch the commotion. Servants walk next to the imperial elephant, driving away flies with peacock feathers stuck into handles of enamelled gold. Others hold perfumes and incense as they walk next to the elephant, so that no offensive smell reaches the exalted passenger. A woman-servant walks in front of the elephant, swinging an incense holder in her hands and shouting out at each step: 'Bismillah! Here comes her highness, Shahzaadi Jahanara Begum! Bismillah!'

Jahanara Begum, eldest daughter and favourite child of Padshah Shah

Jahan is forty years old, unmarried, and at the very height of her glory and power. Known simply as Begum Sahib, she is Padshah Begum of the Mughal empire. The brand-new city of Shahjahanabad, completed by the padshah in 1648, has been shaped in the furnace of Jahanara's ambition. Five of the nineteen imperial buildings in the city have been built by her, including the large central avenue through which the procession now travels. The entire revenue of the territory and port of Surat, all fourteen lakhs rupees of it, is hers to command. The revenue from the estate at Panipat, estimated at over two lakhs of rupees, has also recently been bestowed upon Jahanara. Her ship, the *Sahibi*, sails from the port of Surat under her colours and Jahanara carries out lucrative trade with the Dutch and the English. Her total annual income, including the imperial allowance, is estimated at thirty lakhs rupees (1.5 billion rupees in today's money). In addition, the noblemen at court and the foreign merchants seeking trade favours wrangle to give her the most flawless jewels, the most surprising curiosities. Jahanara is erudite and cultured and has also written two Sufi treatises in Persian, displaying her confidence in the mastery of the Chisthiya faith. 'She was loved by all,' agrees Manucci, 'and lived in state and magnificence.' Her resplendence is unparalleled and she has accomplished more than any single Mughal woman till now. She is especially beloved of Shah Jahan, the padshah, and Dara Shikoh, her brother and heir apparent to the throne, in addition to being deeply respected by all. And yet, in four years from now she will be a prisoner, having been blindsided by her love for her brother and her loyalty to her father. She will lose the finely calibrated game of imperial brinkmanship she plays and then will gallantly accept her loser's lot and follow her father into banishment at the Agra fort. Incarcerated for eight years, she will watch her beloved father slide into decrepitude and terror, undone by his younger son's steely ambition. She will lose her privileges and her power, while her younger sister, Roshanara, will at last claim the glory that was so long, and so humiliatingly, denied her. The convulsions that result in this astonishing reversal of fortunes for the imperial siblings are linked to an ancient Timurid law from Central Asia, one which allows for the accession of any ambitious and successful prince, as opposed to the law of primogeniture, which favours only the oldest son. And so Aurangzeb, only the third son of Shah Jahan, but the most ruthlessly talented and determined, prevails at the bruising war of succession.

This open-ended Timurid law of imperial inheritance has shaped the jagged princely destinies since the time of Babur himself. When the young Babur Mirza rushed to Ferghana to claim his throne upon the death of his father, he knew that any hesitation on his part would mean instant death or banishment at the hands of his own cousins and relatives, who all considered themselves equally deserving of the throne. Timurid mirzas are born to rule, it is all they are trained to do and they are honour-bound to stake a claim to kingship if they can. Later, Humayun too must face his brothers' volatile ambitions and even Akbar must accommodate his half-brother's arrogant demands. For these early Mughal padshahs, however, a brother's blood is sacrosanct and they are all repelled at the thought of shedding royal blood, preferring banishment or a compromise of sorts. But as the Mughal empire expands and attains stability and ever-increasing riches, each succeeding padshah becomes longer-lived and his reign stretches on endlessly while his sons wait in increasingly fractious middle age. It is with Shah Jahan that that ephemeral line is finally crossed and royal shahzaadas are murdered to secure the throne. Shah Jahan will have to pay a price for these deaths, and the psychic freight of this spilt blood will taint the Mughals far into the future generations.

When Shah Jahan becomes padshah at the age of thirty-six, he does everything possible to obliterate the hateful memory of Noor Jahan, whom he blames for turning his once doting father against him. And he makes Arjumand Banu Padshah Begum of the empire. Arjumand Banu is given a befitting title, Mumtaz Mahal (elect of the palace). His eldest daughter Jahanara, at fourteen years of age, is now second in rank to her mother and she is given the title Begum Sahib. She is given an allowance of four lakhs of rupees, while all the other children put together, six surviving siblings, are only allocated a total of six lakh rupees. Within a year, by 1629, Jahanara is given two trade ships, the *Shahi* and the *Ganjawar*. But Mumtaz Mahal doesn't live long as Padshah Begum of Hindustan, dying three years later. The seventeen-year-old Jahanara is a constant presence by the side of the dying empress. The young woman tends to her mother through the endless, bloody hours of her labour, distributing gems and gold coins to the needy in her increasingly desperate and desolate quest for a miracle. But Mumtaz Mahal is beyond saving and dies, probably of postpartum haemorrhage, in an ocean of pain and blood. Jahanara does not have the luxury of grieving very long for her mother, as she has to tend to her father's disarray. 'The pleasures of worldly rule and kingship which were mine with her by my side,' weeps Shah Jahan, 'have now become burdens and increasing sources of grief.' It is not just her father's devastation that Jahanara must deal with, but also the enormous responsibility of running the royal household, for Shah Jahan now declares his eldest daughter Padshah Begum of the Mughal empire, superseding his remaining wives. Her yearly income is fixed at ten lakh rupees and Jahanara now has a veritable army of officers and servants at her command to help her run the enormous, roiling and demanding melee of individuals who make up the household of Padshah Shah Jahan. She is assigned the task of the 'keeper of the imperial seal' and 'from that day, the duty of affixing the great seal to the imperial edicts devolved upon her' writes Shah Jahan's biographer, Inayat Khan. This is the first time an imperial woman, a young and unmarried woman at that, has been given this honour and it is a sign of the enormous faith Shah Jahan has in the talent and loyalty of his eldest daughter. Shah Jahan also gives her half of Mumtaz Mahal's personal estate, the entirety of which is valued at one crore rupees in gold, silver, gems and jewelled ornaments, while the other half is divided between Mumtaz Mahal's six surviving children. An idea of the extravagance of this bequest can be understood when it is compared to the cost of building the Taj Mahal, which amounted to fifty lakh rupees. Jahanara will be padshah begum and the most powerful woman of the Mughal empire for the next twenty-seven years of her life. Her influence and her achievements will never be exceeded by any other Mughal woman and they are the fortuitous result of the enormous wealth of the Mughal empire in the seventeenth century, which is directly available to Jahanara, and the searing ambition and talent of this extraordinary shahzaadi.

For the first ten years after the death of Mumtaz Mahal, Jahanara is completely immersed in the raucous fastness of managing the imperial household. Murad Baksh, her seven-year-old brother, is entrusted into her care and she is responsible for his education and his well-being in addition to organizing all the glittering events at court. The younger children of Mumtaz Mahal continue with their princely education, which includes a thorough grounding in Turkish and Persian literature, as well as an in-depth study of Islamic religious texts. They also learn Hindi, and three styles of handwriting, naskh, nasta'liq and shikasta, which they learn to write with a reed pen on a takhti, or wooden board. The older children soon get married and one of the first great celebrations Jahanara must arrange for is the marriage, in 1633, of her beloved brother Dara Shikoh in Agra. Dara Shikoh is just a year younger than Jahanara and the two siblings share an exceptionally close bond. 'He and I are one soul manifested in two forms', writes Jahanara, 'and we are one life in two bodies.' Dara Shikoh's wedding is the most expensive ceremony ever staged in Mughal history and costs thirty-two lakh rupees. Peter Mundy, an English traveller, describes the fireworks, hidden inside huge puppets shaped like 'great elephants, whose bellies were full of squibs, crackers etc., giants with wheels in their hands then a rank of monsters, then of turrets, then of artificial trees (and other) inventions, all full of rockets'. In the next few years, Jahanara also arranges for the marriages of her brothers Shah Shuja and Murad Baksh as the court keeps wandering, from Agra to the Deccan, through Kashmir and Lahore. There are increasing signs that demonstrate that if Jahanara is the favourite daughter of Shah Jahan, then Dara Shikoh is the favourite son, and therefore the heir presumptive of the Mughal empire. After his grandiose wedding, Dara Shikoh is allowed to pitch a crimson tent, a royal prerogative. Shah Jahan keeps him nearby, at court, and Dara Shikoh is even allowed a seat next to the padshah in his durbar. Adored by his sister, whose influence is endless, and favoured by his father the padshah, Dara Shikoh grows into a young man with talent and charisma, certainly, but one who is extremely leery of the slightest criticism. In time, this will become a fatal tendency towards arrogance. 'The first born son of King Shahjahan,' agrees Manucci, is 'a man of dignified manners, of a comely countenance, joyous and polite in conversation, ready and gracious of speech, of most extraordinary liberality, kindly and compassionate, but over-confident in his opinion of himself, considering himself competent in all things and having no need of advisers.'

Meanwhile, there is a younger son whom everyone seems to be

oblivious of, who is growing up under the claustrophobic shadow of Shah Jahan and Dara Shikoh. This mirza is 'very different from the others, being in character very secretive and serious, carrying on his affairs in a hidden way, but most energetically'. When he is barely fifteen years old this prince, Aurangzeb, momentarily bursts onto the imperial scene. During an elephant fight organized in front of the entire durbar and all the royal princes, Aurangzeb is flung from his horse by an incensed elephant. While the other princes, including Dara Shikoh, maintain a prudent distance, Aurangzeb, helped by Shah Shuja and demonstrating remarkable bravery and sangfroid, confronts the animal on foot with his sword and subdues it. When admonished by Shah Jahan for putting his life at risk, the young mirza sneers at his older brothers claiming, not incorrectly, that 'the shame lay in what my brothers did'. Shah Jahan gives the young prince the title Bahadur, for his exceptional bravery, and not long after, in 1635, Aurangzeb, now a mansabdar of 10,000 horse in rank is sent away on affairs of state, to the Deccan and to other, farther reaches of the empire. Aurangzeb is momentarily recalled, in 1637 when, at the age of nineteen, he is married to Dilras Banu Begum, a descendant of Shah Tahmasp of Persia. Once again, Jahanara and the women of the imperial household are involved in every aspect of the marriage, which now has many Hindustani traditions incorporated into the ceremonies. Aurangzeb's 'hands and feet are stained red with the henna, by ladies concealed behind a screen, and he was robed in the bride's presents, smeared with perfumes and fed with the lucky sugar-candy'. The next day, much before dawn, Aurangzeb arrives from his mansion on the Yamuna to the city palace, taking the river road, and Shah Jahan himself ties a glittering sehra of pearls and precious stones on the groom's turban which covers his face like a veil.

After his wedding, Aurangzeb stays with his father in Agra for three months and then he goes away to the Deccan with his young wife. He will be gone, almost continuously, for twenty-two years. He will disappear from the fierce scrutiny of the court, its ceaseless judgement and appraisal. But while Dara Shikoh inexorably rises at court, surrounded by willing courtiers who pander to his whims, Aurangzeb's trajectory is longer but truer. He spends his wildering years sharpening his military tactics and forging ties of blood and loyalty. He raises an army, he binds men to his cause and he magnifies the flame of his ambition in the cold disregard of his father's neglect.

In Agra, meanwhile, Shah Jahan's enormous energy and wealth is directed to his most favoured means of expression: the building of magnificent structures to adequately reflect his imperial title, Shadow of God on Earth. He adds three major courts to the Agra fort and then begins work on what will become the most famous mausoleum on earth, the Taj Mahal. Jahanara, having spent years organizing her brothers' marriages and taking on the responsibilities of the imperial household, admits to feeling 'trapped and lost' in this gilded cage. 'I am twenty-seven years old,' writes Jahanara, with a sense of malaise at all the empty years, 'and I did not want to lose more time.' In her quest for a deeper meaning in her life outside of the barren tumult of the imperial zenana, Jahanara finds a path that brings both personal solace and reaffirms Mughal imperial legitimacy and grandeur, the Sufi way.

Daughters of the Sun

THAT TIMURID GIRL

The fourteenth-century ancestor of the Mughals of Hindustan, Timur, is one of those men who, like his idol Chinghiz Khan, quite literally shaped the demographics of the human race and altered the trajectory of history. With his semi-nomadic Chagatai Turkish army, Timur's devastating military campaigns caused the death of possibly 5 per cent of the population at the time. An illiterate warrior, he was nonetheless a military genius, politically astute and enormously charismatic. He also sponsored art and architecture of such astounding brilliance that his buildings and cities remained, for a long time, without equal in the world. Though his empire did not long survive his death, his descendants continued to rule over large swathes of the eastern world. Different dynasties in the coming centuries would use select elements of Timurid civilization, depending on their own political traditions, to promote their legitimacy. In Hindustan, the Mughals are careful to nurture this powerful image too and the Timurid element that Jahanara now claims for herself is Sufism.

The Timurids of Central Asia have long had a connection with the Sufi sheikhs of Islam, especially the Naqshbandi silsila. The rulers court the saints as a means to sanctify their claims to kingship and, in return, the Sufis get the protection and patronage of the rulers, in a mutually beneficial relationship. For the Mughals in Hindustan, the Sufi silsila is yet another irrefutable way in which to justify their imperial claims. During the long rule of Akbar, as the power of the Chagatai nobles declines in favour of Rajputs, Hindustani Muslims and Persians, the Naqshbandis lose their pre-eminence in favour of the Chishti order, which has been present in Hindustan for far longer than the Naqshbandis. The Chishti saints are much more accommodating of Akbar's vision in which he sees himself as a truly Hindustani ruler, not a purely Islamic one, and they maintain a more ascetic distance from the dynamics of power and kingship. In the Chishti philosophy, Akbar can see a felicitous similarity to his own religious quest and he becomes an ardent supporter of the order and a regular visitor to Khwaja Moinuddin Chishti's tomb in Ajmer and Nizamuddin Auliya's in Delhi. Sheikh Salim Chishti at Fatehpur Sikri correctly predicts the birth of the much-desired for son for Akbar and now it is to the Chishti saints that Jahanara first turns to for spiritual meaning. 'Since I was twenty years old,' Jahanara says, 'I have been attached in the corner of my faith to the Chishtiyah sect and the circle of the Sheikh tugs at my soul.'

Jahanara is first introduced to the Sufi sheikhs through her beloved brother Dara. When still a very young man, Dara loses his firstborn daughter and he is devastated by this loss. 'I was suffering from a chronic disease', Dara writes of his debilitating sadness. 'For four months the physicians had not been able to cure me.' Shah Jahan, saddened to see his son so broken, introduces him to the Sheikh Mian Meer. 'The saint took my hand into his own', writes Dara, and 'within a week I recovered from the serious malady'. Dara soon becomes a fervent disciple of Mian Meer, experiencing trances and dreams. After Mian Meer's death, Dara becomes a disciple of Mullah Shah Badakhshi, of the Qadiriyya order and in 1637, he introduces Jahanara to the sheikh while they are spending the summer in Kashmir. Blighted by the empty grandeur of her imperial life, Jahanara is soon seduced by the slightly illicit promise of the Sufi sheikhs. She had wanted to join the Chishtiya silsila but 'the Chishti sheikhs do not show themselves in public and remain secluded', she laments. The prosaic reality is that the Chishtis will not ordain a woman, imperial though she may be and 'now that I have joined the qadiriya', Jahanara wonders, 'will I achieve realisation?' It is God Himself, Jahanara claims, who 'created this desire and zeal for me to follow this pull and seek out where it might lead'. In Kashmir, Jahanara spends six months in contemplation of the Qadiriyya order under Mullah Shah Badakhshi. Mullah Shah is an austere sheikh, who has reached enlightenment through extreme breathing exercises, night vigils, fasts and introspection. There are no servants in his home, no cooked meals and no lamps and he lives in an atmosphere of bleak renunciation. Jahanara embraces this notion of sacrifice, of purification of the self and a threadbare existence and writes that 'when I realised that the truth for this existence requires fanaa (sacrifice) I decided to follow what my Peer requires, to die before death, to not wait for death to extinguish me, die before death to become one with the divine'. Jahanara makes four trips in all to Kashmir to be in the presence of Mullah Shah but conscious to a fault of the rules of etiquette, Jahanara keeps a chaste distance from the Shah and all initiations and rituals are conducted through the intermediary of Dara Shikoh. 'The first time I set eyes on the venerable figure of the master, from the cabinet in which I was hiding,' writes Jahanara, was 'when he paid a visit to my father the emperor when he was staying in Kashmir, and when I heard the pearls of wisdom falling from his mouth, my belief in him grew a thousand times stronger than before, and heavenly ecstasy seized my very being.' Jahanara keeps a portrait of Mullah Shah next to her, upon which she meditates, and sends him meals she has cooked herself, naan and saag. Through the course of the intense, blistering months and years of Jahanara's Sufi meditation, she experiences visions and trances equal to those of her illustrious ancestors, with the added, illicit thrill of an erotic ambiguity: 'My beloved came easily into my arms on the nights of parting without efforts,' writes Jahanara, with voluptuous longing. 'Oh Shah! You have finished me with one glance.' Jahanara conflates her love for her sheikh with that for God into a single, radiant, erotic emotion and says, 'my yearning has finally rewarded me with you in embrace. Your passion takes me in embrace and caresses me.' This highly charged language to describe a mystical experience is not unusual in Sufi literature, where a peer or master is often used as a conduit to God, and Sufi imagery routinely describes passionate love, ishq, as a metaphor to explain the peer-murid (Sufi-devout) relationship. What is more disquieting, naturally, is that Jahanara is a shahzaadi and an unmarried one at that, so the transgression is particularly piquant.

In the Sufi tradition, Jahanara finds that her unmarried status is honoured, and even celebrated, as a means to further direct the blazing fire of her desire towards God. There is the provocative example of the spiritually accomplished Bibi Jamal Khatun, sister of Mian Meer who, after six years of conjugal life, deserts the marital bed to direct her attention to the divine and remains 'alone with the remembrance of God'. In Sufi mysticism it is a woman, Rabi'a al-Adawiyya, who, in the eighth century, first expresses the relationship with the divine in hauntingly evocative language: 'God is God', Rabi'a assures us, and 'for this I love God, not because of any gifts but for Itself.' Jahanara evokes the memory of this grace when she writes that 'Mullah Shah has said that about Rab'ia she is not one woman but a hundred men from head to toe.' Through her own acts of devotion, her piety and her mystical visions, Jahanara claims for herself an equally exalted status. 'She has attained so extraordinary a development of the mystical knowledge that she is worthy of being my representative,' agrees Mullah Shah, before adding a dismaying corollary, 'if she were not a woman.' And so Mullah Shah, while acknowledging Jahanara's spiritual powers, denies her the right to be a spiritual guide, or peer, because of her gender. Forsaken by her sheikh, Jahanara then reluctantly abandons her journey to become a Sufi peer. Instead she begins an audacious project, in which she can unfurl the true scope of her Sufi ambition, beyond the derisory limitations of her gender. She writes two books, the *Munis al-Arvah*, which is a biography of Moinuddin Chishti, and the *Risala-i-Sahibiyah*, which is a record of her spiritual journey. The *Risala-i-Sahibiya* remains, to this day, the only autobiography of a Mughal woman from the seventeenth century, and the incandescent scope it describes of Jahanara's ambition is breathtaking.

'When a woman becomes a man in the Path to God', writes Jahanara in the *Risala*, 'she is a man and one cannot anymore call her a woman'. And moreover, 'whoever is honoured by the greatest happiness of knowing and realisation is the perfect human or the absolute essence of the world and is superior amongst all living creatures whether man or woman.' With these few innocuous-seeming words, Jahanara brushes aside the flimsy objections of her peer and of the gathered cohort of objectors in Sufism and mysticism. She writes about her mystical experiences and is fearless about the divine source of her calling; 'The Beloved has placed a noose on my neck', she writes, 'He pulls me wherever He wishes. If I had any control over these things, I would always choose to be around Him.' Jahanara then goes on to claim a remarkable triad of irrefutable powers as witness to her visions. 'I was in a peculiar state which was neither sleep nor wakefulness,' writes Jahanara, 'and it completely overpowered me. I saw the Majlis of the Holy Prophet Muhammad, where the Four friends, noble Companions and great saints were also present. Mullah Shah, was amongst the latter, and had placed his head on the feet of the Holy Prophet, who graciously remarked: "Why have you illuminated the Timurid Lamp?"'

When Gulbadan, that other Timurid woman, sat down to write her *Humayun-nama*, her compulsions were entirely different. 'There had been an order issued', wrote Gulbadan, 'write down whatever you know of the doings of Firdous Makani (Babur) and Jannat-Ashiyani (Humayun)'. This was an imperial directive, given by Akbar himself, and Gulbadan responded by bearing witness to Babur and Humayun. In Jahanara's case the impetus to write comes from no mortal, but from God Himself. 'This fakira', writes Jahanara, referring to herself as a Sufi supplicant, 'only by the assistance and by the favour and approval of God the all-knowing and all-mighty and His beloved messenger Prophet Muhammad, and with the helping grace of my revered master, Mullah Shah, who took my hand, I'm filled with the desire to write this treatise and place it on the mantle with the other accounts of the great ones of religion and the revered ones of certainty'. And so Jahanara invokes, with quite scandalous assurance, divine grace to sanctify and legitimize her mystical quest. She writes her two books as testaments to her own experiences and as guides for those seeking the mystical path. Denied the status of peer because of her gender, she nonetheless claims that very role of spiritual guide through her Sufi texts.

In laying claim to a Sufi legitimacy, Jahanara displays a much more candescent ambition than just that of being a spiritually accomplished woman in a man's domain. Shah Jahan, when he becomes padshah, takes for himself an obscure and ancient title—Sahib Qiran-e-Sani or second Lord of the Auspicious Planetary Conjunction. The first Lord, or Sahib Qiran, is Timur himself and Shah Jahan very consciously styles himself as the second Timur. In the miniatures painted of Shah Jahan his profile, with its fine, strong nose, large eyes and golden complexion speaks more of his Rajput and Persian ancestry than his Turkic one. But every Mughal ruler will be careful to cultivate, in different ways, their celebration of their illustrious Central Asian ancestor Timur. Shah Jahan also bolsters his claims when he aligns himself to some of Timur's cherished ambitions, one of which will be the attempt to recapture Balkh, the Timurid ancestral lands in Central Asia. Jahanara aspires to the same exalted status through her Sufi works, Sufi mysticism being an accepted and vital Timurid link. Through the writing of the *Risala* and the *Munis*, Jahanara reaches beyond just burnishing her imperial identity to claim for herself and for Dara Shikoh, in addition to Shah Jahan, the role of 'lighting the Timurid lamp'. It is only with Dara Shikoh that Jahanara can share the heft of her crackling spiritual ambitions and 'at this time', she writes, 'I had extreme love for Dara Shikoh and the Qadriyya and felt a spiritual and material attachment to him and the order'. When he leaves for Balkh to carry out Shah Jahan's quest for the ancestral lands, Jahanara is confounded by loss. 'When separating' she says, 'I was overcome with disappointment, sadness and restlessness and my brother was greatly saddened and told me to read the Nafabatul Uns.' Indeed Jahanara explicitly claims that even Shah Jahan, in his stricter orthodoxy, 'was always wondering about it (Sufism) and was floundering'. He 'did not know the truth of the importance of this path' writes Jahanara and 'me, the faqira, I constantly told him that Chishti was a Sayyid but he did not believe me until he read the Akbar-nama'. It is Akbar's liberal, mystical and all-embracing theology that Jahanara refers to and she writes that 'in the family of Amir Timur, only we two, brother [Dara Shikoh] and sister are honoured by this enlightened happiness. In our family no one took the step on the path to seek God or the truth that would light the Timurid light eternally.' Only Dara Shikoh and Jahanara are worthy descendants of the illustrious Timur, therefore, and 'there was no end to my happiness', writes the shahzaadi.

In the next few years, as Shah Jahan carries out the project in Agra that will bring him immortality, Jahanara also shapes the contours of various Hindustani cities in the image of her faith. In Agra, she asks for the congregation mosque to be built under her auspices using her personal funds. The mosque is built at a cost of five lakh rupees. Unusually, there is a zenana section to this mosque which is used only by women on Thursday evenings for devotional Sufi rituals. Two years later, in 1650, Jahanara commissions a mosque in Srinagar, the Mullah Shah Badakhshi, in memory of her beloved peer. In Ajmer, at the mosque of the famous

Chishti saint Moinuddin Chishti, Jahanara orders the construction of a pillared marble pavilion in front of the saint's tomb, again for the exclusive use of women. This is known as the Begum Dalani, or Empress' Balcony and it is a sacred, protected space were women can enact their Sufi rituals, uncensored. In all these writings and undertakings, in which she is making momentous, possibly even sacrilegious, claims, Jahanara is always acutely aware of the etiquette within which she must operate, the exquisite adaab which is one of the defining graces of the Mughal court. The inscription above her mosque in Agra, which proudly bears her name, says that Jahanara is 'veiled with chastity, the most revered of the ladies of the age, the pride of her gender, the princess of the realm, the possessor of the world crown, the chosen of the people of the world'. Dara Shikoh, on the other hand, will obscure that fine line between personal ambition and careless outrage and the reckoning, when it arrives, will be brutal.

Dara Shikoh, the urbane, erudite and restless prince, heir to the wealthiest throne in the world, is endlessly distracted by the thrilling and esoteric teachings of the saints and seekers he searches out and surrounds himself with. While his father expands and consolidates the most affluent, opulent and architecturally sublime empire ever seen, Dara Shikoh exhausts his time and attention, scattershot, towards increasingly obscure theories. He becomes negligent of the feelings he bruises and the beliefs and faiths he tramples. 'In the city where a mullah resides', he claims, derisively, 'no wise man is ever found'. While he seems driven by a sincere desire to find a pure filament of truth that runs through all religions, his search is that of a dilettante, never going very much beyond obscurantism and facile esotericism. In one instance he is even ready to give heed to a group that claims to be able to win a battle for him using a potion involving the sacrifice of 'two dancing girls, two thieves, two gamblers, a dog, a sheep, a buffalo, and five chickens'. Meanwhile, Shah Jahan's court is no longer the court of Akbar, with its freewheeling enquiry or even Jahangir's, whose genial interest in religious matters increased as he grew older. Under Shah Jahan, the court is more religiously orthodox and he brings back the Islamic clerics and the scholars who make up the Ulema into the sanctum of the inner court. But Dara Shikoh is the wealthiest of all the princes by far, and he is the beloved of his father and his elder sister. He is surrounded by flatterers and is genuinely adored by the people of the city, being the courtly prince par excellence; he is 'courteous in conversation, quick at repartee, polite and extremely liberal', as Bernier is willing to concede. Despite that, we are told, 'he entertained too exalted an opinion of himself; believed he could accomplish everything by the powers of his own mind, and imagined that there existed no man from whose counsel he could derive benefit'. Even so, for a time, the two eldest children of Mumtaz Mahal live a gilded life, one whose gleaming possibility scorches all those who surround them. Their incandescent destinies are preordained, blessed and inevitable. But in the furthest reaches of the empire, in the Deccan, a maelstrom gathers.

A NEW CITY FOR THE PEACOCK THRONE

By 1638, Agra has been the capital city of five Mughal padshahs. Other cities have been patronised—Lahore, Srinagar, Allahabad, Ajmer and Fatehpur Sikri—but it is to Agra that these padshahs return to build their most magnificent buildings. This great city now has a population of some 660,000 persons and in addition houses an ever-increasing number of foreigners, including the resident Jesuits who have been returning since the time of Akbar. The houses of the noblemen and the gentry are thickly planted all around with trees for shade so 'that if a man behold a City or Town from some conspicuous place, it will seem a Wood rather than a City'. A market is held morning and evening, and Manrique is struck by the 'abundance I noticed of everything in those marts, especially of eatables and household necessaries, as corn, rice, vegetables, sugar-cane, ghee and many kinds of oil'. In Surat, meanwhile, the English have been strengthening their position since the heroic efforts of Sir Thomas Roe. A nineteen-year-old native of Meckleburg, Germany, Johan Albrecht von Mandelslo describes the English trading posts, which have been growing quietly but ominously, every year: 'They have there their Lodges, their Storehouse, their Presidents, their Merchants, and their Secretaries, and indeed have made it one of the most eminent Cities for Traffick of all the East.' The English even seem to have imbibed something of the great state in which the Hindustani nobility live, for Mandelslo admires the English President's hospitality, wherein he serves a 'table of about fifteen or sixteen dishes of meat, besides the Dessert' every night. All the big towns of India are prosperous and bustling with 'a mighty concourse of passengers, horses, elephants and abundance of camels'.

Shah Jahan has added to the magnificence of Agra and has completely rebuilt the fort and now he presides from 'sun-drenched verandahs of the whitest marble' and he is 'glimpsed through apertures of the richest inlay' so that each room and every pavilion shimmers and glitters with saturated colour. He has also, incidentally, built the single greatest monument that the Mughals will be remembered for. But Shah Jahan is King of the World and Shadow of God on Earth and needs a brand-new city, scaffolding on which to create his colossal dreams with all the wealth he has at his disposal. A city which will reflect, to his satisfaction, his glory as the second Timur, the Sahib Qiran-e-Saini, and so Shah Jahan abandons Agra and looks north, to Delhi and the ancient resting places of long-forgotten heroes and eternal saints.

Delhi in 1638 is a city in ruins that silently dreams of its glorious past. Generations of kings and a multitude of dynasties lie in companionable proximity, all enmity forgotten. Great women are buried here as well: Raziya Sultan, warrior princess of the Slave dynasty, as well as Bega Begum and Hamida Begum who are buried in the crypts of Humayun's mausoleum. While kings ruled, and died, and were forgotten, the Sufi flame burns strong in Delhi since the thirteenth century with the presence of the dargahs of two towering Sufi saints, Qutbuddin Bakhtiyar Kaki at Mehrauli and Nizamuddin Auliya at Ghiyaspur. For the Mughals, Delhi enjoys a more bucolic character, having become a familiar stop en route to the northern cities of Srinagar, Lahore and Kabul. The imperial family and the court usually travel by royal barge, sailing on the Yamuna from Agra to Delhi, where they halt for a pleasant stop at the riverside Salimgarh fort, built by Salim Shah Suri, son of Humayun's formidable old nemesis, Sher Shah Suri. From Delhi they then transfer onto elephants, horses or palanquins to continue their northern bound journey—to Srinagar, for the summer, or Lahore, for a military expedition. Delhi is therefore, at this time, a somewhat derelict outpost of empire with a slowly crumbling elegance. All that is about to change for Shah Jahan, his wives and his daughters, are about to conjure up a new vision and in a great, shearing effort will transform Delhi into one of the most magnificent thrumming centres of the world. Their vision is unequivocal and uncompromising; it is to create paradise on earth.

When Shah Jahan decides to build a sparkling new capital city in Hindustan, his empire, one of the largest and richest in the world,

Daughters of the Sun

consists of some 150 million people. Shah Jahan's own entourage of family members, servants, clerks and officials makes up about 7,000 persons while the entire imperial household, including soldiers, servants and dependents, totals a respectable 57,000 people. To accommodate all these people, as well as the seventy or so senior-most great amirs and their own, similarly structured households, a city of monumental scale is required. This city, Shahjahanabad, will be the last great city of the Mughal empire. It is unique in being the vision of a single man, Shah Jahan, and in the number of women who enthusiastically and with enormous ambition, contribute to its creation. Built on the right bank of the Yamuna on a bare plot of land, Shahjahanabad is a city of waterways. The Yamuna is tapped several miles upstream and water is brought by canal to the fort and to the city, where it rushes into stone channels and streams to water gardens and to supply hammams. It whispers down marble waterfalls and fountains in the private apartments of the women to cool the torpid summers and fill the underground pools where perfumed rose petals offer some consolation from the relentless heat.

Before the rest of the city is built, large and roughly circular within high red sandstone walls, work begins, in 1638, on the Qila-e-Mubaarak (the Exalted Fort, better known as Red Fort or Lal Qila) right by the Yamuna, large enough to comfortably house Shah Jahan's huge, rambling household. The fortress itself has high walls and three gateways: a ceremonial main gate which leads into the city, a private one for the use of the imperial family and a riverside gate to the north. From the main gateway and service area is a wide, vaulted passage which leads to the official portion of the fort and is, in fact, a covered bazaar, the first of its kind in India, with arcaded shops on two levels. In this chatta bazaar the ladies of the zenana can shop in complete privacy for all the treasures of the empire. After the vaulted covered bazaar is the naubat khana, or music gatehouse. In the two-storeyed naubat khana, musicians, trumpeters, buglers and drummers wait, and when the padshah is in residence, they shuffle together at regular intervals and sound out a short, abrupt, musical interlude, disturbing the pigeons who fly away in studious synchronicity into the waiting skies. At other times they raucously signal the arrivals of ambassadors, from Persia, Rome, Yemen or Ethiopia. Away from the main gateway and the formal areas are the private spaces for the personal use of the royal household. These include a series of geometric gardens with fruit trees and fragrant, flowering shrubs, supplying fruit for the royal table all year round and flowers to perfume the living spaces. All along the northern wall, overlooking the river, are a series of palaces and pavilions, each more delicately beautiful than the other. There are some twelve distinct pavilions along the riverfront wall, with names echoing the jewel-bright obsession of the imperial family, such as the Hira Mahal and the Moti Mahal. In front of each pavilion is a garden with fountains and water channels while the outer side, facing the river, is a series of 'turrets, kiosks, gilt domes, hanging balconies, oriel windows, arcades, and perforated screens'. The ceilings of the palaces are silver or gilt-plated and every available wall and surface is extravagantly decorated with inlay work, carvings and coloured patterns. One of these palaces is Jahanara's private apartment, and there are palaces also for the favourite wives of Shah Jahan. Jahanara employs architects and painters to paint the walls and ceilings of her mansion, and small pieces of sparkling glass are scattered within the painted walls. She spends seven lakh rupees on her personal mansion in the zenana, including gardens and apartments, while the total cost of the Qila-e-Mubaarak is estimated at sixty lakh rupees. From the perforated screen of her balcony Jahanara can watch the sparkling river and, when the tide is low enough to create a small beach beside the fort, admire the elephant fights which Shah Jahan organizes next to the river. But by 1648, when the entire Mughal household, entourage and amirs move into the completed palace-fortress at Delhi, it is not towards the river that Jahanara and the other imperial women are looking. It is westwards, towards the empty grounds of the city.

Jahanara is now thirty-four years old. She has acquitted herself of all her duties towards her younger siblings, undertaken to complete her mother's unfinished obligations. Her brothers are all married, with children of their own, and so is her youngest sister. She has written her Sufi treatises and anchored her name to her glorious Timurid inheritance. Now, in 1648, Jahanara is richer than ever. In addition to her mother's wealth, her own annual allowance and gifts, she owns the port of Surat and its endless revenue. She also owns the villages of Achchol, Farjahara, Safapur,

Doraha, Medina and Panipat. The revenue from the village of Doraha is used solely for the maintenance of her gardens. With this wealth at her disposal, Jahanara now looks to Delhi, this threshold city about to spin its stories through the erudition, wealth and culture of the Mughal court. She resolves to cleave her name forever into its stones and its romance. Jahanara's blistering ambition is unapologetic and clear. Hers is no creeping tribute to a husband or son. It is a desire to be remembered for all eternity as the most powerful and influential woman of the Mughal empire. And in this vision she is joined by other Mughal imperial women, the wives of Shah Jahan and, to a lesser extent, her sister Roshanara.

Outside of the Qila-e-Mubaarak, Shah Jahan's only great building is the Jami Masjid, an enormous congregational mosque built over fourteen years. The rest of the city is for the noblemen, the amirs, the gentry and the imperial women to mould according to their wealth and ambition. All those with an interest in business, or culture, are invited to add to the wealth and glory of the new city. Shah Jahan invites Dipchand Sah, an Aggarwal Jain merchant of Hisar, to set up his business in Shahjahanabad, for which he is given a large swathe of land near the Qila-e-Mubaarak, and this will transform, in time, to the Dariba neighbourhood of Shahjahanabad. The Jain community is spectacularly successful during the seventeenth century. The most important trade that the EIC conducts is not with the padshah or the nobility, but with a Jain businessman called Virji Vora. He buys all the Company's imports of coral, sells them spices and textiles from Malabar and becomes the Company's banker. The Punjabi Saudagaran community, Hindu Khatris who were converted to Islam by the Sufi cleric Hazrat Shamsuddin, are also invited to the city by Shah Jahan. And so the multi-coloured warp and weft that will make up the tapestry that is Shahjahanabad is spun.

All great cities need an ordered market place and avenues for commerce and now in Shahjahanabad, two women begin the construction of the two large bazaars of the city. Akbarabadi Begum, a wife of Shah Jahan, for the padshah has other wives besides Mumtaz Mahal, who now lies in lonely splendour in the Taj Mahal, undertakes the construction of Faiz Bazaar (Bazaar of Plenty). Faiz Bazaar is 1,050 yards long and stretches out from the Qila-e-Mubaarak to the walls of Shahjahanabad, and has a canal flowing down the centre of the boulevard. Jahanara, meanwhile, lays out the central bazaar of Shahjahanabad, the Chandni Chowk, which is 1,520 yards long and contains 1,560 shops. A large canal, the Paradise Canal, flows down the middle of the avenue, with a row of trees on either side. The shops are small, tucked under an arcaded front over which an awning is stretched with a bamboo frame during the heat of the day. Merchants come to Chandni Chowk from all corners of the empire and even from other countries to sell their goods to the wealthy and discerning nobility of this glorious Mughal city. There are traders from 'Turkey, Zanzibar, Syria, Yemen, Arabia, Iraq, Khurasan, China and Tibet besides Europeans from England and Holland'. The goods sold here include 'rubies from Badakshan, pearls from Oman and fresh fruits from Kashmir and Central Asia'. There are also 'weapons, fine cloth, perfumes, elephants, horses, camels, birds, water pipes, and delicate sweets'.

But the bazaars are not only places of commerce, they are constantly evolving theatres where the people of Shahjahanabad, some four lakh of them when the padshah is in residence, play out their lives. In the sharp morning sun the harried servants and the diligent matrons come to buy fresh fruit and vegetables, meat and fish, and all the spices and grains and dried fruits for the kitchen. There are fragrant heaps of marigold and jasmine, which are threaded into garlands as offerings to the watchful gods in the temples. For there are temples, too, in Shahjahanabad, in the havelis (palaces) of the many Hindu residents who live in the various mohallas (neighbourhoods). But the temples have adapted to their present circumstances and, pragmatic and practical, they are miniaturised and lowered to below the height of the courtyard walls, and the sacred fires burn with restrained fervour. In the pale afternoons of winter, old men warm their emaciated limbs, sitting on clean dhurries along the avenue's pavement, chewing paan and grumbling in companionable groups. In the early evening, furtive sufferers come to consult the physicians and quacks, who sell pungent herbal remedies against impotency, or syphilis, or to consult the astrologers, with their baffling and beguiling possibilities. An unimpressed European deems them to be 'silly women, wrapping themselves in a white cloth from head to toe', who are ready to 'whisper to them [astrologers] all the transactions of their lives, and disclose every secret'. Later in the evening, the young gallants of the city will wander by in freshly perfumed jamas, paan tucked inside their cheeks, ostensibly exchanging verses of poetry but furtively keeping a watchful eye on the famed courtesans who can sometimes be glimpsed from the latticed windows of the first floor kothis. Halfway down the chowk the Paradise Canal opens out into a pool in the middle of a large octagonal piazza. On still summer nights, when the crickets finally quieten, the pool perfectly reflects the light of the moon, giving it its name, Chandni Chowk. 'In its many coffee houses', Dargah Quli Khan, the Persian chronicler of Delhi writes, 'literary personalities gather every day and recite their pieces to each other'. More intoxicating drink is also available and even beautifully crafted goblets and 'they have arranged such attractive (wine) glasses that an austere and pious man, hundred years old, would feel tempted to drink wine'. Aristocratic young men, impeccably dressed and perfumed, linger along the boisterous pavements on their way to the Jama Masjid or the city palace and 'young and pubescent boys are at the fringes of the crowds. Whenever one lifts one's eyes, the gaze glides over the beauty of a moon-faced one and if one extends one's arm it seems to become entangled in some young man's tresses.'

Shahjahanabad, with its endless wealth and tolerant princes, attracts Europeans in increasing numbers. The French are particularly enchanted with the romance of the 'Moghuls' and such is its allure that when Louis XIV's Louvre Palace is renovated a few years later, it is proposed that an apartment in 'the Mughal style' is added. The Mughal court and its entourage attracts mostly artillerymen, but also physicians, jewellers, adventurers and con-men. The mirzas and noblemen who employ these 'firangis' are attracted by their competence and skill, but very often are simply curious about their knowledge of the larger world. François Bernier, a physician who has recently arrived in Shahjahanabad and is employed by the Persian nobleman Danishmand Khan, admits that he becomes sometimes 'weary of explaining to my Agha [Danishmand Khan] the recent discoveries of [William] Harvey and [Jean] Pecquet in anatomy, and of discoursing on the philosophy of [Pierre] Gassendi and [René] Descartes'. When this happens, the ever-curious Danishmand Khan then summons a learned pandit whom he has lured away from the services of Dara Shikoh, and the pandit must do his best to defend the tenets of Hinduism to the Khan. Dara Shikoh, too, is very fond of the various Europeans who roam the city. He has a reputation amongst the firangis of being 'a generous man and friendly to the Europeans'. Jahanara will hear from Dara about the intrepid gumption of the young eighteen-year-old Venetian who arrived in front of him one day dressed like 'a Turk, with a turban of red velvet bound with a blue ribbon and dressed in a satin of the same colour, also a waist-cloth of a gold-flowered pattern with a red ground'. To Dara's amusement, the youngster knows how to pay obeisance by bending from the waist down and placing the back of his right hand on the ground, and is conversant in Persian and Turkish. This decidedly enterprising youth is Niccolao Manucci, who will have a long and illustrious career at the court of the Mughals and whose memoirs will scatter the stories of the great Mughal's magnificence throughout the world. Under Dara's tolerant patronage, the Europeans live in havelis and inns within Shahjahanabad but within a few decades, under Aurangzeb's rule, they will shift to Farangipura, outside the city walls, beyond the Kabuli Darwaaza.

But in 1650, Shahjahanabad is being shaped in the furnace of the imperial women's ambition. Of the nineteen major structures that Mughal women will build in the city, fourteen are completed by 1650 by the wives and daughters of Shah Jahan. It will be fully fifty years before construction work is sponsored again by Aurangzeb's daughter and wife, who between them will build only three structures in 1703. There is a quickening in this mid-seventeenth century, a fortuitous meeting of various elements that leads to this unprecedented, and never to be repeated, cacophony of construction. There is the unimaginable wealth, independently controlled by women, which makes the grandest schemes feasible. There are the slowly accruing previous examples of Mughal women builders: Bega Begum, Maham Anaga, Noor Jahan. There is the example of Shah Jahan himself, the great Mughal builder par excellence. There is also the porosity of the Mughal zenana, wherein the honour of the padshah is not so inviolably linked to the invisibility of his women. In Mughal India the imperial women are allowed a far greater degree of independence than in their other contemporary Muslim empire, the Safavid empire, where imperial women have a much more humble impact on the capital at Isfahan. There is a certain respect, even deference at times, for the opinions and wishes of the Mughal women, which is a cherished reminder of their ancient Timurid, nomadic lineage. Finally, there is the confident, glittering ambition of the women themselves, who are determined to carve their destinies into the stone of this city, which is to be paradise itself, here on earth.

For Jahanara, it is not individual projects that will suffice as testament to her incandescent ambition. It is entire swathes of the city which are hers to shape. North and south of Chandni Chowk, square monumental structures are patronised by her so that this entire central quadrant of the walled city bears her name. At one end of the Chandni Chowk, Jahanara commissions a magnificent double-storeyed caravanserai, following on the example of Noor Jahan. It is a large and imposing arcaded structure, with towers at each corner of the square building and, according to Bernier, it is second only to the Jama Masjid in magnificence. Apart from the ninety rooms for the travellers, beautifully painted and appointed, the serai contains a mosque, a garden and a large courtyard. The garden is planted in the classic Mughal style, with watercourses, flowers and fruit-bearing trees. The caravanserai is a city hotel and 'is the rendezvous of the rich Persian, Uzbek, and other foreign merchants', primarily for the caravans and merchants coming from Iran and Central Asia to be lodged comfortably and safely, 'the gate being closed at night'. Bernier is moved to lament at the lack of such facilities in Paris, for he feels that 'strangers on their first arrival would be less embarrassed than at present to find safe and reasonable lodgings'. With the construction of her Chandni Chowk and caravanserai, as well as her interests in trade and her trading ships, Jahanara is anchoring her name to the commerce of the city. 'I will build a serai,' Jahanara says, 'large and fine like no other in Hindustan. The wanderer who enters its courts will be restored in body and soul and my name will never be forgotten.' The gauntlet has been thrown to posterity: it is immortality that Jahanara seeks.

Having built the Faiz Bazaar, Akbarabadi Begum now also builds a caravanserai, though not as magnificent as Jahanara's, as well as a mosque and a hammam. Her buildings are all concentrated in the area around Akbarabadi gate, near the Jama Masjid, and she is the second most important builder in the city after Jahanara. The Akbarabadi mosque is a particularly fine structure of black, red and creamy white stone and is called the Usrat Panahi (Great Protection). Two other wives of Shah Jahan, Sirhindi Begum and Fatehpuri Begum, also build a further two mosques, a caravanserai and a garden.

The city fizzes and heaves with the changes taking place within it and new buildings coming up seemingly every day in 1650. While the yearly salary of the President of the EIC at Surat is 5,000 rupees, fortunes are spent by the imperial women and marble streams into Shahjahanabad from Kachhawaha in Rajasthan, Harkha Bai's old hometown. Across from the caravanserai at one end of Chandni Chowk, Jahanara builds a public hammam, the largest in the city, 180 feet long. These public baths are greatly appreciated by the gentry and the well-born visitors, and 'many diseases are cured by the bath, such as disorder of the brain, heaviness of the limbs, yawning caused by crop-sickness, and dullness of the system'. While the Chandni Chowk, the bazaar, the caravanserai and the hammam are public structures, for the benefit of the gentry and the citizens of Shahjahanabad, her next and final building is the grandest, and the most personal, of all Jahanara's endeavours. To the north of her caravanserai, in the centre of the walled city, Jahanara develops an enormous pleasure garden, the Sahibabad, 3,000 feet long and enclosing an area of 50 acres. There are towers at the four corners of the walled garden and summer pavilions set within ponds, hidden behind fountains. The gardens are planted thickly with fragrant flowers and fruit trees and thus, right in the middle of the boisterous, roiling city is a cool and secluded place for the women and children of the palace. The fruit from the trees supply the imperial table and all the surplus fruit is sold, for these are not ornamental arrangements of plants but densely planted trees whose interlaced foliage provides a green canopy through which the sunlight filters gently. Just like her ship, the *Sahibi*, and her treatise, the *Risala-i-Sahibiya*, this garden also bears her title—Sahibabad. Shah Jahan's wives, rather cavalierly, are now only known by their city of origin—Fatehpur Sikri, Akbarabad or Sirhind. But Jahanara is almost beyond name, and even gender, and is simply Sahib.

While Sahibabad is the largest green area of the city, there are gardens and trees everywhere in Shahjahanabad. The avenues are dense with shade-giving trees and all the noblemen plant gardens and trees around their havelis—mangoes, neem, pomegranate, champa, ber and guava. This keeps the city relatively cool and fragrant and is only possible due to a wonderful piece of engineering which is the Paradise Canal. This old canal, built 300 years previously by Firoz Shah Tughlaq, had long since fallen to disrepair. Now the canal is expanded and improved and brings water from the Yamuna upstream, crossing the Najargarh Jhil, and enters Shahjahanabad by the Kabul gate. Inside the city, the canal splits into two. One branch flows down the Chandni Chowk, from Fatehpuri Masjid to Faiz Bazar. The other branch enters Sahibabad garden and then runs into the Qila-e-Mubaarak itself from near the Shah Burj. The Paradise Canal brings water from the Yamuna to the city all year round, allowing for the greenery in the suburbs, the city and the city-fort.

Within the Qila-e-Mubaarak, the zenana that firangis like Bernier and Manucci hanker to see is not the enclosed, dark quarter that they imagine it to be. It is, in fact, a city unto itself, with bazaars, hammams and palaces, smaller lodgings, gardens, walkways, courtyards, pleasure halls, libraries, durbars, stables and workshops. It is a place of wide corridors, open skies, shaded gardens, great beauty, waterfalls, canals and fountains. The most exalted of the women, Jahanara, Roshanara and Shah Jahan's principal wives, have mahals, or palaces, of their own, with quarters for their retinue and staff. The lower ranked women have humbler homes and others sleep in verandas and dormitories while the staff have simple mud and bamboo huts. Every woman in the zenana has a clearly defined job to do or a duty to perform. From the dancers and the singers, who are there for the entertainment of the women, to the physicians, wet nurses, teachers, craftswomen and menial staff. Even the old widowed women are valued and cherished, for they keep the precious memories alive and teach the younger children the nuances of language and comportment. There are frequent visitors to the zenana too and these include 'relatives, midwives, astrologers, poets, musicians and dancers, peddlers, and artisans'—all female. Managing the affairs of this huge number of women, their feeding, and clothing, their transportation and all their numberless needs, is an entire complement of female bureaucrats.

As for Roshanara, the only structure she builds is a handsome garden and pavilion, the Roshanara Bagh, which is as far away from Jahanara's central axis of influence as possible. It is four kilometres away, outside the very walls of Shahjahanabad, where the shahzaadi may wander in her gardens with her entourage, her dancers and her musicians. And where she may forget, for a while, the blinding magnificence of her sister.

Meanwhile, the remainder of the city is shaped by the princes and the great amirs of the court. The great camp of Shah Jahan, his ordu-e-mu'alla, numbers between 375,000-400,000 persons. This huge mobile camp, which accompanies Shah Jahan whenever he leaves the city, makes up 80 per cent of the population of Shahjahanabad and some 300,000 of these people, the princes, amirs and their households, live within the walled city. The amirs build magnificent havelis for themselves, miniaturised, self-sufficient versions of the city palace, in distinct mohallas of the city. The most prized locations are those alongside the fort, overlooking the Yamuna and this is where the greatest men of the land, Safdar Jang, Ali Mardan Khan and Dara Shikoh, have their havelis. These huge residences of the great men of the court shape the main mohallas of the city, giving them an ordered, green appearance. Surrounding the large estates of the nobility are hutments of mud with thatched roofs, for the lower tradesmen and craftsmen serving the households of the great houses. The lower ranking great amirs have smaller mansions around the Jami Masjid and the third tier of amirs are further still, towards the outer walls of the city. These are simpler dwellings, of clay and straw, but nonetheless clean and spacious. These noblemen must keep agents at court with carrier pigeons to relay important messages because of their physical distance from the centre of the universe, the imperial Mughal court.

These Mughal women of Hindustan, these wives and unmarried daughters, stand alongside the most glorious of the great Mughals to create the greatest city of their time. Visitors from around the world will be baffled by its size and beauty, and will admit that none of the other great cities of the world, Paris, Isfahan, Constantinople, are comparable to it. The older Timurid women have all disappeared now and there are no longer any direct physical links to that earlier glory. The old insouciance with which the older women were allowed to travel and the irrepressible independence of Hamida Banu and Gulbadan are gone. Jahanara and the wives of Shah Jahan will no longer perform the dangerous and unpredictable Hajj journey. Not just the women, but the entire court is now contained within much stricter rules of etiquette and behaviour. Even Turki, their old mother tongue, has acquired the patina of nostalgia and no one speaks it at court or in the zenana any longer. Shah Jahan, as a child, outright refused to learn how to read and write Turki. Now the language of the zenana is Persian and then Hindustani, a new language born of courtly Persian and Hindi which comes to be known as zabaan-e-ordu (language of the camp).

But despite all these changes, the ineffable connection to the old nomadic ways and the power of their long-ago matriarchs survives. Jahanara maintains that ceaseless vigil over her legacy so that every action she undertakes is first scoured by the ideal of that Timurid vision. She is witness to a glory that seeps into every aspect of courtly life. When Shah Jahan appears at the jharokha (enclosed balcony) of the palace for the darshan at dawn, she can watch from her own latticed balconies the procession of nobles and mansabdars, the cavalry or the elephant fights. Then, precisely at 7.40 a.m., she watches from behind a marble grill as Shah Jahan, accompanied by the raucous sounding of the kettle drums and bugles, enters the durbar of the Deewan-e-aam. The assembled noblemen, amirs and gentry immediately and silently perform the kornish, bending from their waists to place the back of their hand on the floor, then raising it to their heads. There is a great rustling of silk and linen robes, and clinking of jewellery but no other sound, for absolute silence is required. The noblemen wear richly embroidered, diaphanous cotton tunics over colourful, tight churidars. They sparkle with jewels, especially rubies and pearls, and a two-handled dagger is tucked into their cummerbund, which is the most elaborate item of clothing, woven with pure gold threads. Shah Jahan, dressed in jewel-studded robes, seats himself on an astonishing throne, glittering with rubies, garnets, diamonds and pearls. This is the Peacock Throne, 'the richest and most superb throne which has ever been seen in the world'. 'Many gems had been collected by three generations of emperors—Akbar, Jahangir and Shah Jahan', the court annalist Abd al-Hamid Lahawri tells us succinctly. 'Of what use were they if the people could not gaze at them?' So Shah Jahan has devised a way to display Akbar and Jahangir's enormous collection of gems by designing a throne which took seven years to build and cost twice as much as the Taj Mahal. The jewels used to make the Peacock Throne are so luminous that they will pass into legend and have names of their own—the Koh-i-Noor, the Akbar Shah, the Jahangir diamonds and the Timur ruby. Jahanara listens as the affairs of state are discussed and she knows intimately the great amirs of the court, the men of influence and prestige and culture. She may occasionally even voice her thoughts directly to the padshah through the grill, as may some of the other senior women. The Hindustani men are used to the invisible presence of women at court, only the Europeans are startled to learn of these ghostly, but occasionally audible, members of the court. After particularly grand durbars, precious stones are thrown over visitors in a glittering arc—pearls, diamonds and rubies. Paan is passed around on silver platters and itr of roses is rubbed into their palms before they leave.

In the afternoon when Shah Jahan retires to the zenana, Jahanara and Sati-un-Nisa are responsible for the table of the padshah. They supervise the dishes served to him and are present at every meal. In the royal kitchens, the padshah's food has been tasted by the Mir Bakawal, the Head of the Imperial Kitchen. The gold and silver dishes are then sealed and a tally of the dishes made so no dish can be intercepted en route to the padshah. Shah Jahan is haunted by a lifelong fear of being poisoned and in these days when that incorruptible line has been crossed, when brother has killed brother for the throne of Hindustan, then perhaps that fear is not misplaced and the trust in these women is enormous. Indeed, the ritual surrounding each meal eaten by the padshah is branded both by the realization that food is a blessing from the divine and a potential source of malfeasance. Each meal is begun with the recitation of the Bismillah-e-Rehman-o-Rahim, with Sati-un-Nisa standing quietly in attendance. Bearers bring jugs of water and carved basins for the padshah to wash his hands and face before each meal. Shah Jahan dislikes eating in the presence of Europeans, who are considered filthy for not attending to this basic hygienic practice. The dishes are laid out on a spotless dastarkhwan (tablecloth), even the condiments, the sliced mango, ginger and lime pickles and bread having been brought in small sealed dishes. The other members of the zenana may be present, but they are also free to eat their own meals separately. After each meal, fervent exclamations of 'Shukr Allah' are uttered, and the padshah gives thanks to the Almighty.

Jahanara also discusses her architectural plans for Shahjahanabad with the padshah and in the afternoon, or in the early evenings, she pleads the case of deserving, destitute women who have been brought to her attention by Sati-un-Nisa and Shah Jahan dispenses grants. Jahanara's beloved Dara Shikoh is always at court, and he lives a short distance away at his grandiose mansion overlooking the Yamuna. Surrounded by sycophants and immersed in his theological digressions and courtly life, Dara 'assumed that fortune would invariably favour him and imagined that everybody loved him'. The 1650s are years of peace and prosperity for the Mughals. Shah Jahan is almost always at Shahjahanabad, his warrior days finally over, except for the occasional pleasure trip to Kashmir, a couple of short forays to Agra and Ajmer. Elsewhere, in the outposts of empire, and far away from the court, fractures appear in what was the seamless fabric of empire. The other royal princes, Murad Baksh, Shah Shuja and Aurangzeb, are gathering their ambition about them and creating armies of fighting men who are loyal only to them. It is a complicated dawn that rises over Shahjahanabad and its many inhabitants. As the years go by in opulent splendour in Shahjahanabad, there is no way for Dara, Jahanara and the women of the imperial zenana to suspect that their power is as ephemeral as smoke in the wind.

the padshah and in the ...... early evenings, she pleads the case of deserving, destitute women who have been brought to her attention by Sau-un-Nisa and Shah Jahan dispenses grants, Jahanara's beloved Dara Shikoh is always at court, and he lives a short distance

LETTERS BETWEEN A BROTHER
AND A SISTER

It is a day in early November in Shahjahanabad, a day filled with the warm effulgence of a summer finally spent and winter yet to arrive. On his way back from a siege at Kandahar, Aurangzeb arrives at Shahjahanabad and enters the massive red stone walls of the city for the first time since it has been completed. It is 1652, Aurangzeb is thirty-three years old and accompanying him are his household: his wife Dilras Banu Begum and her three daughters, fourteen-year-old Zeb-un-Nisa, nine-year-old Zinat-un-Nisa and one-year-old Zubdt-un-Nisa. There are also some minor wives of Aurangzeb such as the Kashmiri Rajput Nawab Bai and his other children. His two young sons, who have accompanied him into battle at the ages of twelve and eight, are also present: Muhammad Sultan and Muhammad Muazzam. Aurangzeb has been away from the Mughal court and fighting wars for eighteen years, almost continuously, with only occasional visits to court. He is quite unlike his urbane, quick-witted older brother Dara Shikoh, his 'Dada Bhai'. He is 'very different from the others, being in character very secretive and serious, carrying on his affairs in a hidden way, but most energetically'. There is no courtly repartee or risqué humour in his entourage and 'in his company, no improper word, such as of slander or obscenity or falsehood was spoken'. But standing now in the great Qila-e-Mubaarak of Shahjahanabad, Aurangzeb marvels at his father's majestic creation and declares that 'the beauties of that most excellent building are more than one can describe'. He wanders through the enormous complex, admiring the jharoka of the Deewan-e-aam, the mirror-work of the Rang Mahal, the hammams, and the water channels. In the exquisitely laid out gardens, yellow roses bloom, early for the season. He then visits his three sisters, Jahanara, Roshanara and the youngest, Gauhara. The next day he takes Jahanara, 'Nawab Begum Sahib Jiu', with him to his own mansion outside the fort and spends the day with her there, for 1652 has been a momentous year for Aurangzeb and Jahanara is the one counsel whose advice he is always willing to listen to.

Aurangzeb's relationship with Dara Shikoh has been blighted from his early childhood. When he was only eight years old, in 1628, he was separated from his parents and sent, along with Dara Shikoh, to the imperial court of his grandfather Jahangir as hostage. Until then, the boys were part of the household of their parents, Shah Khurram and Arjumand Banu Begum, in the boisterous company of all their other siblings. But Shah Khurram has now become 'bi-daulat', that wretch, to his father Jahangir and his every move is fiercely watched. They two boys lost the tender presence of their mother, their sisters and their kokas, and instead, had to submit to the watchful care of Noor Jahan and the increasingly agonized Jahangir. And so they are made immediately and calamitously aware of the vicious and seductive power of the Mughal throne for which fathers blind their sons and brothers murder their brothers. For in the court of Jahangir, where their uncle Shahriyar Mirza is now being groomed to be padshah, they will have heard of their father's assassination of Khusrau Mirza, beloved of the ladies of the zenana. Whatever affection there may have been between the two young princes would inevitably have corroded into something much more sinister and tainted. They will learn, in those two years at court, that the Mughal throne is now worth any sacrifice, any sacrilege.

The boys rejoin their family in 1628 when Shah Khurram becomes Padshah Shah Jahan. By 1635, at the age of sixteen, Aurangzeb is sent away to war, against the rebellious Raja of Orchha, Jujjhar Singh of Bundelkhand. Aurangzeb defeats Jujjhar Singh and is quick enough to get to the raja's stronghold and prevent the women of the zenana from committing jauhar, a tradition which the Mughals abhor. After this decided success, Aurangzeb is given the governorship of the Deccan, a post which he holds from 1636 to 1644. Even the two other sons of Mumtaz Mahal, Shah Shuja and the youngest, Murad Baksh, are sent away to the provinces, to Bengal and Balkh respectively, but Dara Shikoh remains at court for almost thirty years. It is clear to the courtiers that 'the Emperor from excessive love and partiality, would not allow Dara Shikoh to go away from him'. So Dara Shikoh remains at the court of his father, surrounded by flatterers and courtiers, who will cuirass his self-belief beyond all possibility of doubt or reason. Together with Jahanara, 'one soul in two bodies', the two siblings discuss Sufi theory and share their uninhibited Sufi ecstasies. In a court that is the grandest of the Mughal courts to date, richer by far than any of the existing European monarchies, Dara Shikoh proposes asceticism and without any irony whatsoever makes provocative and disdainful remarks: 'hands soiled with gold begin to stink', Dara claims, 'how bad would be the plight of a soul soiled with gold!' From 1641 onwards, Dara Shikoh begins a search in the Hindu texts for the presence of a 'hidden scripture' since, according to the Quran, no land is bereft of prophetic guidance. He is soon convinced that the Vedas and the Upanishads contain this mystical message and, with the help of Brahmin scholars, begins a study of these ancient Hindu texts. Meanwhile Aurangzeb, in the Deccan, attempts to woo his father in different ways, sending him, in 1642, presents of gems, jewelled handicrafts, rare products of the Deccan and elephants.

In 1644, the entire imperial family is ravaged by a catastrophe that threatens the beloved heart of the Mughal family—Jahanara. It is the Navroz festival and the entire fort of Agra is a ruckus of music, dancing, glittering goods and elaborate tents and decorations. Jahanara is hurrying through the corridors of the palace in the gathering dusk. A eunuch precedes her, holding a jewelled stick with a string of bells at the end. With each step, he thumps down his stick, making the bells jingle, and announces Jahanara's presence: Hoshiyaar! he sings out, Khabardaar! Following Jahanara is her entourage of attendants and servants and ladies in waiting, all effervescent with excitement. The women all wear long jamas of exquisitely fine muslin. So sought-after and valuable are these garments that they have names of their own—aab-e-raawan (running water), shabnam (night dew) and baft hawa (woven air). These cloud-like materials are so thin and transparent that the women wear several layers of dresses, in delicate pastels and embroidered with gold zari work. Some of the most expensive clothes have the famous 'cheent' pattern, from the Hindi word for raindrops. This pattern has recently become resoundingly popular with the Portuguese and English traders, who are always hankering for this 'chintz' cloth. The dresses are also drenched in itr, so that the women leave an intoxicating perfume in the corridors as they pass by, a shadow memory of their presence. But the itr also makes the fine material very flammable and along the floor of the corridors are oil lamps and as Jahanara swishes by, the edge of her muslin jama catches fire and in an instant, Begum Sahib is engulfed by the flames, a living torch. Two of her servant girls die trying to douse the flames on their shahzaadi and by the time the fire is extinguished, Jahanara has extensive and severe burns down her back and her legs and her arms. For many agonized weeks and months the palace fears for the life of Jahanara. So devastated is Shah Jahan that he reaches out to the furthest corners of his empire to find doctors and healers who might help his daughter. Royal hakims are summoned as are mendicants with mystical powers and saints of dubious persuasions. Sufi mystics are asked to pray for her and a visiting Persian physician is also pressed into service. Quacks with doubtful incantations and greedy hands haunt the courtyards outside the palace. Shah Jahan forgets the affairs of state, the daily durbar being reduced to a cursory meeting of a few minutes. Vast sums of money are given away to the destitute and every night a sum of one thousand rupees, five lakhs in today's currency, is placed under the pillow of Jahanara and distributed to beggars the next morning. Shah Jahan weeps and prays and is a constant, anguished presence by his daughter's side.

The shahzaadas, including Aurangzeb, all hurry to the court. But something happens at the court at Agra, some slight perceived, Dara's ascendancy displayed, and Aurangzeb is furious, saying that he will leave the court and his earthly duties, relinquish his sword and retire from rule. It is never clear what leads to Aurangzeb's astonishing actions. Perhaps it is a realization, after years of absence from the imperial court, that Dara Shikoh is favoured and cherished above all and that he is the clear heir in waiting. Dara Shikoh had, after all, been declared Shahzada-e-Buland (Prince of High Fortune), in 1642 and ever since, he has been promoted and his salary increased at a blistering pace. The court historian claims that Aurangzeb was 'misled by the wicked counsels of his foolish companions'. But it is certain that Aurangzeb seems to have been almost mortally wounded in his feelings and in a fit of pique and appalled hurt, hurries away from court, abandoning his duties. 'For a long time,' marvels Manucci, 'he pretended to be a faqir, a mendicant, by which he renounced the world, gave up all claim to the crown, and was content to pass his life in prayers and mortifications.' Aurangzeb will write a very revealing letter to his sister Jahanara ten years later, when he complains of further mistreatment from Shah Jahan, and refers back to this incident:

> If His Majesty wishes that of all his servants I alone should pass my life in dishonour and at last perish in an unbecoming manner, I have no help but to obey... But as it is hard to live and die thus and I do not enjoy [his] grace, I cannot, for the sake of perishable earthly things, live in pain and grief, nor deliver myself up into the hands of others—it is better that by order of His Majesty I should be released from the shame of such a life, so that harm may not be done to the good of the State and (other) hearts may be composed about this matter. **Ten years before this I had realised this fact, and known my life to be aimed at [by my rivals] and therefore I had resigned my post...** so that I might retire to a corner, cause no uneasiness to anybody's heart, and be saved from such harassment.

Shah Jahan is furious and retaliates immediately, depriving his spiky, talented but obdurate son of his governorship and estates, and reducing his allowance. Aurangzeb's disgrace appears complete and Shah Jahan returns to the sickbed of Jahanara.

Eight months after her accident, Jahanara is finally healed and the grateful padshah has her weighed against her weight in gold. This weighing ceremony is an old Mughal custom but it is almost always reserved for the padshah, his sons, or some favourite courtier. For a woman to be so celebrated is an exceptional display of worth in the eyes of the padshah. Shah Jahan also gifts his daughter the port of Surat, its territories and its substantial annual revenues, making her even more immensely wealthy than she already is. A brand-new ship, the *Sahibi*, is built exclusively for the use of the shahzaadi. Like Noor Jahan and Maryam-uz-Zamani before her, the *Sahibi* and the port of Surat are potent reminders of Jahanara's prestige and power. The traders who pay the trade tariffs on goods at

Surat, the merchants who load their cloth onto the *Sahibi* and the pilgrims who use the ship for transportation to Mecca are all witness to the glory of the padshah's daughter.

The English factors write directly to Jahanara, pleading for favour and special farmans because of her authority and her closeness to the emperor. The Europeans are present in ever greater numbers at Surat and Manucci describes the busy, broiling scene, its streets containing multitudes. 'I was much amused when I landed', writes this Venetian traveller, 'to see the greater number of the inhabitants dressed in white clothes, also the many different kinds of people as well men and women'. Interestingly Manucci points out that the women, 'mostly Hindus, do not conceal the face as in Persia and Turkey where women go about with their faces hidden'. The habit of eating paan, which the Mughal court has long loved, has become democratised, and all the people are exceedingly fond of it. Manucci is amazed and 'much surprised to see that almost everybody was spitting something red as blood' and wonders if people in India might routinely have their teeth extracted. When he is informed, by an Englishwoman in Surat, about the aromatic paan he declares that 'the women of India, whose principal business it is to tell stories and eat betel, are unable to remain many minutes without having it in their mouths'.

As soon as she is restored to health, one of the first things Jahanara tends to is the restoration of Aurangzeb in Shah Jahan's good grace. 'Her joyful father,' we are told, 'could refuse her nothing, and, at her entreaty, Aurangzeb was restored to his rank.' For the Europeans, who are present at court and in the various shahzaadas' retinues in different capacities—jewellers, goldsmiths, painters, physicians and soldiers—the influence of Jahanara on her father is positively baffling. In Christian Europe at this time, ideal women are expected to be entirely subservient to their fathers and then to their husbands. Extensive lists are published, explaining how women are meant to serve men faithfully, and detailing their expected characteristics: 'modesty, courtesy, gentleness, affability and good government'. The ideal woman, it is stated, 'obeyed the commandment of the apostle who bideth women be silent and learn of their husbands at home'. Silence in a woman is valued almost above all other virtues except, perhaps, chastity. But Jahanara's influence at court is irrefutable. François Bernier, personal physician to Dara Shikoh, marvels about Jahanara that 'her ascendancy in the court of the Mogul should have been nearly unlimited; that she should always have regulated the humours of her father, and exercised a powerful influence on the most weighty of concerns. This princess accumulated great riches by means of her large allowances, and of the costly presents which flowed in from all quarters, in consideration of numberless negotiations entrusted to her sole management.' Manucci, who also worked for a while for Dara Shikoh, agrees that 'Begom Saeb, the eldest of all...[was] most lovely, discreet, loving, generous, open-minded and charitable. She was loved by all, and lived in state and magnificence.' For some of the Europeans, this influence is grating and unacceptable. They listen to the easy rumours and they add their own sliver of malevolence to the frothing bazaar gossip and accuse the shehzaadi of incest with her brother, Dara Shikoh, and even with Shah Jahan.

The troubling heart of the problem lies in the fact that the two oldest daughters of Mumtaz Mahal, Jahanara and Roshanara, never marry. In time this will give rise to rumours that the Mughal padshahs forbade their daughters from marrying, preferring to keep them to themselves, for purposes lascivious or other. The truth, as ever, is more complex, more prosaic and also tainted with blood and violence. The daughters of the Mughal padshahs have been marrying in every generation of kings. But by the time Shah Jahan becomes padshah, the Mughal empire is a vastly different entity from the one Babur founded. It is now the most glorious, the richest and the most extensive empire on earth. The stakes have altered significantly and now blood is being spilt, royal blood, for access to this throne. Shah Jahan, having murdered his brothers and nephews to secure the throne, does not now wish to add further contenders by having his older daughters marry men from the Persian nobility. The husbands of these daughters, and their in-laws, would become powerful enough by marriage to these shahzaadis to become serious pretenders themselves. Another stark truth is that by the time Shah Jahan's daughters are old enough to marry, there are no suitable grooms for them. The Mughals have long married their daughters within the family, to first cousins and other Timurids. Now, with all their cousins murdered by Shah Jahan, there are no cousins or uncles to marry. As for the Hindustani nobility, while the Mughal men may marry Hindu rajkumaris, Mughal women may not marry Hindu men. It is possible also, for Jahanara, that there is very little incentive to leave the court of her father, where there is limitless wealth and influence, for a lesser home. After all Gauhara, youngest daughter of Shah Jahan, does get married, to Mudam Khan. And daughters will get married into the future generations of the Mughals. But for Jahanara any other alliance would only diminish her radiance, shackle the scope of her ambitions as 'that Timurid girl'. The woman who is most betrayed by these complicated Mughal calculations is Jahanara's sister, Roshanara.

Roshanara is Mumtaz Mahal's second daughter, younger to Jahanara by three years and just one year older to Aurangzeb. Raised in the volatile splendour of Shah Khurram's endlessly roving court, Roshanara is eleven years old when her father becomes padshah and Jahanara is suddenly raised from familiar elder sister to second lady of the empire. Three years later, Mumtaz Mahal dies and now Jahanara is padshah begum. Overnight, she is transformed into an untouchable, radiant presence, who can issue farmans and who no longer has time for girlish pastimes and amusements. Now she is the first lady of the zenana, in lieu of Roshanara's beloved Mumtaz Mahal, with responsibilities and duties but also immense respect and all the other women immediately transfer their loyalties to her. Roshanara's only surviving parent, her father, is so unequivocal in his preference for his eldest daughter, that there is no room in Roshanara's heart for any beguiling comfort. It is made clear that Shah Jahan's exclusive love and concern are for Jahanara and Dara Shikoh, and all the others are remote, somewhat superfluous presences. Roshanara's brittle childhood love is thwarted by something worse even than dislike or disdain—the icy disregard of her imperial father. And yet Roshanara is talented, and vivacious and charming. But in comparison to the perfect shahzaadi, she is always found lacking. She is beautiful, but not as lovely as Jahanara. She is charming and cultured, but without Jahanara's exquisitely refined elegance and taste. 'The Mogol's younger daughter,' confirms Bernier, 'was less beautiful than her sister, neither was she so remarkable for understanding; she was nevertheless possessed of the same vivacity, and equally the votary of pleasure.' Jahanara, however, is 'very handsome, of lively parts, and passionately beloved by her father'. Shah Jahan, wary of most people of influence, implicitly trusts 'his favourite child' and 'she watched over his safety and was so cautiously observant, that no dish was permitted to appear upon the royal table which had not been prepared under her superintendence'. As the two girls grow older, the torque of Jahanara's prestige spirals out from the zenana to the entire court and the world beyond: 'Begom Saeb [Jahanara], whom her father loved to an extraordinary degree, as most lovely; discreet, loving, generous, open-handed and charitable. She was loved by all, and lived in state and magnificence.' Roshanara is also not allowed the grace of anonymity through marriage like her sister Gauhara. Her youngest sister's only noteworthy act in history is to cause the death of her mother through her birth. After that she marries, bows out of the story of the Mughals of Hindustan, and is never heard of again. But Roshanara is the second oldest daughter, too powerful potentially through her Timurid blood, should anything happen to Jahanara. So she must remain at court, an increasingly bitter and restless witness to her sister's glory. There is, however, one other sibling who empathises with Roshanara's broken dreams. Aurangzeb, the closest sibling to Roshanara in age, finds in his sister's ravaged ambitions a kindred spirit. The pair become close over their shared sense of blighted destiny and chafing restrictions. They are both talented and ambitious enough to realize that with Jahanara and Dara Shikoh at court, there is no space for their own, impatient desires. The other two older sons of Mumtaz Mahal never show the calibre required to be contenders for the Mughal throne in these bruising times. Shah Shuja is 'too much a slave to his pleasures', and Murad Baksh 'a man of little wisdom, who could not plan anything beyond his amusements, drinking, singing and dancing'.

When Aurangzeb returns to court in 1652, he is a very different person from the easily wounded, prickly young man who stormed away from his father in 1644 and had to be reinstated through Jahanara's good graces. Returning from the disastrous sieges of Kandahar, he trails behind him an air of scorched desolation. He has just failed his father's cherished ambition of reclaiming Babur's ancestral lands and has suffered such humiliating defeats that they will haunt him even half a century later, when he is a dying man. The Mughals have just lost twelve crores of rupees in the Kandahar campaigns, more than half the gross annual revenue of the entire empire. The wealth of the Mughal empire at this time is estimated at twenty-one crore rupees, or 105 billion rupees in today's money. Aurangzeb realizes that the luxury of the court is just smoke and mirrors, and the supposed invincibility of the Mughal army a myth. But Aurangzeb is also now battle-scarred and battle-proven, having led campaigns in the Deccan, in Gujarat and in Central Asia. He has lived almost a decade away from the court, where no prince or courtier can match the magnificence of Dara Shikoh. A court where he was constantly undermined, his confidence bruised and his talents ignored. He has built an unwavering wall of support and loyalty from men for whom he is first amongst equals. Now he comes bolstered by his wives, his adolescent sons, his many daughters and his liege men.

Jahanara almost does not recognize the sun-darkened, battle-hardened man who walks into her apartments in 1652, after an absence of decades. His long, thin face is almost gaunt now, its length exaggerated by a pointed, black beard. He has made an effort to dress appropriately for the imperial court but he still looks austere in comparison to the amirs and mirzas of Shahjahanabad, and wears almost no jewellery. And yet, when he walks into Jahanara's room, he is still helpless in the face of her contained ardour and impeccable grace. Jahanara is in a room lavishly carpeted with pashmina rugs made in Kashmir. As the terrible days of summer have finally passed, the cool curtains of khas grass have been removed from the awnings and the scattered early winter sun streams into the room. Fresh flowers have been placed in gold vases in the corners, yellow roses from the garden and late-blooming mogra. Jahanara sits on a spotless white takht, her legs folded under her. With her pale complexion and kohl-lined eyes she looks almost like a statue in her absolute immobility as she waits for Aurangzeb, were it not for the diamonds and the rubies that glitter at her throat, and ears and wrists, like constellations. After months and years spent on desolate campaign trails and arid encampments, Aurangzeb pauses to admire the beauty of this room. Every object is exquisite, every colour is in synchrony and understated. He sees the cheetahs embroidered on the edges of the rich red carpets, the soft shahtoosh shawl around Jahanara's shoulders and the gold and jade parrot-shaped ring on her henna-stained finger. On the ground next to her are books and an intricately carved paan box. There is a perfume in the air, something warm and dark like a summer night and it is the fragrance Aurangzeb always associates with Jahanara. Jahanara gets up in a single, seamless motion, gracefully throwing the end of her odhani over her shoulder. The two siblings embrace and then discuss the disastrous Kandahar campaign Aurangzeb has just returned from. No good will come of this hopeless war, Aurangzeb senses, and he wants to explain to Jahanara that it was not for lack of valour or determination on his part that the battle was lost.

When Shah Jahan models himself as the second Qiran-e-Sani and claims to recreate the glory of Timur's empire, there is one ruthless truth he must confront—he does not rule any of Timur's original homeland. And so, 'because they were the heritage of Babur and also lay in the way to Samarqand, the capital of Timur, the founder of the Mughal dynasty', Balkh and Badakhshan must be conquered. Shah Jahan then decides to send his youngest son, twenty-two-year-old Murad Baksh, to conquer Balkh. But in a poignant reversal of Babur's situation when his noblemen wanted to desert the hot and terrible lands of Hindustan for Kabul, Murad Baksh now piteously complains to his father about the stark and uncongenial conditions of Balkh province. Unable to bear the cold, yearning for the warm and lush lands of Hindustan, Murad Baksh writes to his father that he and his nobles 'were dreading the hardships of passing a winter in that clime'. The mirza abandons his post and returns to disgrace and dishonour at his father's court. Next Aurangzeb is sent to war against Balkh where his success is tepid but his reputation for bravery is sealed when he lays out his prayer mat on the battlefield, in the hour of the evening prayer, and says his prayers amidst the noise of the raging battle and on mud glossy with blood. A few years later Aurangzeb is sent to Kandahar, to capture the city. Shah Jahan gifts his son a fine horse, for Aurangzeb loves horses and horse-riding, and he is delighted by the present. 'The Arab horse is very quiet and well-broken, such a horse has rarely been presented to this Murid in recent years,' adds Aurangzeb, in a touching testament to the disregard he always senses in his father, who has gifted him so few horses. The Mughals lay siege to Kandahar but the walls of the city, of packed mud and straw, many feet thick, are more than a match for the primitive Mughal cannons, which can only be fired eight or nine times a day. The soldiers display an astonishing lack of discipline and organization and after two months, the siege is lifted. Despite many assaults, the city walls remain unbreached and Kandahar will never again fall into Timurid hands.

'It astounds us, that after such preparations, the fort was not taken,' writes Shah Jahan bitterly to his son when he hears that the siege has been lifted. Aurangzeb begs for a chance to redeem himself, and to join forces with Dara Shikoh but Shah Jahan's reply is devastating: 'If I had considered you competent to take Kandahar, I would not have recalled your army…every man can perform some work. It is a wise saying that men of experience need no instruction.' Despite Aurangzeb's staunch defence of his reasons, Shah Jahan shows his disappointment clearly. He reduces Aurangzeb's income by 1,700,000 rupees and takes away his rich jagirs in Multan and Bhakkar. Aurangzeb is informed by Shah Jahan that he is to be posted to the Deccan, and after the rich fiefdom of Gujarat this is clearly a demotion for Aurangzeb. Even more provocative to Aurangzeb is the appointment of Dara Shikoh to take over the assault of Kandahar, the allocation to Dara of fertile jagirs in Gujarat, and the naming of Dara Shikoh's son, Suleiman Shikoh, to the governorship of Kabul.

Aurangzeb talks to Jahanara of all these many slights, these grating humiliations. She remains, for Aurangzeb, the woman he will always respect the most in his life, one who was in lieu of a maternal figure for him. He also knows that she is the most likely to influence Shah Jahan in his favour for 'among all these ladies (of the court)' as Manucci confirms, 'the most esteemed and respected was Begam Sahib, because she obtained from her father whatever she liked'. Indeed it is believed that Jahanara influences Shah Jahan to such an extent that she can affect the path of men's careers at court. Even 'the affairs of her brother Dara prospered, and he retained the friendships of the King, because she attached herself steadily to his interest, and declared openly in favour of his party', says Bernier. But when they talk about his old nemesis, Dara Shikoh, and Shah Jahan's treatment of him, Jahanara senses all the old hurt and resentment bristling beneath the surface of his very mannered urbanity. Jahanara reassures Aurangzeb the best she can, praising his 'elegant disposition, noble mind, amiable manners and mildness of tempers' and acknowledges that he has always attempted to please their father. But she misjudges the depth of his bitterness, and the ocean-wide spread of his hatred for Dara. Perhaps Aurangzeb also knows that Jahanara loves Dara Shikoh too dearly to ever consider Aurangzeb a suitable contender for the throne. Jahanara, certainly, will not realize the true extent of Aurangzeb's transgression in his ambitions. 'He was reserved, subtle and a complete master of the art of dissimulation', says Bernier of Aurangzeb. 'When in his father's court, he feigned a devotion which he never felt, and affected contempt for world grandeur while clandestinely endeavouring to pave the way to future elevation.' So Aurangzeb leaves Shahjahanabad in 1652, with turmoil in his heart. He will not meet Jahanara in Shahjahanabad till 1666 but one sister, Roshanara, gauges correctly the warp of his ambition and solders her cause to his. 'She became the ardent partisan of Aurengzebe', admits Bernier and 'she succeeded in conveying, by means of spies, much valuable intelligence to Aurangzebe'.

Aurangzeb heads south to the Deccan, stopping at Agra to meet his other older brother, Shah Shuja. It is possible that having sensed Shah Jahan's inflexible anger towards him, Aurangzeb makes some sort of pact at this point with Shah Shuja, so they would be ready to act when the time came. Ominously, an alliance is made for the marriage of Aurangzeb's son Muhammad Sultan with a daughter of Shah Shuja. He also visits the Taj Mahal, completed a few years earlier, but already showing signs of leakage. Aurangzeb, horrified at the damage, writes immediately to Shah Jahan, with suggestions for improvements and precautions. He then goes to the Deccan, where he is lord of all his domains, his supremacy unquestioned.

In the next few years Shah Jahan will send critical letters and humiliating recommendations to Aurangzeb. He will complain that Aurangzeb sends too few mangoes, too little revenue, and asks for too much. He grumbles that Aurangzeb keeps all the best weavers at Burhanpur at his own private factory and orders all the factories except the imperial one to be closed, thus publicly humiliating Aurangzeb. Ignoring his son's meticulous and laborious efforts at reviving the Deccan, Shah Jahan rebukes him and this is when Aurangzeb writes his letter to Jahanara asking 'to be relieved from the disgust of such a life'. The imperial dak chakki, the post office, is kept busy during these years, carrying fruits and gifts and letters between Aurangzeb and Jahanara and Shah Jahan. Letters are carried in bamboo tubes, stopped at both ends, or in sealed embroidered purses. Gifts come in elegant boxes or in parcels of cloth, also carefully sealed. These goods are often from the karkhaanas (manufacturing centres) which belong to Jahanara and the shahzaadas of the imperial family. Fruits, especially mangoes and pomegranates, are sent for the imperial table. Jahanara sends Aurangzeb gifts of fruits and dry fruit and he, in turn, sends her letters and presents. When Shah Jahan falls off his horse one day, Aurangzeb sends alms to Jahanara, so that she may distribute them for the padshah's health. The letters and gifts are delivered by 'chelas', men who can run up to sixty miles a day, in stages. Riders are rarely used. When horses and elephants are gifted, the valuable animals, unlike the men, are sent at a much slower pace, and rested at regular intervals.

Dara Shikoh, meanwhile, continues to prosper and in 1655 he is named Shah-e-Buland Iqbal (King of High Fortune). In 1657 he is elevated to the extraordinary rank of 50,000 horse and his son, Suleiman Shikoh, has a rank of 20,000 horse. Aurangzeb writes to Jahanara to complain that 'despite twenty years of service and loyalty he [Aurangzeb] is not considered worthy of the same level of confidence as his brother's son'. He lays his many insults and humiliations at her feet—'if it be the wish of the happy heart [Shah Jahan] that I retire into obscurity', he laments, 'Baglana [in Rajasthan] alone would have been enough for me'.

Other aggrieved parties also seek redressment from the powerful shahzaadi. In 1656, when Shah Jahan's armies have been attacking Prithvi Chand, Raja of Srinagar in the Garwhal hills, for two years, the raja writes to Jahanara assuring her of his loyalty to the padshah and Jahanara succeeds in negotiating a royal pardon for him.

While Aurangzeb, in the Deccan, burnishes the flame of his ambition with the many insults he perceives, carefully forwarded from the court by Roshanara, Dara Shikoh is immersed in an altogether different kind of project. In 1655 Dara Shikoh completes his work, the *Majma-ul-Bahrain*, or Mingling of the Two Oceans, in which he seeks to establish the similarity between Sufi and Hindu thought, through an analysis of some of the terms used to describe key concepts in Sufi scriptures and the Upanishads. This is less an attempt to fuse the two religious thoughts than to find, through the use of similar terms such as the Sanskrit 'atma' and the Persian 'ruh', an Upanishadic support for Sufi doctrine. In 1656, assisted by a team of erudite pandit scholars and translators, Dara Shikoh begins 'without any worldly motive, in a clear style an exact and literal translation' of the fifty-two Upanishads from Sanskrit into Persian. Through this work, and his admission that a common thread of thought runs through all scriptures, Dara Shikoh accepts that all religions are equally worthy of study, and that, ultimately, they all support the mystical truth he has found in the Hindustani Sufi movement. The Persian translation of the Upanishads, the *Sirr-e Akbar*, will make this ancient, oceanic religious thought available to the Europeans for the first time and, far in the future, the philosopher Arthur Schopenhauer will be directly influenced by this text and the poet William Blake will own a copy of it. It will not, however, endear Dara Shikoh to the Ulema at Shah Jahan's court. Roshanara keeps Aurangzeb updated about the happenings at this extraordinary court: the increasingly eclectic group of pandits, saints and mystics who drift into Dara's entourage, the arrogant and dismissive way in which he sometimes treats noblemen who will one day become powerful enemies. Dara sneers at Raja Jai Singh, telling him he looks like a musician, a provocative and shocking insult which the raja will not easily forget and Dara thus casually earns himself the wrath of a substantial man. When this mystically inclined shahzaada ecstatically states that 'Thou [i.e. Dara himself] verily art God', it will appal the conservative Muslim clerics and Roshanara will have much to write in her missives to Aurangzeb. In his vulnerable moments, with troubling prescience, Dara confides to his friends that the only one of his brothers who unnerves him is that 'Nemazi', or that prayerful one, Aurangzeb.

In 1657 when Shah Jahan falls ill, so that it is presumed he must die, Aurangzeb makes his inexorable move to claim the throne and his destiny. He seeks the support of his brother Murad Baksh promising to partition the empire in return for his support against Dara Shikoh. Jahanara, horrified, writes once again to her younger brother: 'You should yourself judge how impolite it is on your part to encounter and draw the sword against your own father, in whose obedience lies the pleasure of God and His Prophet', writes Jahanara, in an exact echo of the sentiments of Khanzada or Dildar Begum to Kamran. 'The result of such an action,' she adds, 'will be nothing but disgrace and ultimate ruin.' But Aurangzeb has spent the last decade waiting for just such an occasion. He has gathered his men, sharpened his rage and focused his strength till it has become a clear, luminous beam directing him to the one person he blames for the loss of his father's love: Dara Shikoh. 'The power of the elder Prince [Dara Shikoh] over the affairs of the State is beyond all description', he writes to Shah Jahan in response to Jahanara's letter. 'He is beyond doubt thirsty for our innocent blood.' The message is clear. Dara has sown the wind and must ready to reap the whirlwind which blows towards him: 40,000 of Aurangzeb's well-trained and disciplined soldiers, field artillery manned by European gunners, and a commander who dreams of revenge.

SIBLING RIVALRIES

On an oppressive day in September 1657, Shah Jahan falls so seriously ill that he is not able to present himself for his daily darshan at the jharokha of the Qila-e-Mubaarak at Shahjahanabad for several consecutive days. This seemingly innocuous dereliction of duty will have catastrophic consequences. It will lead to the longest and most bitterly fought war of succession in Mughal history and, in the long run, to the end of Shahjahanabad as glittering imperial capital. It will also bring about an astounding reversal of fortunes for the favoured siblings, Jahanara and Dara Shikoh.

Shah Jahan is now sixty-five years old, and has already lived longer than all his predecessors. His four sons are grown men. Indeed they are middle-aged, and they have adult sons of their own. Shah Shuja is governor of Bengal, Murad Baksh is in Gujarat, and Aurangzeb is governor of the Deccan. Only Dara Shikoh remains close to the padshah, in Shahjahanabad, and has recently completed his theological treatise, the *Majma-ul-Bahrain*, Mingling of the Two Oceans. Just before Shah Jahan falls ill, Dara also completes the translation of the Upanishads into Persian. He also spends considerable time discussing philosophy with an eclectic group of friends, including the Flemish Jesuit priest Father Busee, the astrologer Bhawani Das, as well as provocative dervishes and mystics. His brothers, meanwhile, are occupied in rather more ominous and warlike activities. Aurangzeb especially crackles with ill-contained ferocity and is impatient to solder the Deccan thoroughly to the Mughal empire.

The daily darshan of the padshahs is an old Hindu tradition, revived by the Mughals, and now sacrosanct. In the sacred light of dawn, it is a visible reminder of the padshah's divine magnificence, his benevolent blessing. Brahmins come to bow before Shah Jahan, courtiers throng to the banks of the Yamuna and plaintiffs come to scatter their many woes at his feet, thus feeling unburdened. And the darshan is tangible, irrefutable proof that the padshah still lives. When Shah Jahan fails to appear at the jharoka in 1657, it is the earth itself that shifts in its axis and the infallible order of life for the people of Shahjahanabad is shattered. The assured presence of the padshah anchors their days and guards them against the wasteland of lawlessness and the very gods in their heavens tremble. When Akbar dies, in 1605, a merchant of Agra, Banarsi Das, writes that 'people felt suddenly orphaned and insecure without their sire. Terror raged everywhere, the hearts of men trembled with dire apprehension, their faces became drained of colour.' Banarsi Das himself is so overcome by this catastrophic news that he is physically undone and 'reeled, and losing my balance, fell down the stairs in a faint'. This malaise is widespread and 'everyone closed the doors of his house in panic; shop-keepers shut down their shops. Feverishly, the rich hid their jewels...women shunned finery, dressing in shabby, lustreless clothes.' Half a century later, the reaction of the people is just as tumultuous and 'immediately the wildest rumours spread through the empire; Shah Jahan was dead and Dara was keeping the fact a secret till he had ensured his own succession'.

Fearing just such a reaction to Shah Jahan's illness, and to prevent the royal mirzas from rising in civil war, attempts are made at court to control all flow of information from the palace to the outside world. Dara Shikoh and Jahanara are constantly by Shah Jahan's bedside and all other visitors are strictly forbidden. Jahanara supervises the emperor's food, to guard against poison, and 'soup of mint and manna' are given as remedy for his acute water retention and swelling of limbs. Dara also forbids all couriers from travelling on the roads so as to prevent information from reaching his brothers. The gates to the palace are bolted and only supremely loyal Rajput troops are trusted to guard the palace gates. Dara tries to muzzle the agents at court who are loyal to his brothers and so temporarily imprisons Isa Beg, Aurangzeb's personal vakil at court. But another crucial source of information for Aurangzeb remains at court— Roshanara Begum.

Roshanara is now forty years old. She has lived a muted life in the shadow of her glorious sister, whose every action is celebrated. Jahanara is so universally loved and personally discreet that Roshanara knows she is beyond rumour and scandal. But there is one person who is not so faultless, and who can be brought low—Dara Shikoh. From the zenana of Shahjahanabad, Roshanara observes and forwards to Aurangzeb Dara's many transgressions. She knows he has slowly but steadily antagonized the Ulema and even many of the nobles because of his fascination with mysticism and eclectic Hinduism. He is accused of being 'constantly in the society of brahmins, yogis and sanyasis, and he used to regard these worthless teachers of delusions as learned and true masters of wisdom'. She learns of his scandalous friendship with the naked mystic Sarmad, an Armenian Jew who has converted to Islam, lives with a young Hindu man and taunts the orthodox clerics with his heretical verses. Roshanara is also aware of the fact that Dara Shikoh has made powerful enemies within the nobility due to his arrogance. 'If Dara had a failing', agrees Manucci, it was that he 'scorned the nobles, both in word and deed, making no account of them'. Nor does Dara endear himself to the Ulema when he declares that 'paradise is there where no mullah exists'. Dara himself is ill-advised, being contemptuous of the opinion of others. 'He spoke disdainfully to all those who ventured to advise him, and thus deterred his sincerest friends from disclosing the secret machinations of his brothers.' Roshanara notes all these things about Dara and she bides her time carefully. Amidst the gaunt topography of her life, Roshanara is waiting for her destiny to reveal itself. And few at court suspect the extent of her rancour or the depth of her ambition. Roshanara is 'very clever, capable of dissimulation, bright, mirthful, fond of jokes and amusement, much more so than her sister begum sahib'. Dissimulation, at least, is a trait Roshanara shares with Aurangzeb and 'all was done in great secrecy', says Manucci, of their long-range communications, 'with much craft, so that his brothers could neither know nor suspect anything'. And so, following Shah Jahan's illness, while Shah Shuja and Murad Baksh impetuously declare themselves padshah, Aurangzeb waits. And then in January 1658, he marches north, towards Agra, where Shah Jahan has been moved to, with the purported and pious aim of 'liberating' the old padshah from the noxious influence of the apostate and idolater Dara and establish peace in the empire.

Five months later Aurangzeb, along with his ally Murad Baksh, is advancing upon Agra itself. On a day in May so hot that 'many strong men died from the heat of their armor and want of water', Dara Shikoh and his imperial army have been effectively routed. From within the zenana, Shah Jahan and Jahanara are appalled at the defeat of their beloved shahzaada. Dara sends a disconsolate message to his father and sister, lamenting that 'what has now happened to me is what you foretold'. Shah Jahan had advised Dara to wait for Suleiman Shikoh, his twenty-five-year-old charismatic oldest son, who was fighting Shah Shuja. But Suleiman Shikoh is waylaid and abandoned, and will end up in the stark, rugged hills of Garhwal, under the protection of that raja. Dara is devastated by his loss, the fickle loyalty of his generals who hustle over to Aurangzeb's winning side, by the conflicting orders from his sentimental father who did not want to have his younger sons killed. Jahanara sends out a faithful eunuch with valuable jewels for Dara. She sends a message also expressing 'her deep grief, telling him that she was even more discomfited than he; but she had not lost all hope of some day seeing him reign peacefully'. But Jahanara will never see Dara alive again. He goes to his haveli, takes what precious stones he can carry, and leaves for Delhi with his three wives, his daughter, Jaani Begam, his young son, Siphir Shikoh, and a few servants.

From the zenana, Jahanara sends a long, anguished letter to Aurangzeb, encamped outside the city. 'His majesty is free from all bodily infirmities', she assures Aurangzeb. 'He is devoting all his attention to the improvement of the condition of his subjects and the maintenance of peace in the empire.' She then berates Aurangzeb for his 'unbecoming and improper action' in taking up arms against his brothers. It is clear that Jahanara now understands the true object of Aurangzeb's determined hatred, 'even if your expedition is due to antagonism to prince Dara Shukoh', she acknowledges, 'it cannot be approved by the principle of wisdom, for according to the Islamic law and convention, the elder brother has the status of a father. His majesty holds the same view.' In a distant echo of Humayun she tells Aurangzeb that 'for the life of a few days in this transitory and evil world and its deceitful and deceptive enjoyments are no compensation for eternal infamy and misfortune. Don't, don't, for the virtuous do not behave like this.' She urges Aurangzeb, instead, to write to Shah Jahan so that 'efforts (can) be made for the fulfillment of your wishes'.

But Jahanara has underestimated the corrosive loathing that Aurangzeb has for Dara, whom he blames for his father's cold criticism throughout his career. Obedience to the imperial diktat has been easy for Jahanara, cherished as she has always been. She cannot or will not see how destructive Shah Jahan's constant undermining of Aurangzeb has been. And how, somewhere, Aurangzeb is also a creature of his family's casual disdain. Aurangzeb replies with a meandering letter, blaming Dara for all his ills, claiming, disingenuously, to be acting only in self-defence. He then lays siege to the fort at Agra, cutting off its drinking water in this relentless month of June and the people in the fort capitulate within three days. Aurangzeb and his men take over the fort, its jewels, rich robes, gold and stores. Shah Jahan is, effectively, imprisoned within the zenana of the palace. At this stage, Jahanara goes to meet Aurangzeb in what will be their last meeting in many years. It is clear that Shah Jahan and the women have realized that the stakes have changed considerably. Violence has uncoiled, in the inferno of a June day, and Aurangzeb's ragged ambition will not be denied. There is, possibly, a realization that a reckoning will come for all the thwarted years during which Aurangzeb has been kept from the court and from the love of his father. Perhaps Jahanara guesses that it is for the very life of Dara Shikoh that she must now plead.

When Jahanara reaches Aurangzeb's private apartments, she is not greeted with the customary great signs of deference that are usually shown to her. Instead, she is taken to Aurangzeb's zenana, where she meets with her brother privately. This is the first time that Jahanara has had to ask anything of Aurangzeb, it has always been the other way around. For decades Aurangzeb has laid his many humiliations and slights in front of her, for her sympathy and her validation. Now Jahanara appears before her brother to ask for what is most precious to her, the life of Dara and the honour of her father. But this is not her court and her zenana. It is Aurangzeb's military encampment and he has taken over Dara's imperial red tents. Aurangzeb's men are posted everywhere, battle-hardened men, loud and raucous in their victory, even in the leaching June sun. Jahanara has a proposal for Aurangzeb, to partition the Mughal empire between the four warring brothers and Aurangzeb's oldest son. The Punjab and its territories would go to Dara, Gujarat would continue to be the fief of Murad Baksh, Bengal would be Shah Shuja's, the province of the Deccan would be given to Aurangzeb's oldest son Sultan Muhammad, and the rest of the empire, along with the title of Buland Iqbal and heir apparent is to be Aurangzeb's. This is an old Timurid solution towards warring mirzas, all of whom are equally entitled to rule. Half a century later, on his death bed, Aurangzeb will propose just such a settlement between his fractious sons, all old men themselves. But for now, Aurangzeb is implacable. He will not tolerate Dara, or his claims, in any way whatsoever. He rails against the 'infidel' Dara and claims he will save the empire from such an unbeliever. He refuses to meet with Shah Jahan, will never see his father again, and Jahanara comes away, defeated by the hate in her brother's heart.

Aurangzeb holds a darbar at Agra, distributing mansabs and titles to his noblemen. Murad, wounded after his bravery in battle and therefore a dangerous adversary for Aurangzeb, is imprisoned and will eventually be killed. At the fort in Agra, stripped of his regalia, his soldiers and his court, Shah Jahan, once Shadow of God on Earth, is a prisoner. He is allowed his zenana, and the once-famous women of Shahjahanabad—Aurangabadi Begum, Fatehpuri Begum and Sirhindi Begum—are all incarcerated with the fallen padshah. Shah Jahan is also allowed a few dancing and singing girls, Jahanara Begum, and a view of the Taj Mahal. Aurangzeb allows him his royal cook, and says he may choose a favourite dish which he may eat every day. The cook, pragmatic and surprisingly far-sighted, suggests that Shah Jahan not choose a complicated dish, but that daal can be prepared differently every day of the year. Faithful to her father and tormented by the fate of her beloved Dara, Jahanara is a constant presence by Shah Jahan's side for all the years of his imprisonment. She lays aside her lavish lifestyle, her busy trade and diplomatic dealings, as easily as she would a faded cloak. She is never heard to appeal to Aurangzeb or to complain in any way about her treatment. Just as she had once shared her father's glory, she now shares his destitution and his bitter grief. Her only desire is to console Shah Jahan and ease his burden. The glory and the magnificence of empire are now for Roshanara.

ROSHANARA BEGUM AND
A DANGEROUS BROTHER

In the light blue dawn of a day in May 1659 the residents of Shahjahanabad, who have been living in a state of muted terror this past year, are startled by the distant, raucous din of drums, pipes and trumpets. As the cacophony draws nearer and a dun cloud rises from the south, the people rush to line the streets of the city and watch as a long procession of huge elephants enters Shahjahanabad. The elephants are magnificently draped in velvet and gold cloths and golden bells clash against each other as the animals sway into the city. The elephants are followed by cavalry, smooth, tripping Arab and Persian horses with saddles of gold and gems. Then come the infantrymen, swords flashing in the early morning sun. Finally there is a dense crowd of superbly dressed noblemen surrounding the largest elephant of all. On this elephant, sitting on a golden throne, is a narrow-faced, thin and rather tall man, forty years old. Aurangzeb Alamgir Ghazi, Seizer of the Universe, finally rides into Delhi.

A few weeks later, on a day chosen by astrologers, Aurangzeb is consecrated in a ceremony that is the most lustrous of any of the padshahs before him. The Deewan-e-aam is decorated with gold and silver Persian cloths and Gujarati brocades. Golden chains hung with decorated balls are strung between the pillars and crimson tents cover every open space and the floor is thick with Persian rugs. The assembled men, all the great amirs and noblemen of the land, wait. The astrologers watch their water clocks and sandglasses and when they give a signal, Aurangzeb walks out from behind a screen. He wears a turban of gold cloth studded with diamonds and jewels, and a turban ornament made of pearls. His gleaming white qaba is decorated with fine gold embroidery and a single necklace of enormous pearls hangs down to his waist. There is a hushed and perfumed silence, broken by the syncopated, frantic call of the brain-fever bird. Aurangzeb enters the Deewan-e-aam and mounts the single most expensive object ever created—the Peacock Throne. The royal band immediately lets loose a skirl of sound, as menacing as it is joyous. Musicians begin singing and the dancing girls twirl, their dark skin shining with sweat. The khutba is read out in Aurangzeb's name and he is now officially Padshah Ghazi of Hindustan, sixth of the great Mughals. Trays of pearls and gems are scattered onto the waiting nobles, who each pick one up. They all bend down smoothly to perform the kornish, with loud shouts of 'Khalifa-e-Dauran! Zindabaad!' and imperial servants swing flasks of scented water, sprinkling the assembly with fragrant essences.

After the formal ceremony, Aurangzeb retires to the zenana and holds court there again. All the women, his wives, the wives of the other noblemen, and all his household rush to congratulate him. Roshanara watches him enter the zenana. For once he is smiling, no longer constantly watchful, and all the impatient, lonely years of waiting are forgotten. Aurangzeb is resplendent today and he wants all those who have believed in him and suffered with him to share in his joy. He gives the women gifts and distributes cash, five lakh rupees for Roshanara, and nine lakh rupees to be distributed between his four daughters. The women have worn their finest clothes and shimmer like stars in a constellation. They wear long-sleeved peshwaj in diaphanous gauze, the bodice tightly fitted while the skirt section is long and open in front, showing pajamas which are in contrasting colours, patterns and materials. Their odhanis swirl around their head and shoulders in cloth so fine it is like a cloud. Two hundred years later an Englishwoman will marvel at the inbred elegance of the Mughal women who, when they walk, are 'poetry in motion', straight-backed yet with a 'snake-like, undulating movement' of the hips whereas an Englishwoman, bound up and repressed in her stays and corsets is like a 'German Mannikin'.

Celebrations continue for weeks, with rajas and noblemen and courtiers competing with each other to offer the most gilded presents to the new padshah. Elephants, horses, swords, gems, turban ornaments and jewellery stream into the Qila-e-Mubaarak at Shahjahanabad like moonlight. At night, both banks of the Yamuna are illuminated and noblemen sail down the river past the palace, listening to music on boats alight with diyas (lamps). During all these celebrations, Roshanara is the premier woman of the zenana and of the empire. Aurangzeb's principle wife, a Persian shahzaadi called Dilras Banu Begum, died a few years previously and his few remaining wives are minor ones. Roshanara is now the most celebrated woman of the zenana, an imperial woman from the line of Timur himself, and she is ferociously happy, wanting to make up for the unlovely years spent in the careless neglect of her father. And finally in July comes news that fills both siblings with an excitement that is beyond reason or restraint. Dara Shikoh, on the run these past months, has been captured and is being brought to Shahjahanabad.

By the time Aurangzeb is pronounced Padshah Ghazi of Hindustan, he has neutralized all three brothers. Murad is his prisoner, Shuja and Dara have both been defeated, but Dara has been evading capture, in increasingly desperate circumstances. He has lost all his generals, his soldiers and his allies. Everywhere he goes, accompanied now only by a few women from his zenana and some servants, he is attacked by marauders and betrayed by opportunists. At one point, he plans to flee to Persia as Humayun and Hamida had done in another age but Nadira Banu, his beloved wife and granddaughter of Akbar, cannot bear the thought of exile away from Hindustan. Eventually Nadira Banu commits suicide by drinking poison, unable to bear any further humiliation. Dara is betrayed one last time, captured, and brought to Shahjahanabad.

In Shahjahanabad, in a cruel parody of Dara's once imperial splendour, the shahzaada and his young son Siphir Shikoh are paraded through the streets of the city. Dara is seated on an old, emaciated elephant that lumbers painfully in the torpid August heat. He is wearing tattered rags, no jewellery, a 'dark dingy-coloured turban, such as only the poorest wear'. The contrast with the shahzaada's earlier resplendence is a pointed desecration. Aurangzeb does not only want to humiliate Dara, he wants to annihilate from the very memory of the people his earlier glory. But the people of Shahjahanabad love their shahzaada, who has for so many years lived in the city and represents the best of their tolerant, inquisitive, generous selves. 'The crowd assembled was immense,' writes Bernier, himself overcome by Dara's fate. 'And everywhere I observed the people weeping, and lamenting the fate of Dara in the most touching language. From every quarter I heard piercing and distressing shrieks…men, women and children wailing as if some mighty calamity had happened to themselves.' Dara is paraded through the great boulevards of Shahjahanabad, accompanied by the helpless wails of the people, through Chandni Chowk, and passes in front of Jahanara's great caravanserai, and then through Faiz Bazaar and out into the suburbs, where he is imprisoned. That evening, in the Deewan-e-aam, the fate of Dara is discussed. Danishmand Khan, Bernier's employer, pleads for his life but many other nobles want his death. The most vociferous voice, according to Bernier, is Roshanara and 'her clamours silenced the feeble voice of mercy in a court where most ministers shaped their opinions after their master's inclinations'. Aurangzeb and Roshanara are subsumed by their one desire—Dara will die for the relentless poison that their lives have been. For the blighted dreams, the stifled ambition, the constant rebukes, Dara's vaulting and consuming arrogance and the humiliations at court, especially for Aurangzeb, that ill-loved 'nemazi'. Roshanara gives voice to the primal pain and hate that Aurangzeb, now padshah, cannot. They have never been so united in their purpose before, their hatred for Dara burning away all their differences. They will not falter in their resolve, now, so close to the end, and Dara will die. After a few desultory days of imprisonment, Dara is condemned—he is to be executed as an enemy of the Faith, as an Infidel and an Idolator. Dara is decapitated, and then buried under the dome of Humayun's tomb, in the quiet company of his illustrious ancestors. His daughter, Jaani Begum, is first taken into the zenana of Aurangzeb, but then transferred to Agra, into Jahanara's more resilient care.

Aurangzeb is just as merciless with his remaining brothers and erstwhile allies. After a few years of imprisonment, Murad Baksh is killed. Shah Shuja is forced into exile, where he, too, is murdered. Suleiman Shikoh, eldest son of Dara and heir presumptive to the throne when his father lived, is taken away from the Raja of Garwhal. Imprisoned in Gwalior fort, he is fed posta, a drink made from poppy seeds, every day for a year. He dies a broken, debilitated, raving man, wracked by dementia from the opium poisoning.

With Shah Jahan imprisoned in distant Agra, and Dara Shikoh dead,

Roshanara can finally lead the life in Shahjahanabad that she has yearned to live. She has the wealth, the gems, the regalia and respect, and also the gratitude of the padshah. But her great, visceral need is to overshadow the memory of her sister, to display the same magnificence that was the padshah begum's for so many decades. One of the ways in which she can do this is during the springtime migration to Kashmir.

In December 1662, following a serious illness, Aurangzeb decides to go to Kashmir, to avoid the summer which falls so suddenly in the plains, like a curse. All the preparations are made for this long journey as it can be a full year before they return. Aurangzeb's personal bodyguard, 35,000 horsemen strong, travels with him, as do another 10,000 infantry, artillery and cannon. Anyone connected to the court and household in any manner whatsoever must prepare to leave, no matter their circumstances and Shahjahanabad becomes a ghost town. Two hundred camels, 100 mules, 50 elephants and 100 porters are used to carry the royal tents, of which there are two sets, as one entire set must ride on ahead to be ready for the padshah when he arrives. This mobile city sets off at a leisurely pace, taking over two months to reach Lahore, and at last Roshanara can head this most sparkling of exhibitions—the imperial zenana on the move. Bernier, who takes part in this journey in the train of Danishmand Khan admits that he 'cannot avoid dwelling on this pompous procession of the Seraglio'. This ardent Frenchman, who sometimes finds conditions in Hindustan overwhelming, is clearly awestruck by this great caravan. 'Stretch imagination to its utmost limits', he urges the reader, 'and you can conceive no exhibition more grand and imposing than when Rauchenara-Begum, mounted on a stupendous Pegu [Burma] elephant, and seated in a Mikdember [a large, decorated howdah], blazing with gold and azure, is followed by five or six other elephants with Mikdembers nearly as resplendent as her own, and filled with ladies attached to her household.' Roshanara's elephant is surrounded by the chief eunuchs, and an elite troupe of urdubegis 'fantastically attired and riding handsome pad-horses'. Footmen with large canes lead the way before Roshanara's elephant, clearing the road and driving away any possible miscreants. Behind the royal elephant follow 'one hundred and fifty women, her servants, riding handsome horses and covered from head to foot with their mantles of various colours, each with a cane in her hand'. She is followed by some sixty additional magnificent elephants, all carrying the highest ladies of the court. Bernier stoutly assures us that 'had I not regarded this display of magnificence with a sort of philosophical indifference, I should have been apt to be carried away by such flights of imagination as inspire most of the Indian poets...'

This royal procession, several kilometres long, is a display of all that is most magnificent in the Mughal empire. The Arab war horses, the enormous cavalry and infantry, the falcons and hawks from Central Asia trained for the hunt, the soft-stepping leopards in golden chains, the lions and rhinoceros 'brought merely for parade', the great crimson Mughal tents and all the noblemen of the court, men of the greatest erudition and culture. For Aurangzeb, and now for Roshanara, these long journeys are indispensable in displaying the strength and the glory of the Mughal empire to all its peoples. The pace of the journey is very leisurely, Aurangzeb making frequent detours to hunt. Everywhere they go the people have an opportunity to see this immense tented city of brocade and gold, and the power of the empire, immutable and unchanging as the monsoon winds. Elaborate meals are cooked, bazaars are as well stocked as in the city, and venison from the hunt is plenty. The vast majority of soldiers, however, survive on 'kichery, a mess of rice and other vegetables over which, when cooked, they pour boiled butter'. Bernier himself is brought low when Danishmad Khan's camel is lost, and the oven with it, so that the abject Frenchman 'fears [he] shall be reduced to the necessity of eating the bazar bread'. When they arrive at the foot of the mountains, after many months of travel, only a chosen few are allowed to actually enter Kashmir itself, so as not to overburden the resources of that country. Of the women, Roshanara and 'the intimate friends of Rauchenara-Begum and those women whose services cannot easily be dispensed with', continue the journey. Months are then passed in Kashmir, this 'paradise of the Indies', before the slow return to the plains.

For the first few years of Aurangzeb's rule, the court at Shahjahanabad is largely unchanged. He maintains many of the courtly traditions, even those with clear Hindu traditions such as the darshan at the jharoka and the weighing of the padshah against gold. These are the years of

Roshanara's greatest ascendancy at court, when Aurangzeb is yet uncertain of his grasp on power and keeps his loyal allies close. The women of the zenana enjoy the same opulent lifestyle as they did under Shah Jahan. 'The goldsmiths are almost continuously busy with the making of ornaments' for the women are exceedingly fond of jewellery. Gems are worn uncut and strung on threads and are so large as to look like fruit. They wear several rows of pearls, hanging down to their stomachs, and bunches of pearls as head ornaments on their brow. They wear rings and bracelets and armbands and even the strings on their pajamas are hung with pearls. Their hair is braided, oiled and perfumed and covered in cloths of gold. The shahzaadis sometimes wear turbans adorned with aigrettes. Music is enormously appreciated by the court as well as by the nobility of Shahjahanabad. Mehfils (evenings of courtly entertainment) are organized regularly, and it is Dhrupad, with its rigorous training and sombre tones that is most popular with the discerning elite. Indeed, music is not just entertainment, but a deeply serious science, with treatises being written on theory and performance of Hindustani music, sponsored by royal and noble patrons. Initially Aurangzeb, too, is an enthusiast, giving women musicians and dancers of the zenana evocative names such as Chanchal Bai, Surosh Bai, Dhyan Bai etc. Dance is popular too and all women groups of dancers called Kanchani (the blooming) are even allowed into the zenana, and attend the meena bazaars. They are trained singers and dancers and dance with 'wonderful agility, and were always correct with regard to time'.

As the implacable years go by, a change comes over Aurangzeb. He is increasingly haunted by the steps he has had to take to become padshah, the blood he has spilt and the sacred oaths he has crossed. Most grievous of these sins is that his father, the padshah, is still alive. While brothers have fought over the throne for a long time, it is considered a heinous sin to overthrow one's own reigning father. So abhorrent is this idea that the senior qazi of the Mughal empire refused to sanction Aurangzeb's ascension. Far away in Persia, the Safavid king made a sharply taunting pun when he said that Aurangzeb was less seizer of the world (alam-giri) and more seizer of his father (pidar-giri). Aurangzeb cannot even countenance the charge, always claiming that Shah Jahan has abdicated. He becomes increasingly subsumed by the idea of being seen as a just ruler, an upholder of Islam. Always of 'a melancholy temperament, always busy at something or another, wishing to execute justice and arrive at appropriate decisions', he begins to take on the appearance of an increasingly devout man. He begins to memorize the Quran, and abstains from alcohol and opium, favourite Mughal pastimes. He forbids the dancing Kanchani from entering the zenana and discourages music. 'He was extremely anxious to be recognized by the world as a man of wisdom', agrees Manucci, 'clever, and a lover of the truth'. Time seems to sharpen Aurangzeb's guilt about his father and settles, cold as pebbles, into his sinew and bones. For Roshanara, however, these are incomprehensible doubts. She is free of the rigorous etiquette of her father and sister and her primary concern is to lead the life of an opulent Mughal royal. She drinks wine, as do many Mughal women, and as they have done since the time Babur made a critical note of his drunken woman dining companion. She has an entourage of singing and dancing women and she would prefer fewer restraints, rather than new ones. It was a shared hatred of Dara that united these unlikely siblings and now that he is dead, rifts appear in their unequal camaraderie. It is a sign of their ambivalent partnership that Aurangzeb never does make Roshanara the padshah begum. And then, in 1666, Shah Jahan dies.

For almost eight years, the women of Shah Jahan's zenana have been cloistered behind the high walls of Agra fort. They have been abandoned by all the nobles of the land, who once so assiduously courted them, like the waves of a receding tide. Bereft of all her occupations, Jahanara watches over her dying father, and patience defines the grain of her days. Now she would like a grand funeral for her father, to honour his memory as grandest of the great Mughals, but this is not allowed to her. Instead the corpse, cleaned and then wrapped in a shroud, is taken away from the fort by boat, in the inauspicious dusk, accompanied by just a few nobles and scholars. In Shahjahanabad, the royal zenana wears mourning clothes, as do the shahzaadas, but Aurangzeb does not go to Agra. When he does come, a month later, Jahanara is ready and waiting for him.

Jahanara is a pragmatic woman. As she prepares to meet the murderer of her beloved brother and soulmate, and the jailer of her once mighty father, she knows that her future depends on how she conducts this first meeting. So she banishes her horror and loathing to a place where it will never be found. Perhaps she offers it up to be cleansed by her Sufi masters so that it no longer taints her heart. What she does, instead, is prepare the fort at Agra with all the marks of honour apt for a padshah. Rich brocade tapestries and carpets are laid out at the place where Aurangzeb must alight from his elephant at the entrance of the fort. When he enters the zenana, Jahanara greet him with a large gold basin full of gems, her own as well as Shah Jahan's. 'After the usual obeisances,' writes Manucci, 'she presented to him the letter of pardon that, as she said, she had obtained from Shahjahan, her father, together with the valuable and ancient jewels remaining under his control.' Aurangzeb may have reason to doubt the authenticity of this letter, but he believes it is enough to quell the rancour of the people. He is 'moved by the magnificence of his reception and the affectionate protestations of his sister', and orders all the nobles of Agra to present themselves at the fort with gifts for the ladies of the zenana. Within weeks, Shah Jahan's great zenana is disbanded. Servants and other women who were not widows of Shah Jahan could marry if they wished. The widows are all brought back to Shahjahanabad, into the palace designated for them within the fort, Suhaagpura. And in October 1666, Jahanara rides back to Delhi on an imperial elephant, once again Padshah Begum of the Mughal empire.

Jahanara does not join Aurangzeb's zenana within the fort, but instead is given the mansion of Ali Mardan Khan, one of the highest nobles of the land, now dead. His mansion was built alongside Dara Shikoh's, in the prime position overlooking the Yamuna. It is an enormous estate, and a particularly beautiful haveli because Ali Mardan Khan was an extremely skilful builder. The haveli is a city unto itself, with its large gateway, public and private apartments, and elaborate living quarters for the attending poets, physicians, soldiers, artists, astrologers etc. Jahanara has had the mansion redecorated with her usual inimitable flair and the rooms are bright with curtains and vases of flowers hang from niches in the walls. There are exquisite paintings, brocade cushions and the ceilings gleam with gilding and pieces of glass. Jahanara, unmarried shahzaadi of the Mughal empire, commands her own sprawling household and this is, in its own way, a momentous achievement. Roshanara has long begged for just such an independent arrangement of Aurangzeb but he has always refused. For no matter how wealthy and ambitious the women, there is always the tiresome protocol of the zenana with its mahaldaars and tahwildars, and urdubegis and eunuchs. It is a bitter realization for Roshanara that despite her years of loyalty and support, it is Dara's ally, Jahanara, who has the respect and the power, even now. Aurangzeb gifts Jahanara 100,000 gold pieces and an annual pension of 17 lakh rupees, and restores her title of Padshah Begum.

Jahanara is now fifty-four years old and all her great building works and her philosophical writings, are behind her. There is a slackening of ambition, maybe even a laying down of arms, now that Aurangzeb is padshah instead of Shah Jahan. She concentrates instead on the education of her niece, Jaani Begum, and her literary and musical salons become famous in all Shahjahanabad. In 1669 she organizes the wedding of sixteen-year-old Jaani with Aurangzeb's oldest son, Mirza Muhammad Azam and this is the first imperial wedding of Aurangzeb's reign. A lavish ceremony is organized in her haveli, and 'Begum sahib...to the seed pearls which issued from her eyes at thus losing her beloved niece, added lovely pearls and handsome jewels as a marriage present.' Manucci is eloquent in his description of Jahanara's tears but surely the shahzaadi weeps as much at the recollection of the bride's father's wedding, as at the pain of separation from her niece.

Jahanara establishes herself in the city as the most influential woman patron of literature and poetry. She collects rare and beautiful books and her library is peerless. She donates money to charity, especially Sufi dargahs, and carries on a genteel diplomacy with minor rajas who come to her with grievances and gifts. Budh Prakash, the Raja of Sirmaur in the lower Himalayas, is particularly assiduous, sending gifts such as honey, hill birds and animals, and medicinal herbs. Jahanara writes to the raja, informing him of the arrival of the pomegranates, musk, wild partridges, and delphinium flowers and asking for one more wild partridge. 'As a favour,' she adds, 'from our regal chambers a khillat (robe of honour) is being sent to you as a reward. May it glorify you. Consider me your benefactor.' In another letter, she informs him that 'the taste of the honey was delicious and pleasing' but that 'the falcon is yet juvenile, therefore, we have procured another one in exchange'. She commiserates with the raja when he gets 'dirty, unfrozen ice' from the daroga Abdur Rahman, who manages the ice pits, and assures dire consequences for the negligence. She mediates the somewhat frosty relations between the Raja of Sirmaur, also known as 'burfi raja' as he owns the royal ice pits, and the Raja of Garhwal, about land boundaries.

Towards the end of the 1660s, Aurangzeb introduces a number of measures which subtly but irrevocably alter the nature of the court and the city. He abolishes the daily darshan and the weighing of the padshah against gold, and the use of gold in men's clothes. Aurangzeb himself has begun wearing very plain, inexpensive clothes, and but a few ornaments, in sharp contrast to his father and grandfather. He wears 'nothing but a small plume or aigrette in the middle of his turban and a large precious stone in front; on his stomach another. He wears no strings of pearls.' Many court rituals are pared down, their musical elements forbidden. Imperial patronage for music, especially, is withdrawn and the court at Shahjahanabad is austere and forlorn. Poets and musicians relocate to the courts of the shahzaadas and the nobles, notably Danishmand Khan, and also disseminate to other provinces. These arts will continue to grow, away from the baleful imperial eye. For Roshanara, however, sequestered within the Qila-e-Mubaarak of Shahjahanabad, this is no consolation. She has always been fond of music and dance, and even drinking, and now must submit to the increasingly frugal and abstemious Aurangzeb's diktat. After a few short years of glory, she is relegated again, and forever, to that terrible station: second place. She dies in 1671 and is buried in the garden complex that bears her name.

Jahanara survives her sister by another ten years. But the death of her irrepressible, fun-loving sister shakes her, despite their lifelong differences. A wisp of mortality, perhaps, an acknowledgement of a reckoning to come. For in the same month as the death of her sister, an order is issued to 'equip a ship and bring it to Surat for special use of Sarkar Nawab Ulyatul Alia [Jahanara] who intends proceeding this year to Mecca on pilgrimage, and conveying instructions to Saifulla, Governor of Surat, to provide facilities for the departure of the ship.' Decades after the last great Mughal woman sailed for Mecca, Jahanara intends to make this arduous and unpredictable journey herself, at the age of fifty-seven, and she has Aurangzeb's blessing. No further record exists, however, of this intended journey, and Jahanara never does go to Mecca. The reason for the journey, and its ultimate failure, remains unknown, adding to the mystery around this decidedly enigmatic shahzaadi.

In 1679, Aurangzeb leaves Shahjahanabad for the Deccan, never to return. For almost thirty years, he will roam the Deccan like his nomadic ancestors, in the crimson tents of the padshahs. Of the 400,000 denizens of Shahjahanabad, only some 80,000 remain, the rest leaving in the train of the padshah. Jahanara remains too, and dies, two years later, in 1681. She has given away her money, her gems and her property to her nieces, reserving her favourite jewels for Jaani Begum. She is buried in a tomb of her own design and choosing. The place she has chosen for her grave, after a lifetime spent in the most opulent court in the world, is supremely unostentatious, but it is also the most sacred one, for it ensures immortal life. She is buried at Nizamuddin Auliya's Dargah, between the graves of Nizamuddin and his beloved disciple Amir Khusru, the only woman whose tomb is within the sacred complex. Jahanara has a simple, open air tomb of white marble, so very different from the mausoleum of her parents. An inscription on the tomb, written by Jahanara herself, is perhaps a cryptic answer to the enigma that is this most magnificent, and most elusive, of the women of the great Mughals:

Let nothing cover my tomb save the green grass for
Grass suffices well as a covering for the grave of the lowly.

THE WOMAN IN THE TOWER AND THE LAST PADSHAH BEGUM

When making a weary assessment of his four warring sons' capacity to rule Hindustan, Shah Jahan had said that 'the resolution and intelligence of Aurangzib prove that he (alone) can shoulder this difficult task. But there is great sickness and infirmity in his physical frame.' Shah Jahan was possibly never more wrong than when he misjudged his son's vitality, for though Aurangzeb will always remain very thin, and will appear gaunt and frail in old age, he has a robust vitality which will make him the longest-lived of the great Mughals. Frugal in his habits, he is a vegetarian and renounces alcohol for most of his adult life. In the miniatures of his old age he furls around his Quran like a leaf, insubstantial and pale as regret. But he is ninety when he dies in 1707, with four surviving sons, old men themselves, and nine grandsons. 'Old age is arrived,' he admits in a letter, 'weakness is grown powerful and strength is departed from my joints.' But Aurangzeb shows no fallibility at all, retaining a tight, obsessive control over his sons and their households. Desperate to seek alliances in a crumbling empire threatened with insurgencies by the Jats, Bundelas, Sikhs, Rajputs and Marathas, the shahzaadas revolt and Aurangzeb reacts with scathing speed. He imprisons most of his sons, at one point or the other, and some of the royal women too. 'Never trust your sons,' Aurangzeb writes for baleful posterity, 'nor treat them during your lifetime in an intimate manner, because, if the Emperor Shah Jahan had not treated Dara Shukoh in this manner, his affairs would not have come to such a sorry pass.' Inevitably, as the years turn to decades, the women of the zenana align themselves with a brother, a father or a husband, and, just as inevitably this results in thwarted lives or muted glory.

Zeb-un-Nisa, Aurangzeb's eldest daughter, is born in Daulatabad in

1638 when Aurangzeb is governor of the Deccan. While Daulatabad fort dominates the horizon from a hilltop, Aurangzeb is building a new capital at Khadki town, stronghold of Jahangir's old nemesis, Malik Ambar the 'rebel of black fortune'. Malik Ambar is now long dead, having never allowed the Mughals to claim the Deccan while he lived. Zeb-un-Nisa, daughter of the Persian noblewoman Dilras Banu Begum, grows up in this provincial capital, far from the intrigues of the Mughal court. In the Deccan, the supremacy of her father is unchallenged and Zeb-un-Nisa is given a rigorous education under the supervision of Hafiza Mariam, a scholar from a Khurasani family. Zeb-un-Nisa is an excellent student and excels in the Arabic and Persian languages. Her father is so delighted when she recites the entire Quran from memory as a child that he gifts her 30,000 gold mohurs. In her erudition and her quick wit she is very like her aunt, Shahzaadi Jahanara, whom her father respects above all the other women of the court. When she is fifteen years old, she visits Shahjahanabad with Aurangzeb's zenana as they return from the doomed Kandahar campaign. She is enchanted with the sparkling new city, the elegant women with their refined tehzeeb, their every gesture studied and full of grace. In the travelling court of her father, in these wildering years, it is a more pragmatic and pared down zenana but in 1658, when Zeb-un-Nisa is twenty years old, Aurangzeb deposes Shah Jahan and his household moves to Shahjahanabad.

Dilras Banu Begum, the somewhat haughty senior wife of Aurangzeb, is now dead. Even Aurangzeb, when giving marital advice to a grandson, will later admit that 'in the season of youth', he 'too had this relation with a wife who had extreme imperiousness'. Since the other wives of Aurangzeb have less illustrious backgrounds, the senior women of the royal zenana are Roshanara and her eldest niece, Zeb-un-Nisa.

For twenty years Zeb-un-Nisa will be one of the most influential women of the zenana at Shahjahanabad. Her particular area of interest is poetry and literature. She collects valuable manuscripts and books and her library is one of the most extensive in the country. When Aurangzeb begins to retrench imperial patronage towards music and poetry, it is the royal women, the shahzaadas, the noblemen and then, later still, the wealthy middle class of Shahjahanabad who will continue the patronage of the arts. The governor of Shahjahanabad, Aqil Khan, is himself a poet and writes under the pen name Razi. Indeed, despite Aurangzeb's later disfavour, Shahjahanabad fairly pulses with music. It tumbles from the kothis of the courtesans, the women thoroughly trained singers themselves, who bring Delhi Qawwali singing to mainstream attention. It vaults out of the large mansions of the newly wealthy, who prefer the lighter Khayaal and Thumri styles. In the gloaming of a tropical evening, it throbs out of the immense havelis of the princes and the noblemen, in the tenuous hold that Dhrupad still has amongst the elite of the Mughal court. And the poets keep gathering at Shahjahanabad, despite Aurangzeb's dismissal of them as 'idle flatterers'. They come from very far, like Abd-al-Qader Bidel, whose family is Chagatai Turkic but whose poetry so defines a phase of Shahjahanabadi poetry that he becomes Abd-al-Qader Dehlvi. Some will come from the Deccan, like Wali Dakhni, and some are born in the narrow, winding galis (lanes) of Shahjahanabad itself. They will write in Persian, in Urdu, in Braj and later in Rekhti. They will write in obscure philosophical quatrains, in flamboyant ghazals or in erotic riti styles but many will glow with the high-voltage mysticism of Sufi thought, for the ghosts of Shahjahanabad's Sufi saints will enchant all the poets of the city.

Zeb-un-Nisa, like Jahanara who returns to court as padshah begum in 1666, is instrumental in supporting the work of writers and poets through her patronage. She supports the scholar Mulla Safiuddin Adbeli when he translates the Arabic *Tafsir-i-Kabir* (Great Commentary) into Persian and he dedicates the book to the shahzaadi—Zeb-ut-Tafasir. She also sponsors the Hajj pilgrimage of Muhammad Safi Qazwini. Qazwini will write an extraordinary account of his voyage, the *Pilgrims' Confidant*, unique in its genre and magnificently illustrated and will dedicate it to Zeb-un-Nisa. For a few years, the courts of Jahanara and Zeb-un-Nisa will nurture this eclectic maelstrom of a culture, which has much more in common with Babur and Humayun's camaraderie of artists than it has with Aurangzeb's increasingly austere one. When Aurangzeb bans opium and alcohol, the easy complicity that the noblemen and padshahs shared in the ghusal khaana or the Deewan-e-khaas while drinking wine, is now forbidden. The imperial women, however, continue to drink wine, often made from grapes in their own gardens, flavoured with spices.

In 1669, Zeb-un-Nisa attends the lavish marriage ceremony of her cousin, Jaani Begum, to her brother, Muhammad Azam, at the haveli of Jahanara. There will be other weddings too: her sister Zubdat-un-Nisa will marry Dara Shikoh's youngest son Siphir Shikoh and Mehr-un-Nisa will marry Murad Baksh's son Izad Baksh. But for Aurangzeb's oldest daughters, there are no more cousins to marry. There is an understanding, also, that these oldest daughters, like their aunts, possess a powerful charisma as Timurid shahzaadis and must be kept within the controlling orbit of the imperial zenana. The decades pass and still Aurangzeb rules, as resolute and restless as a young man. His sons, meanwhile, are growing old and impatient. Muhammad Akbar is Zeb-un-Nisa's youngest brother and she is particularly close to him, as their mother Dilras Banu died soon after giving birth to him, when Zeb-un-Nisa was nineteen. The other sons are middle-aged men, and there have been skirmishes, the shahzaadas jostling for power, always subdued immediately by their unforgiving father. In 1681, when Muhammad Akbar decides to challenge his father, with the support of a Rajput alliance including the Rathors of Jodhpur, Zeb-un-Nisa is in a particularly vulnerable position.

In 1681, Jahanara dies. The imperial zenana has glowed with her ambition and talent for more than half a century. If the shahzaadas are uncertain about the future leadership of the Mughal empire, then the stakes are almost as high in the imperial zenana. Zeb-un-Nisa believes she may become the next padshah begum. She is a woman of letters, like Jahanara, with the same Sufi inclinations too. She is the eldest of the Timurid shahzaadis and presides over an astonishingly talented salon. It is time, surely, for a shahzaada to ascend the Peacock Throne as Aurangzeb is already an old man, sixty-three years old. So Zeb-un-Nisa sides with the young prince Muhammad Akbar, hoping to ensure her legacy in the next court.

But Aurangzeb is able to defeat Muhammad Akbar, using a mixture of duplicity and treachery. In the process, he discovers letters which incriminate Zeb-un-Nisa, demonstrating her ardent support for her brother. 'What belongs to you is as good as mine,' Muhammad Akbar writes in a letter to Zeb-un-Nisa, 'and whatever I own is at your disposal.' And in another letter he writes: 'The dismissal or appointment of the sons-in-law of Daulat and Sagar Mal is at your discretion. I have dismissed them at your bidding. I consider your orders in all affairs as sacred like the Quran and Traditions of the Prophet, and obedience to them is proper.' Muhammad Akbar is exiled to Persia, and Zeb-un-Nisa is imprisoned at the Salimgarh fort in Delhi. Her pension of four lakhs rupees a year is discontinued and her property is seized.

Very soon after this rebellion, Aurangzeb leaves Shahjahanabad for the Deccan with an entourage of tens of thousands, all of his sons and his zenana. He will never return to Shahjahanabad, which will slowly be leached of all of its nobility, craftsmen, soldiers and traders. Zeb-un-Nisa will live more than twenty years imprisoned in Salimgarh fort. She will grow old here as Shahjahanabad empties of its people and becomes a shadow of its former self. But the poets and the singers do not desert Shahjahanabad, their fortunes and their hearts are too inextricably linked to the great city, to this paradise on earth. Other patrons take over the role of the nobility, humbler people, so that a critical poet will later write:

> Those who once rode elephants now go barefooted; (while) those
> who longed for parched grains once are today owners of property
> mansions, elephants and banners, (and now) the rank of the lions
> has gone to the jackals.

Not only do the poets remain but their poetry becomes saturated with the haunted longing and nostalgia which becomes the calling card of all the great poets of Delhi. This city of beauty and splendour, abandoned and then desecrated, and then bloodied, will inspire reams of poetry on the twin themes of grief and remembrance. In the future, one of these poets will court eternity when he writes:

> Dil ki basti bhi Sheher Dilli hai;
> Jo bhi guzra usi ne loota

As for Zeb-un-Nisa, she waits for Muhammad Akbar to claim the Peacock Throne but he dies, in 1703, outlived by his father. From her lonely prison on the Yamuna, the shahzaadi can see Shah Jahan's magnificent fort. The Qila-e-Mubaarak remains locked up for decades and the dust and ghosts move in. The bats make their home in the crenelated awnings and sleep as the relentless sun arcs through the lattice windows. Bees cluster drunkenly around the fruit trees in the Hayat Baksh, the overripe fruit crushed on the marble walkways like blood. Moss skims over the canals and the pools, though the waterfall still whispers its secrets to itself in the teh khana (underground chamber) as Zeb-un-Nisa waits. Zeb-un-Nisa writes poetry while she waits for a deliverance that will never come. She is a poet of some repute, and writes under the pseudonym Makhvi, the Concealed One. This is a popular pseudonym, however, and it is difficult to establish which lines are truly written by the shahzaadi but it is likely that the following wistful and delicate lines are hers, written in the grim solitude of Salimgarh fort:

Were an artist to choose me for his model—
How could he draw the form of a sigh?

She dies in 1702, unforgiven by Aurangzeb, and is buried in the Tees Hazari Garden, gifted to her by Jahanara.

◆

Almost a century after Thomas Roe's embassy to the exuberant court of Jahangir and Noor Jahan, William Norris, the newly appointed ambassador from England, arrives in 1702 at the vastly different court of Aurangzeb. This Cambridge man from a distinguished Lancashire family has an endlessly delayed, chaotic and blighted journey to Burhanpur, where Aurangzeb's war camp has been erected. Throughout his journey there are signs of the fin de siècle malaise that corrodes the great Mughal empire. As Norris crosses the country from Surat to Burhanpur, predatory raids by robbers and bands of Marathas who oppose the padshah are a constant menace. On the way he meets another Englishman in Prince Azam Shah's service, who tells Norris of rumours the shahzaada has heard of the ill-health of Aurangzeb who 'was dying and that for three days he had not spoken to anybody'. He crosses rich, fertile fields, rivers with fresh water and rugged mountains with hilltop strongholds. He comes upon a town with strong mud fortifications where the inhabitants are terrified of allowing in strangers because they have recently been attacked by 500 Maratha horsemen. Further down the road, Norris and his party find the bodies of seven slain men, stripped, stabbed and lying face down and killed while on imperial duty. After months of arduous trek across stony hills and arid forests, Norris and his party arrive at last at Burhanpur, where Aurangzeb is waging war against two Maratha hill-fortresses. It is the monsoon season and 'black and dark' clouds hustle across the sky while the hail stones are 'as big as ordinary plums and shaped like young mushrooms' and 'very troublesome'. The people of Burhanpur are fascinated by the English ambassador, massing in large numbers to watch the English soldiers' drill, which they are made to perform every evening. They also come to watch Sunday service, watching in rapt attention so that Norris is moved to admit: 'I have seen many congregations in England behave themselves with less decency than these infidels.'

When the beleaguered party arrive at the imperial camp, Norris is less impressed with the Mughal officials and he finds that even the qazi is corrupt, demanding a fine horse from Norris and the ambassador rails that 'these people are as base as corrupt because they are made up of falsehood themselves believe there is not Truth in anyone else'. Of Aurangzeb's 100,000 strong army, not more than 20,000 are actually fighting men. The imperial coffers are empty and there is no money to pay this excess of men. 'The soldiers were grumbling and beginning to be mutinous, leaving their posts and openly speaking "slightly and reviling" of the Emperor himself.' And yet Aurangzeb 'is very cunning and has spies upon every body and so good intelligence that nobody can move a step or speak a word but he knows it.' When Norris enters the great Mughal mobile camp itself, he finds it 'meaner and poorer than can be expressed or would be believed. Nothing to be seen but confusion and disorder in their encampment and the nastiness and stench of the place very offensive, taking no care to remove any stench but let all sort of nastiness and dead carcasses which at present are pestilential.' This noxious, ill-managed, ragged encampment is particularly shocking given the earlier great luxury of Roshanara and Jahanara's mobile tents.

In the churning mud of the Deccan, suffocated by the stench of dead animals, resides the zenana of the last padshah begum of the great Mughals, Zeenat-un-Nisa. Zeenat-un-Nisa is the younger sister of Zeb-un-Nisa, and is also the daughter of Dilras Banu Begum. When Jahanara dies in 1681 and Zeb-un-Nisa makes the fatal mistake of siding with Muhammad Akbar, Aurangzeb makes Zeenat-un-Nisa padshah begum of the zenana. This educated, cultured shahzaadi will move to the Deccan in the retinue of her father and will remain there as the head of his household till his death in 1707. Hers will be an increasingly lonely place by her father's side, as all the other senior women disappear. After Dilras Banu's early death, it is Aurangzeb's second wife, Nawab Bai, the Kashmiri daughter of Raja Raju of Rajauri, who then falls out of favour. When her son Shah Alam is imprisoned by Aurangzeb, Nawab Bai also follows her son in disgrace, where she dies in 1691, undone by the shame. Aurangabadi Mahal, another wife, also dies in 1688 and the only wife left is Udaipuri Mahal, a young wife who is Zeenat-un-Nisa's age. Udaipuri Mahal's son, Kam Baksh, is the darling of both these women and Zeenat-un-Nisa will often intercede on his behalf with Aurangzeb. There is also another surprising member of this depleted zenana. A Portuguese woman who was initially a slave, Juliana Dias da Costa, is part of Nawab Bai's entourage. Juliana da Costa remains a devout Catholic her whole life and despite a temporary fall from favour, is reinstated by Aurangzeb and is later much respected and appreciated by his heir, Bahadur Shah, Nawab Bai's son.

As for Zeenat-un-Nisa, she remains padshah begum of a crumbling empire, increasingly corrupt and bankrupt at its core. Ambassador Norris never will obtain the farman he hankers for, befuddled by Aurangzeb's impeccable hauteur. In appearance, Aurangzeb's empire is still astoundingly large and magnificent. Indeed, for William Norris it is a far grander empire than that of his own king, William of Orange, who is constantly fending off attacks by the much more powerful Louis XIV of France. But the Mughal empire is now a mirage, the jagirs bringing in no money and the soldiers are unpaid for months at a time. The English will now no longer try desperately to obtain farmans from the Mughal padshahs. They will prefer to quietly strengthen, and then arm their various trade forts. There is no money, either, for ambitious buildings like those of Shah Jahan. But Zeenat-un-Nisa does leave her mark on Shahjahanabad nonetheless. In 1707 she builds a mosque, the Zeenat-al-Masjid, which is the last building built by an imperial woman in Shahjahanabad. Though Zeenat-un-Nisa is not a poet herself, her charming riverside mosque will become a gathering place for the Delhi poets in the early eighteenth century. Here the poets will discuss the new literary rules of ordu-e-mu'alla, the language of the 'army encampment'. This becomes rekhta, 'mixed', with the addition of Indian, Turkish and Persian elements. And so the Urdu of the Delhi poets is born.

Zeenat-un-Nisa survives Aurangzeb by many years. She is witness to the rapid disintegration of the Mughal empire as it recedes away from the Deccan and Bengal and gathers itself around the tombs of the old Sufi saints in Delhi. Zeenat-un-Nisa is the calm constant in a court in which seven padshahs rule in quick succession after Aurangzeb dies, and they are indiscriminately murdered, or blinded, or beheaded. The very last padshah of Zeenat-un-Nisa's long life is Raushan Akhtar Muhammad Shah, great-grandson of Aurangzeb, more commonly known as Muhammad Shah Rangeela. Zeenat-un-Nisa is an old lady of seventy-six when the nineteen-year-old Muhammad Shah becomes Padshah Ghazi. Muhammad Shah is as different from Aurangzeb as it is possible to be. He is a discerning patron of the arts and will preside over a glittering salon where the poets and musicians will create works of endless beauty as Shahjahanabad prepares to burn. He is also, without doubt, something of a bacchanalian, fond of dancing girls and mystifyingly given to wearing a lady's tunic and pearl-embroidered shoes while attending his mushairas (gathering of poets). Like the free-spirited matriarchs who presided over the zenanas of Babur and Humayun, Zeena-un-Nisa is cherished and respected till the end of her long life. But despite the bewildering exuberance of Muhammad Shah Rangeela's court, night approaches for the Mughal empire. Zeenat-un-Nisa will be the last of the padshah begums, a lonely survivor of a golden age, watchful but voiceless guardian of a glorious legacy.

EPILOGUE: THE SUN SETS ON THE MUGHAL EMPIRE

In the 130 years since the death of Aurangzeb, dawn has risen on the age of the 'firangis'. Having defeated the French, Portuguese and Dutch, the British are now effectively rulers of Hindustan. Padshah Akbar II, a descendant of Aurangzeb and the penultimate Mughal padshah, has been demoted to risible 'King of Delhi' by the EIC, who grow weary with the pretence of Mughal supremacy. Even more humiliatingly, other rulers have been encouraged to take the title 'king', on a par with the Mughal padshah, including the Nawab of Awadh whose chief queen is also now padshah begum. Persian is replaced by English on coins, which no longer bear the emperor's name. In Agra, the British employ a band at the Taj Mahal so that visiting Company officials can dance on the marble platform in front of the serene tombs of Mumtaz Mahal and Shah Jahan. 'Can you imagine anything so detestable?' writes a lone sympathetic observer, Fanny Parkes. 'European ladies and gentleman have the band to play on the marble terrace, and dance quadrilles in front of the tomb!' Fanny Parkes herself is overcome by 'feelings of deep devotion; the sacredness of the place, the remembrance of the fallen grandeur of the family of the Emperor' while visiting the Taj Mahal. In the nearby Qila of Agra, 'some wretches of European officers' have converted Noor Jahan's palace into a kitchen, so that 'the ceiling, the fine marbles and the inlaid work, are all one mass of blackness and defilement!' The exquisite hammams of the zenana have been broken up by the Marquess of Hastings, and the marble sold.

In Shahjahanabad, there are still impressive cavalcades of noblemen on elephants accompanied by horsemen, but a muttered proverb decries the true state of the country—Dilli ke dilwali munh chikna pet khali

(The inhabitants of Delhi appear to be opulent when, in fact, they are starving). The 'canal of paradise', which kept Shahjahanabad cool and green, runs dry, the madrasas are empty and the wide steps of the Jami Masjid are riotous with hawkers of cheap goods. A British Resident Officer lives within the qila, effectively controlling the running of the country, and these 'firangis' have finally thrown aside all pretence at being the servants of the Mughals. The zenana from which, in an earlier time, Jahanara and Roshanara influenced the outcomes of battles and designed their monuments for an indifferent posterity, is now found to be a 'queer place, filled with women of all ages; the narrow passages…dirty and wet'. Shahzaadi Hyat-al-Nisa Begum, aunt of Akbar II, is a toothless old woman, who spends her nights and days on a cot within a courtyard of the zenana. Fanny Parkes meets with all the begums of the zenana and 'a plainer set I never met' she writes, astonished. The women appear to live within a few dirty verandas and corridors. Old women lie around on charpais 'looking like hags' and instead of the clear fountains there is 'offensive black water as if from the drains of the cook rooms'. 'Look at what they are,' exclaims Mrs Parkes, fascinated and shocked. 'Look what they have been.' The children who clamour to meet this foreign guest are 'plain' and 'as for beauty, in a whole zenana there may be two or three handsome women and all the rest remarkably ugly. I looked with wonder at the number of plain faces around me.' The shahzaadi herself is a 'clever, intelligent woman' and tries to reassure Mrs Parkes that were she to stay till the evening, there would be nachs (dances) to entertain her. In lieu of the khillats, rubies and gold mohurs of old, all she can offer her British guest is a garland of fresh jasmine. Another Englishwoman, one married to an Indian Muslim herself, also visits the diminished splendour of the Mughal 'raja'. The elderly couple is sitting within a courtyard in the zenana. The begum sits on a takht (bench) on the floor while the padshah sits beside her, on a chair. 'The King's countenance, dignified by age, possesses traces of extreme beauty,' marvels Mrs Meer Hassan. 'His features are still fine, his hair silvery white; intelligence beams upon his brow, his conversation gentle and refined,' she adds. 'He leads a life of strict piety and temperance, equal to that of a durweish of his faith,' writes Mrs Hassan of the descendant of some of the most ostentatious padshahs who ever lived, 'whom he imitates in expending his income on others without indulging in a single luxury himself. The Queen's manners,' she adds, 'are very amiable and condescending.'

At the time of her leave-taking, Mrs Meer Hassan is 'grieved to be obliged to accept the Queen's parting present of an embroidered scarf, because I knew her means were exceedingly limited...' Unwilling to hurt the feelings of her royal hosts, Mrs Meer accepts the gift and a small ring that the queen places on her finger herself. The old padshah shakes her hand, in the English manner. The young Mughal shahzaadas, meanwhile, live lives of aberrant wretchedness, constantly in debt, trying to get by on an allowance of 12 rupees a month, which is equivalent to that of a head servant, and which sneering British officers still have the gall to find 'extravagant'. Deprived of all earnings and carefully humiliated and undermined by the British, the Mughal padshah's influence does not go beyond the high sandstone walls of the Qila-e-Mubaarak. The glittering court disperses, the ateliers are disbanded and the craftsmen, the poets and the painters leave, their craft and their memories still intact.

When Bahadur Shah Zafar becomes padshah two years later at the age of sixty-two, his earnings are so limited that the security of the zenana itself is severely compromised. 'The general impression,' writes William Dalrymple, 'is one of complete chaos, of a once-great establishment unable to maintain basic proprieties in reduced circumstances.' The erstwhile fearsome eunuchs are now unable to prevent intruders from slipping into the zenana and Zafar's concubines become pregnant by lowly court musicians. As for the minor royalty and all the other palace-born princes and princesses, their condition is truly pitiable and they are described as being 'miserable, half naked, starved beings', shut away in a separate quarter of the qila altogether, an unwanted and unloved embarrassment.

To the gentler observer, the Mughals of Hindustan have become voyeuristic objects of pity, and perhaps ridicule. But to most British EIC staffers in Hindustan, the time for admiration and empathy has long gone. Now arrogance and an unshakeable belief in their own superiority has eroded all notions of sympathy towards the diminished Timurids. Very soon, even tolerance will become an outmoded, paltry idea and the Timurid lamp will flicker, and then burn out completely.

History quickened around the Uprising of 1857 and in the furnace of the violence that followed it, the very last traces of Mughal life and culture would be burned away forever. Appalled and incensed beyond all reason at the Uprising that centred around the figure of the old padshah Bahadur Shah Zafar, the British sought to destroy every possible reminder of past Mughal glory. It was Shahjahanabad, Old Delhi today, which suffered the greatest plunder and destruction, including the Qila-e-Mubaarak in which Bahadur Shah Zafar hunkered miserably as his world collapsed in shards around him. Indeed the plan was to raze the city to the ground, every last minaret and mosque and haveli. 'Every civil building connected with the Mohammedan tradition should be levelled to the ground', was Lord Palmerston's direction, 'without regard to antiquarian veneration or artistic predilections'. Fortunately these instructions were not followed to the letter but many precious monuments, including a large number of those built by Mughal women, were wantonly destroyed. Akbarabadi Begum's grand mosque was one of the buildings razed but the greatest fury was directed towards Jahanara's legacy. Her elegant caravanserai in the middle of Old Delhi was destroyed and replaced by a charmless Victorian style Town Hall. Her huge public hammans were also razed and a clock tower built to replace the pool in the middle of the square which gave Chandni Chowk its name. In the Qila-e-Mubaarak, the Red Fort of today, the desecration was almost unimaginable. Fully 80 per cent of the buildings within the fort, the delicate 'turrets, kiosks, gilt domes, hanging balconies, perforated screens', the fragrant gardens, Jahanara's haveli and the entire zenana buildings, amongst other structures, were destroyed in a veritable orgy of violence and replaced by the quite hideous army barracks. What remains is not even a shadow. It is the regret that is felt on waking from a dream.

Apart from the buildings that were destroyed, the entire upper echelon of Muslim nobility was also swept away from Old Delhi, either killed or banished. All Muslim property was confiscated, the mosques deconsecrated and the madrasas locked up. When the Hindu population was slowly allowed back into the city, the mosques and the Muslim properties were sold to Hindu bankers for nominal sums. The few remaining members of the Muslim aristocracy were penniless. For the British would never forget that it was under the banner of the old Mughals of Hindustan that the sepoys, Hindu and Muslims, united, loyal to the memory of a distant past. The British would consistently undermine Muslim influence while promoting Hindu culture, thereby nonchalantly creating fault lines that fracture India to this day.

The last Mughal padshah, Bahadur Shah Zafar, his wives and sons, were sent to exile in Burma where they lived lives of wretched destitution shackled by alcohol and opium addiction and a haunted nostalgia for the things of the past. 'Now there is not a shadow of a doubt,' wrote Bahadur Shah Zafar just before his exile, 'that of the great House of Tim'ur I am the last to be seated [on] the throne of India. The lamp of Mughal domination is fast burning out.' As for the members of Bahadur Shah Zafar's household who remained in Old Delhi, their fate was far worse. 'The male descendants of the deposed King—such as survived the sword,' wrote the poet Ghalib, 'draw allowances of five rupees a month. The female descendants, if old, are bawds; if young, are prostitutes.' As William Dalrymple has described it, when the British reconquered Delhi, there was widespread rape of the women of Delhi by British troops, and an inquiry found that 'perhaps as many as three hundred begums of the royal house—not including former concubines in the Palace'—had been '"taken away by our troops after the fall of Delhi", and that many of those who had not been abducted were now making their livings as courtesans'. Ghalib himself was witness to this final defilement of the women of the Mughal zenana when he wrote, aghast, that they were 'moving about the city, their faces as fair as the moon and their clothes dirty, their pajamas legs torn, and their slippers falling to pieces'.

More insidious was the loss of memory-keeping, of all the ways in which a culture remembers its past and its glory. Manuscripts were burned, libraries despoiled, Urdu and Persian abandoned, and a fortune in artefacts and exquisite objects stolen and removed to Britain. Today most Indian treasures—miniatures, jewellery, statues, gems, books and manuscripts—lie in museums abroad. The disenfranchisement is many-layered and it is deadly. As we forget our languages and can no longer put into context the events and achievements of the past, we grow forgetful and confused.

The phoenix that rose from the ashes of 1857 was not robed in the iridescent peacock feathers of the old Mughal aristocracy. Freedom was won by a new Indian elite, English speaking and educated in the ideals of Western democracy. The memory of the Mughals of Hindustan became somewhat shameful, an unwanted reminder of a past that a new India had outgrown. It became tainted, also, by the colonial interpretation of the Mughal past with all its association of an 'Orientalist' decadence and plundering 'other'. Much was forgotten in this process including the substantial lives of the Mughal women, heavy as sorrow and complicated as birdsong. Mughal history itself became suspect, an alien interlude.

In the 5,000 years of Indian history there have been almost countless dynasties of rulers. Each dynasty, Hindu, Buddhist, Jain and Muslim, has contributed to the great tapestry that is India. The Mughals are closest to us in time and most accessible through the great churning of cultures through which they created some of the most exquisite, syncretic art and an ineffable tehzeeb, or way of being. Though we may not always be aware of it, the influence of these Daughters of the Sun remains in our music, in the food we eat, in the clothes we wear, in an aesthetic vision that colours so much of North Indian art. More changes will come, doubtless, as our pale blue dot swings on its axis through endless space. In reclaiming the past, and the lives of these Mughal women so scalded by beauty, we enrich our present with knowledge and grace so that we may temper our tomorrows.

ACKNOWLEDGEMENTS

Writing is a lonely business and it would have been impossible for me to complete this book without the sympathetic, unwavering and quite selfless support of family and friends. In no particular order: Ayesha Mago, Caroline and Ashwin Juneja, Rathin Mathur, Mandira Mathur, Anjuli Bhargava, Rachna and David Davidar, Arun Kapur, Ashoke Mukhoty, Brijesh Dhar Jayal and Manju Jayal, Niraja Gopal Jayal, and V. Sunil

A special mention to Dr Jyotsna Arora, Deputy Director (Library), Indian Council of Historical Research (ICHR), whose patient explanations helped save me much valuable time and effort. The ICHR is an oasis of quiet erudition and is an invaluable resource for lay scholars.

Thanks also to my friend, scholar, one-time falcon trainer, and native Farsi speaker Sardar Mohammad Ali Khan. To Ali I owe a huge debt of gratitude for his patience and enthusiasm in finding the exact English translation and spelling for long-forgotten Persian words.

A grateful thanks to my talented editors, Simar Puneet and Pujitha Krishnan.

Apart from the original sources and scholarly works on the subject, there has been another source of more ephemeral information on the women of the Mughals; The heritage walks around Delhi conducted by scholars and enthusiasts offer beguiling details not to be found in books, following in the long and venerable tradition of story-telling in India. I am particularly grateful, for their knowledge and generosity, to Asif Khan Dehlvi of Delhi Karavan, Rana Safvi, and Sohail Hashmi.

Thanks always to my daughters, Yashoda and Devaki Jayal, for existing in the world.

And for everything else, and much more besides, Mohit Dhar Jayal, thank you.

IMAGE CREDITS

Babur is reunited with his sister at Kunduz in 1511, © Victoria and Albert Museum, London.

Court lady, attributed to Bishandas, © Freer Gallery of Art, Smithsonian Institution, Washington, D.C.

Gulbadan Begum smoking on a terrace in Delhi, circa 1800. Wikimedia Commons

Akbarnama, Akbar's mother Mariam Makani on boat, outline by Tulsi the Elder, painting by Durga, opaque watercolour and gold on paper, Mughal, circa 1590–95, © Victoria and Albert Museum, London.

The Birth of Prince by Bishandas, circa 1610–15, from the *Jahangirnama*, © Museum of Fine Arts, Boston.

A Lady with Flower and Fly Whisk, Mughal India, circa 1630, © The David Collection, Copenhagen.

Single Leaf of a Portrait of the Emperor Akbar, © The Walters Art Museum, Baltimore.

Akbarnama, scene from marriage entertainment of Baqi Muhammad Khan, outline by La'l, painting by Sanwala, opaque watercolour and gold on paper, Mughal, circa 1590–95, © Victoria and Albert Museum, London.

Akbarnama, Bairam Khan's widow and child are escorted to Ahmedabad after the assassination of Bairam Khan in 1561, circa 1590–95, © Victoria and Albert Museum, London.

A Princess entertained by a dancer, attendants and musicians, © Freer Gallery of Art, Smithsonian Institution, Washington, D.C.

Rang Mahal (women's quarters), the Red Fort, Delhi. Photo: Mogens Krustrup, © The David Collection, Copenhagen.

An Indian princess with a writing tablet, W.668, fol.52b, © The Walters Art Museum, Baltimore.

Single Leaf of a Portrait of the Emperor Jahangir, W.705, © The Walters Art Museum, Baltimore.

Interior of the Mariyam Zamani Begum Mosque, photo credit: Muhammad Ashar. Wikimedia Commons.

Nur Jahan, holding a portrait of Emperor Jahangir by Bishandas, circa 1627, © The Cleveland Museum of Art, Cleveland.

Jahangir and Prince Khurram Entertained by Nur Jahan, circa 1640–50, Gift of Charles Lang Freer, © Freer Gallery of Art, Smithsonian Institution, Washington, D.C.

Silver coin of Nur Jahan, Patna mint. Wikimedia Commons.

Oval portrait of Arjumand Banu Begum (Mumtaz Mahal) from bracelet with portrait miniatures, watercolour on ivory, gold, © The Walters Art Museum, Baltimore.

View of Begum Sahib (Jahan Ara) from *Histoire générale des Voyages* by Antoine François Prévost in 15 volumes (Paris, 1746–1759).

The wedding procession of Shah Jahan's elder son, Dara Shikoh, from the *Padshahnama*, © The Royal Collection Trust.

The marriage procession of Dara Shikoh, © National Museum, Delhi.

Princess Nadira Banu Begum. Wikimedia Commons.

NOTES AND REFERENCES

Peripatetic Queens from Persia to Hindustan: 1494–1569

The Timurids, the Uzbegs and Khanzada's sacrifice

2   **charbagh**: a Persian and Islamic quadrilateral garden layout based on the four gardens of Paradise mentioned in the Quran.

2   **were to come with a large army**: W. M. Thackson Jr., *The Baburnama: Memoirs of Babur, Prince and Emperor*, New York: Random House, 2002.

2   **Mawarannahr**: Also known as Transoxiana, this is the ancient name used for a part of Central Asia corresponding to modern-day Uzbekistan, Tajikistan, southern Krygyzstan and southwest Kazakhstan.

2   **it was not outsiders**: Lisa Ann Balabanlilar, *The Lords of the Auspicious Conjunction: Turco-Mongol Imperial Identity on the Subcontinent*, Columbus: Ohio State University, 2007.

2   **Turco-Mongol yasa**: a set of tribal laws created by Genghis Khan.

3   **Turks that worshipped idols**: Ahmed ibn Arab Shah, *Tamerlane or Timur the Treat Amir*, London; Luzac & Co, 1936.

3   **the valleys and steppes of central Asia**: Amitav Ghosh, 'Love and war in Afghanistan and Central Asia: the life of the Emperor Babur', *amitavghosh.com* <https://amitavghosh.com/essays/love_war.html> [accessed 4 March 2018].

3   **For tactics and strategy**: Thackson, *Baburnama*.

3   **ma'jun**: a narcotic.

4   **I am the wife of Sultan Yunus Khan**: *The Tarikh-i-Rashidi: A History of the Moghuls of Central Asia*, London: Sampson Low, Marston and Company Ltd., 1895.

4   **was with me during**: Thackson, *Baburnama*.

5   **For nearly 140 years**: Thackson, *Baburnama*.

5   **the poor and unfortunate**: Thackson, *Baburnama*.

5   **If you would marry your sister Khanzada Begam to me**: Gulbadan Begum,

The History of Humayun, tr. Annette S. Beveridge, New Delhi: Munshiram Manoharlal Publishers Pvt. Ltd., 2001.

5   **gave the Begam to the khan**: Gulbadan, Ibid.
6   **Wormwood Khan (Shaybani) initiated**: Thackson, *Baburnama*.

Hindustan and the Coming of the Begums and the Khanims

8   **endured much poverty and humiliation**: Stephen Meredyth Edwardes, *Mirza Babur: Diarist and Despot*, London: A. M. Philpot Ltd., 1926.
8   **the little band of homeless fugitives**: Ibid.
8   **So destitute were we**: Thackson, *Baburnama*.
8   **The hungry and lean family**: Ibid.
9   **considering that the days of his youth and manhood**: Edwardes, Ibid.
10   **that she [Zainab Sultan Begum] was not very congenial**: Ibid.
10   **grieving was renewed**: Ibid.
10   **upon first seeing me**: Ibid.
11   **We had been apart for some ten years**: *The Babur-nama in English (Memoirs of Babur)*, translated from the original Turki Text of Zahiru'd-din Muhammad Babur Padhshah Ghazi by Annette Susannah Beveridge, Essex: Luzac & Co, 1922.
11   **In one such painting**: Folio 8b shows Babur meeting Khanzada Begam and other ladies at Quduz, M. S. Randhawa, *Paintings of the Baburnama*, New Delhi: National Museum, 1983.
12   **Some of the sultans and rebels**: Thackson, *Baburnama*.
13   **confirm(s) his ties to the Yusufzai**: Ibid.
13   **whether it be a boy or a girl**: Gulbadan, *History of Humayun*.
14   **up from Hindustan come**: Lucy Peck, *Delhi: A Thousand Years of Building*, New Delhi: Roli Books, 2005.
14   **his Majesty (Babur) and akam (Maham)**: Gulbadan, *History of Humayun*.
14   **the country which from old**: *The Akbarnama of Abu'l Fazl*, translated from the Persian by H. Beveridge, Calcutta: The Asiatic Society, 1939, reprinted 2000.
15   **the whole world's expenditure for half a day**: Gulbadan, *History of Humayun*.
16   **men and women for the most part**: Ibid.
16   **When you go**: Ibid.
17   **one special dancing-girl**: Ibid.
17   **sisters and children and the harams**: According to Beveridge, this is presumably the haram of his kinsmen and of officers whose families were with Babur's in Kabul.
17   **and to the begams and aghas and nurses**: Gulbadan, *History of Humayun*.

17 **to make the prostration of thanks**: Ibid.

17 **Three happy days they remained together**: Ibid.

18 **Although it was a dreadful incident**: Thackson, *Baburnama*.

18 **He sent letters in all directions**: Gulbadan, *History of Humayun*.

19 **unpleasant and inharmonious India**: Thackson, *Baburnama*.

19 **all the begums and khanams went**: Gulbadan, *History of Humayun*.

19 **[He] followed the seasons wandering**: Bernard O'Kane, 'From tents to pavilions: royal mobility and Persian palace design', *Ars Orientalis*, Vol. 23, Pre-modern Islamic Palaces, Freer Gallery of Art, The Smithsonian Institution and Department of the History of Art, University of Michigan, 1993.

Khanzada Begum and the Mystic Feast

20 **Kabul was royal demesne**: Thackson, *Baburnama*.

20 **How can one forget the pleasures**: Lisa Balabanlilar, *Imperial Identity in the Mughal Empire: Memory and Dynastic Politics in Early Modern South and Central Asia*, New York: I. B. Tauris, 2012.

20 **Babur is now,' writes a Timurid refugee**: Lisa Balabanlilar, *The Lords of the Auspicious Conjunction*.

20 **Within the next five years**: Balabanlilar, *Imperial Identity*.

22 **nine troopers, with two sets of nine horses**: Gulbadan, *History of Humayun*.

22 **thus in unpleasant and inharmonious India**: Thackson, *Baburnama*.

22 **All who had acquired lands on the (Jamuna) river**: Thackson, *Baburnama*.

23 **Since the people of India had never seen**: Ibid.

23 **commanded buildings to be put up**: Gulbadan, *History of Humayun*.

30 **there seemed 'to have been no distinction between**: Ruby Lal, *Domesticity and Power in the Early Mughal World*, Cambridge: Cambridge University Press, 2005.

31 **the yurt-type tent**: Caroline Stone, 'Movable palaces', *Saudi Aramco World*, July/August 2010.

Rout at the Battle of Chausa and the Afghan Menace

34 **conduct yourself well with your younger brother**: Thackson, *Baburnama*.

35 **They made a dreadful uproar**: *Private Memoirs of the Moghul Emperor Humayun*, written in the Persian language by Jauhar, translated by Major Charles Stewart.

35 **bade them go quickly**: Ibid.

35 **noble lady Haji Begum**: Bega Begum is usually referred to as Haji Begum in most sources. Only Gulbadan refers to her at this point as Bega Begum in her *History of Humayun*.

36 drank the wholesome sherbet of martyrdom: Fazl, *Akbarnama*.

36 Wicked thoughts did not find their way: Ibid.

36 forbidding the killing or enslavement: S. K. Banerji, *Humayun Badshah*, London: Oxford University Press, 1938.

36 Of many who were in that rout: Gulbadan, *The History of Humayun*.

37 never even heard a word: Lal, *Domesticity and Power*.

37 I am wearing mourning for you: Gulbadan, *The History of Humayun*.

37 My Gulbadan, I used very often to think of you: Ibid.

Dildar Begum and a Marriage Proposal

42 I look on this girl as a sister: Ibid.

42 As for what they have written about alimony: Ibid.

43 It is astonishing that you should go: Ibid.

43 you are speaking very improperly: Jauhar, *Private Memoirs*.

43 After all you will marry someone: Gulbadan, *The History of Humayun*.

43 Oh yes, I shall marry someone: Ibid.

44 horrid journey' in which 'many of our people: Jauhar, *Private Memoirs*.

44 no act of hospitality being shown us: Ibid.

44 that ravening demon: Beveridge, *Akbarnama*.

44 If you leave me, whither will you go?: Gulbadan, *The History of Humayun*.

45 sell our lives as dearly as possible: Jauhar, *Private Memoirs*.

45 people flung themselves on it: Gulbadan.

46 The day was not a fortunate one: Jauhar, *Private Memoirs*.

46 This is all the present I can afford to make you: Ibid.

47 any attempt to assist the Moghuls: Gulbadan.

47 elder kinswoman, and oldest and highest: Ibid.

47 as his Majesty Firdaus-Makani (Babur) decided: Ibid.

48 2000 loads of grain and 300 camels: Ibid.

48 were such that one might say they had not known city: Jauhar, *Private Memoirs*.

48 in the hot season the *Semun* blows: Gulbadan.

48 who were without warm clothing: Ibid.

48 it had snowed and rained: Ibid.

48 Bega Begum is somewhere: Don't know for sure when Bega begum is returned to Humayun.

Hamida Banu and the Persian Escapade

51 we are arrived in your country: Jauhar, *Private Memoirs*.

51 upon his auspicious arrival: William Erskine, *A History of India under the*

First Sovereigns of the House of Taimur, London: Longman, Brown, Green, and Longmans, 1854.

51 **that every person of the city**: Jauhar, *Private Memoirs*.

52 **to receive and entertain the imperial guest**: William Erskine, *A History of India*.

53 **The Persian monarch placed Humayun to his right**: Jauhar, *Private Memoirs*.

53 **they passed the night in feasting and carousing'**: Ibid.

55 **chatr**: Umbrella-shaped tent; **taq**: Round-topped tents or balconies.

56 **300 tents had been fetched**: Jauhar, *Private Memoirs*.

56 **flat, lightly raised breads**: Rachel Laudan, *Cuisine and Empire: Cooking in World History*, Berkeley: University of California Press, 2015.

57 **such is my friendship for you**: Jauhar, *Private Memoirs*.

58 **over which there is constantly a thick fog**: Ibid.

59 **Humayun's new custom of choosing daily the colour of his royal robes**: Ritu Kumar, *Costumes and Textiles of Royal India*, Suffolk: Antique Collectors' Club, 2006.

59 **the begams and ladies made their own [quarters]**: Gulbadan.

60 **All of you go on**: Ibid.

60 **Would to Heaven**: Ibid.

Bega Begum and Humayun's Tomb

62 **The drums of joy beat high**: Fazl, *Akbarnama*.

62 **He remembered the highnesses the Begums**: Ibid.

63 **There were mutual rejoicings**: Ibid.

63 **He was of medium stature**: Annemarie Schimmel, *The Empire of the Great Mughals: History, Art and Culture*, Islington: Reaktion Books, 2006.

63 **As she knew what the state of feeling was**: Fazl, *Akbarnama*.

63 **Everyone who did not know the real facts**: Ibid.

64 **Jinnat Ashiyani**: Ibid.

64 **after she had returned from the holy places**: Ibid

65 **One of his wives had loved Emaumus**: Commentary of Antonio Monserrate, S. J., *On his Journey to the Court of Akbar*, London Bombay Madras Calcutta: Humphrey Milford, Oxford University Press, 1922.

65 **She had taken up her residence**: Fazl, *Akbarnama*.

65 **One of the joyful occurrences of this glorious year**: Ibid.

66 **There were great feasts**: Ibid.

Disappeared Wives and Imperial Splendour: 1556-1631

Maham Anaga and the River of Milk

68 **on account of his nearness to the emperor:** *The Tabaqat-i-Akbari of Khwajah Nizamuddin Ahmad (A History of India from the Early Musalman Invasions to the Thirty-sixth Year of the Reign of Akbar)*, Calcutta: Asiatic Society of Bengal, 1927.

69 **from a divine inspiration:** Fazl, *Akbarnama.*

69 **great hauteur and pride:** *Tabaqat-i-Akbari.*

69 **Son of a fool:** Ibid.

69 **struck him such a blow on the face:** Ibid.

69 **so that his neck was broken:** Ibid.

70 **even-tempered, spiritually-minded:** Ibid.

71 **For the sake of his wives and children:** Gulbadan.

71 **he had attired himself for sport:** Fazl, *Akbarnama.*

72 **a wretchedly puny physique:** John Keay, *India: A History*, London: HarperCollins, 2000.

72 **who, on account of her abundant sense and loyalty:** Fazl, *Akbarnama.*

73 **I am not conscious of having committed any offence:** Ibid.

73 **All the court ladies':** *Tabaqat-i-Akbari.*

74 **Especially Adham Khan:** Abd al-Qadir Badauni, *Muntakhab-ut-Tawarikh.*

74 **Maham Anka thought in her mind:** Ibid.

74 **As long as Bairam Khan:** *The Tabaqat-i-Akbari.*

74 **The Khan Khana would know:** Ibid.

75 **ask the Khan Khanam to excuse:** Ibid.

75 **in concert with Maham Anka:** Fazl, *Akbarnama*

75 **in consultation with Maham Anka:** *The Tabaqat-i-Akbari.*

75 **in her great loyalty, took charge of affairs:** Ibid.

76 **The mosque has an unusual upper story of classrooms:** Monica Juneja, ed., *Architecture in Medieval India*, New Delhi: Orient Blackswan Private Limited, 2008.

77 **carried her honour:** Fazl, *Akbarnama.*

77 **the dancing girls, and nautch-girls:** Ibid.

77 **brought the zenana which had remained behind:** Ibid.

77 **wives, dancing girls and courtesans:** Ibid.

77 **special beauties' of Baz Bahadur's:** Ibid.

77 **the veil over her acts would be raised:** Ibid.

77 **a severed head makes no sound:** Ibid.

78 **distinguished by the honour of rendering service**: *The Tabaqat-i-Akbari*.

78 **regarded herself as substantive prime minister**: Fazl, *Akbarnama*.

78 **Adham killed our Ataga**: Ibid.

78 **She did not complain or lament**: Ibid.

78 **openly critical and even defiant**: T. C. A. Raghavan, *Attendant Lords: Bairam Khan and Abdur Rahim, Courtiers and Poets in Mughal India*, New Delhi: HarperCollins India, 2017.

78 **Between me and Aziz**: Fazl, *Akbarnama*.

Disappeared Wives and the Mystery of Jahangir's Mother

80 **coined and uncoined gold**: Ibid.

80 **strewed the dust of ruin**: Ibid.

80 **obtained honour by being sent to kiss**: Ibid.

81 **'twas better to die with glory**: Ibid.

81 **put armour on her breast**: Ibid.

81 **she drew her dagger**: Ibid.

81 **It is the custom of Indian rajahs**: Ibid.

81 **Whoever out of feebleness of soul**: Ibid.

82 **found two women alive**: Ibid.

82 **Nine queens, five princesses**: Vincent Smith, *Akbar the Great Mogul: 1542-1645*, Oxford: Clarendon Press, 1917.

83 **in a short time the pagan**: Abraham Eraly, *The Last Spring: The Lives and Times of the Great Mughals*, New Delhi: Penguin Books India, 2000.

83 **the crass stupidity of the Hindustanis**: Fazl, *Akbarnama*.

83 **discerning glance read devotion and sincerity**: Ibid.

83 **Harkha Bai arrives at Akbar's court resplendent**: Ritu Kumar, *Costumes and Textiles*.

84 **Hairstyles will change too**: Harbans Mukhia, *The Mughals of India*, New Delhi: John Wiley and Sons, 2004.

84 **Qawwals and eunuchs**: Eraly, *The Last Spring*.

84 **a great terror fell upon the city**: Abraham Eraly, *Emperors of the Peacock Throne: The Saga of the Great Moghuls*, New Delhi: Penguin Books, 2000.

84 **a type of countenance well-fitted**: Monserrate, *Commentary*.

86 **all Jews, Christians, Hindus**: Ibid.

86 **veritable bazaar**: Badauni.

87 **like a female major dome**: Rekha Misra, *Women in Mughal India (1526-1748 A.D.)*, New Delhi: Munshiram Manoharlal, Oriental Publishers and Booksellers,1967.

88 **The inside of the harem**: Gavin Hambly, ed., *Women in the Medieval Islamic World*, New York: Palgrave Macmillan, 1999.

88 **Five hundred beautiful young Turki females**: Ibid.

89 **the unique pearl of the Caliphate**: Lal, *Domesticity and Power*.

89 **The prisoners of the imperial domains**: Ibid.

ever since the reign of Akbar: *The Ain-i-Akbari by Abu'l Fazl Allami*, translated from the original Persian by H. Blochmann, M. A. and Colonel H. S. Jarrett, Calcutta: Asiatic Society of Bengal, 1873-1907.

90 **even the sight or the thought of anything**: Mukhia, *Mughals of India*.

90 **His Majesty cares very little for meat**: Colleen Taylor, *Feasts and Fasts, A History of Food in India*, London: Reaktion Books, 2015.

91 **fasted regularly and gradually increased**: Mukhia, *Mughals of India*.

92 **Like the casting off of the veil**: Ira Mukhoty, *Heroines: Powerful Indian Women of Myth and History*, New Delhi: Aleph Book Company, 2017.

93 **the strange determination of the men**: Mukhia, *Mughals of India*.

93 **here in India among the modest**: Ibid.

93 **was a pleasant sort of control**: Bonnie C. Wade, *Imaging Sound: An Ethnomusicological Study of Music Art and Culture in Mughal India*, Chicago: University of Chicago Press, 1998.

Gulbadan and the Mughal Hajj

96 **long ago made a vow**: Fazl, *Akbarnama*.

97 **burnt the ship and all the people on board**: *Calcoen: A Dutch Narrative of the Second Voyage of Vasco Da Gama to Calicut*, London : B.M. Pickering, 1874.

97 **many Muslims and other infidels**: Ibid.

98 **to ensure friendly treatment**: Ibid.

98 **bore the idolatrous stamp**: Thomas Roe, *The Embassy of Sir Thomas Roe to the Court of the Great Mogul, 1615-1619, as Narrated in His Journal and Correspondence*, London: Printed for the Haklyut Society, 1899.

98 **Its splendour**: The first Christian mission to the court of the great mogul. *Akbar and the Jesuits: An Account of the Jesuit Missions to the Court of Akbar by Father Pierre du Jarric, S. J.*, New York and Oxford: Routledge, 2014.

99 **at great public expense**: John Slight, *The British Empire and the Hajj 1865-1956*, Boston: Harvard University Press, 2015.

99 **is very populous, as all other cities**: Pietro Della Valle, *The Travels of Pietro de la Valle in India; from the Old English Translation of 1664*, London: Printed for the Haklyut Society, 1892.

100 **very disproportionate**: Ibid.

100 'in order to ward off evil: Venetia Porter and Liana Saif, eds., *The Hajj: Collected Essays*, London: The British Museum, 2013.

101 There are enormous pilgrim caravans: Marina Tolmacheva, *Medieval Muslim Women's Travel: Defying Distance and Danger, Forum: Travelers and Traveler's Accounts in World History, Part 2, World History Connected*, Chicago: University of Illinois, 2013.

101 In my opinion: *Travels in Arabia, Comprehending an Account of those Territories in Hedjaz which the Mohammedans regard as Sacred by the Late John Lewis Burckhardt*, London: The Association for Promoting the Discovery of The Interior of Africa, Henry Colburn, 1829.

101 The Meccans are elegant and clean: Ross E. Dunn, *The Adventures of Ibn Battuta: A Muslim Traveler of the Fourteenth Century*, Berkeley: University of California Press; Revised edition, 2004.

102 kill either flea or louse: F. E. Peters, *The Hajj: The Muslim Pilgrimage to Mecca and the Holy Places*, Princeton: Princeton University Press, 1994.

102 Truly it would not be possible: *Buckhard's Travel in Arabia*.

102 I profess, I could not choose but: Joseph Pitts, *A True and Faithful Account of the Religion and Manners of the Mohammetans* (1704) (2nd Edition), Gale ECCO, 2010.

102 when the women are at the stone: Ibid.

103 it is a sight, indeed, able to pierce one's Heart: Pitts, *True and Faithful Account*.

103 it is a matter of sorrowful reflection: Ibid.

103 all that night there is nothing to be heard: Gavin Hambly, *Women in the Medieval Islamic World*.

103 somewhat alarmed by their ostentatious distributions: Ibid.

104 After they are return'd from Meena to Mecca: Pitts, *True and Faithful Account*.

104 they do not think it lawful: Ibid.

104 very small men, and of a dark tawny colour: John Winter Jones, *The Travels of Ludovico di Varthema in Egypt, Syria, Arabia Deserta and Arabia Felix, in Persia, India and Ethiopia*, London: Printed for the Haklyut Society, 1863.

105 is subject to very thick fogs: Hajj essays.

105 each one of us was silently praying: Hajj essays.

105 no longer requiring to be on good terms: Monserrate, *Commentary*.

105 are routed by the Portuguese: Ibid.

105 they pay a gratuitous visit: Badauni.

105 The night of reunion: Beveridge, *Akbarnama*.

105 When his aunt returned from Mekka: Monserrate, *Commentary*.

106 Mahomet is everything here: *The First Christian Mission to the Great Mogul: or The Story of Blessed Rudolf Acquaviva and of his Four Companions in Martyrdom of the Society of Jesus by Francis Goldie*, Dublin: M. H. Gill and Son, London: The Art and Book Company, 1897.

106 whether it was the murmurs of the mullahs: Fazl, *Akbarnama*.

106 his Majesty has made a large enclosure: Ibid.

107 I am dying: Ibid.

Salima Sultan Begum and the Prodigal Son

108 [Akbar] gives very great care and attention: Monserrate, *Commentary*.

108 In Europe,' she will complain: Fanny Parkes, *Begums, Thugs and Englishmen*, New Delhi: Penguin Books India, 2003.

109 After my birth they gave me the name of Sultan Salim: Alexander Rogers, ed. *Tuzuk-I-Jahangiri or Memoirs of Jahangir*, tr. Henry Beverdige, New Delhi: Atlantic Publishers, 1989.

109 his expression is tranquil, serene: Monserrate, *Commentary*.

110 orders his translator's yearly allowance: Badauni, *Muntakhab*.

110 poured into the lap of each the money: Fazl, *Akbarnama*.

111 a very great citie and populous: Ryley, J. Horton, *Ralph Fitch: England's Pioneer to India and Burma*, London: T. Fisher Unwin, 1899.

111 Agra and Fatepore are two very great cities: Ibid.

111 black standards, the sign of war: Monserrate, *Commentary*.

111 the king's mother was to be superior to both of these: Ibid.

111 a few of [Akbar's] principal wives: Taylor, *Feasts and Fasts*.

112 refusing to eat pork or beef: Ibid.

112 dressed in the style of the local nawabs: Ibid.

113 slaughter of cows, and the eating of their flesh: Badauni.

113 it may be suspected that Jalal ud-Din: Monserrate, *Commentary*.

113 these strange-looking, unarmed men: Ibid.

114 The opposition of this party: Ibid.

114 being as much frilled as the waist-band: B. N. Goswamy, *Indian Costumes in the Collection of the Calico Museum of Textiles*, Ahmedabad: Calico Museum, 2008.

115 fed by hand with pellets: Taylor, *Feasts and Fasts*.

115 Queens ride on female elephants: Horton, *Ralph Fitch*.

115 the higher the rank and dignity of these old men: Monserrate, *Commentary*.

116 Shall I describe the severity of the cold: Abu'l Fazl.

116 In his wrath: Ibid.

116 Indeed she is kinder than a mother: Thackston, Wheeler M., ed. and tr.,

The Jahangirnama: Memoirs of Jahangir, Emperor of India, New York: Oxford University Press, Washington, D. C.: Freer Gallery of Art and Arthur M. Sackler Gallery in association with New York: Oxford University Press, 1999.

116 She possessed all good qualities: Ibid.

117 The King's nature: Monserrate, *Commentary.*

117 so submissive that he sometimes did not even dare: Ibid.

117 At his parties, guests drank 'chaghir': Taylor, *Feasts and Fasts.*

117 he sinks back stupefied and shaking: *A Voyage to East-India; wherein some yhings are taken notice of, in our passage thither, but many more in our abode there, within the rich and most spacious Empire of the Great Mogul, observed by Edward Terry*, reprint by BiblioBazaar, 2013.

117 taking the mouth piece into his sacred mouth: Monserrate, *Commentary.*

118 sometimes barbarously cruel: Eraly, *Last Spring.*

118 a pleasing presence and excellent carriage: *A Voyage to East-India.*

118 He both publicly and privately: Thackston, *Jahangirnama.*

118 uttered a cry and became insensible: S. A. I Tirmizi, Mughal documents 1526-1627.

119 When she arrived within two stages of Allahabad: Eraly, *Last Spring.*

119 cleaned the stain of savagery and suspicion: Lal, *Domesticity and Power.*

119 When she had promised the prince: Ibid.

120 Your Majesty, all of the Begims are assembled: Ibid.

Maryam-uz-Zamani, the *Rahimi* and the Perfidious Portuguese

121 a few straggling houses: Samuel Purchas, *Hakluytus Posthumus, or Purchas his Pilgrimes; Contayning a History of the World in Sea Voyages and Lande Travells by Englishmen and Others*, Glasgow: James MacLehose and Sons, 1905-1907.

121 in all necessaries for the use of man: Donald F. Lach, *Asia in the Making of Europe, Volumes 1 and 2*, Chicago: University of Chicago Press, 1965.

122 English East India Company: Hereafter abbreviated to EIC.

122 very richly clad: Ram Chandra Prasad, *Early English Travellers in India: A Study in the Travel Literature of the Elizabethan and Jacobean Periods with Particular Reference to India*, New Delhi: Motilal Banarsidass Publications, 1980.

122 Religion was the first subject they discussed: Ibid.

123 were like madde Dogges: Eraly, *Emperors of the Peacock Throne.*

123 firangi: Firangi is a Persian word derived from the Arabic 'Farenji,' a medieval Arabic pronunciation of 'Frank,' or Frenchman, because 'Franks' had been the most numerous of the Christian Crusaders and Europe itself is known in Hindustan as 'Firangistan.'

123 a kind of uncleanness to mingle with us: Eraly, *The Last Spring*.

124 a small matter more than: *Jahangir and the Jesuits with an Account of The Travels of Benedict Goes and The Mission to Pegu from the Relations of Father Fernao Guerreiro, S.J.* translated by C. H. Payne, London: George Routledge and Sons Ltd., London, 1930.

124 bibbers of wine: Ellison B. Findly, 'The capture of Maryam-uz-Zamani's ship: Mughal women and European traders', *Journal of the American Oriental Society*, Vol. 108, No. 2, Apr-June, 1988.

124 the local merchants wouldn't lade their goods: Ibid.

125 his diamonds, rubies, emeralds: Jonathan Gil Harris, *The First Firangis*, New Delhi: Aleph Book Company, 2015.

125 increased the allowances: *Tuzuk-I-Jahangiri*.

125 according to his estate: Findly.

126 everyone from the Cape of Good Hope: Sagufta Praveen, 'Surat: as a major port-town of Gujarat and its trade history', *Journal of Humanities and Social Science*, Vol 19, Issue 5, Ver. VI, May 2014.

126 Bania: The Hindu 'bania' or merchant class, often spelled 'banian' in European texts.

127 the Banias pitch tents and erect booths : Lach, *Asia in the Making of Europe*.

127 mirroring in miniature: Herbert, foster edition.

127 gold, silver, ivory, pearls: Lach, *Asia in the Making of Europe*.

127 the great pilgrimage ship: Findly.

128 You must know: Chandra Richard de Silva, 'Indian Ocean but not African Sea: the erasure of East African commerce from history', *Journal of Black Studies*, New Delhi: Sage Publications Vol. 29, No. 5, May 1999.

128 If you encounter ships belonging to the aforesaid Moors: Sebastian R. Prange, 'A trade of no dishonor: piracy, commerce and community in the Western Indian Ocean, twelfth to sixteenth century', *The American Historical Review*, Vol. 116, Issue 5, The University of Chicago Press, 2011/12.

128 The King of Portugal commands me: Ibid.

129 Called the 'Portuguese menace': Ibid.

129 but took also 700 persons of all sorts: Findly.

130 The great Mogul's mother was: Ibid.

Noor Jahan, an English Ambassador and the Politics of Colour

131 of a complexion neither white nor blacke: Thomas Coryate, *Thomas Coriate Traueller for the English Vvits: Greetings from the Court of the Great Mogul,*

London: Printed by W. Iaggard, and Henry Fetherston, 1616.

132 in the prime of his life: William, Foster, ed., *Letters Received by the East India Company from its Servants in the East*, London, S. Low, Marston & Company, 1896.

132 quite a dandy: Thomas Coryate, *Traveller*.

132 I saw first their fingers: Eraly, *The Last Spring*.

133 a gentleman of a very lovely presence: Ibid.

133 in excellent formes: Roe, *The Embassy of Sir Thomas*.

134 she shot two tigers with one shot each: Eraly, *The Last Spring*, Terry quote.

134 Habshis: From the Arab word 'Habsh' for Abysinnia, the old name of Ethiopia the centre of the state: Lisa Ann Balabanlilar, 'The begums at the mystic feast: Turco-Mongol influences in the Mughal harem', *The Journal of Asian Studies*, Vol. 69, No. 1, February 2010.

138 sometimes she would sit in the balcony: William Foster, ed., *Letters Received by the East India Company from its Servants in the East*, London: S. Low, Marston & Company, 1896.

138 we could not have come in a more fit time: Ibid.

138 suffered blowes of the porters: Roy Moxham, *The Theft of India: The European Conquests of India, 1498-1765*, New Delhi: HarperCollins India, 2016.

138 here is great store of goods in the country: William Foster, *Letters Received by the East India Company*.

139 the country here is full of commodities: Ibid.

140 two pearl rosaries, two rubies: Ibid.

141 Noormahel fulfills the observation: Ibid.

141 that she had moved the Prince [Khurram]: Niccolaom Manucci, *Storio do Mogor or Mogul India*, tr. William Irvine, London: John Murray, 1907.

142 Jahangir, meanwhile, is most pleased with gifts of alcohol: Abraham Eraly, *The Mughal World-Life in India's Last Golden Age*, New Delhi: Penguin Books India, 2007.

143 the dogs of Hindustan: Ibid.

144 more than that left by the King: Findly.

144 Noor Jahan Begum, whose skill and experience: *Tuzuk-I-Jahangiri*..

145 In truth,' declares the admiring Jahangir: Ibid.

145 and knew what were the requirements: Ibid.

145 suitable kindnesses, such as dresses of honour: Ibid.

145 A few days pass in this manner: Ibid.

146 to twenty cups of doubly distilled-spirits: Ibid.

146 Queen comes with the female slaves: *Jahangir's India, the Remonstrantie of Francisco Pelsaert*, translated from the Dutch by W. H. Moreland, and P.

Geyl, Cambridge: W. Heffer & Sons Ltd., 1925.

146 **they have nor furniture of the kind**: Ellison Banks Findly, *Nur Jahan: Empress of Mughal India*, New York: Oxford University Press, 1993.

147 **kindling a fire with his own hands**: Thomas Coryate, *Traveller*.

148 **that if one drop be rubbed on the palm**: *Tuzuk-I-Jahangiri*.

148 **the emperor used to say**: Shivangani Tandon, 'Negotiating political spaces and contested identities: representation of Nur Jahan and her family in Mughal Tazkiras', *The Delhi University Journal of the Humanities and the Social Sciences*, Vol. 2, 2015.

149 **The reason of the King's special preference for this country**: Pelsaert.

149 **On that night a great wind blew**: *Tuzuk-I-Jahangiri*.

150 **as an intimate friend**: *Tuzuk-I-Jahangiri*.

Mumtaz Mahal and a Love Supreme

156 **as it was necessary to win the heart of Karan**: *Tuzuk-I-Jahangiri*

157 **adorned with an eloquent tongue**: Fergus Nicoll, *Shah Jahan: The Rise and Fall of the Mughal Emperor*, New Delhi: Penguin Books India, 2009.

158 **towards whom I have so much affection**: *Tuzuk-I-Jahangiri*.

163 **assigned grants of land**: Hambly, *Women in the Medieval Islamic World*.

166 **What a pity,' exclaims Aurangzeb**: Flynn, Vincent John Adams, *An English Translation of Adab-i-Alamgiri*, William Foster, ed., *Letters Received by the East India Company from its Servants in the East*, London, S. Low, Marston & Company, 1896.

Ambitious Siblings and a Shahzaadi's Dream: 1631–1721

Shahzaadi

168 **shouting out, pushing and assaulting**: Manucci, *Storio do Mogor*.

171 **which is valued at one crore rupees**: Diana Preston, *A Teardrop on the Cheek of Time: The Story of the Taj Mahal*, New York: Doubleday, 2007.

172 **He and I are one soul manifested in two forms**: Jahanara, *Risala-i-Sahibiya*.

172 **great elephants, whose bellies were full of squibs**: Peter Mundy, edited by Lt-Col Sir Richard Carnac Temple, *Travels of Peter Mundy, in Europe and Aisa, 1608-1667, Vol II*, London: printed for the Hakluyt Society, 1907.

172 **The first born son of King Shahjahan**: Manucci, *Storio do Mogor*.

173 **very different from the others**: Ibid.

173 **the shame lay in what my brothers did**: Jadunath Sarkar, *Anecdotes of Aurangzeb (English Translation of Ahkam-i-Alamgiri Ascribed to Hamid-ud-*

din Khan Bahadur with *A Life of Aurangzib and Historical Notes*, Indian Educational Service, 2nd edition revised, Calcutta: M.C Sarkar & Sons, 1925.

173 hands and feet are stained red with the henna: Jadunath Sarkar, *History of Aurangzeb Based on Original Sources*, 1912. Internet Archive <https://archive.org/details/historyofaurangz01sarkuoft> [accessed: 20 February 2018].

174 I am twenty-seven years old: Jahanara, *Risala-i-Sahibiya.*

That Timurid Girl

176 Since I was twenty years old: Jahanara.

176 I was suffering from a chronic disease: Bikrama Jit Hasrat, *Dara Shikuh: Life and Works*, Allahabad: Visvabharati The India Press Ltd., 1953.

176 The saint took my hand into his own: Ibid.

176 now that I have joined the qadiriya: Jahanara.

177 when I realised that the truth for this existence: Ibid.

177 The first time I set eyes on the venerable figure: Ibid.

177 My beloved came easily into my arms: Ibid.

177 alone with the remembrance of God: Hasrat, *Dara Shikuh.*

178 She has attained so extraordinary a development: John Curry Erik Ohlander, ed., *Sufism and Society: Arrangements of the Mystical in the Muslim World, 1200-1800* Routledge Sufi Series, Oxford 2012.

179 This fakira', writes Jahanara: Jahanara.

180 lighting the Timurid lamp: For more details on the Timurid light, see Mukhoty, *Heroines.*

180 When separating' she says: Jahanara.

180 was always wondering about it (Sufism) and was floundering: Mukhoty, *Heroines.*

181 two dancing girls, two thieves: Munis D. Faruqui, *The Princes of the Mughal Empire, 1504-1719*, Cambridge: Cambridge University Press, 2015.

A New City for the Peacock Throne

183 that if a man behold a City or Town: Lach, *Asia in the Making of Europe.*

183 abundance I noticed of everything in those marts: Michael H. Fisher, *Visions of Mughal India: An Anthology of European Travel Writing*, New York: I. B. Tauris, 2007.

183 table of about fifteen or sixteen dishes: A.V. Williams Jackson ed., *History of India*, London: The Grolier Society, 1906.

183 sun-drenched verandahs: John Keay, *India: A History.*

184 Ghiyaspur: Today known as Nizamuddin colony.

186 **turrets, kiosks, gilt domes**: Juneja, ed., *Architecture in Medieval India.*

187 **Dariba neighbourhood of Shahjahanabad**: Swapna Liddle, *Chandni Chowk: The Mughal City of Old Delhi*, New Delhi: Speaking Tiger Publishing, 2017.

187 **He buys all the Company's imports of coral**: Ibid.

188 **traders from 'Turkey, Zanzibar, Syria**: Mukhoty, *Heroines.*

188 **silly women, wrapping themselves**: Jean Marie Lafont and Rehana Lafont, *The French & Delhi: Agra, Aligarh and Sardhana*, New Delhi: India Research Press, 2010.

189 **they have arranged such attractive (wine) glasses**: Kidwai S. *Dargah Quli Khan: Portrait of a City (Persian)* in Vanita R., Kidwai S. (eds) *Same-Sex Love in India*, New York: Palgrave Macmillan, 2000.

189 **young and pubescent boys are at the fringes of the crowds**: Ibid.

189 **weary of explaining to my Agha**: Jean Marie Lafont and Rehana Lafont, *The French & Delhi.*

190 **a generous man and friendly**: François Bernier, *Travels in the Mogul Empire*, tr. Archibald Constable, Westminster: Archibald Constable and Company, 1891.

190 **a Turk, with a turban of red velvet**: Nicoll, *Shah Jahan.*

191 **is the rendezvous of the rich Persian**: Francois Bernier, *Travels in the Mogul Empire, Vol I*, translated from the French by Irving Brock, London: William Pickering, 1826.

191 **will build a serai**: Balabanlilar, 'The begums at the mystic feast'.

192 **many diseases are cured by the bath**: Jean Baptiste Tavernier, *Travels in India*, translated from the original French edition of 1676 by V.Ball, London: Macmillan and Co., 1889.

197 **assumed that fortune would invariably favour him**: Bernier.

Letters between a Brother and a Sister

198 **very different from the others**: Manucci, *Storio do Mogor.*

198 **in his company, no improper word**: Jadunath Sarkar, *History of Aurangzeb.*

198 **the beauties of that most excellent building**: Letters from Aurangzeb to Shahjahan, letter number 44 from Vincent John Adams Flynn, 'An English translation of the Adab-i-'Alamgiri, the period before the war of succession : being the letters of Prince Muhammad Aurangzib Bahadur to Muhammad Shihabu 'd-din Shah Jahan Sahib-i-Qiran-i-Sani, Emperor of Hindustan', *Open Research Library* <https://openresearch-repository.anu.edu.au/handle/1885/11285> [accessed 4 March 2018].

202 **If His Majesty wishes**: Flynn, *Adab-i-Alamgiri*; emphasis mine.

203 **I was much amused when I landed'**: Manucci, *Storio do Mogor.*

203 **Her joyful father**: Jadunath Sarkar, *Anecdotes of Aurangzib, Translated into English with Notes and Historical Essays.*

203 **modesty, courtesy, gentleness**: Kate Aughterson ed., *Renaissance Woman: A Sourcebook, Constructions of Feminity in England,* London and New York: Routledge, 1995.

204 **her ascendancy in the court of the Mogul**: Bernier.

204 **Begom Saeb, the eldest of all**: Manucci, *Storio do Mogor.*

205 **And daughters will get married into the future generations**: For more details on marriage and the royal princesses, see Mukhoty, *Heroines.*

205 **The Mogol's younger daughter**: Bernier.

206 **trusts 'his favourite child**: Ibid.

206 **Begom Saeb [Jahanara]**: Manucci, *Storio do Mogor.*

206 **too much a slave to his pleasures'**: Sarkar, *History of Aurangzeb.*

206 **The Mughals have just lost twelve crores of rupees**: Jadunath Sarkar, *India of Aurangzib, Compared with the India of Akbar,* Patna: Sanjyal and Co., 1901.

206 **because they were the heritage of Babur**: Edward Terry; *A Voyage to East India.*

208 **were dreading the hardships**: Flynn, *Adab-i-Alamgiri.*

209 **It astounds us, that after such preparations**: Ibid.

209–210 **elegant disposition, noble mind**: Afshan Bokhari, *Imperial Women in Mughal India: The Piety and Patronage of Jahanara Begum,* New York: I. B. Tauris, 2015.

212 **without any worldly motive**: Jonardon Ganeri, 'Migrating texts and traditions: Dara Shukoh and the transmission of the Upanisads to Islam', *Migrating Texts and Traditions,* edited by William Sweet, Ottawa: University of Ottawa Press, 2009.

213 **The power of the elder Prince**: Flynn, *Adab-i-Alamgiri.*

Sibling Rivalries

215 **people felt suddenly orphaned**: Shireen Moosvi, *Episodes in the Life of Akbar, Contemporary Records and Reminiscences,* New Delhi: National Book Trust, India, 2015.

215 **immediately the wildest rumours spread**: Sarkar, *History of Aurangzeb.*

216 **constantly in the society of brahmins, yogis**: Eraly, *The Last Spring.*

216 **He spoke disdainfully to all**: Bernier.

216 **very clever, capable of dissimulation**: Manucci, *Storio do Mogor.*

217 **many strong men died from the heat**: Eraly, *The Last Spring*.

217 **what has now happened**: Manucci, *Storio do Mogor*.

217 **her deep grief, telling him**: Ibid.

217 **His majesty is free from all bodily infirmities**: Khan Bahadur Maulvi Haji Zafar Hasan ed., *The Waqiat-i-alamgiri of Aqil Khan Razi* (an account of the war of succession between the sons of the Emperor Shah Jahan), New Delhi: Mercantile Printing Press,1946.

Roshanara Begum and a Dangerous Brother

221 **poetry in motion**: Fanny Parkes. *Begums, Thugs and Englishmen*.

222 **dark dingy-coloured turban**: Sarkar, *History of Aurangzeb*.

222 **The crowd assembled was immense**: Ibid.

223 **her clamours silenced the feeble voice**: Ibid.

224 **cannot avoid dwelling on this pompous procession**: Bernier.

224 **one hundred and fifty women**: Manucci, *Storio do Mogor*.

225 **had I not regarded this display of magnificence**: Bernier.

225 **kichery, a mess of rice and other vegetables**: Bernier.

226 **Initially Aurangzeb, too, is an enthusiast**: Madhu Trivedi, *The Emergence of the Hindustani Tradition-Music, Dance and Drama in North India, 13th to 19th Centuries*, Gurgaon: Three Essays Collections, 2012.

226 **wonderful agility, and were always correct**: Ibid.

226 **Far away in Persia**: Audrey Truschke, *Aurangzeb: The Man and the Myth*, New Delhi: Penguin Random House India, 2017.

227 **a melancholy temperament**: Manucci, *Storio do Mogor*.

228 **After the usual obeisances**: Ibid.

229 **As a favour**: Mukhoty, *Heroines*.

230 **nothing but a small plume or aigrette**: Manucci, *Storio do Mogor*.

230 **equip a ship and bring it to Surat**: Dr Yusuf Husain Khan ed., *Selected Documents of Auranzeb's Reign, 1659-1706 A.D.*, Hyderabad: Central Records Office, 1958.

The Woman in the Tower and the Last Padshah Begum

232 **the resolution and intelligence of Aurangzib**: *Ruka'at-i-Alamgiri; or, Letters of Aurangzebe, with historical and explanatory notes*, translated from the original Persian by Jamshid H. Bilimoria, London: Luzac & Co., Bombay, Cherag Printing Press, 1908.

232 **Old age is arrived**: Death-bed letters and the last wills of emperor Aurangzeb.

232 **Never trust your sons**: Sarkar, *Anecdotes of Aurangzib*.

235 **What belongs to you is as good as mine**: Ibid.

236 **Those who once rode elephants now go barefooted**: The emergence of the Hindustani tradition.

236 **Dil ki basti bhi**: Mir Taqi Mir—Delhi alone is a city of love; all those who have passed through it have looted it.

237 **Were an artist to choose me**: Annamarie Schimmel, *The Empire of the Great Mughals*.

238 **black and dark**: Harihar Das, *The Norris Embassy to Aurangzib (1699-1702)*, condensed and rearranged by S. C. Sarkar, Calcutta: K. L. Mukhopadhyay Publishers, 1959.

238 **these people are as base as corrupt**: Ibid.

240 **This becomes rekhta**: Annamarie Schimmel.

Epilogue: The Sun Sets on the Mughal Empire

241 **Can you imagine anything so detestable?**: Parkes, *Begums, Thugs and Englishmen*.

242 **The King's countenance, dignified by age**: Hassan Ali, *Observations on the Mussalmauns of India*.

243 **grieved to be obliged to accept**: Parkes, *Begums, Thugs and Englishmen*.

243 **The general impression**: William Dalrymple, *The Last Mughal*, New Delhi: Penguin Books India, 2007.

244 **Every civil building connected with the Mohammedan tradition**: Lord Palmerstone was the Foreign Secretary to the British Government from 1830-1841. Quote appears in Dalrymple.

244 **without regard to antiquarian veneration**: Ibid.

244 **and a clock tower built to replace the pool**: The clock tower inexplicably collapsed in 1950.

245 **Now there is not a shadow of a doubt**: Mukhoty, *Heroines*.

245 **perhaps as many as three hundred begums**: Dalrymple, *The Last Mughal*.

245 **moving about the city**: Ibid.

BIBLIOGRAPHY

Primary Sources

Ali, Meer Hassan, *Observations on the Mussalmauns of India* by Mrs Meer Hassan Ali, New York: Columbia University, 1832.

Anonymous, *Calcoen: A Dutch Narrative of the Second Voyage of Vasco Da Gama to Calicut*, London: B. M. Pickering, 1874.

Babur, Zahiru'd-din Muhammad, *The Babur-nama in English (Memoirs of Babur)*, translated from the original Turki Text of Zahiru'd-din Muhammad Babur Padhshah Ghazi by Annette Susannah Beveridge, Essex: Luzac & Co., 1922.

Bernier, François, *Travels in the Mogul Empire*, tr. Archibald Constable, Westminster: Archibald Constable and Company, 1891.

Beveridge, Henry, ed. *Tuzuk-I-Jahangiri or Memoirs of Jahangir*, tr. Alexander Rogers, New Delhi: Atlantic Publishers, 1989.

Coryate, Thomas, *Thomas Coriate Traveller for the English Wits: Greetings from the court of the Great Mogul*, London: Printed by W. Iaggard and Henry Featherstone, 1616.

Dughlat, Mirza Muhammad Haidar, *The Tarikh-i-Rashidi: A History of the Moghuls of Central Asia,* London: Sampson Low, Marston and Company Ltd., 1895.

Eden, Emily, *'Up the Country': Letters Written to her Sister from the Upper Provinces of India*, London: Richard Bentley, 1867.

Tirmizi, S. A. I, *Edicts from the Mughal Harem*, New Delhi: Idarah-i Adabiyat-i Delli, 1979.

Flynn, Vincent John Adams, *An English Translation of Adab-i-Alamgiri*,

Foster, William, ed., *Letters Received by the East India Company from its Servants in the East*, London, S. Low, Marston & Company, 1896.

Ghulam Yazdani (ed.), *Amal-I-Salih Or Shah Jahan Namah Of Muhammad Salih Kambo*, Calcutta: Asiatic Society of Bengal, 1927.

Gulbadan Begum, *The History of Humayun*, tr. Annette S. Beveridge, New Delhi: Munshiram Manoharlal Publishers Pvt. Ltd., 2001.

Jahanara Begum, *Munis al Arwah*. Citations from Bokhari, Afshan, 'Gendered landscapes: Jahan Ara Begum's (1614–1681) patronage, piety and self-representation in 17th century Mughal India', Vienna: University of Wien, 2009.

————, *Risalah-i-Sahibiya*. Citations from Bokhari, Afshan, 'Gendered landscapes: Jahan Ara Begum's (1614-1681) patronage, piety and self-representation in 17th century Mughal India', Vienna: University of Wien, 2009.

Jauhar, *Private Memoirs of the Moghul Emperor Humayun*, written in the Persian language by Jauhar, translated by Major Charles Stewart.

Jones, John Winter, *The Travels of Ludovico di Varthema in Egypt, Syria, Arabia Deserta and Arabia Felix, in Persia, India and Ethiopia*, London: Printed for the Haklyut Society, 1863.

Jourdain, John, *The Journal of John Jourdain, 1608–1617, Describing his Experiences in Arabia, India and the Malay Archipelago*, Cambridge: Printed for the Haklyut Society, 1905.

Jubayr, Ibn, *The Travels of Ibn Jubayr*, tr. R. J. C Broadhurst, London: Cape, 1952.

Manucci, Niccolaom, *Storio do Mogor or Mogul India*, tr. William Irvine, London: John Murray, 1907.

Monserrate, Antonio, *Commentary of Antonio Monserrate, S. J., On his Journey to the Court of Akbar*, London Bombay Madras Calcutta: Humphrey Milford, Oxford University Press, 1922.

Mubarak, Abu'l Fazl ibn, *The Ain-i-Akbari by Abu'l Fazl Allami*, translated from the original Persian by H. Blochmann, M. A. and Colonel H. S. Jarrett, Calcutta: Asiatic Society of Bengal, 1873–1907.

————, *The Akbarnama of Abu'l Fazl*, translated from the Persian by H. Beveridge, Calcutta: The Asiatic Society, 1939, reprinted 2000.

Parkes, Fanny, *Begums, Thugs and Englishmen*, New Delhi: Penguin Books India, 2003.

Purchas, Samuel, *Hakluytus Posthumus, or Purchas his Pilgrimes; Contayning a History of the World in Sea Voyages and Lande Travells by Englishmen and Others*, Glasgow: James MacLehose and Sons, 1905–1907.

Roe, Thomas, *The Embassy of Sir Thomas Roe to the Court of the Great Mogul, 1615–1619, as Narrated in His Journal and Correspondence*, London: Printed for the Haklyut Society, 1899.

Ryley, J. Horton, *Ralph Fitch: England's Pioneer to India and Burma*, London: T. Fisher Unwin, 1899.

Shah, Abdul-Qadir ibn-i-Muluk known as Al-Badaoni, *Muntakhabu-i-Tawarikh (A History of India)*. English translation selections from Ranking, George S. A., *Histories*, New Delhi: Atlantic Publishers and Distributors, 1990.

Shah, Ahmed ibn Arab, *Tamerlane or Timur the Treat Amir*, London: Luzac & Co, 1936.

Thackson Jr., W. M., *The Baburnama: Memoirs of Babur, Prince and Emperor*,

New York: Random House, 2002.

Thackston, Wheeler M., ed. and tr., *The Jahangirnama: Memoirs of Jahangir, Emperor of India*, New York: Oxford University Press, Washington, D. C.: Freer Gallery of Art and Arthur M. Sackler Gallery in association with New York : Oxford University Press, 1999.

Valle, Pietro Della, *The Travels of Pietro de la Valle in India; from the Old English Translation of 1664*, London: Printed for the Haklyut Society, 1892.

Zeb-un-Nissa, *The Diwan of Zeb-un-Nissa, the First Fifty Ghazals Rendered from the Persian by Magan Lal and Jessie Duncan Westbrook*, London: John Murray, 1913.

Secondary Sources

Asher, Catherine B. and Talbot, Cynthia, *India before Europe*, Cambridge: Cambridge University Press, 2002.

Babur, *The Baburnama: Memoirs of Babur, Prince and Emperor*, Thackston, Wheeler M., (trans. And ed.), New York: The Modern Library, 2002.

Blake, Stephen P., *Shahjahanabad: The Sovereign City in Mughal India 1639-1739*, Cambridge: Cambridge University Press, 2002.

Balabanlilar, Lisa, *Imperial identity in the Mughal Empire: Memory and Dynastic Politics in Early Modern South and Central Asia*, New York: I. B. Tauris, 2012.

————, *The Lords of the Auspicious Conjunction: Turco-Mongol Imperial Identity on the Subcontinent*, Columbus: Ohio State University, 2007.

Beach, Milo Cleveland, *The Imperial Image: Paintings for the Mughal Court*, Freer Gallery of Art, Arthur M. Sackler Gallery and Smithsonian Institution Grantha Corporation, 2012.

Dalrymple, William, *The Last Mughal*, New Delhi: Penguin Books India, 2007.

Dughit, Muhammad Haidar, *The Tarikh-i-Rashidi: A History of the Moghuls of Central Asia*, London: Sampson Low, Marston and Company Ltd., 1895.

Dunn, Ross E., *The Adventures of Ibn Battuta: A Muslim Traveler of the Fourteenth Century*, University of California Press; Revised edition, 2004.

Eraly, Abraham, *The Last Spring: The Lives and Times of the Great Mughals*, New Delhi: Penguin Books India, 2000.

Erskine, William, *A History of India under the Two First Sovereigns of the House of Taimur, Báber and Humáyun*, 1854. Internet Archive <https://archive.org/details/ahistoryindiaun01erskgoog> [accessed: 20 February 2018].

Faruqui, Munis D., *The Princes of the Mughal Empire, 1504-1719*, Cambridge: Cambridge University Press, 2015.

Findly, Ellison Banks, *Nur Jahan: Empress of Mughal India*, New York: Oxford University Press, 1993.

Fisher, Michael H., *A Short History of the Mughal Empire*, New York: I. B.

Tauris, 2015.

Hambly, Gavin, ed., *Women in the Medieval Islamic World*, New York: Palgrave Macmillan, 1999.

Hansen, Waldermar, *The Peacock Throne: The Drama of Mogul India*, New Delhi: Motilal Banarsidass Publications, 1986.

Harris, Jonathan Gil, *The First Firangis*, New Delhi: Aleph Book Company, 2015.

Lach, Donald F., *Asia in the Making of Europe, Volumes 1 and 2*, Chicago: University of Chicago Press, 1965.

Lal, Ruby, *Domesticity and Power in the Early Mughal World*, Cambridge: Cambridge University Press, 2005.

Mathur, Saloni, *India by Design: Colonial History and Cultural Display*, Oakland: University of California Press, 2007.

Moxham, Roy, *The Theft of India: The European Conquests of India, 1498-1765*, New Delhi: HarperCollins India, 2016.

Mukhoty, Ira, *Heroines: Powerful Indian Women of Myth and History*, New Delhi: Aleph Book Company, 2017.

Mukherjee, Soma, *Royal Mughal Ladies and their Contributions*, New Delhi: Gyan Publishing House, 2011.

Mukhia, Harbans, *The Mughals of India*, New Delhi: John Wiley and Sons, 2004.

Peck, Lucy, *Delhi: A Thousand Years of Building*, New Delhi: Roli Books, 2005.

Nicoll, Fergus, *Shah Jahan: The Rise and Fall of the Mughal Emperor*, New Delhi: Penguin Books India, 2009.

Peabody, Norbert, *Hindu Kingship and Polity in Precolonial India*, Cambridge: Cambridge University Press, 2002.

Pearson, Michael, *The Indian Ocean*, New York: Routledge, 2003.

Preston, Diana, *A Teardrop on the Cheek of Time: The Story of the Taj Mahal*, New York: Doubleday, 2007.

Raghavan, T. C. A., *Attendant Lords: Bairam Khan and Abdur Rahim, Courtiers and Poets in Mughal India*, New Delhi: HarperCollins India, 2017.

Randhawa, M. S., *Paintings of the Baburnama*, New Delhi: National Museum, 1983.

Ray, Sukumar, *Humayun in Persia*, Calcutta: Royal Asiatic Society, 1948.

Richards, John F., *The Mughal Empire*, Cambridge: Cambridge University Press, 1995.

Roy, Kaushik, *Military Transition in Early Modern Asia 1400–1750*, London and New York: Bloomsbury Academic, 2014.

Ruggles, D. Fairchild, ed., *Women, Patronage and Self-Representation in Islamic Societies*, New York: State University of New York Press, 2000.

Sarkar, Jadunath, *Anecdotes of Aurangzib, Translated into English with Notes and*

Historical Essays, New York: Scholar's Choice, 2015.

Sarkar, Jadunath, *History of Aurangzeb Based on Original Sources*, 1912, <https://archive.org/details/historyofaurangz01sarkuoft> [accessed: 20 February 2018].

Schimmel, Annemarie, *The Empire of the Great Mughals: History, Art and Culture*, Islington: Reaktion Books, 2006.

Smith, R. V., *Lingering Charm of Delhi: Myth, Lore and History*, New Delhi: Niyogi Books, 2015.

Smith, Vincent, *Akbar the Great Mogul: 1542-1645*, Oxford: Clarendon Press, 1917.

Truschke, Audrey, *Aurangzeb: The Man and the Myth*, New Delhi: Penguin Random House India, 2017.

Wade, Bonnie C., *Imaging Sound: An Ethnomusicological Study of Music Art and Culture in Mughal India*, Chicago: University of Chicago Press, 1998.

Welch, Stuart Cary, *The Emperors' Album: Images of Mughal India*, New York: Metropolitan Museum of Art, 2012.

Wilson, Jon, *India Conquered: Britain's Raj and the Chaos of Empire*, London: Simon & Schuster, 2016.

Architecture

Golombek, Lisa, *The Timurid Architecture of Iran and Turan*, Princeton: Princeton University Press, 1988.

Juneja, Monica, ed., *Architecture in Medieval India*, New Delhi: Orient Blackswan Private Limited, 2008.

Koch, Ebba, 'The Taj Mahal: Architecture, Symbolism and Urban Significance', *Muqarnas Online*, Volume 22, Issue 1, pp 128–149, 2005.

O'Kane, Bernard, 'From tents to pavilions: royal mobility and Persian palace design', *Ars Orientalis*, Vol. 23, Pre-modern Islamic Palaces, Freer Gallery of Art, The Smithsonian Institution and Department of the History of Art, University of Michigan, 1993.

Stone, Caroline, 'Movable palaces', *Saudi Aramco World*, July/August 2010.

Clothes

Condra, Jill, ed., *The Greenwood Encyclopedia of Clothing through World History: 11501-1800*, Westport: Greenwood Press, 2007.

Goswamy, B. N., *Indian Costumes in the Collection of the Calico Museum of Textiles*, Ahmedabad: Calico Museum, 2008.

Kumar, Ritu, *Costumes and Textiles of Royal India*, Suffolk: Antique Collectors' Club, 2006.

Neutres, Jerome and Hutheesing, Umang, *Les Derniers Maharajas: Costumes du*

Grand Durbar a l'independance 1911–1947, Paris: Editions de la Martinière, 2010.

Tilke, Max, *Costume Patterns and Design*, New York: Rizzoli, 1990.

Food

Dehlvi, Sadia, *Jasmine and Jinns: Memories and Recipes of My Delhi*, New Delhi: HarperCollins India, 2017.

Taylor, Colleen, *Feasts and Fasts, A History of Food in India*, London: Reaktion Books, 2015.

Medieval Hajj Travel

Pearson, M. N., *Pious Passengers: the Hajj in Earlier Times,* London, Hurst & Company, 1994.

Ryad, Umar, ed., *The Hajj and Europe in the Age of Empire*, Boston: Brill, 2016.